S0-BBC-842

THE JOHANNINE SCHOOL:

AN EVALUATION OF THE JOHANNINE-SCHOOL

HYPOTHESIS BASED ON AN INVESTIGATION

OF THE NATURE OF ANCIENT SCHOOLS

Society of Biblical Literature

Dissertation Series

Edited by

Howard C. Kee

and

Douglas A. Knight

Number 26

THE JOHANNINE SCHOOL:
AN EVALUATION OF THE JOHANNINE-SCHOOL
HYPOTHESIS BASED ON AN INVESTIGATION
OF THE NATURE OF ANCIENT SCHOOLS

by

R. Alan Culpepper

SCHOLARS PRESS
Missoula, Montana

THE JOHANNINE SCHOOL:

AN EVALUATION OF THE JOHANNINE-SCHOOL

HYPOTHESIS BASED ON AN INVESTIGATION

OF THE NATURE OF ANCIENT SCHOOLS

by

R. Alan Culpepper

Published by

SCHOLARS PRESS

for

THE SOCIETY OF BIBLICAL LITERATURE

Distributed by

SCHOLARS PRESS
University of Montana
Missoula, Montana 59801

THE JOHANNINE SCHOOL:
AN EVALUATION OF THE JOHANNINE-SCHOOL
HYPOTHESIS BASED ON AN INVESTIGATION
OF THE NATURE OF ANCIENT SCHOOLS

by

R. Alan Culpepper
The Southern Baptist Theological Seminary
2825 Lexington Road
Louisville, Kentucky 40206

Ph.D., 1974
Duke University

Adviser:
D. Moody Smith, J

Library of Congress Cataloging in Publication Data

Culpepper, R   Alan.
  The Johannine school.

  (Society of Biblical Literature. Dissertation series
; no. 26)
  Originally presented as the author's thesis, Duke, 1974.
  Bibliography: p.
  Includes index.
  1. Johannine school. 2. Bible. N.T. John — Author-
ship. 3. Philosophy, Ancient. I. Title. II. Series.
BS2615.2.C86   1975   226'.5'061   75-34235
ISBN 0-89130-063-5

PRINTED IN THE UNITED STATES OF AMERICA
1 2 3 4 5
Edwards Brothers, Inc.
Ann Arbor, Michigan 48104

TO JACQUE

TABLE OF CONTENTS

ABBREVIATIONS

AA	*Archäologischer Anzeiger*
AGSU	Arbeiten zur Geschichte des Spätjudentums und Urchristentums
AJP	*American Journal of Philology*
ALUOS	*Annual of Leeds University Oriental Society*
Ant.	Josephus *Jewish Antiquities*
ATR	*Anglican Theological Review*
BBB	Bonner biblische Beiträge
BJRL	*Bulletin of the John Rylands Library*
BWANT	Beiträge zur Wissenschaft vom Alten und Neuen Testament
BZ	*Biblische Zeitschrift*
BZNW	Beihefte zur Zeitschrift für die neutestamentliche Wissenschaft
CBQ	*Catholic Biblical Quarterly*
CP	*Classical Philology*
CQ	*Classical Quarterly*
CR	*Classical Review*
CRAI	*Comptes rendus de l'Académie des inscriptions et belles lettres*
CTM	*Concordia Theological Monthly*
CW	*Classical Weekly* [through Vol. L (1956-57)] *Classical World* [beginning with Vol. LI (1957-58)]
DJD	Discoveries in the Judaean Desert
D. L.	Diogenes Laertius
D. S.	Diodorus Siculus
EBib	Études bibliques
EncJud	*Encyclopaedia Judaica*
EncPhilos	*Encyclopedia of Philosophy*
EstBib	*Estudios Bíblicos*
FRLANT	Forschungen zur Religion und Literatur des Alten und Neuen Testaments
HNT	Handbuch zum Neuen Testament

HTCNT	Herder's Theological Commentary on the New Testament
HTKNT	Herder's theologischer Kommentar zum Neuen Testament
HTR	*Harvard Theological Review*
HUCA	*Hebrew Union College Annual*
Iamb.	Iamblichus
ICC	International Critical Commentary
IDB	*Interpreter's Dictionary of the Bible*
IG	*Inscriptiones Graecae*
JBC	*Jerome Biblical Commentary*
JBL	*Journal of Biblical Literature*
JBR	*Journal of Bible and Religion*
JdI	*Jahrbuch des deutschen archäologischen Instituts*
JEH	*Journal of Ecclesiastical History*
JHS	*Journal of Hellenic Studies*
JJS	*Journal of Jewish Studies*
JOAI	*Jahreshefte des Österreichischen archäologischen Institutes in Wien*
JP	*Journal of Philology*
JQR	*Jewish Quarterly Review*
JR	*Journal of Religion*
JSS	*Journal of Semitic Studies*
JTS	*Journal of Theological Studies*
LSJ	Liddell, H. G., and Scott, R., eds. *A Greek-English Lexicon.* Revised by H. S. Jones and R. McKenzie.
LXX	Septuagint
M.	Mishnah
Mand.	*Mandates* (in *The Shepherd of Hermas*)
MT	Masoretic Text
MusHelv	*Museum Helveticum*
NovT	*Novum Testamentum*
NovTSup	Novum Testamentum, Supplements
NTS	*New Testament Studies*

NTSMS	New Testament Studies Monograph Series
NTTS	New Testament Tools and Studies
OCD	*Oxford Classical Dictionary*
Porph.	Porphyry
RAC	*Reallexikon für Antike und Christentum*
RB	*Revue biblique*
RE	*Paulys Real-Encyclopädie der classischen Altertums-wissenschaft*
REG	*Revue des études grecques*
RevExp	*Review and Expositor*
RGG	*Die Religion in Geschichte und Gegenwart*
RHPR	*Revue d'histoire et de philosophie religieuses*
RQ	*Revue de Qumran*
RSR	*Recherches de science religieuse*
SBBerl	*Sitzungsberichte der königlich Preussischen Akademie der Wissenschaften zu Berlin*
SBMun	*Sitzungsberichte der Bayerischen Akademie der Wissenschaft: Philosophisch-historische Klasse,* Munich
SBS	Stuttgarter Bibelstudien
SBT	Studies in Biblical Theology
SBVien	*Sitzungsberichte der kaiserlichen Akademie der Wissenschaften: Philosophisch-historischen Classe,* Vienna
Sim.	*Similitudes* (in *The Shepherd of Hermas*)
SJT	*Scottish Journal of Theology*
StANT	Studien zum Alten und Neuen Testament
Str-B	Strack, H., and Billerbeck, P. *Kommentar zum Neuen Testament aus Talmud und Midrasch*
SUNT	Studien zur Umwelt des Neuen Testaments
TAPA	*Transactions of the American Philological Association*
TB	Babylonian Talmud
TDNT	*Theological Dictionary of the New Testament*
ThRu	*Theologische Rundschau*
TLZ	*Theologische Literaturzeitung*

TP	Palestinian Talmud
TS	*Theological Studies*
TU	Texte und Untersuchungen zur Geschichte der altchristlichen Literatur
TWNT	*Theologisches Wörterbuch zum Neuen Testament*
USQR	*Union Seminary Quarterly Review*
VA	*Vita Apollonii*
Vorsokr.	Diels, H., and Kranz, W. *Die Fragmente der Vorsokratiker*
VP	*De Vita Pythagorica liber* (Iamblichus) *Vita Pythagorae* (Porphyry)
VT	*Vetus Testamentum*
VTSup	Vetus Testamentum, Supplements
WMANT	Wissenschaftliche Monographien zum Alten und Neuen Testament
WUNT	Wissenschaftliche Untersuchungen zum Neuen Testament
ZAW	*Zeitschrift für die alttestamentliche Wissenschaft*
ZNW	*Zeitschrift für die neutestamentliche Wissenschaft*
ZTK	*Zeitschrift für Theologie und Kirche*

ACKNOWLEDGMENTS

No work of this scope can be produced without the assistance of a great many persons. Special acknowledgment and gratitude must be expressed to: my advisor, Dr. D. Moody Smith, Jr., for his interest, keen observations, and willingness to allow me a great deal of latitude in developing the thrust and conclusions of the dissertation, while guiding my work with insight and erudition; Dr. John F. Oates, whose interest in this work was a great encouragement and whose guidance helped me to work into areas not often touched by New Testament studies; Dr. W. D. Davies, for encouragement and suggestions; and Mr. R. Michael Casto, whose meticulous proofreading helped me eliminate embarrassing errata; Mrs. Anne Izard, for carefully retyping the dissertation for publication. Professors Franklin W. Young, Orval Wintermute, and James H. Charlesworth have been most supportive and have made valuable suggestions which strengthened this work. Special thanks is also due to The Southern Baptist Theological Seminary for allowing me to finish the dissertation before assuming my teaching duties, and for underwriting the cost of retyping the dissertation for publication. Acknowledgment must also be made of the way in which I was stimulated by my fellow graduate students; their friendship, questions, suggestions, and criticisms have been immeasurably helpful and supportive. My wife, Jacque, contributed her typing skill lovingly and with ardent attention to accuracy; without her encouragement and patience this work would not have been possible.

ABSTRACT

The question of the precise nature of the Johannine community has received increased significance in the light of recent
studies which suggest that the content of the Gospel of John
was shaped not by a lone writer but by the situation of the
community in which it was composed. This dissertation addresses
the problem of whether or not the Johannine community was a
school as the widely used expression "the Johannine school"
implies. The "Johannine-school hypothesis" is used to designate
theories that the Gospel of John was composed by one or more
members of a school.

In the first chapter the history of the Johannine-school
hypothesis is traced and analyzed. The "school of John" was
first explicitly so called by E. Renan. Subsequently, the
Johannine community has been called a school by numerous
scholars who used the term "school" in a variety of ways and
held varied positions on the question of the authorship of the
Fourth Gospel. Nevertheless, no study has yet been primarily
concerned with the question of whether or not the community was
a school. Three basic arguments have been advanced in support
of the Johannine-school hypothesis: 1) The linguistic and
theological similarities and dissimilarities among the Johannine
writings can be best explained by assuming that they were written by several persons working in one community--hence probably
a school; 2) the patristic writings which refer to John and his
disciples suggest that there was a Johannine school; and 3)
John's use of the Old Testament suggests that the Gospel was
composed in a school. Previous attempts to confirm or deny the
Johannine-school hypothesis, however, have been vitiated by an
imprecise or unsubstantiated use of the term "school." The
writer has developed a fourth argument: if the Johannine
community can be shown to have shared the characteristics of
ancient schools, then it probably was a school.

The nature of a variety of ancient schools is investigated
(Chapters II - X): the Pythagorean school, the Academy, the
Lyceum, the Garden, the Stoa, the school at Qumran, the House
of Hillel, Philo's school, and the school of Jesus. Only
schools which traced their origin to a founder are chosen for
study, since the Beloved Disciple appears to have functioned
as a founder within the Johannine community. A list of nine

characteristics of the schools studied is compiled (Chapter XI) and used to define what is meant by an ancient "school."

In the last chapter (XII) the perspectives gained from the study of ancient schools are applied to the study of the Johannine community. Theses are advanced regarding the nature of the community and its history (especially concerning the role of the Beloved Disciple in the community and the relationship between him and the Paraclete). The Johannine community is found to have shared the characteristics which define ancient schools; hence the dissertation concludes that the Johannine community was a school.

Chapter I

THE JOHANNINE-SCHOOL HYPOTHESIS

Introduction

The popularity of the term "Johannine school" has allowed
scholars to use it uncritically. Actually, "school" is used in
a confusing variety of ways; hence the hypothesis that John is
the product of a school must now be examined. Hereafter "the
Johannine-school hypothesis" designates theories that John was
produced by one or more members of a community which can be
called a school. The definition of this hypothesis, however,
is a goal, not a presupposition, of the dissertation. When and
how did the concept of the Johannine school arise? What evidence supports the contention that there was a school or that
John was composed by one or several of its members? What
approaches have been taken in arguing for and against the
school hypothesis?

This chapter attempts to supply answers to these questions
by surveying the history of the Johannine-school hypothesis.
Once these questions are answered we may consider whether we
should continue to speak of the Johannine school, and if so how
it should be understood. We shall deal with the relevant literature chronologically and summarize the approaches, method-
ologies, and conclusions of the writers who discuss the Johannine school. Particular attention will be paid to the evidence
cited and the various ways in which "school" is understood.
Finally, we shall analyze the current status of the Johannine-
school hypothesis.

History of the
Johannine-school hypothesis

Many of the elements of the Johannine-school hypothesis
were developed prior to 1863.[1] Dionysius of Alexandria denied

---

[1]It is not our purpose to trace the history of the debate over the
authorship of John, but the issue cannot be avoided entirely. We shall
deal with only those scholars who contributed to the development of the
Johannine-school hypothesis. Fuller discussions of Johannine scholarship
prior to 1875 can be found in Christoph E. Luthardt, *St. John the Author of
the Fourth Gospel* (Edinburgh: T. & T. Clark, 1875), pp. 15-25; this book
was revised, translated, and enlarged by C. R. Gregory, who added a valuable
appendix--a partially annotated bibliography of the "Literature of the
Disputed Origin of the Fourth Gospel from 1792 to the Present" [1875]; James
Drummond, *An Inquiry into the Character and Authorship of the Fourth Gospel*
(London: Williams and Norgate, 1903), pp. 67-71; Paton J. Gloag, *Introduction to the Johannine Writings* (London: James Nisbet and Co., 1891),

that Revelation was written by John the Apostle.[2] In 1641 Hugo
Grotius claimed that chapter 21 was added by the Ephesian church
after the Apostle's[3] death.[4] In 1792 E. Evanson denied the
apostolic authorship of John and attributed the Gospel[5] to the
work of a Platonist in the second century.[6] J. C. R. Eckermann
in 1792 said that the evangelist, a friend of the Apostle, collected information for his gospel from the Apostle and his
friends.[7] 1820 marks a significant point in Johannine scholarship because in that year K. G. Bretschneider marshalled the arguments against apostolic authorship.[8] Bretschneider's work
provoked severe criticism which temporarily resulted in the
triumph of the traditional view. L. A. Dieffenbach[9] and H. E.
G. Paulus,[10] however, defended the view that John was written
by a disciple of the Apostle. D. F. Strauss[11] continued the

---

pp. 123-30; and Vincent H. Stanton, *The Gospels as Historical Documents*,
Part III: *The Fourth Gospel* (Cambridge: University Press, 1920), pp. 1-16.
Christoph E. Luthardt, *St. John's Gospel: Described and Explained Accord-
ing to Its Peculiar Character*, trans. by C. R. Gregory (3 vols.; Edinburgh:
T. & T. Clark, 1876-78), I, ix-xiii, contains a list of commentaries on
John published between 1517 and 1875, and III, ix-xvii, contains a list of
books on John dating from A.D. 230-1878. David Friedrich Strauss, *Das
Leben Jesu für das deutsche Volk bearbeitet* (Leipzig: F. A. Brockhaus,
1864), pp. 90-114, traces the history of scholarship from Bretschneider to
Baur.

[2]Eusebius *Ecclesiastical History* VII. xxv. 1-24.

[3]Herein "the Apostle" refers to John the son of Zebedee.

[4]Cited by Stanton, *The Gospels as Historical Documents*, Part III:
The Fourth Gospel, p. 17.

[5]When capitalized "the Gospel" refers to John.

[6]Edward Evanson, *The Dissonance of the Four Generally Received
Evangelists and the Evidence of Their Authenticity Examined* (Ipswich, 1792),
cited by Gregory in Luthardt, *St. John the Author of the Fourth Gospel*, p.
283.

[7]Jacob C. R. Eckermann, "Ueber die eigentlich sichern Gründe des
Glaubens an die Hauptthatsachen der Geschichte Jesu, und über die wahrscheinliche Entstehung der Evangelien und der Apostelgeschichte," *Theologische Beiträge*, Bd. V, St. 2 (1796), 106-256, cited by Gregory, ibid., p. 284.

[8]Karl G. Bretschneider, *Probabilia de evangelii et epistolarum
Joannis Apostoli, indole et origine* (Leipzig, 1820), cited by Gregory,
ibid., p. 293.

[9]Ludwig A. Dieffenbach, "Ueber einige wahrscheinliche Interpolationen
im Evangelium Johannis," *Kritisch. Journ. d. neuest. theol. Lit.*, V (1816),
1-16, cited by Gregory, ibid., p. 292.

[10]Heinrich E. G. Paulus, "Bretschneider de Origine Ev. et Epist.
Joann.," *Heidelberg Jahrbücher der Literatur*, (1821), 112-42, cited by
Gregory, ibid., p. 295.

[11]David F. Strauss, *Das Leben Jesu kritisch bearbeitet* (Tübingen:
C. F. Osiander, 1835-36).

attack on the traditional view, and C. H. Weisse[12] concluded
that the followers of the Apostle wrote the Gospel using notes
which the Apostle left when he died. L. F. O. Baumgarten-
Crusius appears to be the first to have used the idea of a
Johannine circle in defense of the "authenticity" of the Gospel.
C. R. Gregory summarized Baumgarten-Crusius' position as
follows:

> Gospel genuine [sic]; even if written down by some one else
> or worked up by some one else than John, this must have been
> done in John's own circle, and so early as to be in his mind
> and tone.[13]

F. C. Baur emphasized the concept of Logos and the polemical interests of John and dated the Gospel in the second century, but added little to the development of the Johannine-
school hypothesis.[14] In 1864 both M. Nicholas[15] and C. H. von
Weizsäcker[16] asserted that the Gospel was written by a pupil of
John or a member of the Ephesian church.

Thus, by the 1860's many of the bases of the Johannine-
school hypothesis had been proposed. It was understood that
the five writings attributed to John are closely related to
each other, and some of those who denied the common authorship
of these writings postulated their composition within a common
circle or group.[17] Many of the scholars cited above held that
John is the work of more than one man and that it is at least
partially the work of a pupil or disciple of John. Therefore,
the idea of disciples of the Apostle, or a Johannine circle,
developed before the term "Johannine school."

---

[12]Chr. Hermann Weisse, *Die evangelische Geschichte kritisch und
philosophisch bearbeitet* (2 vols.; Leipzig, 1838), II, 225-300, cited by
Drummond, *An Inquiry into the Character and Authorship of the Fourth Gospel,*
p. 404.

[13]Ludwig F. O. Baumgarten-Crusius, *Theologische Auslegung der
johanneischen Schriften* (Jenai, 1843), I, cited by Gregory in Luthardt, *St.
John the Author of the Fourth Gospel*, p. 308.

[14]Ferdinand C. Baur, "Ueber die Composition und Charakter des
johanneischen Evangeliums," *Theologische Jahrbücher*, (1844), 1-191, 397-475,
615-700, cited by Gregory, ibid., p. 309.

[15]Michel Nicolas, *Études critiques sur la Bible* (Paris, 1864), pp.
127-221, cited by Gregory, ibid., p. 334.

[16]Carl H. von Weizsäcker, *Untersuchungen über die evangelische Geschichte ihre Quellen und den Gang ihrer Entwicklung* (Gotha, 1864), I, iii,
220-302, cited by Gregory, ibid., p. 335.

[17]See the list of scholars compiled by James Moffatt, *An Introduction
to the Literature of the New Testament*, International Theological Library
(New York: Charles Scribner's Sons, 1918), pp. 589-90.

4

The first occurrence known to this writer of the phrase "school of John" appears in E. Renan's *Vie de Jésus* (1863). Renan hypothesized that while the Apostle John wrote notes, his disciples revised them and added passages, such as chapter 21, to the gospel.[18] The strangeness of the Gospel is explained in part by the claim that the school absorbed the syncretistic atmosphere of Ephesus; "tous les germes du gnosticisme y existaient déjà."[19]

J. B. Lightfoot was apparently the next scholar to propose the existence of a Johannine school. This proposal was made in a series of articles published in 1875 and 1876.[20] Lightfoot defended the traditional view of authorship by emphasizing that many of the Church Fathers who maintained that John was written by the Apostle had actually been his disciples. Polycarp and Papias were members of John's school:

> . . . at the fall of Jerusalem a remnant of the Apostolic company, together with other primitive disciples, sought a new home in Asia Minor. Of this colony Ephesus was the headquarters, and St. John the leader. Here he is reported to have lived and laboured for more than a quarter of a century, surviving the accession of Trajan, who ascended the imperial throne A.D. 98. In this respect his position is unique among the earliest preachers of Christianity. While St. Peter and St. Paul converted disciples and organized congregations, St. John alone was the founder of a school. . . . Hence the traditions of St. John are more direct, more consistent, and more trustworthy, than those which relate to the other Apostles.
>
> Thus we may, without any great impropriety, speak of the 'school of St. John.' The existence of such a body of disciples gathered about the veteran teacher is indicated by notices in various writers.[21]

Even in Lightfoot's writings, however, we find "school" being used in two different senses. He spoke of the schools of John and Paul, but claimed that John was different from Peter and Paul in that only he founded a school.[22] Apparently Lightfoot

---

[18]Ernest Renan, *Vie de Jésus* (9th ed.; Paris: G. Paetz, 1864), pp. xxii-xxxii.

[19]Ibid., p. xxviii.

[20]J. B. Lightfoot, *Essays on the Work Entitled Supernatural Religion* (London: Macmillan and Company, 1889), originally published in *Contemporary Review*, XXV-XXVII (1875-76). Cf., [Walter Richard Cassels], *Supernatural Religion: An Inquiry into the Reality of Divine Revelation* (2 vols.; London, 1874).

[21]Lightfoot, *Essays on the Work Entitled Supernatural Religion*, p. 217.

[22]Ibid., pp. 95, 217.

intended for his readers to understand the reference to the
school of Paul as merely designating men in some loose sense
associated with Paul. His vision of the school of John was
quite different: John was the head of this school for a quarter of a century; he wrote at least the gospel and epistles
attributed to him; other disciples of Jesus lived in the area
and probably visited John's school; John taught his students,
and they passed on his teachings and certified the authenticity
of his writings.

The next decade brought little development in the school
hypothesis. In a thorough, carefully prepared series of articles H. J. Holtzmann investigated the relationship between John
and I John giving special attention to the verbal parallels
and concluded that they were not written by the same author.[23]
B. F. Westcott held that all five Johannine writings were written by the Apostle and referred to the school only in a footnote.[24] Apparently he was substantially in agreement with
Lightfoot but placed no emphasis on the school.

The hypothesis next appeared in a rather ambiguous statement made by J. Martineau:

> . . . I am at last more impressed by a few fundamental dif-
> ferences of religious conception pervading the two writings
> [Jn. and I Jn.], than by several agreements in terminology
> and secondary categories of thought, which point to some
> common relation to the same school.[25]

Martineau did not mention the school again, but proceeded to
list five characteristic features of the two writings which
could not co-exist in the same mind. He appealed to the school
hypothesis in an attempt to hold in close relationship the two
writings which he could not ascribe to the same author.

The references which J. V. Bartlet made to "John's companions" and the ". . . circle of responsible associates in
Ephesus" and his conclusion that the appendix (John 21) was
added by the Johannine "circle" indicate that he should be
included among the early proponents of the school hypothesis.[26]

---

[23]H. J. Holtzmann, "Das Problem des erstens johanneischen Briefes in
seinem Verhältnis zum Evangelium," *Jahrbücher für protestantliche Theologie*,
VII (1881), 690-712; VIII (1882), 128-52, 316-42, 460-85, esp. p. 152.

[24]B. F. Westcott, *The Gospel According to St. John* (London: John
Murray, 1882), p. xxxi.

[25]James Martineau, *The Seat of Authority in Religion* (3rd ed.; London:
Longmans, Green and Co., 1891), p. 509.

[26]James Vernon Bartlet, *Ten Epochs of Church History: The Apostolic*

6

The work of C. von Weizsäcker gave a new form and prominence to the idea of the Johannine school. The evidence he
cited is interesting. First, Christianity confronted Justin
Martyr in Ephesus as a superior kind of philosophical school.[27]
Then, in the controversies with Monarchianism and in the Passover dispute the church of Asia Minor appealed to the Johannine
school's traditions:

> All this falls into the second half of the second century;
> but the men of that time at least believed that their school
> reached back into the period of the Apostle himself. While
> the vigour of the Church of Asia Minor is therefore no proof
> of the existence of an Apostolic school there, it yet points
> in that direction.[28]

The close relationship between the Gospel and the Apocalypse
encouraged Weizsäcker to think that they both come from the
Johannine school[29] but that neither of them is the work of the
Apostle himself.[30] The way in which the Gospel portrays faith
in Christ as faith in the Logos of God also indicates that it
is not the work of the Apostle who knew Jesus, but of one of
his disciples. The Gospel's assertion that the Apostle was
Jesus' most trusted disciple and that the Apostle stood directly
behind the teaching of the Gospel itself, however, points most
clearly to its origin in an apostolic school. Yet, Weizsäcker
held the Apostle in contact with the school:

> On the other hand, the conclusion is without doubt warranted
> that the author of the book and the school of which he was a
> member were able to lay claim to the name of the Apostle,
> because he had belonged to, and been the head of, their
> Church.[31]

This school's controversy with a form of Judaism that ". . .
developed after the destruction of Jerusalem . . ." reflects
views which could not have developed prior to this time.[32] Finally, the school was threatened by Gnosticism:

> The Johannine school found cause to combat Gnosis. The first
> of the letters ascribed to John in our Canon belongs to the

Age, Its Life, Doctrine, Worship and Polity (New York: Charles Scribner's
Sons, 1899), pp. 436-38.

[27]Carl von Weizsäcker, The Apostolic Age of the Christian Church,
trans. by J. Millar (2 vols.; New York: G. P. Putnam's Sons, 1899), II, 169.

[28]Ibid., p. 170.

[29]Ibid., p. 172.

[30]Ibid., p. 174.

[31]Ibid., pp. 211-12, cf. pp. 234-36.

[32]Ibid., p. 226.

school; it represents the spirit and thought of the Gospel, but overwhelming indications show that it was written later.[33]

In view of the positions taken by T. Zahn in his later works,[34] his early work "Apostel und Apostelschüler in der Provinz Asien" is especially interesting. He began by defining the terms in the title of his work broadly:

> Die Worte "Apostel" und "Apostelschüler" im Titel dieser Abhandlung verstehe ich in dem weiteren Sinne, welchen beide in der alten Kirche vielfach hatten. Apostelschüler soll nur ein kurzer Ausdruck dafür sein, dass einer sich mit dem einen oder anderen Gliede des Apostelkreises persönlich berührt hat, ohne dass damit eine dauernde Lebensgemeinschaft und ein förmliches Schülerverhältnis behauptet würde.[35]

Nevertheless, Zahn proceeded to say that during the controversy with the *alogoi* I John was regarded as the Apostle's work--at least it was regarded as the work of John of Ephesus from the beginning by his "Schülern."[36] H. H. Wendt spoke of both a "circle of communities in Asia Minor" and a "circle of disciples" around the Apostle John. It was from the circle of disciples that the Gospel appeared after the death of the Apostle.[37] The Apostle wrote a source of I John. The evangelist used this source--the Apostle's memoirs--and other traditions. Chapter 21 was not written by the evangelist.[38]

By 1903 the idea that the Gospel was the work of a disciple of the Apostle was popular enough for J. Drummond to devote a chapter of his book to an attempt to refute it.[39] In particular, Drummond took issue with the assertions that the evangelist refers to "the disciple whom Jesus loved" as one other than himself and that the evangelist wished to exalt his master

---

[33]Ibid., p. 238.

[34]Theodor Zahn, *Introduction to the New Testament*, trans. by M. W. Jacobus and C. S. Thayer (3 vols.; Edinburgh: T. & T. Clark, 1909); and his *Kommentar zum Neuen Testament*, Bd. IV: *Das Evangelium des Johannes* (5 und 6 Aufl.; Leipzig: A. Deichertsche Verlagsbuchhandlung, 1921).

[35]Theodor Zahn, "Apostel und Apostelschüler in der Provinz Asien," in *Forschungen zur Geschichte des neutestamentlichen Kanons*, Vol. VI (Leipzig: A. Deichert'sche Verlagsbuchhandlung, 1900), p. 6.

[36]Ibid., p. 177.

[37]Hans Hinrich Wendt, *The Gospel According to St. John: An Inquiry into Its Genesis and Historical Value*, trans. by E. Lummis (Edinburgh: T. & T. Clark, 1902), p. 236. H. H. Wendt, *Die Johannesbriefe und das johanneische Christentum* (Halle: Buchhandlung des Waisenhauses, 1925), was unavailable to the writer.

[38]Wendt, *The Gospel According to St. John*, p. 251.

[39]Drummond, *An Inquiry into the Character and Authorship of the Fourth Gospel*, pp. 394-408.

(John) above Peter. In opposition to the position of "mediate authorship" Drummond asked why a disciple would have withheld the name of John. Having raised these objections primarily in opposition to the work of Weizsäcker, Drummond turned his attention to Wendt's theory. According to Drummond, Wendt's position is based on two observations about the Gospel: ". . . the presence of primary and secondary elements in the narrative, and the breaks and apparent dislocations."[40] Neither of these observations persuaded Drummond. Rather, he found the similarity of style between John and I John to be so close that they must be the work of the same man. Moreover, there is no external evidence for the kind of source of memoirs and sayings which Wendt proposed.[41]

In 1905 N. Schmidt presented his theory of the origin of John. Very early John the Apostle was confused with the Presbyter. Actually, John was martyred long before the beginning of the second century:

> The champions of Peter's primacy, who by their addition to the gospel made it acceptable to the Catholic Church, were convinced that it came from the hand of "the beloved disciple," unable to distinguish between the two Johns, but anxious to prevent any rival claims by the Johannine school based on the widely reported saying of Jesus and the developing legend of John's continued existence on earth or translation. It is impossible to prove that this presbyter John who is known through Papias only as a transmitter of oral tradition had anything to do with the composition of the Fourth Gospel, is identical with "the presbyter" of the epistles whose name is not given, or is the author of the Apocalypse or any part of it.[42]

From this statement one surmises that Schmidt used the term "Johannine school" loosely and had in mind only those Christians who traced their brand of Christianity to John.

P. W. Schmiedel proposed an elaborate theory in 1908. All five Johannine writings were written in Ephesus by a community of writers who venerated John the Elder, who was once the head of their community. The Elder may have been the redactor of Revelation. The two small epistles were written by his followers

---

[40]Ibid., p. 400.

[41]Ibid., p. 403. Ernest De Witt Burton, *A Short Introduction to the Gospels* (Chicago: University of Chicago Press, 1904), pp. 117-122, 127, adopted a similar position.

[42]Nathaniel Schmidt, *The Prophet of Nazareth* (New York: The Macmillan Company, 1905), p. 211.

and published under his name. The community of writers realized, however, that the Elder's influence was not widespread,
so they published their subsequent writings, the Gospel and
First Epistle, in the name of a higher authority--John the
Apostle. Eventually the origin of these writings was obscured,
and all five were attributed to the Apostle.[43] Perhaps the
most interesting points about Schmiedel's proposal are that he
thought not just of a community of disciples but of writers,
and he separated them from any direct connection with John the
Apostle. C. K. Barrett's theory bears obvious resemblances to
Schmiedel's.[44]

E. F. Scott used "school" very loosely; John and I John
were not written by the same author but by men of ". . . the
same school of thought."[45] Regarding the authorship of Revelation, Scott stated only that it was ". . . written in the same
neighbourhood, under the same outward conditions as our Gospel."[46]

J. Wellhausen was primarily interested in the literary
strata of John but viewed the Gospel as a unity because of its
relation to a particular community:

> Trotz seiner verschiedenen Schichten lässt es sich doch his-
> torisch als wesentliche Einheit betrachten. Es ist anzuneh-
> men, dass die Erweiterungen zumeist aus dem selber Kreise
> stammen, innerhalb dessen die Grundschrift entstanden ist
> und ihre ersten Leser gefunden hat.[47]

Perhaps Wellhausen was the first to see the significance of the
Kreise or school in which the Gospel originated for the study of
its sources and literary strata.

In an important article in 1909 W. Bousset claimed that
the figure of the Beloved Disciple was created in order to place
the Gospel under the authority of an unknown disciple.[48] Then,

---

[43]Paul W. Schmiedel, *The Johannine Writings*, trans. by M. A. Canney
(London: Adam and Charles Black, 1908), p. 217; see also p. 191.

[44]C. K. Barrett, *The Gospel According to St. John* (London: S. P. C. K.,
1955), pp. 113-14; see below p. 23.

[45]Ernest F. Scott, *The Fourth Gospel: Its Purpose and Theology* (2nd
ed.; Edinburgh: T. & T. Clark, 1908), p. 88. The first edition was published in 1906.

[46]Ibid., p. 116.

[47]J. Wellhausen, *Das Evangelium Johannis* (Berlin: Georg Reimer, 1908),
p. 119. For Wellhausen's view of the relationship between the Gospel and I
John see his earlier work, *Erweiterungen und Änderungen im vierten Evangelium*
(Berlin: Georg Reimer, 1907), esp. p. 38.

[48]W. Bousset, "Ist das vierte Evangelium eine literarische Einheit?"
ThRu, XII (1909), 47-48.

after surveying the literary seams in John, Bousset concluded prophetically: "Vielleicht werden wir uns gewöhnen müssen das Evangelium als das Werk einer Schule, nicht eines einzelnen Mannes zu betrachten."[49] Bousset, therefore, was the first to raise the possibility that the Gospel may be the product of the joint effort of a school of writers.

In 1909 R. Law presented a carefully documented study of the linguistic evidence for the common authorship of John and I John. Since he rejected the idea that one writer was saturated with the manner of expression and theology of the other, he did not deal with the school hypothesis.[50]

Relying heavily on the evidence assembled by Holtzmann, A. E. Brooke argued for the common authorship of the Gospel and First Epistle. His only mention of the school hypothesis is instructive: ". . . it is practically impossible to *prove* common authorship, as against imitation, or similarity produced by common education in the same school of thought."[51] Brooke recognized that it is more difficult to refute the school hypothesis than the theory that the two writings were written by two authors not related to a common school.

J. Weiss subscribed to the view that John was written in a close-knit community without placing much emphasis on it:

> Around the author of the original work stood the circle of his disciples, influenced by him, and quite congenial to him in spirit. And it was from this circle, with the consent of a majority, that someone took up the work of redaction and edited the whole work; cf. in 21:24 the testimony of his students to the Disciple.[52]

Weiss seems to have been drawn to the school hypothesis both because of the evidences within the Gospel that it was redacted and because he interpreted 21:24 as referring to the evangelist's disciples.

---

[49]Ibid., p. 64. See the discussion of Bousset's later work below, p. 12.

[50]Robert Law, *The Tests of Life: A Study of the First Epistle of St. John* (Edinburgh: T. & T. Clark, 1909), esp. p. 345.

[51]A. E. Brooke, *A Critical and Exegetical Commentary on the Johannine Epistles*, ICC (Edinburgh: T. & T. Clark, 1912), p. xviii.

[52]Johannes Weiss, *The History of Primitive Christianity*, completed by R. Knopf, ed. by. F. C. Grant (2 vols.; New York: Wilson-Erickson Inc., 1937), II, 788. Weiss is discussed at this point because his position in the work cited is the same as that which he took in an earlier (1912) article: "Literaturgeschichte des N.T.," *RGG*, erste Aufl., III, 2199-201.

W. Heitmüller arrived at the school hypothesis by beginning with the Papias tradition. He first concluded that Papias
had no direct contact with John the Presbyter.[53] He was merely
instructed by the Presbyter's pupils:

> Aus den Mitteilungen, die dem Papias zuteil wurden, entneh-
> men wir, dass--vor seiner Generation--in Kleinasien ein Kreis
> von Leuten (vielleicht eine Art von Schule) vorhanden war,
> die den Ehrentitel "Presbyter" in Anspruch nahmen, als
> Schüler von Herrenjüngern galten.[54]

This circle promoted John and the Apocalypse and appealed to
the authority of a disciple of the Lord, the Presbyter John.
This man was probably not John the son of Zebedee. Gradually
he became the basis of authority for the traditions of this
circle (school).[55] The Gospel of John developed in three stages
within this circle:

> Wir würden also drei Stadien erkennen: 1. eine Schrift oder
> Einzelstücke ohne oder ohne deutliche Beziehung auf den Lieb-
> lingsjünger; 2. der Lieblingsjünger als Zeuge; 3. der Lieb-
> lingsjünger als Verfasser: c. 1-21 in der heutigen Gestalt.[56]

An analysis of the Gospel yields a clear parallelism to the
Papias tradition, i.e., both refer to a long-lived disciple:
"Der langlebige (21,22f.) Lieblingsjünger hier, der langlebige
Herrenschüler Johannes dort."[57] Heitmüller, therefore, claimed
that the two men are one and the same and that the "we" of John
21:24 refers to essentially the same circle known to Papias.[58]
In the tradition of the circle one also finds the statement of
the Presbyter John that Mark was written by a disciple of Peter.
Perhaps this statement is evidence that John was composed in a
similar manner:

> In dieser Schule, die sich an den Presbyteros Johannes
> anlehnte, wurden--so dürfen wir annehmen--Herrenworte,
> Erklärungen, längere Ausführungen kolportiert, die man mit
> Recht oder Unrecht auf diesen Johannes zurückführte. Sie
> wurden niedergeschrieben. So sind vielleicht Materielen
> entstanden, einzelne Worte, kürzere oder längere abgerundete
> Stücke--gedeckt von der Autorität des Johannes--die dann zu
> einer Evangelienschrift verarbeitet wurden.[59]

---

[53]W. Heitmüller, "Zur Johannes-Tradition," *ZNW*, XV (1914), 201.

[54]Ibid.

[55]Ibid., p. 203.

[56]Ibid., p. 205.

[57]Ibid., p. 206.

[58]Ibid., p. 207.

[59]Ibid., pp. 207-08.

Finally, near the end of the second century, the Presbyter John
was taken to be John the Apostle. Heitmüller argued his case
forcefully, but his vacillation between the terms "circle" and
"school" indicates his uncertainty as to the exact nature of
the community. He based his argument almost completely on the
patristic sources and evidences gathered from the Gospel itself,
making almost no use of the other Johannine writings. Ultimately
however, Heitmüller's weakest point may be the great credence
he required from his readers regarding the stages by which an
unknown figure, "John," was called presbyter, became the head
of a circle or school, became the basis of their authority, and
finally, was incorrectly understood to be John the son of Zebedee

In 1915 W. Bousset studied the schools of Philo and Clement
of Alexandria in order to illuminate the profile of early Christian teachers. In connection with our present study his work is
helpful because of the interpretation he gave to the term
πρεσβύτερος:

> Die πρεσβύτεροι, welche Papias als seine Autoritäten zitiert,
> resp. die παρηκολουθηκότες τοῖς πρεσβυτέροις sind herumzieh-
> ende Wanderlehrer. Wenn unter ihnen ὁ πρεσβύτερος Ἰωάννης
> und Aristion erscheinen, so haben wir in ihnen jedenfalls
> derartige inoffizielle Autoritäten zu sehen. Wir gewinnen
> überhaupt den Eindruck, als stünden die Kreise, die in den
> johanneischen Schriften zu Wort kommen, gleichsam als eine
> Schule mehr ausserhalb der organizierten Kirche, man denke
> an den 3. Johannesbrief mit seiner Polemik gegen den
> φιλοπρωτεύων Diotrephes. Der Kreis der φίλοι, der uns am
> Schluss dort entgegentritt, die Polemik gegen die falschen
> Hirten Joh. 10, das Kapitel 21 des Evangeliums, alles deutet
> in diese Richtung.[60]

In a footnote on the same page, Bousset added that he was in
agreement with the conclusions reached by Heitmüller in the
article discussed above. Bousset is important because he was
the first to use the study of relatively contemporary schools
and teachers as the way he approached the Johannine school.
And, his work seems to have had a notable influence on later
scholars: Kragerud[61] seized upon the idea of the *Wanderlehrer*,
and Käsemann[62] upon the relevance of the polemic against
Diotrephes for the task of describing the Johannine community.

---

[60]W[ilhelm] Bousset, *Jüdisch-Christlicher Schulbetrieb in Alexandria
und Rom: Literarische Untersuchungen zu Philo und Clemens von Alexandria
Justin und Irenäus*, FRLANT, n.F., Hft. VI (Göttingen: Vandenhoeck & Ruprecht,
1915), p. 316.

[61]See below, pp. 25-26.

[62]See below, p. 21.

H. L. Jackson proposed in 1918 that the Gospel is the product of an inner circle from the Johannine school which finished it after the author had died.[63] James Moffatt's *An Introduction to the Literature of the New Testament*, published in the same year, added little to the development of the Johannine-school hypothesis but endorsed what seems to have been the standard form of the hypothesis at that time. Using the Papias and Irenaeus traditions and the argument from silence, he concluded that John and the Apocalypse were both written in the Johannine school. John the Presbyter was the head of this school. The Apocalypse was probably the first writing to be attributed to John the Apostle. Later all five writings were attributed to him, and the Apostle replaced John the Presbyter as the traditional head of the school in Ephesus.[64]

In 1920 R. H. Charles arrived at the Johannine-school hypothesis as a result of his study of Revelation and the Jewish writings which form its background. He first asserted that the linguistic evidence points decisively to the conclusion that John and Revelation were not written by the same author. But, the two writers were related to each other ". . . either as master and pupil, or as pupils of the same master, or as members of the same school."[65] This hypothesis is further supported by evidence for similar schools in which some of the Jewish writings originated:

> We find perfect parallels to the latter relationship in earlier days. The authors of the Testaments of the XII Patriarchs and of the Book of Jubilees, . . . , studied clearly in the same school; for the text of the one has constantly to be interpreted by that of the other. . . . The second parallel is to be found between 4 Ezra and 2 Baruch. . . .
> In the Seer and the Evangelist we have got just such another literary connection. But the literary connection is much less close than in the case of the Jewish authors just mentioned, . . .[66]

---

[63]H. Latimer Jackson, *The Problem of the Fourth Gospel* (Cambridge: University Press, 1918), cited by Wilbert F. Howard, *The Fourth Gospel in Recent Criticism and Interpretation* (London: The Epworth Press, 1931), pp. 51-52.

[64]Moffatt, *An Introduction to the Literature of the New Testament*, pp. 589-619.

[65]R. H. Charles, *A Critical and Exegetical Commentary on the Revelation of St. John*, ICC (2 vols.; Edinburgh: T. & T. Clark, 1920), I, xxix.

[66]Ibid., I, xxxiii.

14

Charles' analysis of the relation between these Jewish writings
and the similarity between the situations in which they were
composed and the one in which the Johannine writings were written may require revision. His insight into the value of the
study of comparable schools for the study of the origin of the
Johannine writings, however, remains undiminished.

V. H. Stanton, writing in the same year as Charles, opposed
the Johannine-school hypothesis. In an attempt to refute
Wellhausen, Stanton maintained that it is unlikely that any
early Christian community ". . . should have contained several
members with the qualities of mind and spiritual temper which
would have made them capable of writing pieces of the Fourth
Gospel."[67] In this way he minimized the importance of the
aporias in John and did not consider the differences between
the Johannine writings to be sufficiently strong to warrant any
departure from the traditional view of their authorship.

In spite of his earlier work on the apostles and their
disciples,[68] T. Zahn repudiated the theory of the Johannine
school in his commentary. John was written for a specific community that knew the author,[69] but it is unthinkable that the
John of the Papias tradition should have been confused with the
Apostle.[70] No silhouettes like "Presbyter John" or "Johannine
school" can hide the apostolic authorship of the Gospel.[71]

J. Grill supported the school hypothesis by claiming that
the Presbyter and Papias were fellow students (*Mitschüler*) of
the Apostle.[72] But, he developed the hypothesis no further.

In an interesting study of the use of "we" in the Johannine
writings, A. von Harnack outlined the possible referents:

I.   ein indifferenter schriftstellerischer Plural, oder
II. der Plural. majest., bzw. autorit. (potenziertes "Ich")
     oder

---

[67]Stanton, *The Gospels as Historical Documents*, Part III: *The Fourth Gospel*, p. 48.

[68]See above, p. 7.

[69]Zahn, *Kommentar zum Neuen Testament*, Bd. IV: *Das Evangelium des Johannes*, p. 3.

[70]Ibid., p. 14.

[71]Ibid., p. 16.

[72]Julius Grill, *Untersuchungen über die Entstehung des vierten Evangeliums* (2 vols.; Tübingen: J. C. B. Mohr, 1902-23), II, 309.

III. der Plural. communic.
    (a) Der Schriftsteller und seine Genossen, seien es
           mitschreibende oder sei es ein bestimmter Kreis,
           dem er angehört und in dessen Namen er schreibt,
    (b) der Schriftsteller und seine adressaten,
    (c) der Schriftsteller und die Gemeinde der Gläubigen[1],
    (d) der Schriftsteller und, mehr oder weniger bestimmt,
           alle Menschen.

---

[1]Diese Bedeutung des "Wir" kann der des potenzierten "Ichs"
(II) sehr nahekommen.[73]

Then he investigated the use of "we" in the two small epistles.
The most important result of this investigation for the present
study is that the Presbyter never linked himself with unknown
persons who, in contrast to his readers, had a share in his
authoritative position.[74] Harnack then studied the use of "we"
in I John. The investigation yielded results similar to that
derived from the smaller epistles:

Doch bevor wir zu diesem übergehen, ist als Ergebnis unserer
Untersuchung hervorzuheben, dass das "Wir" der drei Johannesbriefe nirgendwo "Ich und alle Mitapostel" oder "Ich und alle
persönlichen Jünger Jesu und Augenzeugen" oder "Ich und mein
kleinasiatischer Kreis von Augenzeugen" bedeutet, sondern
entweder die in den Lesern angeschaute Gemeinde der Gläubigen
zusammen mit dem Verfasser oder das potenzierte Ich des Ver-
fassers allein, ...[75]

After a detailed study of the Gospel, Harnack finally concluded
that the author never introduced a "kleinasiatische Zeugengruppe"
or a special group of eye-witnesses of the historical Jesus,
that he distinguished himself from the Beloved Disciple, John,
and that he had never seen Jesus.[76] The evangelist looked upon
the Apostle as his "Gewährsmann."[77] Harnack denied that the
Johannine writings refer to a group of eye-witnesses but recognized that they were related to a "streitenden Kreise" in Asia
Minor.[78]

    B. H. Streeter asserted: "The word 'school' is one of
those vague seductive expressions which it is so easy to accept

---

[73]Adolf von Harnack, "Das 'Wir' in den johanneischen Schriften,"
Sitzungsberichte der Preussischen Akademie der Wissenschaften, XVII (1923),
96.

[74]Ibid., p. 99.

[75]Ibid., p. 105.

[76]Ibid., pp. 112-13.

[77]Cf. Adolf von Harnack, "Zum Johannesevangelium," in *Erforschtes und
Erlebtes* (Giessen: Alfred Töpelmann, 1923), p. 43.

[78]Harnack, "Das 'Wir' in den johanneischen Schriften," p. 113.

as a substitute for clear thinking."[79] He made this statement
in the midst of a discussion of the authorship of II and III
John. These epistles are either the work of one man or a teacher and his pupil. But, if the small epistles are not by the
author of the Gospel and I John, they must be secondary to the
larger works. The author of John cannot be dated a generation
earlier than John the Elder, nor can he be seen as a docile
pupil--he is a man of prestige and authority. The school hypothesis cannot be used to explain similarities in style, thought,
and general outlook. Moreover, in art and philosophy a school
". . . comes into existence when there is a considerable body
of work by the founder which serves as a model and a standard
for the pupils."[80] This is not the case with the Johannine literature except with respect to the Acts of John which is ". . .
obviously what artists call 'school work,' an inferior imitation."[81] Hence, Streeter concluded that all four writings are
the work of one man, the Elder.

R. Bultmann's article published in 1925 stressed the community background of the Fourth Gospel and located this community in Syria but did not deal with the Johannine-school hypothesis directly.[82] E. Gaugler, in a study of the Church in the
Johannine writings, proposed that because the author dealt so
freely with the synoptic gospels and the *logia* tradition he must
have stood in close relation to the Apostle John. Perhaps he
was a member of John's "Schülerkreis," which represented his
personal tradition. Furthermore, Gaugler made the interesting
observation that the residence of the Apostle John in Ephesus
is more strongly supported by the tradition than is his authorship of John.[83]

C. F. Nolloth allowed for the possibility that the Johannine writings are the product of a circle or school but claimed

---

[79]Burnett Hillman Streeter, *The Four Gospels: A Study of Origins*
(London: Macmillan and Co., Ltd., 1924), p. 459.

[80]Ibid., p. 460.

[81]Ibid.

[82]Rudolf Bultmann, "Die Bedeutung der neuerschlossenen mandäischen
und manichäischen Quellen für das Verständnis des Johannesevangeliums," *ZNW*,
XXIV (1925), 100-46.

[83]Ernst Gaugler, *Die Bedeutung der Kirche in den johanneischen
Schriften* (Bern: Gedruckt bei Stämpfli & Cie., 1925), pp. 9-10. Reprinted
from *Internationale kirchliche Zeitschrift*, XIV (1924), 97-117, 181-219; XV
(1925), 25-42.

that the impression that they are the work of one mind is stronger. He noted especially the ". . . intensely personal note . . ." which each writing strikes and the reference to the experience of the Word in the prefaces of each of the three major writings.[84] The single mind reflected in the prefaces ". . .--if not responsible for the writings as a whole--was, at any rate, the force that lay behind the school or group in which they had their origin."[85]

In 1929, in his introduction to the New Testament, H. Pope presumed to identify the members of the Johannine school.[86] J. Carpenter, writing a year later, mentioned the school hypothesis in a footnote[87] and noted that the writer of the prologue was ". . . not a trained metaphysician, nor a theologian of the schools."[88] J. H. Bernard did not adopt the school hypothesis, but his solution approached it: the Apostle wrote Revelation; the Presbyter sat at the feet of the Apostle and wrote John and the three epistles.[89] Likewise, M. Dibelius, in his article in RGG^2 asserted only that John depended upon the circle in which it originated.[90] The John of Ephesus was not the Apostle, but he drew about himself a circle of followers and wrote the Apocalypse.[91] The author of John, who was a member of the circle, appealed to this John as his "Gewährsmann" and regarded his authority as apostolic.[92]

H. Windisch's commentary on the catholic epistles contained a useful list of conceptual parallels between the Gospel and I John. He concluded that the two writings were composed in the same circle but have no literary connection with each other.

---

[84]Charles F. Nolloth, *The Fourth Evangelist: His Place in the Development of Religious Thought* (London: John Murray, 1925), pp. 99.

[85]Ibid., p. 101.

[86]H. Pope, *The New Testament* (London, 1926), pp. 268-74, cited by J. Edgar Bruns, *The Christian Buddhism of St. John: New Insights into the Fourth Gospel* (New York: Paulist Press, 1971), p. 8 n. 2.

[87]J. Estlin Carpenter, *The Johannine Writings: A Study of the Apocalypse and the Fourth Gospel* (Boston: Houghton Mifflin Co., 1927), p. 456.

[88]Ibid., p. 313.

[89]J. H. Bernard, *A Critical and Exegetical Commentary on the Gospel According to St. John*, ed. by A. H. McNeile, ICC (2 vols.; Edinburgh: T. & T. Clark, 1928), I, lxviii-lxx.

[90]Martin Dibelius, "Johannesevangelium," *RGG*, zweite Aufl., III, 357.

[91]Ibid., cols. 360-62.

[92]Ibid., col. 362.

Much speaks for their having been written by different authors, but common authorship cannot be ruled out.[93]

C. H. Dodd's famous article in the *Bulletin of the John Rylands Library* compared the style, language, and thought of the Gospel and I John. He concluded that they were written by different authors, but the author of I John was:

> . . . quite possibly a disciple of the Fourth Evangelist, and certainly a diligent student of his work. He has soaked himself in the Gospel, assimilating its ideas and forming his style upon its model.[94]

So, while Dodd did not explicitly speak of a Johannine school, his view of the authorship of these writings fit comfortably with the school hypothesis. The following year, 1938, P. Gardner-Smith published his *Saint John and the Synoptic Gospels*. In it he left open the question of whether John 21 was added to the Gospel by ". . . the original author or by 'one of his school.'"[95]

W. J. Burghardt examined the evidence for Ignatius of Antioch's knowledge of the Fourth Gospel or acquaintance with its author. Although he did not claim certainty, he thought that Ignatius shows dependence upon the author of the Fourth Gospel rather than the text of the Gospel itself.[96] Ignatius absorbed the substance of the Gospel ". . . either through the medium of personal discipleship, or through contact with a Johannine School, or by oral tradition."[97] Burghardt acknowledged the possibility of a Johannine school and used it to argue for the existence of a "well-formed" oral tradition which Ignatius may have known. He concluded that the hypothesis that Ignatius depended on the text of John is most likely, but ". . . we cannot at present see our way clear to a flat rejection of

---

[93]Hans Windisch, *Die katholischen Briefe*, HNT, Bd. XV, 2 Aufl. (Tübingen: J. C. B. Mohr, 1930), p. 110. See also his "Das johanneische Christentum und sein Verhältnis zum Judentum und zu Paulus," *Die christliche Welt*, XLVII (1933), 98-107, 147-54.

[94]C. H. Dodd, "The First Epistle of John and the Fourth Gospel," *BJRL*, XXI (1937), 129-56.

[95]P. Gardner-Smith, *Saint John and the Synoptic Gospels* (Cambridge: At the University Press, 1938), p. 85.

[96]Walter J. Burghardt, "Did Saint Ignatius of Antioch Know the Fourth Gospel?" *TS*, I (1940), 152.

[97]Ibid., p. 154.

the hypothesis of oral tradition or (less likely) a Johannine School."[98]

In a neglected book H. E. Dana argued forcefully for the transmission of an oral tradition containing Palestinian elements in Ephesian Christianity.[99] He referred to the tradition of teaching in the synagogue and pointed out that teaching and teachers played a significant role in early Christianity. Surprisingly though, he did not use the term "school." Instead he referred to "Ephesian Christianity," or "the Ephesian tradition," or occasionally the "Ephesian circle."[100] Still, much of his argument might be used equally well as support for the Johannine-school hypothesis.

Bultmann's commentary on John added little to the development of this hypothesis. He claimed that the evangelist belonged to a group of disciples of John the Baptist who went over to the Christian community and that he relied upon the traditions of this group.[101] Although Bultmann held that 21:24 refers to a ". . . definite circle, namely the author and the group to which he belongs; . . .,"[102] he added a footnote which weakened the force of this assertion:

> Goguel is right, Introd. II 309ff.: a definite circle cannot be meant. For either the readers know the circle which is editing the gospel, and then the appeal is superfluous, or they do not know it, and then it is meaningless.[103]

In his commentary on the Johannine epistles (1946) Dodd reaffirmed the position which he had taken earlier[104] but did not go beyond it. He suggested that II and III John were probably written by the same man and that this man can hardly have been ". . . a subordinate figure of a Johannine school . . ." because of the great authority and responsibility which he

---

[98]Ibid., p. 156.

[99]H. E. Dana, *The Ephesian Tradition: An Oral Source of the Fourth Gospel* (Kansas City: The Kansas City Seminary Press, 1940).

[100]Ibid., p. 123.

[101]Rudolf Bultmann, *The Gospel of John: A Commentary*, trans. by G. R. Beasley-Murray, R. W. N. Hoare, and J. K. Riches (Philadelphia: The Westminster Press, 1971), pp. 18, 108. First published in German in 1941.

[102]Ibid., p. 717.

[103]Ibid., p. 718.

[104]See above, p. 18.

exercised.[105] Moreover, the author of these epistles also wrote
I John but not the Gospel. Finally, he observed that "the
epistles can be attributed to the Presbyter John only at the
cost of withdrawing his candidature for the authorship of the
Fourth Gospel, ..."[106] Thus, Dodd left his readers the
following view: the Epistles were written by a disciple (perhaps John the Presbyter) of the evangelist but not by a subordinate member of the Johannine school.

In the year following the publication of Dodd's commentary,
W. F. Howard attempted to refute Dodd's position point by point
and thus to reassert the common authorship of the Gospel and
three epistles.[107] W. G. Wilson[108] and A. P. Salom[109] examined
the linguistic evidence and reached the same conclusion. It is
interesting to observe that the scholars who have opposed the
Johannine-school hypothesis have usually done so by arguing that
the Johannine writings (at least the Gospel and epistles) were
written by one man and thereby implying (at least by their silence on the question of a school) that such a hypothesis is
unnecessary. Ironically, J. B. Lightfoot, one of the first to
affirm the existence of the Johannine school, also supported
the common authorship of the Johannine writings. The point
is that few scholars have argued directly against the existence
of a Johannine school.

E. Stauffer maintained that the John at Ephesus was the
Apostle and ascribed to him all five Johannine writings. Still,
he interpreted John 21 and the Papias tradition to mean that
the Apostle had disciples and agreed that these disciples may
have taken part in ". . . the transcription, the shaping, and
the publication of the writings themselves."[110] But, since he
could not separate the work of the disciples from their master,

---

[105]C. H. Dodd, *The Johannine Epistles*, The Moffatt New Testament Commentary (New York: Harper and Brothers, 1946), p. lxiv.

[106]Ibid., p. lxxxi.

[107]W. F. Howard, "The Common Authorship of the Johannine Gospel and
Epistles," *JTS*, XLVIII (1947), 12-25.

[108]W. G. Wilson, "An Examination of the Linguistic Evidence Adduced
against the Unity of Authorship of the First Epistle of John and the Fourth
Gospel," *JTS*, IL (1948), 147-56.

[109]A. P. Salom, "Some Aspects of the Grammatical Style of I John,"
JBL, LXXIV (1955), 96-102.

[110]Ethelbert Stauffer, *New Testament Theology*, trans. by J. Marsh (New
York: The Macmillan Company, 1955), p. 41. The book was first published in
German in 1947.

he ascribed the writings ". . . to the apostle John or to his influence."[111] Stauffer also emphasized the role of "systematic theological instruction," the discussions between Christian schools, and their common struggle against heretical schools.[112] Specifically, he found evidence for a Pauline, Johannine, Roman, and later an Alexandrian "school."[113]

While the 1930's and 1940's produced relatively little literature on the Johannine school, discussion of this hypothesis blossomed in the next two decades. The wide acceptance which the Johannine-school hypothesis gained in the 1950's is indicated by the way in which authors accepted it without making a case for it. C. B. Hedrick referred to "St. John and his school" as though there were no longer any need to justify or explain the idea.[114] The hypothesis also gained support from those scholars who argued that the Johannine tradition was as old as the synoptic.[115]

In "Ketzer und Zeuge" E. Käsemann provisionally held the common authorship of the Gospel and Epistles but indicated that his thesis would not be affected if one had to distribute the writings ". . . auf den Kreis einer Schule."[116] His thesis was that the Presbyter was a Christian gnostic who was recognized as such by Diotrephes and excommunicated from the orthodox Church.[117] Yet, Diotrephes did not want to prevent the Johannine writings (perhaps after an ecclesiastical revision) from entering triumphantly into the orthodox community.[118] Even if

---

[111]Ibid.

[112]Ibid., p. 236.

[113]Ibid., p. 320 n. 751.

[114]Charles Baker Hedrick, "The Christianity of the Fourth Gospel," *ATR*, XXXIII (1951), 218. See also Philip Carrington, *The Primitive Christian Calendar: A Study in the Making of the Marcan Gospel* (Cambridge: University Press, 1952), I, xiv-xv.

[115]See, for example, Oscar Cullmann, "The Significance of the Qumran Texts for Research into the Beginnings of Christianity," *JBL*, LXXIV (1955), 213-26.

[116]Ernst Käsemann, "Ketzer und Zeuge," in *Exegetische Versuche und Besinnungen* (Göttingen: Vandenhoeck & Ruprecht, 1960), I, 174. This article was first published in *ZTK*, XLVIII (1951), 292-311. Käsemann later assigned the Gospel and Epistles to different writers: *Exegetische Versuche und Besinnungen*, II, 133 n. 1.

[117]Ibid., I, 174, 178.

[118]Ibid., I, 178.

the Gospel and Epistles were written by only one man, they still
reflect a community which saw itself as "living in the truth":

> Ebensowenig ist es zufällig, dass später gerade Konventikel-
> frömmigkeit immer wieder diese Prädikate als Bezeichnung der
> wahren Kirche aufgegriffen hat. Die johanneischen Schriften
> weisen auf eine ecclesiola in ecclesia als sie tragende
> Gemeinschaftsform hin. . . . und die Briefe insofern auch
> mit einem gewissen sachlichen Recht als die ersten Zeugnisse
> christlicher Konventikelbildung angesprochen werden dürfen.[11]

Although Käsemann did not embrace the school hypothesis, he illuminated the nature of the community in which the Johannine
writings developed.

R. Gyllenberg claimed the root of the diversity between
the gospel traditions could be traced directly to the striking
differences among the disciples around Jesus: "Also haben wir
es nicht mit einer Urgemeinde zu tun, sondern von Anfang an mit
mehreren von einander abweichenden kleinen Kreisen, die alle
von Jesus entscheidende Eindrücke bekommen hatten."[120] Apparently the Johannine tradition developed in one of these
"Kreisen," but what did Gyllenberg mean by this term? B. Noack
also stressed the oral tradition upon which the Fourth Gospel
is based but did not adopt the school hypothesis explicitly.[121]

In 1954 K. Stendahl strengthened the Johannine-school
hypothesis considerably by his study, *The School of St. Matthew*.
He recognized schools as the possible "creative milieu of the
gospels" and then attempted to show how the Old Testament quotations in Matthew reflect the work of the Matthean school.
The same method, he asserted, can be used to demonstrate the
work of the Johannine school:

> As in Revelation he seems to work on his own, showing acquaint-
> ance with the Hebrew text as well as with the LXX. This is
> exactly what might be expected in a gospel which developed in
> the School of St. John, a school where the Scriptures were
> studied and meditated upon in the light of the preaching,
> teaching and debating in which the church was involved.[122]

For Johannine research Stendahl's contribution is twofold: he

---

[119]Ibid., I, 179.

[120]Raffael Gyllenberg, "Die Anfänge der johanneischen Tradition," in
Neutestamentliche Studien für Rudolf Bultmann, BZNW, XXI (Berlin: Alfred
Töpelmann, 1954), p. 146.

[121]Bent Noack, *Zur johanneischen Tradition: Beiträge zur literarkri-
tische Exegese des vierten Evangeliums* (Copenhagen: Rosenkilde, 1954).

[122]Krister Stendahl, *The School of St. Matthew: And Its Use of the
Old Testament* (2nd ed.; Philadelphia: Fortress Press, 1968), p. 163; see
also p. 31. First published in 1954. (Hereinafter referred to as *School*.)

demonstrated (1) that other Christian schools probably existed at the time John was written and (2) that the work of such schools can be seen in their quotations from the Old Testament.

C. K. Barrett presented the school hypothesis in an elaborate form. John the Apostle went to Ephesus and gathered pupils. Revelation is based on his written words. The evangelist, the author (or authors) of the Epistles, and the final editor of Revelation were all pupils of the Apostle. The Gospel was later edited, chapter 21 was added, and the whole Gospel was ascribed to the Apostle John.[123]

In a sense, F. W. Young's article provided support for the Johannine-school hypothesis. Young found within John a very sophisticated use of Isaiah, i.e., a form of exegesis which Stendahl would probably regard as the work of a school. John drew upon his knowledge of an "Isaiah tradition": "There is good reason to believe that the author of the Fourth Gospel was one of a group who related themselves to Isaiah in a unique way, and drew upon his book for religious inspiration."[124] While Young never suggested that this "group" was a school, his article supported rather than weakened the hypothesis.

The papers presented by H. Riesenfeld, J. A. T. Robinson, and S. Schulz to the International Congress on "The Four Gospels in 1957" are all important in the history of debate over the Johannine school. Riesenfeld stressed the importance of teaching and memorization in the early Church and stated that Matthew and John ". . . issued from the formative influence of a school."[125] Robinson concluded his paper by saying that the fundamental distinction of "the new look on the Fourth Gospel" is that it sees the origin of the Johannine tradition and its continuity with the earliest days of Christianity in ". . . the life of an on-going community."[126] Schulz characterized this community as a *ḥaburah* similar to other heterodox, late-Jewish

---

[123]Barrett, *The Gospel According to St. John*, pp. 52, 113-14.

[124]Franklin W. Young, "A Study of the Relation of Isaiah to the Fourth Gospel," *ZNW*, XLVI (1955), 231.

[125]Harald Riesenfeld, "The Gospel Tradition and Its Beginnings," in *Studia Evangelica*, TU, Bd. LXXIII (Berlin: Akademie-Verlag, 1959), p. 44. Reprinted in his *The Gospel Tradition* (Philadelphia: Fortress Press, 1970), cf. p. 3.

[126]John A. T. Robinson, "The New Look on the Fourth Gospel," in *Studia Evangelica*, p. 350. Reprinted in his *Twelve New Testament Studies*, SBT, XXXIV (Naperville, Ill.: Alec R. Allenson, Inc., 1962), pp. 94-106.

24

ḥaburoth. The members of this *ḥaburah* came predominantly from
". . . Mitgliedern der Qumran--wie Täufergemeinden und Vertre-
tern der Apokalyptic, . . ." who entered the early Christian
community.[127] The nucleus of the community consisted of ". . .
schriftkundige und midraschgewandte . . ." priests who stood in
a closed front against the official, pharisaic Judaism. These
educated priests produced the Johannine writings with their
anti-pharisaic polemic. Schulz developed this position further
in a later writing.[128] He distinguished three different kinds
of *ḥaburoth*: the pharisaic *ḥaburoth* of the time of Jesus, the
yaḥad of Qumran, and the Rabbinic *ḥaburoth* after the destructio
of the temple. The first and third cannot be considered as
models for the Johannine *ḥaburah*, but the similar *ḥaburoth* of
the Baptist, apocalyptists, and Urmandeans must be considered.
So, the Johannine *ḥaburah* emerges as a kind of mixing pot
("Sammelbecken") of the various sectarian groups of late Judais
and Schulz saw evidence of their various traditions in the
Johannine writings. Thus, while the synoptic tradition relies
upon a more strongly pharisaic type of Jewish-Christianity, the
Johannine tradition goes back to a sectarian, syncretistic, and
gnosticizing Jewish-Christianity.

W. Wilkens studied the use of sources and traditions in
John and concluded that the Gospel was left unfinished by the
evangelist and put in circulation after his death by a
"Schülerkreis" (21:24f.).[129] F.-M. Braun viewed the Johannine
school in a slightly different way. The Apostle John decided
to produce a gospel from the small units of his kerygma. In
this effort he used the help of secretaries and disciples.
After some preparatory work he enlisted the services of a scrib
(secretary) who could write Greek correctly, but the scribe did
not finish the work before the Apostle died. Thereafter the
scribe added a few finishing touches but left certain aporias

---

[127]S[iegfried] Schulz, "Die Komposition des Johannesprologs und die
Zusammensetzung des 4. Evangeliums," in *Studia Evangelica*, pp. 361-62.
Schulz was not the first to suggest that the Johannine community was a
ḥaburah: see: A. Fridrichsen, *Johannesevangeliet* (Stockholm, 1939), cited
by Stendahl, *School*, p. 31.

[128]Siegfried Schulz, *Komposition und Herkunft der johanneischen Reden*,
BWANT, V, 1 (Stuttgart: W. Kohlhammer Verlag, 1960), pp. 182-87.

[129]Wilhelm Wilkens, *Die Entstehungsgeschichte des vierten Evangeliums*
(Zollikon: Evangelischer Verlag A.G., 1958), p. 172.

in the text.[130] R. Schnackenburg endorsed Braun's hypothesis
with some modifications.[131]

A. Kragerud raised serious objections to the Johannine-
school hypothesis:

> Mit dem allgemeinen Urteil, das johanneische Schrifttum
> stamme aus derselben "Schule", können wir uns nicht begnügen.
> Denn sofern der Begriff der "Schule" hier ein geistesge-
> schichtlicher ist, so ist dabei nur die Wurzelverwandschaft
> der Schriften als solche gekennzeichnet, sofern er ein his-
> torischer Begriff sein will, so vermissen wir darin gerade
> die wesentliche Bestimmung, wie wir uns diese "Schule" vorzu-
> stellen haben.[132]

In a footnote Kragerud charged that the Johannine school is too
often spoken of as a private theological seminary. He traced
the progressive development of the concept of school from
Heitmüller, to Bousset, to Stendahl[133] and observed that
Stendahl's concept of a school approximated the *ḥaburoth* discussed by Jeremias.[134] All of these theories have the same
fault; they are not derived ("gewonnen") from the writings themselves. The "we" in John 21:24 and the manner in which the Old
Testament is quoted cannot be used to this end.[135] Kragerud's
reservations must be taken seriously. If the Johannine-school
hypothesis is to be accepted it must be solidly based on the
evidence provided by the Johannine writings themselves, and the
concept of the "school" must be defined in accordance with what
we know of first-century institutions.

Having expressed these reservations, Kragerud proceeded to
develop an elaborate theory about the origin of the Johannine
writings. All five writings originated in a circle of traveling prophets, an ". . . apostolischen Kollegs von Wanderpredi-
gern."[136] This circle was an organized "Gemeinschaft,"[137] which

---

[130]F.-M. Braun, *Jean le Théologien*, EBib (3 vols.; Paris: Librairie
Lecoffre, 1959-66), I, 40-41, and 396-97.

[131]See below, p. 28 n. 153.

[132]Alv Kragerud, *Der Lieblingsjünger im Johannesevangelium* (Oslo:
Osloer Universitätsverlag, 1959), p. 93.

[133]See the discussions of the work of these men above.

[134]Joachim Jeremias, *Jerusalem in the Time of Jesus: An Investigation
into the Economic and Social Conditions during the New Testament Period*,
trans. by F. H. and C. H. Cave (Philadelphia: Fortress Press, 1969), pp.
247-56.

[135]Kragerud, *Der Lieblingsjünger im Johannesevangelium*, p. 93.

[136]Ibid., p. 104. Cf. the work of Bousset discussed above, p. 9.

[137]Ibid., p. 105.

sent its members out from a central community on missionary tours. The occasion for writing III John arose when some of these traveling preachers were rejected by Diotrephes and his congregation and reported the difficulty to the Presbyter when they returned. This community had ". . . dem höchst denkbaren pneumatischen Selbstbewusstsein."[138] Since it saw itself as the true mediator between Christ and the Church, the community referred to itself as the Beloved Disciple.[139]

M.-É. Boismard traced the development of various stages of Johannine eschatology. He referred to Johannine "circles" and conceded that Dodd had made a strong case for diversity of authorship, but still held that the evolution of style and theology could be accounted for by stages of redaction by one man over a period of several decades.[140] Gerhardsson's work, though relevant, did not deal with the Johannine-school hypothesis.[141]

B. Lindars, guided by his study of the use of the Old Testament in the New, embraced the Johannine-school hypothesis. Several writers worked to produce the Johannine writings, but the author of Revelation did not have "a close personal contact" with the evangelist:

> This school, like that of Matthew, has the common store of scriptural material for its catechetical and apologetic work, and also its own local developments. John's relation to this school seems to be less formal than that of Matthew's.[142]

Nevertheless, John was familiar with the "rabbinic type of disputation" at the school and sifted its traditions.[143]

O. Merlier developed a multiple-stage hypothesis about the composition of John but did not claim that it was the work of a school.[144] Echoing Dodd, G. B. Caird asserted that the author-

---

[138]Ibid., p. 100.

[139]For the full discussion see Kragerud, ibid., pp. 93-112, 149-50.

[140]M.-É. Boismard, "L'Évolution du thème eschatologique dans les traditions johanniques," *RB*, LXVIII (1961), 523-24.

[141]Birger Gerhardsson, *Memory and Manuscript: Oral Tradition and Written Transmission in Rabbinic Judaism and Early Christianity*, trans. by E. J. Sharpe, Acta Seminarii Neotestamentici Upsaliensis, XXII (Uppsala: C. W. K. Gleerup, 1961).

[142]Barnabas Lindars, *New Testament Apologetic: The Doctrinal Significance of the Old Testament Quotations* (Philadelphia: Westminster Press, 1961), pp. 265-66.

[143]Ibid., pp. 266 and 272.

[144]Octave Merlier, *Le Quatrième Évangile: La question johannique* (Paris: Presses Universitaires de France, 1961), pp. 432-48.

ity of the Presbyter is such that he cannot have been ". . . a subordinate member of the Johannine school."[145] Caird assumed the existence of the Johannine school without supporting or clarifying the hypothesis.

The following statement suggests that L. Goppelt assumed that the disciple referred to in John 21:24 was the evangelist:

> Today one can say with a degree of certainty about the back-ground of the Fourth Gospel that the author left it behind in its unfinished form, and it was·published by a circle of men who were intimately connected with him (John xxi.24f.).[146]

Goppelt also declared that this circle was neither a congrega-tion nor a *ḥaburah* but ". . . a school comparable to that which we find around Paul and Peter and like the one which stands behind Matthew's Gospel."[147] The school formed around the Apostle John, engaged in missionary struggles with the Samaritans, disputed with Gnosticism, and preserved the common tradition which we find in John and Revelation.[148] The way in which Goppelt assumed the validity of the school hypothesis, asserted that the school was not a *ḥaburah* and likened it to "schools" which developed around other prominent figures indicates the need for a detailed clarification of the evidence in favor of the Johannine-school hypothesis and an attempt to determine the nature of this "school."

In his study of the earliest Christian confessions, V. H. Neufeld concluded that the function of the *homologia* in the Johannine literature is threefold:

> (1) As a confession of faith the *homologia* was the test or criterion of true inspiration and belief (I Jn. 4.1-3). . . .
> (2) As a profession of faith the *homologia* was the test of personal belief and conviction. . . . (3) As a statement of "orthodoxy" the *homologia* was not only a test of true faith but also a weapon used polemically against heretical movements (I Jn. 2.18-23; 4.1-3; II Jn. 9-11).[149]

With footnotes to Stauffer and Bousset, Neufeld stated that in the third function we see the effect of the Johannine school's

---

[145]G. B. Caird, "John, Letters of," *IDB*, II, 951. Cf. The quotation from Dodd above, p. 19.

[146]Leonhard Goppelt, *Apostolic and Post-Apostolic Times*, trans. by R. A. Guelich (London: Adam and Charles Black, 1970), p. 128. The German edition was published in 1962.

[147]Ibid., pp. 128-29.

[148]Ibid., pp. 129-30.

[149]Vernon H. Neufeld, *The Earliest Christian Confessions*, NTTS, Vol. V (Grand Rapids, Mich.: Wm. B. Eerdmans, 1963), pp. 106-07.

struggle with heretical views.[150] His work is important because
it opened a new approach to the school hypothesis, i.e., the
possibility that the Johannine *homologia* serve as evidence in
favor of the hypothesis.

In his commentary on the Johannine epistles, published
before his commentary on John, R. Schnackenburg stated that the
differences between the Gospel and First Epistle can be resolved
by the considerations proposed by W. F. Howard. So, common
authorship is possible; but he could also understand why other
authors, even Catholic authors, deny common authorship.[151] He
wrote of a circle and agreed that those who claim that John was
written by the Apostle encounter no difficulty in ascribing I
John to one of his disciples.[152] In the following year, 1965,
Part I of his commentary on John appeared. In this volume
Schnackenburg endorsed F.-M. Braun's position with modifications
at the following points: he rejected the "secretary" hypothesis
denied that the writer of the body of the Gospel also wrote
21:24, and allowed ". . . the Hellenistic disciple of the Apostl
who committed the Gospel to writing . . ." far more independence
than Braun.[153] Schnackenburg also contended that the Johannine
discourses of Jesus may reflect the influence of ". . . the
venerable preacher, who remains in the background, . . ." the
evangelist, the redactor, or ". . . the theological school or
trend . . . to which the rest of the 'Johannine' writings must
also be ascribed."[154] This hypothesis allows one to attribute
the references to the Beloved Disciple to the evangelist, who
along with the other disciples was accustomed to referring to
his master, John, in this way.[155]

---

[150]Ibid., p. 104.

[151]Rudolf Schnackenburg, *Die Johannesbriefe*, HTKNT, Bd. XIII, Fasz. 3,
3 Aufl. (Freiburg: Verlag Herder, 1965), p. 38.

[152]Ibid., p. 41.

[153]Rudolf Schnackenburg, *The Gospel According to St. John*, trans. by
K. Smyth, HTCNT (New York: Herder and Herder, 1968), I, 101-02. Published
in German in 1965. For Braun's position see above, p. 24. Schnackenburg
did not use the term "school" in "The Church in the Johannine Writings
Including the Apocalypse," in *The Church in the New Testament* (New York:
Herder and Herder, 1965), pp. 103-17.

[154]Schnackenburg, *The Gospel According to St. John*, I, 103, cf. p. 95.

[155]See also Rudolf Schnackenburg, "On the Origin of the Fourth Gospel,"
in *Jesus and Man's Hope* (2 vols.; Pittsburgh: Pittsburgh Theological Seminary, 1970), I, 223-46, in which Schnackenburg attempted to relate the texts
which refer to the Beloved Disciple to their contemporary background in
". . . the Johannine circle and the Johannine communities."

E. D. Freed agreed with Lindars that John's use of the Old Testament makes it "extremely likely" that John originated in an early Christian school. There is evidence for the use of the Hebrew text along with the Greek and the tradition of the Targums, and the evangelist's method ". . . presupposes and reveals a thorough training in the Jewish scriptures and tradition and a thorough knowledge of their content."[156] P. Borgen's study of the homily in John 6:31-58 agreed with Freed's findings: ". . . John's environment seems to have been a 'school' of a church after the break with the synagogue had become a definite fact."[157] John 6 reflects the situation of the Johannine church; the threat comes from gnostic docetism, and the quotation in 6:45 and its interpretation point to a ". . . conscious scholarly effort."[158]

D. M. Smith, Jr. observed that if ". . . the Johannine literature is the work of a school or circle of disciples, . . ." then it is not surprising to find an indication in Jn. 19:35 of the ". . . real or alleged source of their distinctive witness."[159] The Gospel and Epistles are not the work of one man, and ". . . some as yet undefined relation may very well exist between them and Revelation."[160]

R. E. Brown has advanced the most highly developed form of the Johannine-school hypothesis to date. He posited five stages and suggested that the Gospel's pre-history may be even more complicated. Stage one is simply ". . . a body of traditional material pertaining to the words and works of Jesus."[161] This material was independent of the synoptic tradition. Stage two

---

[156]Edwin D. Freed, *Old Testament Quotations in the Gospel of John*, NovTSup, Vol. XI (Leiden: E. J. Brill, 1965), pp. 129-30, and p. xi.

[157]Peder Borgen, *Bread from Heaven: An Exegetical Study of the Concept of Manna in the Gospel of John and the Writings of Philo*, NovTSup, Vol. X (Leiden: E. J. Brill, 1965), p. 3.

[158]Ibid., p. 86.

[159]Dwight Moody Smith, Jr., *The Composition and Order of the Fourth Gospel: Bultmann's Literary Theory*, Yale Publications in Religion, X (New Haven: Yale University Press, 1965), p. 233.

[160]Robert A. Spivey and D. Moody Smith, Jr., *Anatomy of the New Testament: A Guide to Its Structure and Meaning* (2nd ed.; New York: Macmillan Publishing Co., 1974), p. 427.

[161]Raymond E. Brown, *The Gospel According to John*, The Anchor Bible, Vols. XXIX and XXIXa (Garden City, New York: Doubleday & Company, Inc., 1966-70), p. xxxiv. The following sentences summarize the theory he developed on pp. xxxiv-xxxix.

is ". . . the development of this material in Johannine patterns, . . ." which was accomplished over several decades
through preaching and teaching. Toward the end of this stage
units of the developing oral tradition were written down. The
preaching and teaching was probably the work of more than one
man, but one man may have been principally responsible for it:

> Since the general traits of Johannine thought are so clear,
> even in the units that betray minor differences of style, we
> should probably think of a close-knit school of thought and
> expression. In this school the principal preacher was the
> one responsible for the main body of Gospel material. Per-
> haps, too, in such a school we may find the answer to the
> problem of other Johannine works, like the Epistles and Rev-
> elation, which share common thoughts and vocabulary, but
> betray differences in style.[162]

Stage three is the composition of a consecutive Gospel. The
". . . dominant or master preacher and theologian . . ." of
stage two organized this first edition of the Gospel and thus
may be called the evangelist. Stage four is the ". . . secondary edition by the evangelist." The evangelist may have worked
over his Gospel more than once, but only one editing seems to
be required. The Gospel was edited to meet new goals as the
situation of its readers changed. Stage five is the final
editing by the redactor:

> We think that the most likely supposition is that the redac-
> tor was a close friend or disciple of the evangelist, and
> certainly part of the general school of thought to which we
> referred in Stage 2.[163]

The redactor preserved material from stage two which was derived
from the evangelist but not included in the Gospel earlier.
Nevertheless, Brown attributed the inclusion of a great deal of
material to the work of the redactor: 3:31-36; 6:51-58; 12:44-
50; 16:4-33 (and possibly much more of chapters 15-17), chapters
11-12; the redactor also added material that had not come from
the evangelist: chapter 21, and the prologue ("a once-independen
hymn composed in Johannine circles"), and possibly minor element
taken from the synoptic tradition. In spite of this elaborate
hypothesis, Brown was noticeably vague about the nature or
organization of the Johannine school. He referred to it as "a
close-knit school of thought and expression," "the general
school of thought," and, regarding the origin of the prologue,
"Johannine circles." Furthermore, the central figure in this

---

[162]Ibid., p. xxxv.

[163]Ibid., p. xxxvi.

school of thought is a "preacher and theologian," not a teacher.
One wonders whether Brown was really thinking of a school or of
a church or group of churches. Perhaps his view of the Johannine school will be clarified in his forthcoming commentary on
the Johannine epistles.

E. Käsemann used the theology of John 17 as the means for
studying the Johannine community. The self-designations "disciples," "brothers," and "friends" characterize the community.[164]
Käsemann called the community "the Johannine school," but only
once and only while writing about I John.[165] Usually he used
the words "community" or "Christian conventicle." Käsemann concluded that John's theology reflects its origin in a conventicle
with gnosticizing tendencies,[166] possibly located in Syria,[167]
which existed on or was ". . . being pushed to, the Church's
periphery."[168]

W. G. Kümmel published his comprehensive *Introduction to the
New Testament* in 1966.[169] In view of the thoroughness of this
work and the number of scholars who have adopted the Johannine-
school hypothesis one is amazed that Kümmel did not discuss this
hypothesis at all.

J. C. O'Neill proposed that I John was written by a member
of a Jewish sectarian group. Most of the members of this sect
had become Christians, but a few refused to do so. I John ". . .
consists of twelve poetic admonitions belonging to the traditional writings of the Jewish movement, . . ."[170] and is a
polemic against those who refused to join the Christian movement. John is ". . . a later development within the same tradition."[171]

_____

[164]Ernst Käsemann, *The Testament of Jesus: A Study of John in the
Light of Chapter 17*, trans. by G. Krodel (Philadelphia: Fortress Press,
1968), pp. 30-32. Published in German in 1966.

[165]Ibid., p. 60.

[166]Ibid., pp. 70, 73.

[167]Ibid., pp. 24, 36.

[168]Ibid., p. 39.

[169]Werner Georg Kümmel, *Introduction to the New Testament*, trans. by
A. J. Mattill, Jr., founded by P. Feine and J. Behm (14th ed.; New York:
Abingdon Press, 1966).

[170]J. C. O'Neill, *The Puzzle of I John: A New Examination of Origins*
(London: S. P. C. K., 1966), p. 6.

[171]Ibid., pp. 66-67.

In his article in the *Jerome Biblical Commentary*, J.-L. D'Aragon tentatively followed the school hypothesis as proposed by C. K. Barrett, F.-M. Braun, and A. Feuillet. John the Apostle resided in Asia Minor and ". . . inspired all the Johannine writings, perhaps through a catechetical school at Ephesus, but the redaction would have been carried out by different disciples, more or less familiar with his thought."[172]

H. Leroy attempted to study the Johannine milieu by studying the Gospel's use of the technique of misunderstanding. He emphasized the eschatological awareness of the community and referred to the Johannine "Traditionskreis," but he did not mention a school. The community was short-lived, mid-way between enthusiasm and early Catholicism, and in conflict with the synagogue.[173]

Recent research on John has contributed much to our understanding of its background. J. L. Martyn, for example, illuminated an important aspect of John's milieu, but did not refer to the Johannine community as a school.[174] B. Vawter stated that in a broad sense at least "I Jn can be considered a commentary on the Gospel as taught in the Johannine school."[175] H. Conzelmann claimed that the Epistles ". . . derive from the school of the evangelist,"[176] and that the Johannine community has ". . . the appearance of a sect, which cultivates its religious life by retreating from the world."[177] Nevertheless, this "enclosed brotherhood" still confronts the world with revelation and the offer of faith.[178] W. E. Hull accounted for the dissimilarities among the Johannine writings by assigning

---

[172]Jean-Louis D'Aragon, "The Apocalypse," *JBC*, II, 469.

[173]Herbert Leroy, *Rätsel und Missverständnis: Ein Beitrag zur Formgeschichte des Johannesevangelium*, BBB, XXX (Bonn: R. Hanstein, 1968), pp. 191-95.

[174]J. Louis Martyn, *History and Theology in the Fourth Gospel* (New York: Harper and Row, 1968), and "Source Criticism and *Religionsgeschichte* in the Fourth Gospel," in *Jesus and Man's Hope*, I, 247-73.

[175]Bruce Vawter, "The Johannine Epistles," *JBC*, II, 405. Vawter maintains that I John is earlier than John and is a commentary on its oral history.

[176]Hans Conzelmann, *An Outline of the Theology of the New Testament*, trans. by J. Bowden (New York: Harper & Row, Publishers, 1969), p. 321. Published in German in 1967.

[177]Ibid., p. 355.

[178]Ibid., p. 356.

them to "a number of individuals" who contributed to their composition ". . . over a period of perhaps one or two decades, . . . " and for the similarities among them by claiming that these individuals all contributed their efforts to ". . . the same Christian 'school' or community, ..."[179] G. Johnston referred to the Johannine-school hypothesis several times in his study of the Spirit-Paraclete. But, although his discussion of the Spirit-Paraclete as the inspired teacher complements the hypothesis, he seems to have had reservations about calling the community a school.[180]

G. Klein examined the theological perspective of, and relationship between, John and I John from the standpoint of their concept of time. In this way, he claimed, we can see some of the theological development which occurred in the Johannine school, a "theologische Schule."[181]

> So komplex ist die vom Verfasser des I Joh zu bewältigende überlieferungsgeschichtliche Situation: Die eschatologische Qualifikation der Gegenwart, der Johannesschule anvertrautes zentrales Vermächtnis ihres Lehrers, muss nunmehr notwendig vermittelt werden mit der inzwischen aufgebrochenen Erfahrung, dass der Ablauf der Zeit als theologisches Problem damit noch nicht bewältigt ist.[182]

In another attempt to understand the background of John by examining its theology, J. E. Bruns found Buddhist influence upon the Johannine school.[183] More significantly, J. L. Price[184] and J. H. Charlesworth[185] both adopted the Johannine-school hypothesis in their contributions to a collection of studies on John and Qumran.

A formidable attempt to understand the Johannine community was recently made by W. A. Meeks. Meeks used the word "school"

---

[179]William E. Hull, "John," in *The Broadman Bible Commentary* (Nashville: Broadman Press, 1970), IX, 190-91.

[180]George Johnston, *The Spirit Paraclete in the Gospel of John*, NTSMS, XII (Cambridge: At the University Press, 1970), cf. pp. 110, 116-18, 125, 132, 134.

[181]Günter Klein, "'Das Wahre Licht scheint schon': Beobachtungen zur Zeit- und Geschichtserfahrung einer urchristlichen Schule," *ZTK*, LXVIII (1971), 302.

[182]Ibid., p. 325.

[183]Bruns, *The Christian Buddhism of St. John*.

[184]James L. Price, "Light from Qumran upon Some Aspects of Johannine Theology," in *John and Qumran*, ed. by James H. Charlesworth (London: Geoffrey Chapman, 1972), p. 11.

[185]James H. Charlesworth, "Qumran, John and the Odes of Solomon," in *John and Qumran*, pp. 128-29.

to describe the Johannine community only once, and then in
parentheses and in reference to the role of several writers in
the composition of John.[186] Nevertheless, he used the motif
of ascending and descending to show that John was written within
and for a group or community which had separated itself from
the world. The Johannine metaphorical system was well understood by the insiders of this group for whom true faith in Jesus
meant joining the Johannine community. In fact, the Gospel
". . . defines and vindicates the existence of the community."[187]
John is not a missionary tract; one of its primary functions was
". . . to provide a reinforcement for the community's social
identity which appears to have been largely negative."[188]
John presents the Christological motifs which this community
developed and which in turn drove it into further isolation.
The Johannine letters show us a later stage of the isolation,
estrangement, and disruption of this community.[189] Thus, Meeks
has provided yet another perspective from which to view the
Johannine community, a perspective which again forces us to
raise the question: should we call the Johannine community a
school?

Analysis of the
Johannine-school hypothesis

So many authors have discussed the Johannine school that
one may easily assume that a consensus has been reached. This
assumption is false, but generally accepted. Not one book or
article has been found which deals primarily with the question
of whether the Johannine-school hypothesis is warranted or not;
and even among those who agree that John is the product of the
Johannine school the diversity of opinion is astonishing. In
this section we shall analyze the various understandings of the
term "school" and the ways in which the Johannine school has
been studied.

Even though we are primarily concerned about the second
word of the designation "Johannine school," it is instructive
to notice the various ways in which scholars have used the first

---

[186]Wayne A. Meeks, "The Man from Heaven in Johannine Sectarianism,"
JBL, XCI (1972), 48.

[187]Ibid., p. 70.

[188]Ibid.

[189]Ibid., p. 71

word. "Johannine school" was first used to indicate the school
which formed around the Apostle John.[190] When others held that
the Gospel was written by John the Presbyter or the unknown John
of the Apocalypse, "Johannine school" was used to refer to the
community of which this John was the head or a member.[191] Scholars who wish to study the origin of the Johannine writings
without becoming involved in the question of authorship use the
term to refer simply to the community in which the writings
attributed to John were composed. Finally, those who limit their
study to the origin of the Gospel alone may use the designation
to refer only to the community in which John was composed. The
latter two uses are often hard to identify. Obviously these
uses are not mutually exclusive and in fact appear in interesting combinations. One might even be able to say that there was
a Johannine school, but John was not composed in it. In this
study "Johannine school" refers to the community in which the
Gospel and Epistles were composed.

The term "school" is also used in various ways. The
loosest use appears in the phrase "school of thought."[192]
Often this means no more than that the evangelist had affinities
with some other writers of his age. Occasionally, this phrase
may mean something more, but its precise denotation is usually
difficult to determine. A different level of usage is reached
when one uses "Johannine school" to mean that the evangelist
was a member of a particular group or "circle." Usually "circle"
designates a group of individuals,[193] but occasionally a writer
has in mind a group of congregations.[194] Some scholars indicate
that the members of the group were writers.[195] For others the

---

[190]The scholars and works cited in the following footnotes are all
discussed and fully documented above. Therefore, we cite only the author's
name and the number of the footnote in which the bibliographical information
is given. Whenever there is some question about the inclusion of a scholar
in one of the lists a question mark is placed after his name. Renan (18);
Lightfoot (21); Stauffer (110); Hedrick (114); Barrett (123); Braun (130);
D'Aragon (172); Charlesworth (185).

[191]Harnack (77); Schmiedel (43); Heitmüller (54); Moffatt (64);
Dibelius (91); Käsemann (117).

[192]Schmidt? (42); Scott (45); Brooke (51).

[193]Cf. n. 17; Harnack (77); Bartlet (26); Wendt (37); Wellhausen (47);
Weiss (52); Heitmüller (54); Dibelius (90); Windisch (93); Bultmann (102);
Gyllenberg (120); Kragerud (136); Goppelt (146); Schnackenburg (151); Price
(184); Charlesworth (185).

[194]Wendt (37); Harnack? (78); Boismard? (140).

[195]Schmiedel (43); Streeter? (80); Braun? (130).

school may be described as a (heretical?) sect or conventicle.[196]
Still others compare it with the *ḥaburoth*.[197] Finally, many
New Testament scholars have understood the Johannine school to
be a community or group of individuals whose primary corporate
activities are teaching, studying, writing, and worshiping,
though not necessarily in that order.[198] These scholars have
the most highly-developed concept of a Christian school. Whether
such a community would have been very different from the Christian churches of the first century, whether such communities
existed at all, and whether John was composed in such a community are questions which we must leave for consideration in the
final chapter.

Scholars also differ in their understanding of the relationship of the evangelist to the school or community. Many
have assumed that he was the head of this community.[199] Usually
this view is coupled with the assertion that the evangelist was
the Apostle John. Others have thought that the evangelist was
a student of the Apostle.[200] Two other positions may be associated with either of these possibilities: various members of the
school wrote different ones of the Johannine writings,[201] and/or
several members of the school collaborated in writing the
Gospel.[202]

All too often apologetic interests have determined a
scholar's use of the Johannine-school hypothesis: it has been
used in defense of the traditional view of apostolic authorship[203]
and in an effort to establish a mediating position which denies

[196]Käsemann (117 and 164); Kragerud (136); O'Neill (170); Conzelmann (177); Meeks (189).

[197]Cf. n. 127; Schulz (127 and 128).

[198]Lightfoot? (21); Schmiedel? (43); Heitmüller? (59); Stauffer (112); Stendahl (122); Riesenfeld (125); Goppelt (147); Freed (156); Price (184); Charlesworth (185).

[199]Lightfoot (20); Zahn (36, cf. 71); Stauffer (110); Hedrick (114); Braun? (130); Brown (162).

[200]Wendt (37); Gaugler (83); Bernard (89); Barrett (123); Schnackenburg (153).

[201]Weizsäcker (29); Charles (65); Barrett (123); Lindars (142); Brown? (162); D'Aragon (172); Hull (179).

[202]Bousset (49); Jackson (63); Barrett? (123); Brown? (163); Charlesworth (185); Meeks (186). This position was opposed by Stanton (67).

[203]Baumgarten-Crusius (13); Lightfoot (20); Zahn (36, cf. 71).

apostolic authorship but maintains a relationship to the Apostle through his school.[204] Hopefully the era in which apologetic interests ruled historical investigation has now passed.

Many approaches have been taken in attempts to study the Johannine school. 1) The external evidence provided by the Church Fathers has been analyzed.[205] 2) The verbal parallels and stylistic features of the Johannine writings have been investigated,[206] and the conceptual parallels or developments have been set forth.[207] 3) Various scholars have also examined the use of the Old Testament,[208] the use of "we,"[209] the *homologia*,[210] terms like "friends" or "disciples,"[211] and polemical interests[212] in John in an attempt to learn something about the community in which the Gospel was composed. No one, though, has studied other ancient schools with the purpose of illuminating the Johannine community.[213]

Conclusion

Today most Johannine scholars are convinced that John was written in and for a definite community and that at least I John was written in the same community, if not by the same man. One of the cutting edges of Johannine research is the effort to learn more about this community. Many scholars are willing to call the community a school, but they describe it in a variety of ways. Our study shows that the variety of descriptions and definitions is endless. This variety is indicative of how little we know about the Johannine community. Whether or not

----

[204]Cf. n. 200; Nicolas (15); Weizsäcker (16 and 31); Barrett (123).

[205]Lightfoot (20); Weizsäcker (27); Zahn (35); Heitmüller (53); Bousset (60); Moffatt (64); Burghardt (96).

[206]Holtzmann (23); Wendt (37); Wellhausen (47); Brooke (51); Weiss (52); Charles (65); Dodd (94); Howard (107); Wilson (108); Salom (109).

[207]Martineau (25); Windisch (93); Dodd (94); Klein (181); Meeks (187).

[208]Stendahl (122); Lindars (142); Freed (156).

[209]Heitmüller (58); Harnack (73).

[210]Neufeld (149).

[211]Käsemann (164).

[212]Weizsäcker (33); Bousset (60); Schulz (127); Kragerud (136); Neufeld (150); Leroy? (173); Martyn (174); Meeks (187).

[213]The following men have studied first-century schools from various perspectives, but none of them has been primarily interested in the Johannine school: Bousset (60); Charles (66); Stendahl (122); Gerhardsson (141).

the community may properly be called a school has yet to be
determined.

What is needed now is a thorough study of the schools or
school-like communities which were roughly contemporary with
the composition of John. Such an investigation might: 1) establish the common characteristics of ancient schools so as to give
some basis for determining whether the Johannine community was
a school; 2) produce insights into the most productive ways to
study ancient schools, insights which could be used in the study
of the Johannine community; and 3) provide the background against
which one would be able to see more clearly the ways in which
the Johannine community was similar to or different from ancient
schools. If these objectives can be achieved, we will be in a
much better position to attempt to determine the nature of the
Johannine community. In the succeeding chapters the following
schools will be studied: the Pythagorean school, the Academy,
the Lyceum, the Garden, the Stoa, the school at Qumran, the
House of Hillel, Philo's school, and the school of Jesus.[214]   In
order to increase the likelihood that the results of this study
will be relevant for the study of John, the following principles
were followed in the selection of these schools: 1) they were
all established prior to the composition of John; 2) they all
trace their origin to a founder (except the school of Philo);[215]
and 3) they all have the potential of informing us about the
factors which influenced, or which may illuminate for us, the
nature of the Johannine community. Schools of elementary education, schools of rhetoric, and the Gnostic communities (which
probably postdate the composition of John) have been omitted
because of restrictions of space and time, but they probably
also form part of John's milieu.

---

[214]The following works on ancient schools have been especially helpful: M. L. Clarke, *Higher Education in the Ancient World* (Albuquerque:
University of New Mexico Press, 1971), (Hereinafter referred to as *Higher
Education*); and H[enri] I[rénée] Marrou, *A History of Education in Antiquity*, trans. by G. Lamb (New York: Sheed and Ward, Inc., 1965).

[215]After several schools had been studied the writer realized that they
shared certain characteristics because they traced their origins to founders.
The writer further realized that the role of either Jesus or the Beloved
Disciple in the Johannine community might be comparable to that of the
founders of ancient schools, and this characteristic guided the selection
of the remaining schools. Although Philo is different in many respects
from the other teachers and schools chosen for study, it was felt that he
could not be omitted from a study of the background of John.

Chapter II

THE PYTHAGOREAN SCHOOL

The importance of the
Pythagorean school

The school of Pythagoras is difficult to study since the
writings which describe it are late and unreliable. If the
sources can be trusted at all, though, a closely-knit association or brotherhood formed around Pythagoras. This school was
probably the earliest philosophical school. If there was an
earlier school at Miletus, which produced Thales, Anaximander,
and Anaximenes we know nothing about it. The Pythagorean
school, however, is exceptionally important because it probably
influenced the organization of later philosophical schools.

The sources for the study
of the Pythagorean school

The focus of this study is on the Pythagorean *school*.
Information about Pythagorean *philosophy* is available in relatively early sources, but is relevant only when it contributes
to our understanding of the nature of the *school*. The basic
collection of the earliest sources is Hermann Diels and Walther
Kranz, *Die Fragmente der Vorsokratiker*,[1] but the sources which
tell us most about the school are those furthest removed from
Pythagoras. It has been observed that "the evidence for a
brotherhood is as overwhelming in its gross weight as it is a
hodgepodge of hearsay."[2] Because the sources date from the
third century A.D., one can argue that they describe contemporary
Neoplatonic schools but tell us nothing about the Pythagorean
school. Hence, the question of the reliability of our sources
is crucial for this study.

Pythagoras himself probably wrote nothing.[3] According to
some sources, none of the Pythagorean traditions were published

---

[1](3 vols.; 12th ed.; Dublin: Weidmann, 1966). (Hereinafter referred
to as *Vorsokr*.) G. S. Kirk and J. E. Raven, *The Presocratic Philosophers:
A Critical History with a Selection of Texts* (Cambridge: University Press,
1963), is also indispensable. (Hereinafter referred to as *Presocratic Philosophers*.) Texts and translations of classical sources are taken from the
Loeb Classical Library unless otherwise indicated. Dates for classical
authors are taken from the *OCD* unless otherwise indicated.

[2]Howard Baker, "Pythagoras of Samos," *Sewanee Review*, LXXX (1972), 34.

[3]Porph. *VP* 57 (*Vorsokr*. 46. 2); Iamb. *VP* 252; for tradition to the
contrary see D. L. VIII. 6-7 (*Vorsokr*. 14. 19). Cf. James A. Philip,
Pythagoras and Early Pythagoreanism, Phoenix supplementary volume VII
(Toronto: University of Toronto Press, 1966), pp. 192-94.

40

until the time of Philolaus (b. *ca.* 470 B.C.).[4] The extant
fragments of the pre-Socratic writers tell us virtually nothing
about the school.[5] Plato describes Pythagoras as:

> . . . presiding over a band of intimate disciples who loved
> him for the inspiration of his society and handed down a way
> of life which to this day distinguishes the Pythagoreans
> from the rest of the world.[6]

Aristotle refers to the Pythagoreans but tells us nothing about
the school.[7] The fourth century B.C. historians[8] Timaeus (*ca.*
356-260 B.C.),[9] Aristoxenus (b. *ca.* 375-360 B.C.),[10] and

---

[4]See p. 50 n. 84 and p. 55 n. 115 below.

[5]For a summary of the evidence they provide see: J. S. Morrison,
"Pythagoras of Samos," *CQ*, N.S. VI (1956), 135-41. See the fragment attributed to Heracleitus (*ca.* 500 B.C.) of Ephesus (*Vorsokr.* 14. 19):
"Pythagoras, son of Mnesarchus, practised research most of all men, and
making extracts from these treatises he compiled a wisdom of his own, an
accumulation of learning, a harmful craft." Translation from Kathleen
Freeman, *Ancilla to the Pre-Socratic Philosophers: A Complete Translation
of the Fragments in Diels, Fragmente der Vorsokratiker* (Oxford: Basil
Blackwell, 1948), p. 33.

[6]*Republic* 600AB (*Vorsokr.* 14. 10):
ὥσπερ Πυθαγόρας αὐτός τε διαφερόντως ἐπὶ τούτῳ ἠγαπήθη, καὶ οἱ ὕστεροι
ἔτι καὶ νῦν Πυθαγόρειον τρόπον ἐπονομάζοντες τοῦ βίου διαφανεῖς πη
δοκοῦσιν εἶναι ἐν τοῖς ἄλλοις.
Translation from Kirk and Raven, *Presocratic Philosophers*, p. 216.

[7]Esp. *Metaphysica* 984-1093. Cf. Philip, *Pythagoras and Early Pythag-
oreanism*, p. 19:
"In the present study I have taken as a basis for reconstruction the
testimony of Aristotle. He is the principal 'watershed' in our tradition
and he is almost alone in having no Pythagorean axe to grind."
See also Walter Burkert, *Weisheit und Wissenschaft: Studien zu Pythagoras,
Philolaus und Platon*, Erlanger Beiträge zur Sprach- und Kunstwissenschaft,
Bd. X (Nürnberg: Verlag Hans Carl, 1962), pp. 26-46.

[8]For recent appraisals of the value of traditions which can be traced
to these writers see: Kurt von Fritz, *Pythagorean Politics in Southern
Italy: An Analysis of the Sources* (New York: Columbia University Press,
1940), pp. 3-67 (Hereinafter referred to as *Pythagorean Politics*.); Kurt von
Fritz, "Pythagoras," *RE*, XXIV (1963), 172-77; Morrison, "Pythagoras of
Samos," pp. 141-43; C. J. de Vogel, *Pythagoras and Early Pythagoreanism: An
Interpretation of Neglected Evidence on the Philosopher Pythagoras*, Philosophical Texts and Studies, Vol. XII (Assen: Van Gorcum & Co., 1966), pp.
7, 68-69; Philip, *Pythagoras and Early Pythagoreanism*, pp. 8-19.

[9]For discussions of Timaeus see Burkert, *Weisheit und Wissenschaft*,
pp. 92-94; Isidore Lévy, *Recherches sur les sources de la légende de Pythagore*, Bibliothèque de l'École des hautes études, Vol. XIV (Paris: Éditions
Ernest Leroux, 1926), pp. 53-59. Lévy also discusses the other fourth-
century and Neo-Platonic writers.

[10]D. L. VIII. 46 (*Vorsokr.* 44 A 4); note the comment of Edwin L. Minar
Early Pythagorean Politics in Practice and Theory, Connecticut College Mono-
graph, No. II (Baltimore: Waverly Press, Inc., 1942), p. 96:
"Aristoxenus was the friend, confidant, and admirer of the 'last of the
Pythagoreans,' as he calls them. He represents his accounts of Pythag-
orean history and doctrine as having been communicated to him by these

Dicaearchus (fl. *ca.* 326-296 B.C.)[11] collected Pythagorean traditions; and while only fragments of their writings have survived, source criticism has enabled scholars to trace many traditions back to them.[12] Aristoxenus had first-hand information from "the last of the Pythagoreans," but Timaeus gives us a less biased account in his general history of southern Italy. Diodorus Siculus (*ca.* 60-30 B.C.) also wrote a section on the Pythagoreans.[13]

The writings of Diogenes Laertius (early 3rd c. A.D.),[14] Porphyry (A.D. 232/3-*ca.* 305),[15] and Iamblichus (*ca.* A.D. 250-*ca.* 325)[16] provide the fullest account of the Pythagorean school. They are late, however, and Iamblichus, at least, compiled his account with notorious carelessness. At points they relied directly or indirectly on written sources going back to the fourth century B.C. historians. Scholars disagree about whether these Neoplatonic writers tell us anything about the Pythagorean school. Most scholars now claim that where they rely on earlier sources they must be taken seriously.[17] Some, however, maintain

---

friends, and thus his expositions seem to have the authority of the authentic tradition of the Pythagorean school. There is no reason to doubt that he also made use of written sources."
(Hereinafter referred to as *Early Pythagorean Politics*.) Cf. Fritz Wehrli, *Die Schule des Aristotles: Texte und Kommentar*, Heft II: *Aristoxenus* (Basel: Benno Schwabe & Co., 1945).

[11]Cf. Fritz Wehrli, *Die Schule des Aristotles: Texte und Kommentar*, Heft I: *Dikaiarchos* (Basel: Benno Schwabe & Co., 1944).

[12]Cf. von Fritz, *Pythagorean Politics*, pp. 3-67.

[13]D. S. X. 3-11.

[14]For discussion see: J[ames] A. Philip, "The Biographical Tradition--Pythagoras," *TAPA*, XC (1959), 191; M. Wellmann, "Eine pythagoreische Urkunde des 4. Jahrhunderts vor Chr.," *Hermes*, LIV (1919), 225-48, traces D. L. VIII. 25-33 (*Vorsokr.* 58 B 1a) back to a fourth century source.

[15]Text: "Vita Pythagorae," *Porphyrii Philosophii Platonici: Opuscula selecta*, ed. by A. Nauck (Leipzig: B. G. Teubneri, 1886), pp. 17-52. Translation: Moses Hadas and Morton Smith, *Heroes and Gods: Spiritual Biographies in Antiquity* (New York: Harper and Row, 1963), pp. 105-28. Discussions of Porphyry's sources: Philip, "The Biographical Tradition--Pythagoras," pp. 185-94; Burkert, *Weisheit und Wissenschaft*, pp. 86-97.

[16]Text: *De Vita Pythagorica liber*, ed. and trans. by M. von Albrecht (Zürich: Artemis Verlags A. G., 1963); *De Vita Pythagorica liber*, ed. by L. Deubner (Leipzig: B. G. Teubneri, 1937). Translation: *Iamblichus' Life of Pythagoras, or Pythagoric Life*, trans. by T. Taylor (London: John M. Watkins, 1965). Discussions of Iamblichus' sources: Vogel, *Pythagoras and Early Pythagoreanism*, pp. 299-303; and the discussions by von Fritz, Philip, and Burkert cited above, n. 12 and n. 15.

[17]Cf. von Fritz, *Pythagorean Politics*, pp. 29-32, 65-67; Morrison, "Pythagoras of Samos," p. 135; Vogel, *Pythagoras and Early Pythagoreanism*, pp. 68-69, 153-54.

that even there they cannot be trusted because by the fourth century B.C. legends had already obscured the tradition about Pythagoras.[18] Festugière concludes that their description of the Pythagorean school is really a portrait of contemporary Neo-platonic schools.[19] On the other hand, the Pythagorean school probably served as the guardian of the Pythagorean tradition.

The decision regarding the trustworthiness of the Neo-platonic writers when they are using earlier sources is crucial for the study of the development of schools. If one accepts their accounts, he may argue that the Pythagorean school was the model for Plato's Academy and all subsequent philosophical schools. But, if one rejects their testimony even when it derives from the fourth century B.C., then the Pythagorean school is merely a reflection of later philosophical schools cast back onto the Pythagorean era by writers eager to attribute the organization of their school to a venerable founder. In short, the question is whether the Pythagoreans influenced later schools or the later schools were the model used by the writers who purport to tell us about the Pythagorean school.

While we acknowledge that much of what the sources tell us about the Pythagorean school is legendary, two related consid-erations prompt us to take them seriously.[20] 1) One of the dis-tinguishing characteristics of the Pythagoreans was their empha-sis on secrecy. Hence, we should not expect to find much informa-tion about them in our earliest sources. 2) The Pythagoreans were remembered for their emphasis on memory. Their traditions were not committed to writing but were memorized and handed on.

The picture which results from this approach to the sources must remain open to question. Many of the details are legendary, but the general outlines of their description of the Pythagorean school may be accurate. This line of argument will be supported and documented as specific points are considered below, but it seems wise to emphasize for the reader the importance of one's approach to the sources and to indicate in general the approach

---

[18]Cf. J[ohn] Burnet, *Early Greek Philosophy* (4th ed.; London: Adam & Charles Black, 1930), p. 87; Kirk and Raven also place little credence in the fourth-century sources. Philip, "The Biographical Tradition--Pythagoras," argues that Porphyry and Iamblichus did not have access to secret sources of school tradition.

[19]R. P. Festugière, *La révélation d'Hermès Trismégiste* (2nd ed.; Paris: Librairie Lecoffre, 1949), II, 33-47.

[20]The evidence on which these considerations are based is cited below in the description of the Pythagorean school.

to be followed here. The reports of the later writers are important for this dissertation because even if the Pythagorean school was not as developed as they describe it to be, they may give us an accurate picture of what some schools were like during the first century A.D.[21] Nevertheless, the dates of the sources will be indicated.

The origin of the Pythagorean school

Since the Pythagorean school is probably the earliest philosophical school, the factors which led to its formation are of special interest. The most important factors are the person—Pythagoras—and the historical situation. Orphism and the Greek clubs (ἑταιρεῖαι) may also have influenced its organization.

What do we know about Pythagoras and his era? Kirk and Raven state that we know he was not merely a legendary figure but that we can add little to the bare fact of his existence.[22] Nevertheless, even they can write a short paragraph about the relatively certain facts of his life.[23]

Pythagoras, the son of Mnesarchus,[24] was born on Samos.[25] Questionable traditions link his education to two masters: Pherecydes and Hermodamas.[26] Many legends describe Pythagoras' travels and study abroad, but even the legend of his journey to Egypt remains suspect.[27] These legends probably reflect the awareness that Pythagoras doctrines had affinities with some foreign teachings.[28] Pythagoras later left Samos because of his opposition to the tyrant Polycrates, and some have inferred from this that he was connected with the aristocracy.[29] The widely-

---

[21]Even Philip traces the tradition back as far as Nicomachus (*ca.* A.D. 100) or Timaeus; cf. *Pythagoras and Early Pythagoreanism*, pp. 140-41, 145.

[22]Kirk and Raven, *Presocratic Philosophers*, p. 219.

[23]Ibid., p. 217.

[24]Herodotus IV. 95 (*Vorsokr.* 14. 2); Heraclitus (*Vorsokr.* 22 B 129); D. L. VIII. 1 (*Vorsokr.* 14. 8).

[25]Isocrates *Busiris* 28 (*Vorsokr.* 14. 4); *Vorsokr.* 14. 8.

[26]Cf. Philip, *Pythagoras and Early Pythagoreanism*, pp. 188-89.

[27]Isocrates *Busiris* 28 (*Vorsokr.* 14. 4).

[28]Cf. Philip, *Pythagoras and Early Pythagoreanism*, pp. 189-91; Kirk and Raven, *Presocratic Philosophers*, p. 224.

[29]Aristoxenus according to Porph. *VP* 9 (*Vorsokr.* 14. 8)--when Pythagoras was about 40 years old; D. L. VIII. 3; Iamb. *VP* 11. Cf. Minar, *Early Pythagorean Politics*, pp. 4, 7.

44

known story of Zalmoxis may indicate that Pythagoras was already known as a σοφιστής before he left Samos.[30] Upon his arrival at Croton[31] in about 530 B.C. Pythagoras is alleged to have delivered speeches which attracted a group of followers and led to the formation of his school.[32] The nature of the school and its political influence will be considered in detail below. Although various traditions about his death have survived, there is a general consensus that he died at Metapontum following the first revolt against the Pythagoreans.[33] The dates of Pythagora life cannot be fixed with certainty, but the generally-accepted dates are:[34]

Birth	570 B.C.
Arrival at Croton	530
Flight to Metapontum	509
Death	503–490

Although the influence of Pythagoras cannot be measured, the power of his personality was probably the central cohesive facto of the Pythagorean school.

Another factor which may have influenced the Pythagorean school is Orphism.[35] The relationship between Orphism and Pythagoreanism is exceedingly difficult to determine, however,

---

[30]Herodotus IV. 95 (Vorsokr. 14. 2); Morrison, "Pythagoras of Samos," pp. 139-41, 144.

[31]For discussions of the political situation at Croton ca. 530 B.C. see: T. J. Dunbabin, The Western Greeks: The History of Sicily and South Italy from the Foundation of the Greek Colonies to 480 B.C. (Oxford: Clarendon Press, 1948), pp. 355-75; Minar, Early Pythagorean Politics, pp. 8-14.

[32]Iamb. VP 30, 37-57. The speeches are referred to by Antisthenes Odysseus I; cf. Vogel, Pythagoras and Early Pythagoreanism, pp. 70-147, 249-50; Werner Jaeger, Aristotle, trans. by R. Robinson (2nd ed.; Oxford: Clarendon Press, 1948), p. 456 n. 3.

[33]D. L. VIII. 39-40 gives four accounts. See also Porph. VP 55-57; Iamb. VP 248-58; Vorsokr. 14. 16. For analysis see: Isidore Lévy, La légende de Pythagore de Grèce en Palestine, Bibliothèque de l'École des hautes études, No. CCL (Paris: Édouard Champion, 1927), pp. 62-77; Minar, Early Pythagorean Politics, pp. 72-73.

[34]Cf. Minar, Early Pythagorean Politics, pp. 133-35; von Fritz, Pythagorean Politics, pp. 47-93; Vogel, Pythagoras and Early Pythagoreanism, pp. 20-27; Philip, Pythagoras and Early Pythagoreanism, pp. 195-96.

[35]Regarding Orphism see: Vittorio D. Macchioro, From Orpheus to Paul: A History of Orphism (New York: Henry Holt and Co., 1930); W. K. C. Guthrie, The Greeks and Their Gods (London: Methuen and Co., Ltd., 1950), pp. 307-32; M. P. Nilsson, "Early Orphism and Kindred Religious Movements," HTR, XXVIII (1935), 181-230; Robert Böhme, Orpheus: Der Sänger und seine Zeit (Bern: Francke Verlag, 1970).

because of the dearth of reliable evidence.[36] Although Orphism
dates from the sixth century B.C., its origins are shrouded in
mystery. Nevertheless, the Orphic discipline appears to have
been established at Croton by the time Pythagoras arrived.[37]
Orphism and Pythagoreanism shared many doctrines; both were
concerned with the deliverance of the soul and emphasized ascetic practices and ritual purity to achieve this end.[38] By the
fifth century B.C. similarities between the two movements were
recorded.[39] Ion of Chios (*ca.* 490-before 421 B.C.) reported
that Pythagoras wrote some Orphic poems,[40] and Plato refers to
an Orphic way of life.[41] The doctrine of the transmigration of
the soul is ascribed to Pythagoras on relatively solid evidence;
Xenophanes (6th c. B.C.) records the story of Pythagoras recog-
nizing the voice of a friend in a dog's yelp.[42]

Some early writers seem to have confused the two movements,[43] but there were striking differences. Von Fritz claims
that whereas Orphism was a religion of the "*kleine Leute*"; in
its earliest period Pythagoreanism was a thoroughly aristocratic

---

[36]For an extreme estimate of our ignorance about Orphism see: Philip,
Pythagoras and Early Pythagoreanism, p. 154.

[37]There was an Orphic Necropolis nearby at Thurii. Cf. Otto Kern,
*Orpheus: Eine religionsgeschichtliche Untersuchung mit einem Beitrag von
Josef Strzygowski* (Berlin: Weidmannsche Buchhandlung, 1920), p. 5.

[38]James Adam, *The Religious Teachers of Greece*, ed. by A. M. Adam
(Edinburgh: T. & T. Clark, 1908), pp. 192-94. For discussions of the differences between Orphic and Pythagorean asceticism see: Philip, *Pythagoras
and Early Pythagoreanism*, p. 168; Pierre Boyancé, *Le Culte des muses chez
les philosophes Grecs: Études d'histoire et de psychologie religieuses*,
Bibliothèque des Écoles françaises d'Athènes et de Rome, Fasc. CXLI (Paris:
E. de Boccard, 1937), pp. 82-83 (Hereinafter referred to as *Culte*). Regarding the emphasis on ritual purity see: Guthrie, *Greeks and Their Gods*, p.
327; Philip, *Pythagoras and Early Pythagoreanism*, pp. 149 n. 4, 167.

[39]Herodotus II. 81 (*Vorsokr.* 14. 1); cf. Iamb. *VP* 145.

[40]D. L. VIII. 8; Clement of Alexandria *Stromateis* I. 131 (*Vorsokr.* 15).

[41]*Laws* 782CD.

[42]D. L. VIII. 36 (*Vorsokr.* 21 B 7); cf. Herodotus II. 123 (*Vorsokr.*
14. 1). Compare the contrasting views of the following scholars regarding
the origin of the doctrine of the transmigration of souls: von Fritz,
"Pythagoras," *RE*, XXIV, 191 (Pythagorean); Nilsson, "Early Orphism and
Kindred Religious Movements," p. 212 (Orphic).

[43]Macchioro, *From Orpheus to Paul*, p. 167, cites Herodotus II. 81
(*Vorsokr.* 14. 1); Iamb. *VP* 151; Proclus *In Platonis Timaeum* V. Erich Frank,
*Plato und die sogenannten Pythagoreer: Ein Kapitel aus der Geschichte des
Griechischen Geistes* (Halle: Verlag von Max Niemeyer, 1923), p. 68, agrees,
but Minar, *Early Pythagorean Politics*, p. 126, denies that the two movements
were confused.

movement.[44] Von Fritz lists four further differences: 1) the
Orphics lacked the fixed organization of the Pythagoreans; 2)
the Pythagoreans were more active politically; 3) the religious
practice of the Pythagoreans was not only ritualistic, but also
contained strong ethical elements; and 4) although Pythagorean
doctrine was certainly "*mystisch*," it was not "*mythologisch*" in
the sense that Orphic doctrine was.[45] Orphism was distinct from
Pythagoreanism, but many of the earliest Pythagoreans were probably Orphics.

A crucial question for this study is whether there were
Orphic associations (θίασοι) which might have influenced the
Pythagorean school.[46] The evidence regarding the Pythagorean
organization, however, is more solid than that concerning the
Orphic communities. Orphism was a way of life with prescribed
rituals; hence it is questionable whether it could have survived
apart from a community or association to enforce its prescrip-
tions.[47] The earliest real evidence, though, comes from the
later practice of burying adherents to Orphism in their own
cemetery.[48] Thus, if there were separate Orphic communities in
Croton at the time Pythagoras arrived there, we know almost
nothing about them.[49]

Orphism may have influenced the organization of the Pythagorean school, but our sources do not enable us to describe its
influence. The most we can say is that Orphism and Pythagoreanism shared common doctrines; some members of the school were
probably Orphics; Orphic communities may have influenced the

---

[44]von Fritz, "Pythagoras," *RE*, XXIV, 244. Guthrie, *Greeks and Their
Gods*, p. 328, argues to the contrary: ". . . , Orphism was not especially
a religion of the lower, underprivileged classes." For discussion
regarding the association of Pythagoreanism with the aristocracy see below,
p. 52 n. 96.

[45]von Fritz, "Pythagoras," *RE*, XXIV, 245-46.

[46]Cf. A[rthur] D[arby] Nock, *Conversion: The Old and the New in Religion from Alexander the Great to Augustine of Hippo* (Oxford: Clarendon
Press, 1933), pp. 28-32.

[47]W. K. C. Guthrie, *Orpheus and Greek Religion: A Study of the Orphic
Movement* (2nd ed.; London: Methuen and Co., Ltd., 1952), p. 205. Burnet,
Early Greek Philosophy, p. 82, affirms that adherents of Orphism were organ-
ized in communities.

[48]Kern, *Orpheus*, p. 5 n. 2. There is no evidence of Orphic communities
in fourth or fifth-century Greece; cf. Guthrie, *Orpheus and Greek Religion*,
pp. 11, 204.

[49]Adam, *Religious Teachers of Greece*, p. 93.

Pythagorean school; and Orphism may have been spread by the popularity of Pythagoreanism.[50]   Still, Orphism was probably a
major tributary of the first philosophical school.

Political clubs are another possible source of influence
on the Pythagorean school.[51]   Both the clubs and the Pythagoreans
are called ἑταιρεία.[52]   G. M. Calhoun defines the term as follows:

> Ἑταιρεία, as an abstract noun, signifies the relationship of
> ἑταῖροι, the bond which united the members of a political
> club.   As a concrete noun, it became the customary and defi-
> nite designation of a club of which the interests were chief-
> ly political, and which was devoted either wholly or in
> part to the support of its members in politics and
> litigation.[53]

The origin of these clubs is difficult to determine.
Ἑταῖρος is used in Homer,[54] but the first clear reference to a
club is in Herodotus (d. before 420 B.C.).[55]   Plutarch (before
A.D. 50-after A.D. 120) refers to ". . . the Pythagorean societies [ἑταιρεῖαι] throughout the different cities . . ."[56] and
Thucydides (460/55-ca. 400 B.C.) mentions members of political
clubs on Samos, the home of Pythagoras.[57]   The membership of
the clubs was usually composed of about 20 to 30 aristocratic
men of similar age and social position.[58]   Members submitted to
rites of initiation and vows of friendship.   They held frequent

---

[50]Macchioro, *From Orpheus to Paul*, p. 168.

[51]The basic study of clubs is: G. M. Calhoun, *Athenian Clubs in
Politics and Litigation*, Bulletin of the University of Texas, Humanistic
Series, No. XIV (Austin: University of Texas, 1913).   (Hereinafter referred
to as *Athenian Clubs*.)   The results of this study were related to the Pythagoreans by Minar, *Early Pythagorean Politics*, esp. pp. 18-28.   See also
Erich Ziebarth, *Das Griechische Vereinswesen* (Wiesbaden: Dr. Martin Sändig
oHG., 1969 [originally published in 1896]), pp. 69-74.

[52]Cf. n. 56 below.   Further examples are cited by Minar, *Early Pythagorean Politics*, pp. 19-20.

[53]Calhoun, *Athenian Clubs*, pp. 5-6.

[54]Cf. Ibid.

[55]V. 71.   A. D. Godley, trans., *Herodotus*, Loeb Classical Library
(London: William Heinemann, 1928), III, 79, dates the event Herodotus
refers to between 620 and 600 B.C.   Cf. Calhoun, *Athenian Clubs*, pp. 13, 30.

[56]*Moralia* 583A (*Vorsokr.* 44 A 4a):   . . . αἱ κατὰ πόλεις ἑταιρεῖαι τῶν
Πυθαγορικῶν . . .   Cf. Calhoun, *Athenian Clubs*, p. 6 n. 2.   Minar, *Early
Pythagorean Politics*, p. 19, asserts that the passage is ". . . undoubtedly
taken over at least in great part from an early source."

[57]VIII. 48. 3.   Cf. Calhoun, *Athenian Clubs*, p. 20.

[58]G[uy] C[romwell] Field, *Plato and His Contemporaries: A Study in
Fourth-Century Life and Thought* (3rd ed.; London: Methuen & Co. Ltd., 1967),
p. 81, refers to political clubs in Athens as ". . . the chief organs of the
anti-democratic movements."

48

banquets, and some secrecy may have surrounded their activities.
Many of these characteristics recur in the Pythagorean school.
The similarities between the school and clubs are strong, but
the two organizations were not identical.

> The Pythagorean Society was not the same as the ordinary
> political club. It was bound together by religious as well
> as by political and social ties and much more closely organ-
> ized than the often ephemeral groups which made their influ-
> ence felt in the political field.[60]

Nevertheless, Minar concludes that clubs were probably active
in Magna Graecia and that ". . . the Pythagorean Society was
built on a foundation of already existing organizations of this
type."[61] The evidence is tenuous, but Minar's conclusion at
least carries the force of probability.

In conclusion, it appears that three formative factors
influenced the organization of the Pythagorean school: Pythagoras
himself, Orphism, and political clubs. Our sources do not allow
us to be dogmatic about any of these factors; but just as the
school united religious and political elements, so it appears to
have been influenced by religious and political organizations.

The nature of the Pythagorean school

Many terms are used by the doxographers to describe the
Pythagoreans: θίασος and ἑταιρεία have already been mentioned.
Diogenes Laertius uses μαθηταῖς (VIII. 3) and σύστημα (VIII.
45). Iamblichus, *Vita Pythagorica* uses: διατριβή (74),
διατριβῶν (178), διδασκαλεῖον (104 and 114), αἵρεσις (191 and
241), κοινωνία (241), σχολή (265), and σύστημα (266). Not surprisingly, the task of describing the Pythagoreans is no easier
today. Philip argues that there was a Pythagorean political
association but no school or brotherhood.[62] Von Fritz, however,
asserts that there was an organized Pythagorean order, while
acknowledging that much of what the sources tell us about it is
apocryphal.[63]

59Calhoun, *Athenian Clubs*, pp. 10-39.59Calhoun, *Athenian Clubs*, pp. 10-39.

60Minar, *Early Pythagorean Politics*, p. 22.60Minar, *Early Pythagorean Politics*, p. 22.

61Ibid., p. 24.61Ibid., p. 24.

62Philip, *Pythagoras and Early Pythagoreanism*, p. 24.62Philip, *Pythagoras and Early Pythagoreanism*, p. 24.

63K[urt] von Fritz, "Mathematiker und Akusmatiker bei den alten Pythag-63K[urt] von Fritz, "Mathematiker und Akusmatiker bei den alten Pythagoreern," *SBMun*, (1960), Heft XI, p. 6:
"Dass Pythagoras in Italien eine Art Orden mit strengen Regeln und wohl
auch einer Art Hierarchie geschaffen hat, ist wohl kaum zu bezweifln, wenn

Pythagoras came to Croton as a reformer, calling the people from luxury to simplicity.[64] The Crotonians were drawn to him, and he was venerated even before his death.[65] Guthrie perceptively observes: "Anecdotes may not be true, but their existence is revealing."[66] The number of his followers is variously assessed as 300,[67] 600,[68] and 2,000.[69] Those who desired membership were questioned about their way of life, and their physical form and mode of walking were observed. They were neglected for a while to test their desire for learning and then ordered to observe a five-year period of silence. Finally, they underwent rites of purification and were initiated into the brotherhood.[70] Women were also eligible for membership.[71] Among the members there were two ranks: the μαθηματικοί were given the full teaching, while the ἀκουσματικοί were given only a summary.[72] The Pythagoreans observed taboos about beans[73] and wool,[74] and submitted to dietary restrictions.[75] They were also

---

auch die einzelnen Nachrichten darüber sehr cum grano salis [sic] aufzunehmen sind."
(Hereinafter referred to as "Mathematiker.") Cf. von Fritz, "Pythagoras," *RE*, XXIV, 192.

[64]Justinus *Epitome* XX. 4. 1; translation available in Morrison, "Pythagoras of Samos," pp. 143-44. The source for this passage is Timaeus; cf. von Fritz, *Pythagorean Politics*, p. 41. See also D. S. X. 3. 3, and X. 7. 1.

[65]Porph. *VP* 18-20; Iamb. *VP* 30-31, 255. Statements regarding the veneration of Pythagoras are characteristic of the Neoplatonic writers.

[66]Guthrie, *History of Greek Philosophy*, I, 149.

[67]D. L. VIII. 3; Iamb. *VP* 254, 260.

[68]Iamb. *VP* 29; D. L. VIII. 15.

[69]Porph. *VP* 20; Iamb. *VP* 30.

[70]Iamb. *VP* 71-74. The source of this important section is unknown. Minar, *Early Pythagorean Politics*, p. 28, attributes it to Timaeus, but von Fritz, "Mathematiker," p. 7, states that it is anonymous. Cf. D. L. VIII. 10; Gellius I. 9. 3-4; Iamb. *VP* 94-95.

[71]D. L. VIII. 41; Porph. *VP* 18-19 (*Vorsokr.* 14. 8a); Iamb. *VP* 30, 54, 132, 267 (*Vorsokr.* 17. 1).

[72]Porph. *VP* 37 (*Vorsokr.* 18. 2); Iamb. *VP* 29-30, 80-81, 87. Cf. von Fritz, "Mathematiker;" Burkert, *Weisheit und Wissenschaft*, pp. 187-202; Guthrie, *History of Greek Philosophy*, I, 184-93. See p. 55 n. 119 below.

[73]Aristotle is the authority for this tradition according to D. L. VIII. 34 (*Vorsokr.* 58 C 3); cf. D. L. VIII. 24 (*Vorsokr.* 58 B 1a) and 45 (*Vorsokr.* 14. 10); Porph. *VP* 44 (*Vorsokr.* 58 C 6).

[74]Iamb. *VP* 100, 149; Philostratus *VA* I. i, VI. xi.

[75]D. L. VIII. 12-13, 19-20; Philostratus *VA* I. i, VI. xi; Porph. *VP* 7, 15, 34; Iamb. *VP* 25, 68-69, 106-07.

known for their "friendship":

> According to Timaeus, he was the first to say, "Friends have all things in common" and "Friendship is equality"; indeed, his disciples did put all their possessions into one common stock.[76]

Silence was practiced as a virtue,[77] and the memory was trained by recalling each day the master's teaching.[78] They transmitted the teachings orally with careful attention to accuracy and spoke and wrote in such a way that their meaning would not be obvious to an outsider.[79] Those who violated the secrecy of their doctrines were punished or expelled.[80]

Some forms of music were used for edification,[81] and Homer was probably studied.[82] To what extent the earliest Pythagoreans studied science and mathematics is vigorously debated,[83] but of little consequence for this study. It is also difficult to determine whether the Pythagorean school produced any writings prior to the time of Philolaus.[84] Their later works were

---

[76]D. L. VIII. 10:
εἶπέ τε πρῶτος, ὥς φησι Τίμαιος, κοινὰ τὰ φίλων εἶναι καὶ φιλίαν ἰσότητα. καὶ αὐτοῦ οἱ μαθηταὶ κατετίθεντο τὰς οὐσίας εἰς ἕν [ποιούμενοι].
Cf. D. S. X. 8. 1; Iamb. *VP* 101-02, 230-31 (*Vorsokr*. 58 D 9); Vogel, *Pythagoras and Early Pythagoreanism*, pp. 150-59. See also Aristotle *Nicomachean Ethics* VIII. ix. 1:
"Again, the proverb says 'Friends' goods are common property,' and this is correct, since community is the essence of friendship. Brothers have all things in common, and so do members of a comradeship; . . . ."
καὶ ἡ παροιμία "κοινὰ τὰ φίλων," ὀρθῶς· ἐν κοινωνίᾳ γὰρ ἡ φιλία. ἔστι δ' ἀδελφοῖς μὲν καὶ ἑταίροις πάντα κοινά, ...

[77]Iamb. *VP* 68-69, 94; Isocrates *Busiris* 29 (*Vorsokr*. 14. 4); Philostratus *VA* VI. xi and xx.

[78]D. S. X. 5. 1; D. L. VIII. 23; Proph. *VP* 40; Iamb. *VP* 164-66 (*Vorsok*. 58 D 1), 226-27.

[79]D. L. VIII. 15, 17-18; D. S. X. 8. 3; Iamb. *VP* 94, 162, 226-27, 246-47 (*Vorsokr*. 18. 4).

[80]Iamb. *VP* 199 (*Vorsokr*. 14. 17), 247 (*Vorsokr*. 18. 4); cf. Kathleen Freeman, *The Pre-Socratic Philosophers: A Companion to Diels, Fragmente der Vorsokratiker* (3rd ed.; Oxford: Basil Blackwell, 1953), pp. 74-76.

[81]Porph. *VP* 32-33; Iamb. *VP* 64-65, 68, 110-14 (*Vorsokr*. 58 D 1, 31 A 15).

[82]Porph. *VP* 32; Iamb. *VP* 111-12; D. L. VIII. 21; cf. Marcel Detienne, *Homère, Hésiode, et Pythagore: Poésie et philosophie dans le pythagorisme ancien*, Collection Latomus, LVII (Brussels: Latomus, 1962); Boyancé, *Culte*, pp. 121-31.

[83]W. A. Heidel, "The Pythagoreans and Greek Mathematics," *AJP*, LXI (1940), 1-33; Burkert, *Weisheit und Wissenschaft*, pp. 379-456; von Fritz, "Mathematiker," pp. 19-24.

[84]D. S. X. 8. 3; D. L. VIII. 15, 24 (*Vorsokr*. 58 B 1a), 84-85 (*Vorsokr* 44 A 1); Porph. *VP* 58; Iamb. *VP* 199 (*Vorsokr*. 14. 17); see p. 55 n. 115 belo

ascribed to Pythagoras, and they used the formula Αὐτὸς ἔφα
when they referred to their doctrines.[85]

Iamblichus describes the daily routine of the Pythagoreans.[86] Whether or not the members actually lived together,[87]
communal meals were an important feature of their corporate
life.[88] The sources claim that they held all goods in common,[89] but there are indications that either this practice was
short-lived or applied only to the innermost group.[90] Although
there is a tradition that only the highest rank of Pythagoreans
had access to Pythagoras,[91] it is more probable that he was
interested in the education of the Crotonians and actively
involved in their political life.[92]

---

[85]D. L. VIII. 46 (*Vorsokr.* 14. 10); Cicero *De Natura Deorum* I. 10.

[86]Iamb. *VP* 96-100. Vogel, *Pythagoras and Early Pythagoreanism*, pp.
185-87, attributes the description to Aristoxenus; and Clarke, *Higher Education*, p. 57, summarizes it as follows:
"In a Pythagorean community the day began with solitary walks in quiet
places. After the morning walk the group met together, if possible in a
temple, and devoted themselves to study. There followed a time for rec-
reation and exercise. After a light luncheon of bread and honey they
engaged in affairs of state. In the evening they went for another walk
in groups of two or three, after which they dined, and after dinner there
were readings by the youngest members of the group under the presidency
of the oldest."
Iamb. *VP* 256 adds that the Pythagoreans rose early and adored the rising sun.

[87]Vogel, *Pythagoras and Early Pythagoreans*, p. 187, contends that the
Pythagoreans did not live together. Morrison, "Pythagoras of Samos," p. 146,
cites fragments from Justinus and Timaeus which state that the Pythagoreans
lived apart from the rest of the city, but he observes: "They must have
lived at home and spent by no means all their time with their *hetairoi* "
(p. 151). Porph. *VP* 20, states: "They did not return home, but together
with children and wives, establishing a great school of fellow hearers, built
a city in that country everyone calls Magna Graecia in Italy." (Translation
by Hadas and Smith, *Heroes and Gods*, pp. 113-14.)

[88]Herodotus IV. 95 (*Vorsokr.* 14. 2); cf. Morrison, "Pythagoras of
Samos," pp. 139-40, 151. Minar, *Early Pythagorean Politics*, pp. 25-26,
claims that the common meal as practiced by the clubs must have been modi-
fied by the rather Spartan Pythagoreans. D. S. X. 5. 2 reports that the
Pythagoreans cultivated their self-control by having a banquet served,
gazing on it, and then leaving without having eaten anything.

[89]D. S. X. 3. 5; D. L. VIII. 10; Porph. *VP* 33; Iamb. *VP* 30, 72, 168.
Cf. above, p. 50 n. 76.

[90]Iamb. *VP* 89; cf. von Fritz, "Mathematiker," p. 9; Morrison,
"Pythagoras of Samos," p. 151.

[91]Iamb. *VP* 72.

[92]Vogel, *Pythagoras and Early Pythagoreanism*, pp. 62-63.

Scholars once debated whether the Pythagoreans were active politically during the lifetime of their founder,[93] but as Dunbabin correctly observes, ". . . no thinker in the small society of a city-state could avoid playing some part in public affairs; . . . ."[94] Guthrie persuasively argues that Pythagoras role as a reformer of society was his motive for acquiring power,[95] but one need only recognize that political clubs were composed of aristocratic citizens active in political affairs.[96] The members of the Pythagorean school merely continued to exercise their influence in Croton when they became associated with Pythagoras.

The debate now centers on the extent of their influence and whether the school ever ruled directly as Pythagoreans. Von Fritz has pointed out that the Pythagoreans could not have observed the strict rules of the order and been active politically at the same time; so they must have either been loosely affiliated with the school, excused from the observance of the rules while in political office, or both.[97] He concludes that they never ruled *as* Pythagoreans,[98] and Morrison agrees: the Pythagorean rule actually consisted of little more than ". . . the gradual concentration of all offices into the hands of men who had been Pythagoras' pupils and thus formed a kind of *hetaireia*."[99] Vogel[100] and Minar, however, argue to the contrary: "Pythagorean control is too definite and absolute to be regarded as merely semi-official."[101] Minar's next point makes the question almost inconsequential:

> . . . the fact that a revolt against the government in power was the same thing as an attack against the [Pythagorean] Society, or at least involved such an attack as an integral

---

[93]Eduard Zeller, *A History of Greek Philosophy: From the Earliest Period to the Time of Socrates*, trans. by S. F. Alleyne (London: Longmans, Green, and Co., 1881), I, 349-60.

[94]Dunbabin, *The Western Greeks*, p. 361.

[95]*History of Greek Philosophy*, p. 361.

[96]See above, p. 47. Burnet, *Early Greek Philosophy*, pp. 89-91, argues unsuccessfully that the Pythagoreans were not aristocratic.

[97]von Fritz, "Mathematiker," p. 12.

[98]Ibid.; cf. von Fritz, *Pythagorean Politics*, pp. 95-96.

[99]"Pythagoras of Samos," p. 149.

[100]*Pythagoras and Early Pythagoreanism*, pp. 189-91.

[101]*Early Pythagorean Politics*, p. 17.

part, strongly suggests that the Pythagorean Society was recognized as the real ruler in Croton and most of the cities of Magna Graecia.[102]

The Pythagoreans were influential in the life and politics of Croton from about 529 to 509 B.C.[103]

Dunbabin concludes that although the Pythagoreans dominated Croton during the lifetime of Pythagoras, they did not exercise much control in other south Italian cities until later.[104] Still, they probably used the existing form of government to direct the affairs of Croton and most of the other south Italian cities through the first half of the fifth century.[105] How were the Pythagoreans at other cities related to the school at Croton? Minar claims that they were controlled by the school and that ". . . the entire foreign policy of Croton from 510 to 460 B.C. was one of territorial expansion."[106] After analyzing the literary sources and the numismatic evidence, von Fritz maintained:

Ancient tradition does not provide the slightest evidence for the existence of anything like a real rule of the Pythagoreans in any of the cities of Southern Italy at any time.[107]

Morrison would agree.[108] Vogel, however, claims that there was no "Pythagorean rule" during the sixth and the beginning of the fifth century, but there was during the middle of the fourth

---

[102]Ibid., p. 18.

[103]The basic sources for our knowledge of Pythagorean political activity are the fragments of early tradition found in the following passages: Polybius II. 39. 1-4 (*Vorsokr*. 14. 16); D. L. VIII. 3; Porph. *VP* 54; Iamb. *VP* 97. Aristoxenus, however, was pro-Pythagorean and probably exaggerated their political influence. Cf. above, p. 40 n. 9.

[104]*The Western Greeks*, p. 361.

[105]Ibid. Philip, *Pythagoras and Early Pythagoreanism*, p. 39 n. 3, claims that Dunbabin's account of the political influence of the Pythagoreans is more accurate than those of von Fritz or Minar. Cf. the analysis of Iamblichus' catalogue of Pythagoreans in Freeman, *Pre-Socratic Philosophers*, pp. 244-45; Kirk and Raven, *Presocratic Philosophers*, p. 221 n. 5.

[106]*Early Pythagorean Politics*, p. 48, cf. p. 38; Minar regards the Pythagoreans as ". . . a sort of reactionary international."

[107]*Pythagorean Politics*, p. 95. See Guthrie, *History of Greek Philosophy*, I, 176-77, for an appraisal of the suggestion that Pythagoras designed the Crotonian coinage.

[108]"Pythagoras of Samos," p. 152:
"These non-Crotoniate *synedria* were not sub-ordinate in any way to Croton, nor were they vehicles for Crotoniate power. The influence of Pythagoreanism at Metapontum and Tarentum did not, as a matter of historical fact, carry with it any economic or political ties with Croton."

54

century.[109] The variety of positions summarized in this paragraph indicates how much remains obscure and debatable regarding
the political activity of the Pythagoreans.

The history of the
Pythagorean school

The increasing political influence of the Pythagoreans
eventually encountered bitter hostility. Neanthes (3rd c.
B.C.) probably confused the revolt which occurred during the
life of Pythagoras with a later revolt. His confusion was
compounded by later writers.[110] In about 509 B.C. a Crotonian
who had been denied admission to the school led a revolt
against it.[111] Pythagoras escaped, however, and the incident
did not hinder the further growth of Pythagoreanism.[112]
Following this rebellion, Clinias ruled as tyrant over Croton.[11]

In the middle of the next century (*ca.* 450 B.C.) a much
more serious anti-Pythagorean movement developed. The house of
Milo, the Pythagorean athlete, was burned, and many prominent
Pythagoreans perished. Events spanning a generation of hostility have probably been compressed into this incident by our
sources.[114] Led by Philolaus (b. *ca.* 470 B.C.) and Lysis,

---

[109]*Pythagoras and Early Pythagoreanism*, pp. 189-91.

[110]Porph. *VP* 55.

[111]Porph. *VP* 54-55; Aristoxenus according to Iamb. *VP* 248-51 (*Vorsokr.*
14. 16); Timaeus according to Iamb. *VP* 254-64.

[112]See above, p. 44 n. 33. For discussion of Pythagoreanism during
the period immediately following 509 B.C. see von Fritz, *Pythagorean Politics*, pp. 68-93, esp. p. 92.

[113]Cf. Dunbabin, *The Western Greeks*, p. 367; Minar, *Early Pythagorean
Politics*, pp. 71-73.

[114]D. L. VIII. 39; Porph. *VP* 55, 58; Iamb. *VP* 249 (*Vorsokr.* 14. 16).
These accounts probably derive from Aristoxenus (see Minar, *Early Pythagorean
Politics*, p. 75), Polybius II. 39. 1-4 (*Vorsokr.* 14. 16) is probably a
separate account of the same general rebellion:
"When, in the district of Italy, then known as Greater Hellas, the club-
houses of the Pythagoreans were burnt down, there ensued, as was natural,
a general revolutionary movement, the leading citizens of each city having thus unexpectedly perished, and in all the Greek towns of the district
murder, sedition, and every kind of disturbance were rife."
καθ' ὃς γὰρ καιροὺς ἐν τοῖς κατὰ τὴν Ἰταλίαν τόποις κατὰ τὴν Μεγάλην
Ἑλλάδα τότε προσαγορευομένην ἐνεπρήσθη τὰ συνέδρια τῶν Πυθαγορείων, μετὰ
ταῦτα γενομένου κινήματος ὁλοσχεροῦς περὶ τὰς πολιτείας, ὅπερ εἰκός, ὡς
ἂν τῶν πρώτων ἀνδρῶν ἐξ ἑκάστης πόλεως οὕτω παραλόγως διαφθαρέντων,
συνέβη τὰς κατ' ἐκείνους τοὺς τόπους Ἑλληνικὰς πόλεις ἀναπλησθῆναι φόνου
καὶ στάσεως καὶ παντοδαπῆς ταραχῆς.
For discussion of Polybius' (*ca.* 200-after 118 B.C.) account see: F. W.
Walbank, *A Historical Commentary on Polybius* (2 vols.; Oxford: Clarendon

Pythagoreans then grouped at Phlius, Thebes, and Rhegion.[115]
According to von Fritz's reconstruction, ". . . the final
exodus of the Pythagoreans from Italy" occurred about 390.[116]
At about this same time the Pythagoreans began to appear in
Attic literature.[117]

By sometime in the fourth century two kinds of Pythagoreans were known. Whether this split derived from ranks within
the earliest period of the school is uncertain.[118] It is more
likely that the cleavage reflects a polarizing of the Pythagoreans according to their interests: one group interested in
the philosophy of science and mathematics, and the other in
the religious traditions of the school.[119] Archytas (first half of
4th c. B.C.), whose interests were more philosophical than
religious, remained in Tarentum, and through him Pythagoreanism
had its most direct influence on Plato.[120]

The Pythagorean communities disappeared by the end of the
fourth century B.C., but reappeared in Rome during the first
century B.C. What happened to the Pythagorean tradition during
the intervening centuries? H. Thesleff has attempted to prove
that:

> . . . Pythagorean schools continued to live on in Southern
> Italy, that they flourished there in a cultural isolation,
> and produced a whole literature of school texts, written in
> the Doric of Archytas, in the course of the third and second
> century. According to this theory Pythagoreanism then

Press, 1957-67), I, 222-24; von Fritz, *Pythagorean Politics*, pp. 72, 75-78.
For discussion of this rebellion see: Minar, *Early Pythagorean Politics*, p.
34; Vogel, *Pythagoras and Early Pythagoreanism*, pp. 24-26; Burkert, *Weisheit
und Wissenschaft*, pp. 181-82.

[115]Iamb. *VP* 251 (*Vorsokr.* 14. 16); cf. Guthrie, *History of Greek
Philosophy*, I, 329-33; Philip, *Pythagoras and Early Pythagoreanism*, pp. 32-
33; Burkert, *Weisheit und Wissenschaft*, pp. 203-77. For opposing views
regarding the authenticity of the Philolaus fragments (*Vorsokr.* 44 B) see:
Kirk and Raven, *Presocratic Philosophers*, pp. 307-13; and G. B. Kerferd,
"The Pythagoreans," review of *Pitagorici: testimonianze e frammenti*, by
Maria Timpanaro Cardini, in *CQ*, N.S. XIV (1964), 27. See above, p. 50 n. 84.

[116]*Pythagorean Politics*, pp. 75-79, 92.

[117]Vogel, *Pythagoras and Early Pythagoreanism*, p. 227.

[118]See above, p. 49 n. 72.

[119]For discussion see: von Fritz, "Pythagoras," *RE*, XXIV, 193, 264;
Kirk and Raven, *Presocratic Philosophers*, p. 227; F. M. Cornford, "Mysticism
and Science in the Pythagorean Tradition," *CQ*, XVI (1922), esp. pp. 137-38.

[120]*Vorsokr.* 47; Plato *Epistles* VII. 339DE, 350A; D. L. VIII. 79-83
(*Vorsokr.* 47 A 1); Iamb. *VP* 104, 127 (*Vorsokr.* 58 D 7), 197 (*Vorsokr.* 47 A 7),
250 (*Vorsokr.* 14. 16), 266-67.

spread from Southern Italy to Rome where it was connected with King Numa.[121]

Von Fritz takes a similar position, arguing that small, sectarian, Pythagorean communities persisted even after they lost their political influence.[122] The evidence for the survival of Pythagorean communities through the third and second centuries is extremely weak, and Vogel is probably correct when he claims that the tradition is emphatically against Thesleff; ". . . the 'last of the Pythagoreans' who Aristoxenus knew, did not live in Southern Italy, but in Northern or Central Greece."[123] Albin Lesky addresses himself to Thesleff's evidence directly and probably interprets it more accurately:

> And so the Pseudopythagorica discussed here form part of a sort of pseudo-philosophical Koine. Obviously they have nothing in common with the cult and the community of the Pythagorean conventicles, and Burkert's phrase goes straight to the heart of the matter: "In the Hellenistic age there is a deluge of Pythagorean literature, but there are no Pythagoreans."[124]

The continued existence of a formal Pythagorean school like the one which flourished at Croton cannot be demonstrated; there was a break in the tradition from the fourth century to the first.

The factors which led to the revival of Pythagoreanism have not been clearly established, nor are they of great significance for this study.[125] Other aspects of Neopythagoreanism are noteworthy: 1) it emphasized the religious traditions of Pythagoreanism; 2) it venerated Pythagoras; and 3) it may have had some influence on Judaism and Christianity at Rome and Alexandria.[126]

---

[121]Vogel, *Pythagoras and Early Pythagoreanism*, p. 28. Cf. Holger Thesleff, *An Introduction to the Pythagorean Writings of the Hellenistic Period*, Acta Academiae Aboensis, Humaniora, XXIV, 3 (Abo: Åbo Akademi, 1961); Holger Thesleff, *The Pythagorean Texts of the Hellenistic Period*, Acta Akademiae Aboensis, Humaniora, XXX, 1 (Abo: Åbo Akademi, 1965).

[122]von Fritz, "Pythagoras," *RE*, XXIV, 219, 268-70, cf. col. 270: "Die Wahrscheinlichkeit spricht daher mehr dafür, dass der P., ohne in der Offentlichkeit aufzufallen, in kleinen Gruppen sektenartig weiter bestand."

[123]Vogel, *Pythagoras and Early Pythagoreanism*, p. 28.

[124]*A History of Greek Literature*, trans. by J. Willis and C. de Heer (New York: Thomas Y. Crowell Company, 1966), pp. 798-99.

[125]For discussion see: Thesleff, *Introduction to the Pythagorean Writings of the Hellenistic Period*, pp. 46-71; R. Festugière, "Sur une Nouvelle Édition du 'de Vita Pythagorica' de Jamblique," *REG*, L (1937), 470-94.

[126]Moses Hadas, *Hellenistic Culture: Fusion and Diffusion* (New York:

The crucial question is whether there were Neopythagorean schools. The accounts of Neopythagoreanism which we find in Philostratus' *Life of Apollonius*[127] and Seneca[128] do not provide any evidence that the Neopythagoreans formed schools like the one at Croton.[129] If there were Neopythagorean schools, they probably attempted to imitate the original Pythagorean school, and Porphyry and Iamblichus would have been influenced by them. The strongest evidence for the existence of Neopythagorean schools is provided by Carcopino's suggestion that the basilica discovered at the Porta Maggiore in Rome was used by Pythagoreans in the first century B.C.[130] Even if Carcopino is right, the evidence about Neopythagorean schools is too sparse to add anything to our understanding of ancient schools.[131]

Chiefly through the work of Numenius (2nd c. A.D.), Neopythagoreanism was subsumed by Neoplatonism.[132] After Pythagoreanism ceased to be an independent stream of tradition, Pythagoras was studied in the Neoplatonic schools.[133]

The influence of the Pythagorean school

The influence of the Pythagoreans was carried into the Hellenistic world not by any small Pythagorean communities which may have survived, but by Plato and the Academy. The

---

Columbia University Press, 1959), pp. 193-94; von Fritz, "Pythagoras," *RE*, XXIV, 275-76; Lévy, *La légende de Pythagore de Grèce en Palestine*, pp. 211-34; Jérôme Carcopino, *De Pythagore aux Apôtres: Études sur la conversion du monde romain* (Paris: Flammarion, 1956). Whether the model of the Pythagorean school influenced Philo will be considered later.

[127]I. 18, IV. 37; cf. Clarke, *Higher Education*, p. 83.

[128]*Epistulae* CVIII. 17.

[129]von Fritz, "Pythagoras," *RE*, XXIV, 274: "Denn der entscheidende Punkt altpythagoreischer Lebensführung konnte nicht wieder verwirklicht werden: das Zusammenleben in enger Wohngemeinschaft."

[130]Jérôme Carcopino, *La basilique pythagoricienne de la Porte Majeure* (Paris: L'Artisan du Livre, 1926); cf. Nock, *Conversion*, p. 168.

[131]Ulrich von Wilamowitz-Moellendorff, *Der Glaube der Hellenen* (2 vols.; Berlin: Benno Schwabe & Co. Verlag, 1959), II, 438-39, doubts that Carcopino is right.

[132]Clarke, *Higher Education*, p. 84; H. Dörrie, "Ammonios der Lehrer Plotins," *Hermes*, LXXXIII (1955), 444 n. 3; cf. H. Dörrie, "Der nachklassische Pythagoreismus," *RE*, XXIV, 268-77.

[133]Clarke, *Higher Education*, pp. 105-106.

influence of Pythagoreanism on Platonism and the extent to
which doctrines developed in the Academy were attributed to
Pythagoras cannot be investigated here.[134] Nevertheless, the
form of the Pythagorean school probably influenced Plato's
organization of the Academy. First, the example of the
Pythagoreans convinced Plato that the school was an effective
means for combining philosophy and politics;[135] and secondly,
Plato continued the Pythagorean preoccupation with both religion and mathematics.[136] The Pythagorean ideas probably made
their impact upon Plato when he became acquainted with Archytas
during his first trip to the West in 388/7.[137] Shortly after
his return he organized the Academy.[138]

Since early in the nineteenth century scholars have
noticed similarities between the Pythagoreans and the Essenes.[139]
The similarities are emphasized in Josephus' description of the
Essenes;[140] both schools are characterized by an emphasis on
"friendship" among the members, a community of goods, the
practice of silence, prayer at the rising and setting of the
sun, common meals, ranks among the members, a probationary
period prior to initiation, punishment of severe offenses by
expulsion, and the veneration of their founder. In addition,
both regarded the number fifty (*nun*) as sacred and advocated

---

[134]Cf. von Fritz, "Pythagoras," *RE*, XXIV, 226-36; Vogel, *Pythagoras and Early Pythagoreanism*, esp. pp. 192-202; Philip, *Pythagoras and Early Pythagoreanism*, pp. v, 10-14; Burkert, *Weisheit und Wissenschaft*, esp. pp. 74-85. See also A[lfred] E[dward] Taylor, *A Commentary on Plato's Timaeus* (Oxford: At the Clarendon Press, 1928), p. 11.

[135]J. S. Morrison, "The Origins of Plato's Philosopher-Statesman," *CQ*, N.S. VIII (1958), esp. 199, 210-12; Burkert, *Weisheit und Wissenschaft*, p. 74 n. 3, disagrees with Morrison: "(der aber Platons Absicht in der Formulierung 'realize his political ambitions through the academy' gewiss nicht gerecht wird)."

[136]John Burnet, *Greek Philosophy: Thales to Plato* (London: Macmillan and Co., Ltd., 1950), pp. 88, 213; F. A. G. Beck, *Greek Education 450-350 B.C.* (London: Methuen & Co., Ltd., 1964), pp. 227-28; Boyancé, *Culte*, pp. 249-75.

[137]Plato *Epistles* VII; see p. 55 n. 120 above; Morrison, "The Origins of Plato's Philosopher-Statesman," pp. 199, 201-02, 213-16; Field, *Plato and His Contemporaries*, pp. 175-87.

[138]See below, p. 70.

[139]For a summary of the debate see: Isidore Lévy, *Recherches esséni-ennes et pythagoriciennes*, Hautes études du monde greco-romain, III, 1 (Genève: Librairie Droz, 1965), pp. 57-63.

[140]*War* II. 119-61; *Ant.* XVIII. 18-22.

the abolition of blood sacrifices.[141]   Josephus, who describes
Jewish groups as philosophical schools,[142] claims that the
Essenes are ". . . a group which follows a way of life taught
to the Greeks by Pythagoras; . . ."[143] and Aristobulus shows
that Alexandrian Judaism at the beginning of the second century
B.C. knew Pythagoreanism.[144]

Prior to the discovery of the Qumran scrolls, Pythagorean
influence on the Essenes was stressed by Zeller,[145] Schürer,[146]
Levy,[147] Cumont,[148] and Lagrange.[149]   Subsequent to their
discovery the primary advocate of Pythagorean influence has
been Dupont-Sommer.[150]   Vermès[151] and Hengel,[152] however, find

---

[141]For discussion of these similarities see the works cited in footnotes 144-152.

[142]*War* II. 119.

[143]*Ant.* XV. 371: γένος δὲ τοῦτ' ἔστιν διαίτη χρώμενον τῆ παρ' Ἕλλησιν
ὑπὸ Πυθαγόρου καταδεδειγμένη.   Compare Josephus *War* II. 137-42 with the process of admission to the Pythagorean school described above, p. 49.

[144]Cf. Martin Hengel, *Judentum und Hellenismus: Studien zu ihrer
Begegnung unter besonderer Berücksichtigung Palästinas bis zur Mitte des 2.
Jh. v. Chr.*, WUNT, X (2 Aufl.; Tübingen: J. C. B. Mohr, 1973), p. 320 n.
379a, and p. 449.

[145]Eduard Zeller, *Die Philosophie der Griechen in ihrer geschichtlichen
Entwicklung* (6th ed.; Hildesheim: Georg Olms Verlagsbuchhandlung, 1963),
III, 2, pp. 89, 359, 365-77.

[146]Emil Schürer, *Geschichte des jüdischen Volkes im Zeitalter Jesu
Christi* (3rd ed.; Leipzig: J. C. Hinrichs'sche Buchhandlung, 1898), II,
573-84.

[147]*La légende de Pythagore de Grèce en Palestine*, pp. 264-93; *Recherches
esséniennes et pythagoriciennes*.

[148]Franz Cumont, "Esséniens et Pythagoriciens d'après un passage de
Josèphe," *CRAI*, (1930), 99-112.

[149]M.-J. Lagrange, *Le Judaïsme avant Jésus-Christ* (Paris: Librairie
Lecoffre, 1931), pp. 325-28.

[150]A[ndré] Dupont-Sommer, *The Dead Sea Scrolls: A Preliminary Survey*,
trans. by E. M. Rowley (Oxford: Basil Blackwell, 1952), pp. 97-98; A[ndré]
Dupont-Sommer, *The Jewish Sect of Qumran and the Essenes: New Studies on
the Dead Sea Scrolls*, trans. by R. D. Barnett (London: Vallentine, Mitchell
& Co., Ltd., 1954), esp. pp. 112-17, 161-62; André Dupont-Sommer, "Le
problème des influences étrangères sur la secte juive de Qoumrân," *RHPR*,
XXXV (1955), 75-94. See also: Michel Testuz, *Les idées religieuses du livre
des Jubilés* (Genève: Librairie E. Droz, 1960), pp. 134-37; T. Francis
Glasson, *Greek Influence in Jewish Eschatology: With Special Reference to
the Apocalypses and Pseudepigraphs* (London: S. P. C. K., 1961), pp. 48-56;
A. R. C. Leaney, *The Rule of Qumran and Its Meaning: Introduction, Translation and Commentary* (Philadelphia: Westminster Press, 1966), pp. 28, 47,
62, 87-89; Hadas, *Hellenistic Culture*, pp. 195-96.

[151]Géza Vermès, *Discovery in the Judean Desert* (New York: Desclee
Company, 1956), pp. 60-61.

[152]*Judentum und Hellenismus*, pp. 445-53; cf. Georg Molin, "Qumran --
Apokalyptik -- Essenismus," *Saeculum*, VI (1955), 280.

less evidence of Pythagorean influence on the Essenes.

Although the similarities between the two schools remain striking, they are probably not to be explained by direct Pythagorean influence on the Essenes. Three considerations help to explain the similarities: 1) the Essenes absorbed and re-minted foreign influences.[153] 2) Josephus was acquainted with traditions about the Pythagorean school and intentionally emphasized (and exaggerated?) elements common to the two groups.[154] 3) Indirectly the Essenes may have colored the Pythagorean tradition so that characteristics of the Essenes came to be ascribed to the Pythagoreans by Neoplatonic writers. Still, it is possible that the influence of the Pythagorean school (filtered through later philosophical schools and Hellenism) left its mark upon the Essenes.

Marrou admirably summarizes the significance of the Pythagorean school:

> This, as we see it at Metapontus or Croton, was no longer a simple "hetairia" of the ancient type, with the master and his pupils all on the same level; it was a real school, taking charge of the whole man and forcing him to adopt a particular way of life. It was an organized institution, with its own buildings and laws and regular meetings--a kind of religious brotherhood devoted to the cult of the apotheosized Pythagoras. And it set the type: modelled on it later were Plato's Academy, Aristotle's Lyceum and the school of Epicurus, and it was always to remain the standard pattern of the Greek school of philosophy.[155]

---

[153]Ibid., pp. 450-51:
"Dass die Essener--wie schon die Chasidim--in beträchtlichen Masse fremde Einflüsse der hellenistischen Umwelt sowohl aus Babylonien und dem Iran wie auch aus dem ptolemäischen Ägypten aufgenommen und verarbeitet haben, lässt sich nach angeführten Beispielen kaum mehr bestreiten, typisch pythagoräisch sind sie nicht."

[154]*Apion* I. 163-65, indicates that Josephus knew a life of Pythagoras by Hermippus (3rd c. B.C.).

[155]Marrou, *A History of Education in Antiquity*, p. 77.

Chapter III

THE ACADEMY

The importance of the Academy

The Academy marks a new stage in the development of ancient schools. Prior to the Academy the sophists dominated higher education. No other form of training was available to ambitious young Greeks except in areas like mathematics, astronomy, and medicine.[1] The Academy was also the first permanent philosophical school. It remained near or in Athens for over 900 years and attracted many of the ablest minds of the Hellenic world.[2] After leaving the Academy many of its students played influential roles in the history of the Hellenistic world, and Aristotle, who spent his formative years in the Academy, later established his own school.

The sources for the study of the Academy

The study of the Academy has been facilitated by the bibliographies compiled by T. G. Rosenmeyer[3] and H. Cherniss.[4] In addition, Konrad Gaiser has collected the important primary sources.[5] The extent of the information provided by our sources is disappointing. If we were confined to the writings produced by members of the Academy during Plato's life (including Plato's dialogues and letters), we would not know that the Academy was anything more than a garden.[6]

> In our sources the Academy is a gymnasium, a garden, a
> school, a sect, and a literary convention. . . . Symbol,

---

[1]Gilbert Ryle, *Plato's Progress* (Cambridge: At the University Press, 1966), p. 103.

[2]Ronald B. Levinson, *In Defense of Plato* (Cambridge, Mass.: Harvard University Press, 1953), p. 43.

[3]"Platonic Scholarship: 1945-1955," *CW*, L (1957), 172-82, 185-96, 197-201, 209-11.

[4]"Plato 1950-1957," *Lustrum*, IV (1959), 5-308; V (1960), 323-648.

[5]*Platons ungeschriebene Lehre: Studien zur systematischen und geschichtlichen Begründung der Wissenschaften in der Platonischen Schule* (Stuttgart: Ernst Klett Verlag, 1963), pp. 443-557, esp. pp. 446-51.

[6]The problem of using the writings produced by members of the Academy to describe the school is similar to that of using the Johannine writings to describe the community in which they originated. The difference is that we know from other sources that the Academy was a philosophical school, but we have no such evidence for the Johannine school. This observation is surprising in view of the importance of the Academy.

tradition, institution, and legend have so played into one another's hands that the imagination is sorely tried when it tries to picture with confidence the kind of school Plato founded and the manner of life and teaching that there prevailed. We get no help from sources immediately contemporaneous with Plato.[7]

Nevertheless, even though Plato never refers to the Academy directly, his writings must be examined.

Although ". . . we have the unusual good fortune to possess intact everything that he wrote for publication,"[8] it is difficult to assess the relation of Plato's writings to his work in the Academy. None of the dialogues purport to have taken place in the Academy,[9] and they are neither lecture notes nor textbooks.[10] Do the dialogues contain Plato's "real teaching" or only ". . . what he thought fit to give a wider public?"[11] When and how did members of the Academy become familiar with the dialogues? Were some of them withheld from the Academy? Were the dialogues copied and "published" by the Academy?[12] Friedländer correctly asserts that there must be some ". . . functional relationship between Plato's literary activity and his teaching, . . ." but he also notes the difficulty of deducing anything about the Academy from the dialogues:

The attempts to penetrate from these general considerations to something more concrete have resulted in altogether different interpretations. Those who were inspired by the *Symposium* saw the Academy as a festive society governed by divine madness and singing hymns to Eros or discussing the nature of love. It was in this spirit that the Florentines attempted to resurrect it. But suppose we look at the *Phaedo*: the Academy becomes a religious sect of salvation around the figure of the executed savior.[13]

---

[7]Frederick J. E. Woodbridge, *The Son of Apollo: Themes of Plato* (Boston: Houghton Mifflin Company, 1929), p. 26

[8]Harold Cherniss, *The Riddle of the Early Academy* (Berkeley and Los Angeles: University of California Press, 1945), p. 4. (Hereinafter referred to as *Riddle*.)

[9]R. E. Wycherley, "Peripatos: The Athenian Philosophical Scene," *Greece and Rome*, VIII (1961), 159.

[10]Clarke, *Higher Education*, p. 65.

[11]Burnet, *Greek Philosophy*, p. 214, claims the latter; Cherniss, *Riddle*, pp. 9-10, disagrees.

[12]Cf. Ryle, *Plato's Progress*, pp. 216-17.

[13]Paul Friedländer, *Plato*, trans. by H. Meyerhoff, Bollingen Series, LIX (2nd ed.; Princeton, N.J.: Princeton University Press, 1969), I, 87. Cf. Cherniss, *Riddle*, p. 62.

In spite of the difficulties, attempts have still been
made to glean information about the Academy from the dialogues.
It is commonly assumed that the progressive stages of education
and the disciplines prescribed for the guardians in the *Republic*
are an ideal program which was attempted, though not fully
accomplished, in the Academy.[14] Levinson, responding to the
charge that the Academy was organized for revolutionary purposes, claims that *Phaedrus* 276E-277A ". . . expresses *in nuce*,
. . . , Plato's aim in establishing and maintaining his school
throughout the years."[15] Ryle asserts that it ". . . announces
to Hellas that the Academy is now going to teach rhetoric,"[16]
and Friedländer finds that the *Phaedrus* is consistent with the
other dialogues in portraying the Academy as ". . . a community
of teachers and disciples united by *Eros*. . . . Indeed, the
Academy is a historically unique embodiment of *Eros*."[17] The
Phaedo, Ryle conjectures, is Plato's farewell to Athens and the
Academy with his counsel regarding how to find a successor
should he fail to return from his second trip to Sicily.[18] The
Parmenides, Philebus, Sophist, and *Politicus* have also been
interpreted as reflections of exercises or discussions which
arose within the Academy,[19] and Ryle claims that: "The *Timaeus*
was not issued to the world in book-form until after Plato's
death. It was reserved for the instruction of students in the
Academy."[20] The *Symposium* has been regarded as a model of the

---

[14]Cf. Paul Shorey, *What Plato Said* (Chicago: The University of Chicago
Press, 1933), p. 30; Levinson, *In Defense of Plato*, p. 365; Friedländer,
Plato, I, 86-87, 92; Hans Joachim Krämer, "Die Platonische Akademie und das
Problem einer systematischen Interpretation der Philosophie Platons," *Das
Platonbild: Zehn Beiträge zum Platonverständnis*, ed. by K. Gaiser
(Hildesheim: Georg Olms Verlagsbuchhandlung, 1969), p. 204. Ryle, *Plato's
Progress*, pp. 53-54, offers a less probable alternative:
"On the present hypothesis Plato did not during his lifetime release his
text of our *Republic* to the world at large, and therefore not even to
members of the Academy. Aristotle and his pupils never heard or read our
Republic until after Plato's death, though members of the postulated
reading clubs had heard it, probably again and again, during the 350's
and maybe the late 360's."

[15]*In Defense of Plato*, pp. 363-64.

[16]*Plato's Progress*, p. 97.

[17]*Plato*, I, 90.

[18]*Plato's Progress*, p. 227.

[19]Shorey, *What Plato Said*, p. 30. Cf. A. E. Taylor, *Plato: The Man
and His Work* (5th ed.; London: Methuen & Co. Ltd., 1948), p. 410.

[20]*Plato's Progress*, p. 83; cf. pp. 12-13.

banquets at the Academy,[21] and it has been claimed that Plato
gave to characters in the dialogues traits of his students in
the Academy.[22] Similarly, Jaeger finds in *Theatetus* 173C-E a
description of the men of the Academy.[23] Even though many of
these conjectures do not command general acceptance, they
exemplify the attempts that have been made to describe the
Academy on the basis of Plato's dialogues.

Plato's letters are another important source. Of the
thirteen letters the seventh is the most important and the one
with the greatest claim to authenticity. In past decades it
was commonly regarded as genuine,[24] but recently a more skeptical
view has emerged.[25] In the most recent and exhaustive study of
this letter, Ludwig Edelstein concludes that it was not written

---

[21]Hans Herter, *Platons Akademie* (2nd ed.; Bonn: Verlag Bonner Univer-
sitäts-Buchdruckerei Gebr. Scheur, 1952), p. 9. Harold Cherniss, Review of
Platons Akademie, by Hans Herter, in *CP*, XLIII (1948), 130, warns:
". . . as an account of the nature of the Academy and of Plato's teaching
  it [*Platons Akademie*] cannot be said to be an improvement upon the highly
  fictional or enthusiastically conjectural expositions which on account of
  the very number and professional dignity of the authors have during the
  last hundred years come to be widely accepted as a satisfactory substitut
  for historical evidence."
For discussion of the symposia in the Academy see below, p. 78.

[22]E. Salin, *Platon, Dion, Aristoteles, Robert Boehringer: Eine Freundesgabe* (Tübingen, 1957), pp. 525-42, cited by Cherniss, "Plato 1950-1957,"
p. 25.

[23]Werner Jaeger, *Paideia: The Ideals of Greek Culture*, trans. by G.
Highet (New York: Oxford University Press, 1943), II, 274-75.

[24]The acceptance of the authenticity of the *Seventh Letter* by the
following scholars indicates the extent of its acceptance: Franz Egermann,
*Die Platonischen Briefe 7 und 8: Eine Untersuchung ihrer historischen
Voraussetzungen sowie ihres Verhältnisses zueinander* (Berlin: Dissertation,
1928), [This work was unavailable. See the review of it by U. v. Wilamowitz
Moellendorff, *Gnomon*, IV (1928), 361-64]; Glenn R. Morrow, *Studies in the
Platonic Epistles: With a Translation and Notes*, Illinois Studies in Lan-
guage and Literature, Vol. XVIII, Nos. 3-4 (Urbana, Ill.: The University of
Illinois, 1935); R. S. Bluck, *Plato's Life and Thought: With a Translation
of the Seventh Letter* (London: Routledge & Kegan Paul Ltd., 1949), p. 189;
Jaeger, *Paideia*, II, 83; Bertha Stenzel, "Is Plato's Seventh Epistle Spuri-
ous?" *AJP*, LXXIV (1953), 383-97; Field, *Plato and His Contemporaries*, pp. 19
201; Walter Bröcker, "Der philosophische Exkurs in Platons siebentem Brief,"
Hermes, XCI (1963), 416-25; Kurt von Fritz, "Die philosophische Stelle im
siebten platonischen Brief und die Frage der 'esoterischen' Philosophie
Platons," *Phronesis*, XI (1966), 117-53.

[25]The following recent works reject the *Seventh Letter*: Cherniss,
Riddle, p. 13; Levinson, *In Defense of Plato*, p. 41; Karl R. Popper, *The
Open Society and Its Enemies*, Vol. I: *The Spell of Plato* (5th ed.; Princeto
University Press, 1966), p. 208 n. 5; Ryle, *Plato's Progress*, p. 47; John
Herman Randall, Jr., *Plato: Dramatist of the Life of Reason* (New York:
Columbia University Press, 1970), pp. 9-10.

by Plato[26] but reflects changes in the Academy subsequent to
his death: "Plato's immediate pupils stressed the practical
virtues more than had their teachers."[27] Probably due to the
precedent of Aristotle's school, the Academy had come to place
more emphasis on education by the time the letter was written.[28]
The author ". . . must have been a younger contemporary of
Xenocrates, ..."[29] Edelstein further observes that the
most important consequence of accepting the *Seventh Letter* has
been to overestimate the political involvement of the Academy.[30]
Still, the letter is an important source; the author was well
informed about the Academy and Plato's activities. The following statement provides the guidelines to be followed here in
the use of the *Seventh Letter*:

> Even for those few who remain doubtful of the Platonic
> authorship, among whom the present writer wishes to count
> for one, the *Letters* contain much valid historical and
> biographical material, as shown by their consistency with
> trustworthy ancient sources. But in dealing with those
> passages in the *Letters* in which Plato's inner thoughts and
> feelings and private conversations purport to be revealed,
> only those for whom Plato is the unquestioned author will
> presume to employ them as the basis for judging his
> character.[31]

The *Seventh Letter* does not refer to the Academy explicitly,
but relevant passages are cited below.

Although Plato's contemporaries often refer or allude to
the Academy, they seldom provide much solid information. The
most informative contemporary writer is Isocrates (436-338 B.C.),
not Aristotle. As Ryle observes: "Hardly one whisper of the
tutorial voice of Plato is relayed to us by Aristotle, even on
philosophical matters."[32] On the other hand, one may infer
from Isocrates' polemic against the Academy that eristic became
part of its curriculum prior to Plato's death.[33] Isocrates also

---

[26]*Plato's Seventh Letter*, Philosophia Antiqua, Vol. XIV (Leiden: E. J.
Brill, 1966), cf. pp. 1, 166.

[27]Ibid., p. 67.

[28]Ibid., p. 163.

[29]Ibid.; cf. p. 67.

[30]Ibid., pp. 160, 165.

[31]Levinson, *In Defense of Plato*, p. 41.

[32]Gilbert Ryle, "Plato," *EncPhilos*, VI, 315.

[33]Philip Merlan, "Isocrates, Aristotle and Alexander the Great," *Historia*, III (1954-55), 64-72, summarizes Isocrates' polemic against the
Academy. Cf. Ryle, *Plato's Progress*, p. 108.

condemns the Academy for being impractical and unpolitical.[34]
Specifically, *Antidosis* 258-69 appears to be directed against
the Academy.

References to the Academy in Middle Comedy constitute
another allusive source.[35] The most famous description of one
of Plato's "seminars" survives in a fragment of an unnamed play
by Epicrates.[36] Aristophanes (457/45-385 B.C.) refers to the
Academy as a race track,[37] and in a fragment from Ephippus'
Shipwrecked we find a satirical description of a student at the
Academy:

> Then up there rose a youth of lucky wit,
> Mock-Platonist of the Academy, who, smit
> With Bryso-Thrasymachian itch for pence,
> Being of a trade that lives by eloquence
> And able to say things that sound quite smart,
> His hair a triumph of the barber's art,
> His beard to decent length descending whole,
> His feet well shod in shoes of shaven sole,
> With criss-cross latchets halfway to his waist,
> And cloak bunch bravely in the best of taste,
> Struck a fine attitude upon his stick,
> And using what I think 's another's trick,
> Cried 'Men of Attic.'[38]

As the above survey indicates, the earliest sources tell
us very little about the Academy. Most of what is commonly

---

[34]Levinson, *In Defense of Plato*, pp. 364-65. For discussion of the
differences between the Academy and the school of Isocrates see: Field,
Plato and His Contemporaries, pp. 31-34; Ryle, "Plato," *EncPhilos*, VI, 318.

[35]See T. B. L. Webster, *Studies in Later Greek Comedy* (Manchester:
University Press, 1953), pp. 51-56; John Maxwell Edmonds, *The Fragments of
Attic Comedy: After Meineke, Bergk, and Kock* (3 vols.; Leiden: E. J. Brill
1959).

[36]See below, p. 75 n. 112.

[37]*Clouds* 1005. This play was written in 423 and revised in 418/16.

[38]Athenaeus XI. 509cd:
ἔπειτ' ἀναστὰς εὔστοχος νεανίας
τῶν ἐξ Ἀκαδημείας τις ὑποπλατωνικὸς
Βρυσωνοθρασυμαχειοληψικερμάτω
πληγεὶς ἀνάγκη, ῥιφολομίσθω τέχνη
συνὼν τις, οὐκ ἄσκεπτα δυνάμενος λέγειν,
εὖ μὲν μαχαίρα ξύστ' ἔχων τριχώματα,
εὖ δ' ὑποκαθιεὶς ἄτομα πώγωνος βάθη,
εὖ δ' ἐν πεδίλω πόδα δεθεὶς ὑποξύρω
κνήμη γ' ἱμάντων ἰσομέτροις ἑλίγμασιν,
ὄγκω τε χλανίδος εὖ τεθωρακισμένος
σχῆμ' ἀξιόχρεων ἐπικαθεὶς βακτηρία,
ἀλλότριον, οὐκ οἰκεῖον, ὡς ἐμοὶ δοκεῖ,
ἔλεξεν· '"Ανδρες τῆς Ἀθηναίων χθονός.'
Translation and text from Edmonds, *The Fragments of Attic Comedy*, II, 152-
55. For other descriptions see: pp. 176-77, and Friedländer, *Plato*, I, 99,
and 354-55 n. 23.

accepted as evidence for the description of the Academy comes
from later sources which include legendary material. Athenaeus
(fl. *ca.* A.D. 200) preserves informative references to the
Academy in *The Deipnosophists*.[39] Diogenes Laertius (first half
of 3rd c. A.D.) is the sole authority for much of what we know
about Plato's life and the Academy.[40] Other sources include:
Apuleius (b. *ca.* A.D. 123) *De Platone et eius dogmate*,[41] an
Anonymous Prolegomena to Platonic Philosophy,[42] a Herculaneum
papyrus,[43] and references in the Suda (10th c. [date from LSJ]),
and Hesychius (5th c.).

The origin of the Academy

Plato's personality must have exerted a powerful influence
on the Academy during his lifetime. His disciples even imitated
his stoop.[44] It is reasonable that Socrates, the sophists, and
the Pythagoreans had some influence on Plato's "founding"[45] the
Academy. These influences may be assessed in the course of a
brief survey of Plato's life. The above review of the sources
available for this task supports Woodbridge's conclusion:
"That the life of Plato cannot now be written as the biography
of a man, is the one solid conclusion to be drawn from our
sources of information."[46]

Plato, the son of Ariston, and an Athenian citizen, was
born about 429 B.C. Diogenes Laertius traces his ties with old

---

[39]Hereinafter referred to by name of author.

[40]See above, p. 41 n. 14.

[41]*Opera quae supersunt*, Vol. III: *De philosophia libri*, ed. by Paulus
Thomas (Stuttgart: B. G. Teubneri, 1970), pp. 82-134.

[42]L. G. Westerink, *Anonymous Prolegomena to Platonic Philosophy*
(Amsterdam: North-Holland Publishing Company, 1962). (Hereinafter referred
to as *Anonymous Prolegomena*.)

[43]Segofredus Mekler, ed., *Academicorum philosophorum index Herculanensis*
(Berlin: Weidmann, 1902). Cf. Ingemar Düring, *Aristotle in the Ancient
Biographical Tradition*, Göteborgs Universitets Årsskrift, Vol. LXIII, 2
(Göteborg: Elanders Boktryckeri Aktiebolag, 1957), p. 467: "Philodemus is
generally held to be the author of the *Index Academicorum philosophorum
Herculanensis*, containing precious information from old reliable sources."
(Hereinafter referred to as *Biographical Tradition*.)

[44]Clarke, *Higher Education*, p. 65, citing Plutarch *Moralia* 26b, 53c.

[45]The term "found" is probably misleading, since we cannot be sure
that the Academy was not just an unintentional by-product of Plato's teaching activity.

[46]*The Son of Apollo*, p. 29.

Attic nobility.[47] He was trained in letters and wrestling, wrote poetry early in his life,[48] and was active in political movements in his youth.[49] When he was twenty he became a pupil of Socrates.[50] It is impossible to assess the importance of the influence of Socrates on Plato, but Clarke's observation is illuminating:

> The Socratic belief that virtue is knowledge implied that it could be taught and it was on this assumption that the later schools were based.[51]

Speaking through Alcibiades, Plato acknowledges his role as mediator of the personality and doctrine of Socrates: "Let me tell you that none of you knows Socrates; but I shall reveal him to you."[52] Whatever the extent of Socrates' influence, it cannot be said that he had a formal school which Plato emulated. After Socrates' death, Plato withdrew to Megara. He was about 28 at the time.[53] Euclides seems to have had a school at Megara, and it is possible that this school suggested the idea of the Academy to Plato.[54]

During the next ten years Plato probably wrote some of his early dialogues. In 390/89 Plato left Greece. It is possible that he visited Egypt and probable that he met Archytas in Southern Italy before arriving at Sicily.[55] The *Gorgias* reflect enough knowledge of the Pythagoreans to make it plausible that Plato made the journey in order to study the discoveries of

---

[47]III. 1. Cf. Lesky, *A History of Greek Literature*, p. 506.

[48]D. L. III. 4-5.

[49]Plato *Seventh Letter* 324c; cf. Lesky, *A History of Greek Literature*, p. 508.

[50]D. L. III. 6. Randall, *Plato*, pp. 10-11, notes the artificial neatness with which Plato's life falls into 20-year periods.

[51]*Higher Education*, p. 59. Was the mediation of this doctrine to Judaism through the spread of Hellenism influential in the development of the Jewish schools? See below, p. 184.

[52]*Symposium* 216c: εὖ γὰρ ἴστε ὅτι οὐδεὶς ὑμῶν τοῦτον γιγνώσκει· ἀλλὰ ἐγὼ δηλώσω. Translation by Friedländer, *Plato*, I, 89. The similarity to passages like Matt. 11:27 and John 17:25 is merely superficial and coincidental.

[53]D. L. III. 6.

[54]Cf. Ryle, "Plato," *EncPhilos*, VI, 315; Burnet, *Greek Philosophy*, p. 213.

[55]D. L. III. 6. See above, p. 55 for discussion of the role of Archytas in mediating the influence of Pythagoreanism to Plato.

Pythagoras.[56] This contact seems to have persuaded him that a school like that of the Pythagoreans would provide ". . . the trustworthy friends and supporters. . ." necessary for effective political activity.[57]

In Sicily, Plato met Dionysius I (405-367 B.C.) and his brother-in-law, Dion, who showed some aptitude for philosophy. Plato's views on tyranny so offended Dionysius that he seized Plato and held him as a political prisoner until Anniceris paid the ransom. Anniceris would not accept repayment for the ransom from Plato's friends, ". . . but bought for Plato the little garden which is in the Academy."[58]

In 387 Plato returned to Athens and lived at the Academy. The origin of the name "Academy" is obscure; the garden and gymnasium received its name from the nearby shrine of the hero or god *Academus* or *Hecademus*.[59]

> The use of the name in later writers is very flexible; it meant primarily the shrine, but by natural extension it was used of the gymnasium, the school of Plato, of course, or of the district; and sometimes, improperly, of the cemetery on the way to the Academy, or of the Kerameikos.[60]

Until its "beautification" by Cimon (5th c. B.C.), the Academy had been "a waterless and arid spot."[61] Subsequently, it was known as a particularly pleasant place.[62] Hipparchos had built a wall there ". . . which became proverbial for an expensive job,"[63] and the gymnasium may have pre-dated Solon.[64]

----

[56]Cicero *De Finibus* V. xxix. 87; cf. Morrison, "The Origins of Plato's Philosopher-Statesman," p. 211.

[57]Plato *Seventh Letter* 325D. Cf. Edelstein's caution about the use of the *Seventh Letter*, above p. 65. Friedländer, *Plato*, I, 90, notes two significant differences between the Platonic and the Pythagorean schools: 1) The spirit of Socrates humanized philosophy, and 2) the Platonic school was characterized by conversation rather than decree from the master.

[58]D. L. III. 20.

[59]D. L. III. 7. Plutarch *Theseus* XXXII. 3, records that when the Lacedaemonians invaded Attica and wasted the country, they spared the Academy for the sake of *Academus*.

[60]Wycherley, "Peripatos," p. 2. On "Academy" as a place-name see, Otto Seel, *Die Platonische Akademie: Vorlesung und eine Auseinandersetzung* (Stuttgart: Ernst Klett Verlag, 1953), pp. 13-14.

[61]Plutarch *Cimon* XIII. 8.

[62]Aristophanes *Clouds* 1005; Horace *Epistles* II. ii. 45. Cf. Jean Delorme, *Gymnasion: Étude sur les monuments consacrés à l'éducation en Grèce (des origines à l'empire romain)*, Bibliothèque des Écoles françaises d'Athenes et de Rome, Fasc. 196 (Paris: Éditions E. de Boccard, 1960), pp. 51-54.

[63]Wycherley, "Peripatos," p. 2.

[64]Demosthenes XXIV. 114.

The olive trees at the Academy were considered sacred.[65]
Sporadic excavations have unearthed part of the gymnasium and a
tantalizing inscription.[66]   The Academy was purchased for 3,000
drachmae, and Plato made his residence there.[67]   Tradition has
it that he placed before the Museum [μουσεῖον] the inscription:
ἀγεωμέτρητος μηδεὶς εἰσίτω ("Nobody untrained in geometry may
enter.").[68]

The events which led to the establishment of the Academy
are unknown.   According to the traditional reconstruction,
Plato began teaching in his house or nearby immediately after
his return from Sicily in 387.[69]   As a result of his teaching,
Plato and his followers soon came to dominate the Academy and
formalized their association by dedicating a shrine to the
Muses.[70]   This action gave the school an acceptable religious
status in the Athenian society.

The traditional position has recently been challenged by
Gilbert Ryle, who observes that there is no evidence that the
Academy was founded during the 380's or early 370's.   He dates
its founding after Isocrates' *Helen* but before the death of
Theaetetus in 369 and the arrival of Aristotle at the Academy
in 367.[71]   During the 380's and 370's Plato taught elenctic
debating to young men, and for this he was prosecuted in the

---

[65]Cf. Edmonds, *The Fragments of Attic Comedy*, II, 54-55.   For further
descriptions of the physical site of the Academy see: Pausanias *Attica* I.
xxix. 2, xxx. 1-3; Plutarch *Solon* I. 4; Walther Judeich, *Topographie von
Athen*, Handbuch der Altertumswissenschaft, Abt. III, t. 2, Bd. 2 (2nd ed.;
Munich: C. H. Beck'sche Verlagsbuchhandlung, 1931), p. 404; C. B. Armstrong,
"Plato's Academy," *Proceedings of the Leeds Philosophical and Literary
Society*, VII (1952-55), 90-92.

[66]Cf. H. G. G. Payne, "Archaeology in Greece, 1930-1931," *JHS*, LI
(1931), 186; G. Karo, "Archäologische Funde von Mai 1932 bis Juli 1933:
Griechenland und Dodekanes," *AA* (Supplement to *JdI*), XLVIII (1933), cols.
208-10; Wycherley, "Peripatos," pp. 6-8.

[67]Plutarch *Moralia* 603B.   Cf. Clarke, *Higher Education*, p. 59.

[68][Elias], *Eliae in Porphyrii Isagogen et Aristotelis Categorias:
Commentaria*, ed. by Adolfus Busse, Vol. XVIII, Pt. I of *Commentaria in
Aristotelem Graeca*, ed. by Academiae Litterarum Regiae Borussicae (23 vols.
in 29; Berlin: Typis et impensis Georgii Reimeri, 1900), p. 118 lines 18-
19.   Cf. Gaiser, *Platons ungeschriebene Lehre*, pp. 446-47; Athenaeus XI.
508c, alludes to the inscription.

[69]See, for example, Field, *Plato and His Contemporaries*, p. 36.   Cf.
D. L. III. 7.

[70]*Anonymous Prolegomena* 4. 14-26; D. L. IV. 1; cf. Armstrong, "Plato's
Academy," p. 91.

[71]Ryle, *Plato's Progress*, p. 8.

370's. Thus, the real martyr of the *Apology* was not Socrates, but Plato himself.[72] The prosecution resulted in ". . . the suppression of this teaching" and indirectly in ". . . the cessation of his eristic dialogues."[73]

> It was now or very soon afterwards that Plato joined forces with Theaetetus, who had had a mathematical school at Heraclea on the Black Sea, and Eudoxus, who had had a mathematical and astronomical school at Cyzicus. The Academy was formed as a merger between Plato's suppressed school of eristic and the other two immigrant schools.[74]

By this dating, the Academy was founded only three or four years before Aristotle joined it in 367, not twenty years as is generally supposed.[75] This reconstruction also explains why Plato did not teach his *forte*, eristic, in the Academy. In fact, eristic was not taught there until Aristotle introduced it in the 350's.[76] Ryle's argument for a later date for the founding of the Academy is pushed to the extreme by Randall:

> There is, in fact, no real evidence that Plato ever established an Academy, or that there was one until later times. . . . Not until much later do we find evidence of a flourishing school--. . . .[77]

We must conclude that we know virtually nothing about the "founding" of the Academy, but that at least by 370 Plato and his associates were recognized as a school.

Apparently in an effort to put his political philosophy into practice by teaching Dionysius II, Plato made two more trips (367-66 and 361-60) to Syracuse. The *Seventh Letter* is the principal source for this episode of his life. Ryle argues that Plato probably took Aristotle with him on his third trip.[78] The adventure was a disaster, and in 354 Dion was assassinated by a fellow member of the Academy.[79] In 348/47 Plato died and was buried near the Academy.[80] Significantly, his will does not mention the school.[81]

---

[72]Ibid., p. 152.

[73]Ibid., p. 153.

[74]Ibid., p. 154.

[75]Ibid., p. 225; cf. Ryle, "Plato," *EncPhilos*, VI, 318.

[76]Ryle, *Plato's Progress*, pp. 18, 109-10.

[77]*Plato*, p. 11.

[78]*Plato's Progress*, p. 90.

[79]Plutarch *Dion* XIV. 2; XVII. 1; Athenaeus XI. 508ef; cf. Lesky, *A History of Greek Literature*, pp. 510-11.

[80]Pausanias *Attica* I. xxx. 3; D. L. III. 2-3, 41.

[81]D. L. III. 41-43. See below, p. 79.

The nature of the Academy

The dearth of evidence about the Academy has permitted
scholars of various countries and decades to describe it in
terms of their own universities.[82] It is now clear that the
outlines of a modern university cannot be forced back upon the
Academy. Still, Plato's school can be viewed from several
perspectives. Legally it was a religious cult of the Muses,
and Socrates and Plato became its heroes.[83] Politically it was
a training-ground for tyrants, and scholastically it was an
association of scholars. The relative emphasis one gives to
each of these perspectives determines his understanding of the
Academy.

The Academy was probably founded as a cult (θίασος) of
the Muses more from necessity than religious fervor. The
"bigoted democracy" which had executed Socrates was soothed by
this concession to conformity, and the religious associations
of the place may have influenced Plato's selection of the
Academy.[84] Whether the Academy--as a legal entity--owned
property during Plato's life is unclear, but this was doubtless
the case later.[85]

The political purpose and activity of the Academy is
extremely difficult to assess. One's conclusions regarding
this facet of the Academy are dependent to a large extent on
his decision concerning the authenticity of the Platonic letters.[86] They tell us that Plato was active politically during
his youth,[87] that he realized the need for ". . . trustworthy
friends and supporters,"[88] and that rulers turned to the

---

[82]Cherniss, *Riddle*, p. 62; cf. Hans Joachim Krämer, *Arete bei Platon
und Aristoteles: Zum Wesen zur Geschichte der platonischen Ontologie*
(Amsterdam: Verlag P. Schippers N.V., 1967), p. 448; H. Leisegang, "Platon,"
RE, XX, 2352-53.

[83]Cf. Boyancé, *Culte*, pp. 261-69; Olivier Reverdin, *La religion de la
cité platonicienne*, École française d'Athenes, travaux et mémoires, Fasc. VI
(Paris: E. de Boccard, 1945).

[84]Marrou, *A History of Education in Antiquity*, p. 103.

[85]The legal status of the Academy has been the subject of an extended
debate: Ulrich von Wilamowitz-Moellendorff, *Platon* (2 vols.; 2nd ed.;
Berlin: Weidmannsche Buchhandlung, 1920), I, 271-72; Theodor Gomperz, *Greek
Thinkers: A History of Ancient Philosophy*, trans. by G. G. Berry (4 vols.;
London: John Murray, 1901-12), II, 272; III, 308; Field, *Plato and His
Contemporaries*, pp. 46-47; Ryle, *Plato's Progress*, p. 67; Clarke, *Higher
Education*, pp. 59-60.

[86]See above, p. 65.

[87]*Seventh Letter* 324C.

[88]See above, p. 69 n. 57.

Academy for advice.[89] Furthermore, the Academy was notorious
for the tyrants it produced (e.g., Timaeus of Cyzicus and
Chaeron of Pellene).[90] These references have led to an interest
in (and perhaps an exaggeration of) the political role of the
Academy. Morrow concludes that ". . . the Academy was founded
to accomplish, among other things, this definitely political
purpose: it was intended to serve as a training-school for
statesmen and public-spirited citizens."[91] Winspear maintains
a similar position: ". . . the Academy was first of all a
political organization, . . . its primary function and purpose
was the defense of international conservatism, ..."[92]
Levinson responds to similar claims by noting that Isocrates
criticized the curriculum of the Academy for ". . . its impractical and unpolitical character. . . ."[93] Nevertheless, it
appears that members of the Academy (including Plato) were
deeply interested in both the theory and application of political philosophy.[94] The Academy exerted political influence but,
ironically, not in Athens.[95]

We do not know by what means students came to be associated with the Academy. Some scholars have suggested that there
were entrance requirements or even an entrance examination.[96]
Such conclusions are drawn either from Plato's resolve to test
Dionysius' devotion to philosophy[97] or from the later practice
of the Academy.[98] All we know is that many of Plato's students

---

[89]*Sixth Letter*; cf. Plutarch *Moralia* 1126C.

[90]Athenaeus XI. 509AB; Plutarch *Moralia* 1126CD; Popper, *The Open
Society and Its Enemies*, I, 268 n. 25.

[91]*Studies in the Platonic Epistles*, p. 134.

[92]Alban Dewes Winspear, *The Genesis of Plato's Thought* (2nd ed.; New
York: S. A. Russell, 1956), p. 306.

[93]*In Defense of Plato*, p. 365.

[94]Edelstein, *Plato's Seventh Letter*, p. 165, disagrees: ". . . , and
Plato was greatly interested in questions of politics. But it was the
theory of Politics, not practical politics that captivated him."

[95]Cf. Friedländer, *Plato*, I, 102; Field, *Plato and His Contemporaries*,
p. 43.

[96]Friedländer, *Plato*, I, 86-87; Field, *Plato and His Contemporaries*,
pp. 34-35; Herter, *Platons Akademie*, p. 10.

[97]*Seventh Letter* 340B-341A.

[98]Cf. Clarke, *Higher Education*, p. 3: "But whatever may have been the
case with Plato, the Academy after his time certainly required its pupils to
have completed a course of general education before entry."

74

were from cities other than Athens,[99] Plato did not charge a
fee,[100] and Aristotle joined the Academy when he was seventeen.[101] There is some evidence that two women were included
among his pupils[102] and that a student was not required to
devote himself to the activities of the Academy exclusively.[103]
While we do not know the size of the school, Ryle conjectures
that: "The Academy's students in a given year could probably
have been counted in two figures, and very likely in the not
very high two figures."[104] Plato and some of his successors
lived at the Academy, but the students probably did not.[105]
There seems to have been no prescribed length of residence.
Some students would stay for a year or two, while others devoted
their life to study in the Academy.[106] This arrangement led to
differences in status among Plato's associates: ". . .
Speusippus and others were thought of as associated with Plato
as teachers, and distinguished from the crowd of youthful
students under instruction."[107] Plato did not attempt to
establish an "orthodoxy of opinion" in the Academy.[108] Rather,
the more mature members pursued investigations of their own,[109]
and Eudoxus seems to have brought his own students to the
Academy.[110] In spite of this diversity, a fraternal spirit
existed among the members.[111]

---

[99]D. L. III. 46. Cf. Bluck, *Plato's Life and Thought*, p. 32; Ryle,
"Plato," *EncPhilos*, VI, 318.

[100]D. L. IV. 2; *Anonymous Prolegomena* 5. 25; Athenaeus VII. 279.

[101]Düring, *Biographical Tradition*, pp. 254-55.

[102]*Anonymous Prolegomena* 4. 25-26. Cf. Cherniss, *Riddle*, p. 62.

[103]Edelstein, *Plato's Seventh Letter*, pp. 161-62.

[104]"Plato," *EncPhilos*, VI, 318.

[105]Plutarch *Moralia* 603BC; D. L. IV. 3, 19. According to Plutarch
Dion XVII. 1, while studying at the Academy, Dion lived ". . . in the upper
city of Athens with Callippus, one of his acquaintances, but for diversion
he bought a country-place, . . ." which he later gave to Speusippus.

[106]Cf. Clarke, *Higher Education*, p. 64.

[107]Field, *Plato and His Contemporaries*, p. 35.

[108]Ibid., pp. 39-40; Cherniss, *Riddle*, p. 81.

[109]Levinson, *In Defense of Plato*, p. 367.

[110]For discussion of the relation between Plato and Eudoxus see:
Friedländer, *Plato*, I, 353 n. 15; Field, *Plato and His Contemporaries*, pp.
36-37, 45-46.

[111]Cf. Marrou, *A History of Education in Antiquity*, p. 100; see below,
p. 78, for discussion of symposia.

The most valuable glimpse of the activities at the Academy comes from a satirical comedy by Epicrates.

> At the Panathenaea I saw a troop of lads . . . at the playground of the Academy I heard words unutterable, extraordinary. For they were making definitions about nature, and separating into categories the ways of beasts, the nature of trees, the kinds of vegetables; and in the course of it they were seeking to determine what species the pumpkin belonged to. . . . Well, then; in the first place, they all in silence took their station and with heads bowed low they reflected a long time. Then suddenly, while the lads were still bending low in study, one said it was a round vegetable, another said it was grass, a third a tree. On hearing that, a physician from Sicily could contain himself no longer, and snapped his fingers at them for a pack of lunatics. . . . No, the lads didn't mind it at all. And, Plato, who was standing by, very mildly, and without irritation, told them to try again to define the species to which the pumpkin belongs. So they set to inquiring.[112]

In this scene Plato is portrayed as a tolerant, fatherly teacher. Popper believes he was more aloof.[113] The Herculaneum papyrus describes Plato as posing problems for his students and "acting as architect."[114] Cherniss, however, finds evidence from Simplicius (6th c. A.D.) that Plato was not the "master" or

---

[112]Athenaeus II. 59d-f:

Παναθηναίοις γὰρ ἱδὼν ἀγέλην
μειρακίων . . . .
ἐν γυμνασίοις 'Ακαδημείας
ἤκουσα λόγων ἀφάτων, ἀτόπων.
περὶ γὰρ φύσεως ἀφοριζόμενοι
διεχώριζον ζώων τε βίον
δένδρων τε φύσιν λαχάνων τε γένη.
κἆτ' ἐν τούτοις τὴν κολοκύντην
ἐξήταζον τίνος ἐστὶ γένους. . . .
πρώτιστα μὲν οὖν πάντες ἄναυδοι
τότ' ἐπέστησαν καὶ κύψαντες
χρόνον οὐκ ὀλίγον διεφρόντιζον.
κἆτ' ἐξαίφνης, ἔτι κυπτόντων
καὶ ζητούντων τῶν μειρακίων,
λάχανον τις ἔφη στρογγύλον εἶναι,
ποίαν δ' ἄλλος, δένδρον δ' ἕτερος.
ταῦτα δ' ἀκούων ἰατρός τις
Σικελᾶς ἀπὸ γᾶς
κατέπαρδ' αὐτῶν ὡς ληρούντων. . . .
οὐδ' ἐμέλησεν τοῖς μειρακίοις.
ὁ Πλάτων δὲ παρὼν καὶ μάλα πράως,
οὐδὲν ὀρινθείς, ἐπέταξ' αὐτοῖς
πάλιν ἐξ ἀρχῆς τὴν κολοκύντην
ἀφορίζεσθαι τίνος ἐστὶ γένους.
οἱ δὲ διῄρουν.

Cf.Edmonds, *The Fragments of Attic Comedy*, II, 354-57. Cherniss discounts the value of this fragment, but Levinson adduces significant reasons for taking it more seriously; cf. *In Defense of Plato*, pp. 365-66 n. 283.

[113]*The Open Society and Its Enemies*, I, 42-43.

[114]*Academicorum philosophorum index Herculanensis*, pp. 15-16; cf. Clarke, *Higher Education*, p. 66.

even "seminar director," but that he merely offered "general advice and methodical criticism" to those who respected his insight.[115]

The question of whether Plato lectured in the Academy has been a major issue since the publication of Cherniss' *The Riddle of the Early Academy*. Previously it was generally assumed that Plato lectured regularly or even offered courses of lectures. Debate over Plato's oral teaching has been heated because Cherniss challenged the use of Aristotle's writings as a source for supplementing our understanding of Plato's theory of Ideas. If Plato did not give oral instruction to his students and interpret his writings, then Aristotle himself was dependent on the writings we possess.[116] Cherniss emphasizes that even though Plato worked in the Academy for forty years we have evidence of only one lecture;[117] Aristoxenus reports that Plato gave a public lecture on "the Good" and that it was a disaster.[118] Ryle couples his theory that Plato did not teach dialectic in the Academy with Cherniss' conclusions.[119]

Although Cherniss succeeded in demonstrating the paucity of evidence for claiming that Plato lectured in the Academy, more recent publications have amassed arguments to show that he did, nevertheless, give some esoteric teaching.[120] Sir David Ross cites two passages in which Plato professes to prefer oral communication to writing. On the basis of these he claims "it is really unthinkable . . ." that Plato did not enter into conversation with members of the Academy in which he discussed what he had written or was in the process of writing.[121] Thus far Ross is persuasive; then he reaches the following dubious conclusion:

---

[115]*Riddle*, p. 65; Taylor, *Plato*, p. 410, sees Plato functioning like ". . . the 'moderator' in the schools of the Middle Ages. . . ."

[116]*Riddle*, p. 78.

[117]Ibid., p. 2.

[118]*The Harmonics of Aristoxenus* 30-31, ed. and trans. by Henry S. Macran (Oxford: At the Clarendon Press, 1902), pp. 122-23, 187. Cf. Taylor, *Plato*, p. 503; Krämer, *Arete bei Platon und Aristoteles*, p. 409; Düring, *Biographical Tradition*, pp. 355-61; Cherniss, "Plato 1950-1957," pp. 28-31.

[119]Ryle, *Plato's Progress*, pp. 173-74.

[120]For the history of this debate see: Krämer, *Arete bei Platon und Aristoteles*, pp. 380-85; Gaiser, *Platons ungeschriebene Lehre*, pp. 16-18.

[121]*Phaedrus* 275C-277A; *Seventh Letter* 341C-342A; *Plato's Theory of Ideas* (Oxford: At the Clarendon Press, 1951), pp. 142-43.

It is certain, then, that Plato did give oral instruction on philosophy, and therefore we need not hesitate to accept what Aristotle says about Plato merely because we find no support for it in the dialogues.[122]

In his ground-breaking work, Krämer overturns Cherniss' hypothesis.

Das richtige Verständnis der platonischen Schriften fordert geradezu die Existenz des esoterischen Platon, und die Behauptung von Cherniss, die Hypothese eines esoterischen Platonismus habe sich erst durch Rückprojektion der aristotelischen Berichte gebildet, ist wissenschaftshistorisch unzutreffend.[123]

Relying mainly on the *Seventh Letter* and the *Phaedrus*, Krämer seeks to establish not only that there was a decisive difference between the content of Plato's oral and written teaching but also that Plato attempted to keep his esoteric teaching secret.[124]

Gaiser regards it as certain that Plato gave esoteric teaching to the circle of his friends and students and attempts with great erudition to recover that teaching.[125] The following statement may be true for ancient schools in general:

Wie in vergleichbarer Form schon bei dem Bund der Pythagoreer, so ergibt sich auch bei Platon das nebeneinander einer innerschulischen Forschung und Lehre (esoterik) und einer für die politische Offentlichkeit bestimmten Schriftstellerei (Exoterik) von selbst aus der *Lebenssituation der 'Schule'*; . . .[126]

Plato's teachings were probably graded, tests may have been given, and the whole of Plato's thought was probably known to only a few students.[127] Whether Plato lectured or not, he

---

[122]Ibid., pp. 150-51.

[123]*Arete bei Platon und Aristoteles*, p. 399.

[124]Ibid., p. 396; and Krämer, "Die Platonische Akademie und das Problem einer systematischen Interpretation der Philosophie Platons," pp. 204-05.

[125]*Platons ungeschriebene Lehre*, p. 1.

[126]Ibid., p. 3. Debate over the issue of the esoteric teaching continues with Krämer and Gaiser opposed by von Fritz. Cf. Hans Joachim Krämer, "Retraktionen zum Problem des esoterischen Platon," *MusHelv*, XXI (1964), 137-67; and von Fritz, "Die philosophische Stelle im siebten platonischen Brief und die Frage der 'esoterischen' Philosophie Platons," esp. pp. 144-45, 153. If a division between esoteric and exoteric teaching can be established as common in ancient schools, the result may be important for Johannine studies. Both Leroy and Meeks have recently suggested that the Johannine metaphors were meant to be understood only by those within the Johannine community. See above p. 34. The implications of this observation will be developed below, see p. 262.

[127]Ibid., p. 7. Cf. Ernst Moritz Manasse, Review of *Platons ungeschriebene Lehre*, by K. Gaiser, *AJP*, LXXXVI (1965), 439.

probably discussed and interpreted his teachings for his associates in the Academy.[128]

The study of division and definition and of mathematics
probably preceded the study of dialectic;[129] and even if Plato
did not teach it, the students probably practiced dialectic and
wrote dialogues of their own.[130] It was natural for others to
imitate Plato's writings. Some of these non-Platonic dialogues
were preserved in the Academy, and some may have later been
attributed to Plato.[131]

Regular "banquets" or "drinking parties" (συμπόσια) were
also characteristic of the Academy. Simple food and orderliness
marked these occasions,[132] and Plato asserted that they were an
essential element of education.[133] Later, rules were established and responsibility for these occasions was delegated on
a rotating basis.[134]

The Academy may also have had a library, but there is no
direct evidence on this point. Gomperz argued that the Academy
could not legally own a library but that manuscripts were
bequeathed by the head of the school to whom ever he wished.[135]
Although no manuscripts are mentioned in Plato's will,[136]
inferences may be drawn from scattered references. While
residing at the Academy, Aristotle was nick-named "the Reader,"[137]
and Vogel claims: ". . . the fourth century Academy possessed

---

[128]Cicero refers to ". . . Plato's practice of holding discussions
. . ." in the Academy: *De Finibus* V. i. 1-2; *Academica* I. iv. 17. Cf.
D. L. III. 28, 46.

[129]Cf. Ryle, *Plato's Progress*, pp. 138-39; Levinson, *In Defense of
Plato*, p. 367.

[130]Cf. Levinson, *In Defense of Plato*, p. 366 n. 284; Gilbert Ryle,
"Dialectic in the Academy," *New Essays on Plato and Aristotle*, ed. by
R. Bambrough (New York: The Humanities Press, 1965), p. 67.

[131]Jaeger, *Aristotle*, p. 24; Field, *Plato and His Contemporaries*,
pp. 49-50. The Johannine corpus may have originated in a similar manner.

[132]Plato *Republic* 372BC; *Laws* 639E-641D; Cicero *Tusculan Disputations*
V. xxxii. 91, xxxv. 100; Athenaeus IV. 137F; XII. 547D.

[133]*Laws* 641D.

[134]D. L. V. 4; Athenaeus V. 186B.

[135]Theodor Gomperz, "Platonische Aufsätze II: Die angebliche platonische Schulbibliothek und die Testamente der Philosophen," *SBVien*, CXLI
(1899), Abhandlung VII, pp. 1-11.

[136]D. L. III. 41-43.

[137]See below, p. 87 n. 21.

79

a collection of Pythagorean texts."[138] The crucial argument, however, rests on the purity of the textual tradition of Plato's writings.

> But the consideration of chief weight is the testimony of those concerned with textual criticism that the condition of the text of Plato's works is far superior to that of other writers, even those edited in Alexandrian times. This argues that from the beginning they must have been preserved with peculiar care, and it would be natural to suppose that that must have been in the Academy.[139]

Thus, the Academy may have functioned as a guardian of the Platonic writings, attempting to preserve the purity of their text and maintain their distinction from non-Platonic dialogues.[140] While it is possible that the Academy had a rudimentary library, Wilamowitz-Moellendorff's assertion that it possessed ". . . mathematische Modelle und Instrumente, Karten und vor allen Dingen Bücher" is unlikely.[141]

The history of the Academy

There are great gaps in our knowledge of the history of the Academy. For our purposes, however, it is necessary only to observe the way in which the Academy perpetuated itself as a school.

The absence of any provision for the continuation of the Academy in Plato's will probably indicates that such provisions had already been made by other means. As a cult of the Muses, the legal means for the survival of the Academy had already been established. Still, Ryle is probably too influenced by contemporary institutions when he claims: "Plato's will seems to show that the Academy became, some time before Plato's death, an endowed foundation, controlled by trustees."[142] Plato chose Speusippus (Head of the Academy 347-339) to be his

---

[138]*Pythagoras and Early Pythagoreanism*, p. 182.

[139]Field, *Plato and His Contemporaries*, p. 47. Antigonus Carystus (fl. 240 B.C.) wrote (according to D. L. III. 66) that when Plato's writings were first edited with critical marks, their owners charged a fee to anyone wishing to read them.

[140]This possibility suggests the interesting question of whether a study of the textual purity of the Johannine writings would support the argument that they were preserved by a school.

[141]*Platon*, I, 273. On the history of libraries see: Carl Wendel, "Das Griechisch-Römische Altertum," *Handbuch der Bibliothekswissenschaft*, Bd. III: *Geschichte der Bibliotheken*, ed. by F. Milkau and G. Leyh (Leipzig: Otto Harrassowitz, 1940), pp. 1-63.

[142]"Plato," *EncPhilos*, VI, 319.

successor, and as a result Xenocrates and Aristotle left the
Academy when Plato died.[143]   The atmosphere of the Academy
changed; Speusippus carried further Plato's "Pythagorean tendencies" by rejecting the theory of forms and substituting
numbers for them.[144]   Legends arose about the birth of
Plato,[145] and efforts were made to complete his works.   Philip
of Opus (fl. *ca*. 350 B.C.) allegedly edited the *Laws* and added
a supplement to it entitled *Epinomis*.[146]

> The Academy must have entrusted him with this task because
> he knew the manuscripts Plato had left and the plans he had
> had in mind, so that we cannot call the *Epinomis* a forgery.
> It is rather a supplement to *The Laws*, which Plato's own
> school therefore considered to be incomplete.[147]

When Speusippus died, the younger members of the Academy
first asked Aristotle to succeed him.   Aristotle, however, was
"in Macedonia," so they elected Xenocrates (Head of the Academy
339-314).[148]   The Head of the Academy normally held the position until his death, though there were at least two who
resigned.   Either the Head of the Academy chose his successor
himself, or he was elected by the *younger* members of the school.
The process of election seems to have been abandoned in the
later history of the Academy.[149] Xenocrates ". . . systematized
Plato's philosophy; in his hands it became a doctrine that
could be taught and learnt."[150]   The rotating position of
archon was also formalized under Xenocrates.   The *archon* super-
vised the religious rites and symposia.[151]   Furthermore, at

---

[143]D. L. IV. 1.

[144]D. A. Rees, "Platonism and the Platonic Tradition," *EncPhilos*, VI,
336.   Cf. [Julius] Stenzel, "Speusippos," *RE*, 2nd ser., IIIA$_2$, cols. 1636-
69.

[145]D. L. III. 2.

[146]Cf. D. L. III. 37.

[147]Jaeger, *Paideia*, III, 214.   John 21 was probably composed under
similar circumstances.

[148]*Academicorum philosophorum index Herculanensis*, pp. 38-39; D. L.
IV. 3.   Cf. Philip Merlan, "The Successor of Speusippus," *TAPA*, LXXVII
(1946), 103-11.

[149]Cf. Clarke, *Higher Education*, pp. 63-64.

[150]Edelstein, *Plato's Seventh Letter*, p. 163; cf. Cherniss, *Riddle*,
p. 82; Richard Heinze, *Xenocrates: Darstellung der Lehre und Sammlung der
Fragmente* (Leipzig: B. G. Teubner Verlagsgesellschaft, 1892; reprinted by
Hildesheim: Georg Olms Verlagsbuchhandlung, 1965).

[151]D. L. V. 4; Athenaeus XII. 547EF.

least by the time of Xenocrates, it was the practice of the
Head of the Academy to give formal lectures.[152] In contrast to
Speusippus, Xenocrates and his successor lived at the Academy.[153]

While Polemo was Head of the Academy (314/313-270) his
students ". . . made themselves little huts and lived not far
from the shrine of the Muses and the lecture-hall."[154] Under
Arcesilaus (d. 242/241) the Academy entered a period of skepti-
cism.[155]

> Lacydes [Head of the Academy 241/40 to at least 224/23] used
> to lecture in the Academy, in the garden which had been laid
> out by King Attalus, and from him it derived the name of
> Lacydeum.[156]

The Academy was probably destroyed by Philip about 200
B.C.,[157] but according to Cicero, Carneades (Head of the Academy
from before 155 until he resigned in 137-36) lectured there.[158]
During the first century B.C., the Academy was again a victim
of military violence:

> . . . , he [Sulla] laid hands upon the sacred groves, and
> ravaged the Academy, which was the most wooded of the city's
> suburbs, as well as the Lyceum.[159]

> His wood he cut in the grove of the Academy, where he con-
> structed enormous engines. He also demolished the Long
> Walls, and used the stones, timber, and earth for building
> the mound.[160]

As a result of this destruction the school may have abandoned
Academe and moved into the city.[161] Nevertheless, the Academy

---

[152]D. L. IV. 16; cf. Clarke, *Higher Education*, p. 67.

[153]Plutarch *Moralia* 603BC.

[154]D. L. IV. 19: . . . , παρ' ὃν οἱ μαθηταὶ μικρὰ καλύβια ποιησάμενοι κατῴκουν πλησίον τοῦ μουσείου καὶ τῆς ἐξέδρας.

[155]Plutarch *Moralia* 1120C.

[156]D. L. IV. 60:
Ὁ γοῦν Λακύδης ἐσχόλαζεν ἐν 'Ακαδημείᾳ ἐν τῷ κατασκευασθέντι κήπῳ ὑπὸ 'Αττάλου τοῦ βασιλέως, καὶ Λακύδειον ἀπ' αὐτοῦ προσηγορεύετο.

[157]Livy XXXI. xxiv. 18.

[158]*De Finibus* V. 4, 8; cf. Clarke, *Higher Education*, p. 60.

[159]Plutarch *Sulla* XII. 3:
. . . ἐπεχείρησε τοῖς ἱεροῖς ἄλσεσι, καὶ τήν τε 'Ακαδήμειαν ἔκειρε δενδροφορωτάτην προαστείων οὖσαν καὶ τὸ Λύκειον.

[160]Appian *Mithridatic Wars* V. 30:
ὕλην δὲ τῆς 'Ακαδημείας ἔκοπτε, καὶ μηχανὰς εἰργάζετο μεγίστας. τά τε μακρὰ σκέλη καθῄρει, λίθους καὶ ξύλα καὶ γῆν ἐς τὸ χῶμα μεταβάλλων.

[161]Clarke, *Higher Education*, p. 60, claims that it did; Wycherley, "Peripatos," p. 19, argues that it did not.

is referred to as a living school by later writers, and it maintained some claim to a continuous history until it was closed by Emperor Justinian in A.D. 529.[162]

The influence of the Academy

The influence of the Academy can scarcely be assessed. Politically it played a significant role in the Hellenistic world. Men who had studied there became rulers and counsellors-of-state. The most important recipient of the legacy of the Academy was Aristotle. Aristotle's role in the Academy and its influence on him are discussed in the following chapter. The transfer of influence from the Academy and Lyceum to the Epicureans, Stoics, and Museum at Alexandria is also traced below.[163]

During the early part of this century many scholars emphasized the influence of the Academy on the modern university.[164] This emphasis has now been justly abandoned, but the sentiment it embodied is beautifully conveyed by F. J. E. Woodbridge:

Plato may or may not have held school in the Academy for well-nigh the last forty years of his life until he died at a marriage feast or otherwise. We may never know. He has held school in the Academy ever since for many of his disciples. This may be of more consequence than anything he himself ever taught by word of mouth to eager students.[165]

---

[162]For the later history of the Academy see: Clarke, *Higher Education*, pp. 79, 101-02; Rees, "Platonism and the Platonic Tradition," *EncPhilos*, VI, 336.

[163]See esp. pp. 100, 117-21, 141-42.

[164]See above, p. 72.

[165]*The Son of Apollo*, pp. 28-29.

Chapter IV

THE LYCEUM

The importance of the Lyceum

Aristotle's influence on the evolutionary development of
the philosophical schools was epoch-making. As the principal
heir of the Platonic system he transformed the earlier attempts
at collaboration in the pursuit of knowledge into a well-
organized effort by a scholarly community to assemble all that
could be learned in most of the areas of science, literature,
and politics. He was the first schoolmaster to organize his
students for the achievement of goals in research and the
production of written materials. He was also the first to base
his work ". . . on access to libraries and collections of study
material, on archive research and field-work, and on the full
use of a well thought-out scientific method."[1] The effect of
this innovative approach on later schools and libraries makes
Aristotle and his associates important for our study of ancient
schools.

The sources for the study of the Lyceum

As has been true of the earlier schools, our primary
source, the Aristotelian corpus, tells us less about the school
than the biographical tradition about Aristotle. Ingemar
Düring's work, *Aristotle in the Ancient Biographical Tradition*,
is an indispensable collection and analysis of the traditions
about Aristotle.[2]

Before proceeding to the biographical tradition, however,
the Aristotelian corpus must be examined. A literary division
among the writings attributed to Aristotle was noticed as early
as Cicero (106-43 B.C.);[3] and it is the "treatises" (λόγοι
κατὰ φιλοσοφίαν) as opposed to the "dialogues" (ἐξωτερικοὶ
λόγοι or ἐδεδομένοι λόγοι) which are of primary importance to
us.[4] The dialogues were composed early in Aristotle's life--

---

[1]Ingemar Düring, "Aristotle the Scholar," *Arctos*, N.S. I (1954), 61.

[2]First cited above p. 67 n. 43.   See also: Herbert S. Long, "A Bibliographical Survey of Recent Works on Aristotle," *CW*, LI (1957-58), 47ff.

[3]*De Finibus* V. 5, 12; cf. Jaeger, *Aristotle*, p. 32 n. 1; see below
p. 92 n. 56.

[4]Cf. Lesky, *A History of Greek Literature*, p. 552.

some while he was still at the Academy--and survive only in
fragmentary form. The treatises are generally connected with
the lectures and research projects at the Lyceum. In his work
which marked the beginning of a new era in the study of
Aristotle, Jaeger claims:

> There is no school of learning of which we have so complete
> a picture as the Lyceum. The very lectures that were given
> there are mostly preserved to us in the writings of Aristotle

Although this statement is essentially true, it conceals a
snarl of critical problems. What is the relationship between
the lectures and the treatises? It was once popular to hold
that the treatises are lecture notes taken by students. This
theory has now been discarded.[6] Many scholars now trace the
treatises to Aristotle himself even though it is universally
agreed that he made use of research done by his associates and
that the treatises have been revised, supplemented, and edited
by later hands. Moreover, certain treatises attributed to
Aristotle are pseudonymous.[7] Indeed, the treatises are the
product of a living school-tradition: ". . . many peripatetic
lecturers contributed to almost every part of what is known as
Aristotle's works."[8] Nevertheless, all of the contributors
were ". . . dominated by a single great mind."[9] While they
tell us little about the organization and communal life of the
Lyceum, the treatises reflect a community of scholars indus-
triously analyzing and compiling information in a wide variety
of fields.[10] Furthermore, the suggestion that these writings

---

[5]*Aristotle*, p. 314.

[6]See for example: Philip Wheelwright, *Aristotle* (New York: The
Odyssey Press, 1951), pp. xix-xx; G. E. R. Lloyd, *Aristotle: The Growth
and Structure of His Thought* (Cambridge: At the University Press, 1968),
p. 15; Marjorie Grene, *A Portrait of Aristotle* (London: Faber and Faber
Limited, 1963), p. 32, calls it a "quaint theory."

[7]Lloyd, *Aristotle*, p. 16:
"One example is the treatise entitled *On Mechanics*, though in this and
several other similar cases the author was probably a member of the
Lyceum and a pupil of Aristotle."

[8]Felix Grayeff, "The Problem of the Genesis of Aristotle's Text,"
Phronesis, I (1956), 109-10; cf. Lesky, *A History of Greek Literature*, p.
575; E. Jos. Schächer, *Ist das Corpus Aristotelicum nach-Aristotelisch?*
Salzburger Studien zur Philosophie, Bd. II (Munich: Anton Pustet, 1963).

[9]John Herman Randall, Jr., *Aristotle* (New York: Columbia University
Press, 1960), pp. 25-26: "In other words, there is to be found in the
corpus the activities of a whole school, dominated by a single great mind."

[10]The usefulness of the Aristotelian corpus for describing the Lyceum
is not seriously affected by one's decision about the accuracy of Strabo's
account of the transmission of these writings. See below, p. 96.

85

were intended to serve as ". . . some sort of permanent record within the school . . ." and that to some extent they reflect the curriculum of the Lyceum is intrinsically probable.[11]

As was the case with the schools of Pythagoras and Plato, so with that of Aristotle, the biographical tradition which developed around the "founder" carried with it important traditions and legends about the school. Düring's analysis of the biographical traditions about Aristotle provides us with significant insights for understanding the history of the tradition about the Lyceum.[12] A politically and doctrinally inspired antagonism toward Aristotle developed even before his death. Aristotle was engaged in a bitter polemic with Isocrates and his followers and was the subject of anti-Macedonian hatred. He was also the victim of sharp jabs from rival schools, especially the Epicureans and Academicians. Fragments of the work of Aristocles of Messina (2nd c. A.D.) contain much of this early unfavorable tradition. Philochorus (before 340 - shortly after 261/60 B.C.) in his *Atthis* was the first to attempt to offer a more favorable account of Aristotle, and we are probably indebted to him for our understanding of the chronology of Aristotle's life:

> He also refuted some of the accusations brought against Aristotle: it was not true that Aristotle was an ὀψιμαθής and he had not seceded from the Academy or opened a school rivaling that of Plato.[13]

Ariston of Ceos, who probably succeeded Lyco as head of the Lyceum *ca.* 225 B.C., wrote a life of Aristotle. From a phrase in Diogenes Laertius ". . . it has been inferred that Ariston's work was based on the archives of the Peripatos and the oral tradition, and that it contained the four Wills which we now possess."[14] In the third century B.C. there also developed a literature composed for entertainment. Hermippus (fl. 3rd c.

---

[11]G. R. G. Mure, *Aristotle* (New York: Oxford University Press, 1964), p. 257; cf. Grene, *A Portrait of Aristotle*, p. 32.

[12]What follows is a summary of Düring, *Biographical Tradition*, pp. 462-76. Cf. Olof Gigon, "Interpretationen zu den antiken Aristoteles-Viten," *MusHelv*, XV (1958), 147-93. Assuming for the moment that there was a Johannine school, one reason why we have so little information about it is that no biographical tradition about its "founder" (or at least very little) has survived. Jesus, not the founder, was the figure of chief interest in the Johannine school, and what tradition there was about the founder may be embedded in the Gospel of John.

[13]Düring, *Biographical Tradition*, p. 463.

[14]Ibid., p. 464.

B.C.) probably used Ariston's work when he compiled his own
biography of Aristotle in the library at Alexandria. As a
Peripatetic, ". . . he has had a great influence on the biographical tradition: he wanted to extol Aristotle as the
founder of the Peripatetic school in the Lyceum."[15] He linked
Aristotle to the tradition of an attempt to start a rival
school while Plato was in Sicily in 361/60, and claimed that
when Aristotle later returned to Athens

> . . . , he "founded his own school in the Lyceum". This
> legend, together with the aetiological explanation of the
> name "Peripatetics", is Hermippus' chief contribution to the
> biographical tradition.[16]

Artemon (probably not later than 2nd c. B.C.) collected
Aristotle's correspondence, but most of the letters are probably
forgeries. Hermippus' work survives mainly in the fragments
used by Diogenes Laertius, who appears to have been ". . . an
erudite amateur, isolated and without personal connections with
the contemporary schools of learning."[17] Surprisingly, Diogenes'
work was not known to Ptolemy, who wrote the life of Aristotle
known to the Neoplatonic schools. We possess three epitomes of
this work, the aim of which appears to have been to glorify
Aristotle. In spite of his biased approach, Ptolemy may still
preserve for us valuable bits of information from his sources:
Artemon's collection of letters, and Hermippus. Düring concludes that ". . . Ptolemy was a member of Porphyry's and
Iamblichus' school and that he wrote his life of Aristotle in
the first half of the fourth century.[18] This summary of Düring's
reconstruction of the growth of the biographical tradition
indicates that one should be cautious about claiming that
Aristotle founded a school at the Lyceum in opposition to the
Academy.

The origin of the Lyceum

The biographical tradition about Aristotle is significant
in another respect; what we know about Aristotle's life illu-
mines the origin of the Lyceum and the influences which shaped
it. Aristotle was born in 384 in Stagira, the son of a physi-

---

[15]Ibid., p. 465.

[16]Ibid.

[17]Ibid., p. 469. Cf. Paul Moraux, "La composition de la 'vie d'
Aristote' chez Diogene Laerte," *REG*, LXVIII (1955), 124-63.

[18]Düring, *Biographical Tradition*, p. 475.

cian.[19] At the age of seventeen (367/66) he came to the Academy
where he was influenced by Plato, Eudoxus of Cnidos, and to a
lesser extent Philistion and Isocrates.[20] Eudoxus and Philistion
were especially interested in empirical research and the natural
sciences. While at the Academy, Aristotle also began to read
and probably began collecting books.[21] Ryle suggests that
Aristotle accompanied Plato on his third trip to Syracuse
(361), but this remains conjectural.[22] Nevertheless, shortly
after this event Aristotle began to write dialogues and teach
rhetoric in the Academy.[23] He is reported to have said: "It
is a shame to remain silent while allowing Isocrates to speak."[24]

Interesting attempts have been made to learn more about
this period of Aristotle's life. Henry Jackson has attempted
to describe Aristotle's lecture room in the Academy on the
basis of objects referred to in his early writings.[25]

> As Jackson points out, Aristotle in some of these examples
> speaks as if pointing with his finger towards some represen-
> tation on the wall. Was it a painting, with the central
> figure in white? Does it not in fact seem very natural that
> the main lecture-room in the Academy was decorated with
> wall-paintings representing two famous scenes: Socrates at
> the meeting of the sophists in Callias' house, and Socrates
> sitting on his bed in jail on the day of his death, talking
> with his friends?[26]

In a separate study Philip Merlan suggests that a group of
Academicians was meeting regularly in the Lyceum at this
time.[27] Isocrates was spurred to a polemic by this development,

---

[19]D. L. V. 1, 9; Düring, *Biographical Tradition*, pp. 263-72.

[20]D. L. V. 6; Düring, "Aristotle the Scholar," pp. 62-64.

[21]Düring, "Aristotle the Scholar," p. 64; Frederic G. Kenyon, *Books and Readers in Ancient Greece and Rome* (Oxford: At the Clarendon Press, 1932), pp. 24-25.

[22]*Plato's Progress*, p. 90.

[23]Ingemar Düring, "Aristotle and Plato in the Mid-fourth Century," *Eranos*, LIV (1956), 113, 120; Ryle, *Plato's Progress*, p. 97; Philip Merlan, "Isocrates, Aristotle and Alexander the Great," *Historia*, III (1954-55), 65.

[24]Cicero *De Oratore* III. xxxv. 141; *Tusculan Disputations* I. iv. 7; Quintilian III. i. 14; cf. Clarke, *Higher Education*, p. 68. Some manuscripts read "Xenocrates" instead of "Isocrates."

[25]"Aristotle's Lecture-Room and Lectures," *JP*, XXXV (1920), 191-200; cf. Marrou, *A History of Education in Antiquity*, p. 104.

[26]Düring, *Biographical Tradition*, p. 372.

[27]Merlan, "Isocrates, Aristotle and Alexander the Great," pp. 69-70, bases his argument on Isocrates *Panathenaicus* 18-19, and 33. The *Panathenaicus* was begun in 342 and completed in 339 (*OCD*, p. 554).

adding credence to the suggestion that this group was associated with Aristotle.

> It may be that the people who used to meet there [in the Lyceum] represented a pro-Aristotelian faction within the Academy, opposed to Speusippus, and thus the nucleus of the Peripatos.[28]

If Merlan's theory is correct, we have a natural explanation of why Aristotle "founded his school" in the Lyceum a few years later. Still, while there may be some truth to this hypothesis, the evidence is too weak to allow one to build a theory of the pre-history of the Lyceum on it. Merlan's theory is related to the question of when Aristotle broke from Plato philosophically—a question which is still being debated.[29]

When Plato died in 347, Speusippus became head of the Academy, and Aristotle and Xenocrates withdrew to Assos. There Aristotle spent three years in the company of other Platonists under the protection of Hermias, and it is possible that Aristotle taught in a school there. Josephus hands on a tradition from Clearchus, a pupil of Aristotle, that Aristotle met and talked with a Jewish sage. The sage spoke Greek and came to test Aristotle's learning. Aristotle is reported to have said: "But as one who had been intimate with many cultivated persons, it was rather he who imparted to us something of his own."[30] Hans Lewy locates this meeting at Assos but is rightly skeptical about the authenticity of the narrative.[31] The Jewish sage was probably a fictitious character, one which excited contemporary imaginations. If such a meeting did occur, however, it was the first direct contact of which we have a record between a representative of the philosophical schools and a learned Jew.

---

[28]Merlan, "Isocrates, Aristotle and Alexander the Great," p. 69 n. 2.

[29]In contrast to the thesis developed by Jaeger in his *Aristotle*, Düring, "Aristotle the Scholar," p. 65, argues that Aristotle never held to the theory of ideas and ". . . at a very early stage of his development, he followed his own course." Cf. *Biographical Tradition*, pp. 315-36; D. L. V. 2:

> "He seceded from the Academy while Plato was still alive. Hence the remark attributed to the latter: 'Aristotle spurns me, as colts kick out at the mother who bore them.'"
> Ἀπέστη δὲ Πλάτωνος ἔτι περιόντος· ὥστε φασὶν ἐκεῖνον εἰπεῖν,
> "'Ἀριστοτέλης ἡμᾶς ἀπελάκτισε, καθαπερεὶ τὰ πωλάρια γεννηθέντα τὴν μητέρα."

[30]Josephus *Apion* I. 181: ὡς δὲ πολλοῖς τῶν ἐν παιδεία συνωκειῶτο, παρεδίδου τι μᾶλλον ὧν εἶχεν.

[31]"Aristotle and the Jewish Sage According to Clearchus of Soli," *HTR*, XXXI (1938), 205-35.

Accompanied by Theophrastus, Aristotle moved to Mytilene where in 343/42 he accepted the invitation of Philip to become Alexander's tutor. We know very little about Aristotle's activities in Macedon. When Speusippus died, Aristotle was nominated to succeed him, but the office fell to Xenocrates.[32] Although the evidence is scant, it appears that during his absence from Athens Aristotle began investigations in the natural and social sciences which he continued for the rest of his life.[33]

In 335/34 he returned to Athens and began teaching in the Lyceum. As a non-citizen he could not buy property in Athens, but he enjoyed the protection of his Macedonian friend, Antipater. In the course of their investigations and teaching Aristotle and Theophrastus attracted others to their "school."[34] Nevertheless, there is no evidence that Aristotle ever offi- cially "founded" a school:

> As the years passed the circle of collaborators and students probably became more closely united, but the Peripatos as a school in the same sense as the Academy was not established until after Aristotle's death.[35]

Thus, it is difficult to argue that Aristotle intentionally established a school to rival the Academy; his pursuits were merely alien to the direction which the Academy had taken during his absence. In the aftermath of Alexander's death anti-Macedonian feeling surfaced in Athens and led to charges of impiety against Alexander's former tutor. Consequently, after thirteen years at the Lyceum, Aristotle withdrew to Chalcis where he died a few months later in 322.[36]

The terms "Lyceum" and *"Peripatos"* are customarily used to designate Aristotle's school, but neither term carried this meaning during Aristotle's life. The Lyceum was a shrine of

---

[32]See above, p. 80 n. 148.

[33]For further discussion of Aristotle's travels see: Düring, *Biographical Tradition*, pp. 272-99; Jaeger, *Aristotle*, pp. 105-23; Lesky, *A History of Greek Literature*, pp. 549-51.

[34]D. L. V. 3: "In time the circle about him grew larger; he then sat down to lecture, ..." Ἐπειδὴ δὲ πλείους ἐγένοντο ἤδη, καὶ ἐκάθισεν . . .

[35]Düring, *Biographical Tradition*, p. 461. Lloyd, *Aristotle*, pp. 7-8; and Boyancé, *Culte*, p. 299, agree: the school did not acquire the legal status of a θίασος until after Aristotle's death. Field, *Plato and His Contemporaries*, p. 46, follows Gomprez in concluding that the Lyceum did not become a legal entity until after the death of Theophrastus.

[36]D. L. V. 6.

Apollo Lykeios which lay to the east of the city. It was one
of Socrates' favorite places,[37] and ". . . since long ago well
known as a place where foreign sophists and teachers gave
lectures."[38] It had the usual *Mouseion*, stoas, and running-
tracks; and it was used as a parade ground.[39] What was possibly a boundary marker of the Lyceum has recently been identified.[40] More detailed descriptions are given in the wills of
the later Peripatetics.

How *peripatos* came to refer to the school of Aristotle is
not clear. The original meaning of the word was a "covered
walk,"[41] and the Lyceum probably contained one. K. O. Brink
traces the way in which this term came to be applied to philosophical schools and to the Aristotelian school in particular.[42] Hermippus derived the name from Aristotle's practice of
walking while teaching:

> . . . , when he saw the school [the Academy] under a new
> head, he made choice of a public walk [περίπατον] in the
> Lyceum where he would walk up and down discussing philosophy
> with his pupils until it was time to rub themselves with
> oil. Hence the name 'Peripatetic.' But others say that it
> was given to him because when Alexander was recovering from
> an illness and taking daily walks, [ἐκ νόσου περιπατοῦντι]
> Aristotle joined him and talked with him on certain
> matters.[43]

The tradition which associates the term with Alexander is
certainly legendary, and Protagoras is reputed to have taught
peripatetically long before Aristotle.[44] G. B. Kerferd claims
that the derivation of the term from Aristotle's alleged

---

[37]Cf. Plato *Euthyphro* 2a; *Lysis* 203a; *Euthydemus* 271a.

[38]Düring, *Biographical Tradition*, p. 461. Aristophanes (4th c. B.C.)
refers to the sophists in the Lyceum as "thin, worthless starvelings," in
fragments preserved in Athenaeus III. 98f; XIII. 565f. Cf. Delorme,
Gymnasion, pp. 54-58.

[39]Wycherley, "Peripatos," p. 10.

[40]Ibid., pp. 11-12.

[41]LSJ, p. 1382.

[42]"Peripatos," *RE*, Suppl. VII, cols. 899-900; cf. Düring,
Biographical Tradition, pp. 404-11.

[43]D. L. V. 2:
. . . ἐλθόντα δὴ αὐτὸν καὶ θεασάμενον ὑπ' ἄλλω τὴν σχολήν, ἐλέσθαι
περίπατον τὸν ἐν Λυκείω καὶ μέχρι μὲν ἀλείμματος ἀνακάμπτοντα τοῖς
μαθηταῖς συμφιλοσοφεῖν· ὅθεν περιπατητικὸν προσαγορευθῆναι. οἱ δ', ὅτι
ἐκ νόσου περιπατοῦντι Ἀλεξάνδρω συμπαρὼν διελέγετο ἅττα.
Düring, *Biographical Tradition*, p. 406, claims: "It was probably Hermippus
himself who concocted this story." For other references to teaching peripatetically see: Cicero *Academica* I. 17; Athenaeus IV. 163b.

[44]Plato *Protagoras* 314E-315B.

practice of teaching while walking is ". . . now generally
regarded as a mistaken reference, based on nothing more than
the name itself; . . ."[45] i.e., a covered walking place.

The nature of the Lyceum

We have already observed that the school at the Lyceum
evolved from an informal relationship between Aristotle, his
associates, and his pupils. It was not until Demetrius of
Phalerum became governor of Athens and made legislative changes
". . . under Theophrastus' influence (317/16-316/15). . ." that
the school was recognized legally and began to acquire property.[46] Nevertheless, even under Aristotle the school bore
some resemblance to the Academy in terms of its veneration of
the Muses[47] and symposia.[48] Even so, the differences between
the Academy and the Lyceum are striking. The Lyceum was a
research center surpassed only by the Museum in Alexandria
during the next century. Aristotle organized his associates
and probably assigned areas of research. Lloyd cites the
following projects which were initiated by Aristotle: compiling
a complete list of the winners of the Pythian games, writing
histories of various branches of speculative thought, a history
of Greek medicine, a collection of political constitutions,
full botanical treatises, and the list continues.[49] Some of
the achievements have survived in the Aristotelian corpus and
fragments of the writings of his students, but much has been
lost. Even though some of these projects were completed only
after Aristotle's death, the breadth and intensity of the work
done at the Lyceum is staggering.

In addition to this research activity, a regular program
of instruction was conducted. Aulus Gellius (*ca.* A.D. 130 -
ca. 180) reports that Aristotle delivered two kinds of lectures.[50] He gave acroatic lectures [ἀκροατικά] in the morning
which dealt with the more profound elements of philosophy.

---

[45]G. B. Kerferd, "Peripatetics," *EncPhilos*, VI, 92.

[46]Frank William Walbank, "Demetrius," *OCD*, p. 325; see above, p. 87
n. 26, and Marrou, *A History of Education in Antiquity*, p. 291.

[47]Cf. Boyancé, *Culte*, pp. 299-322. Aristotle's hymn to Hermias
[D. L. V. 7-8.] in which he refers to the Muses as "the daughters of Memory"
is relevant to this point.

[48]See below, p. 93.

[49]Lloyd, *Aristotle*, pp. 98-102.

[50]*Attic Nights* XX. v. 1-12.

Attendance of these lectures was limited to the advanced students. The exoteric lectures [ἐξωτερικά] were held in the same place in the evening. These were open to any young man and offered instruction in rhetoric and politics. Other sources note that Aristotle habitually debated both sides of every question.[51] Aulus Gellius states that he walked while delivering both kinds of lectures and: "He also divided his books on all these subjects into two divisions, calling one set 'exoteric,' the other 'acroatic.'"[52] The same writer preserves correspondence between Alexander and Aristotle which he found in the works of Andronicus (1st c. B.C.) in which Alexander rebukes Aristotle for publishing the acroatic books. Aristotle responds:

> You have written to me regarding my acroatic lectures, thinking that I ought to have kept them secret. Know then that they have both been made public and not made public. For they are intelligible only to those who have heard me.[53]

The letters are obviously fictitious, and Düring traces the legend that ". . . the afternoon lectures were 'exoteric' and the morning lectures 'acroatic', . . ." to the work of Andronicus.[54] He also suggests that Andronicus forged the letters to support this idea.[55] The assertion that secret doctrines were given in the morning lectures did not develop until later. Thus, Andronicus appears to have fabricated the two kinds of lectures as an explanation for the two kinds of writings: the dialogues (exoteric) and the treatises (esoteric) The division of the writings predates Andronicus.[56] Still, the tradition that Aristotle lectured regularly remains firm, and the difference between the dialogues and the treatises at least allows for the notion that there was some distinction between esoteric teaching (for advanced students) and exoteric (open to

---

[51]Cicero *Tusculan Disputations* II. iii. 9.

[52]Aulus Gellius *Attic Nights* XX. v. 6: Libros quoque suos, earum omnium rerum conmentarios, seorsum divisit, ut alii "exoterici" dicerentur, partim "acroatici."

[53]Ibid., XX. v. 12:
Ἔγραψάς μοι περὶ τῶν ἀκροατικῶν λόγων, οἰόμενος δεῖν αὐτοὺς φυλάττειν ἐν ἀπορρήτοις. ἴσθι οὖν αὐτοὺς καὶ ἐκδεδομένους καὶ μὴ ἐκδεδομένους. ξυνετοὶ γάρ εἰσιν μόνοις τοῖς ἡμῶν ἀκούσασιν. ἔρρωσο, Ἀλέξανδρε βασιλεῦ

[54]*Biographical Tradition*, p. 432.

[55]Ibid., p. 434.

[56]Ibid., p. 432; see above, p. 83 n. 3.

anyone). There is, nevertheless, no evidence that there was
any secrecy about the esoteric doctrines.[57]

By the time Aristotle moved back to Athens he had probably
acquired a considerable library. This library was his personal
property and was probably kept in his house rather than in the
Lyceum, a public gymnasium.[58] Nevertheless, it must have
played an important part in the work of the Lyceum.

> Even if it were not actually related that Aristotle pos-
> sessed a library, the fate of which after his death is on
> record, [Strabo XIII. i. 54] it would be obvious from the
> mere list of his works that it must have been so. His great
> compilations could not have been produced without a ref-
> erence library; and his practice set an example which was
> followed by his disciples, such as Theophrastus and Menon,
> and which profoundly influenced the course of Greek liter-
> ary history.[59]

Aristotle's will does not mention his books, but Strabo reports
that he left his library to Theophrastus.[60] Theophrastus then
willed his library to Neleus.[61]

Aristotle continued Plato's practice of holding symposia,
and ". . . following the example of Xenocrates, he made it a
rule in his school [σχολῇ] that every ten days a new president
[ἄρχοντα] should be appointed."[62] Under Lyco this office
became a burden to its recipient.[63] Athenaeus preserves an
interesting fragment about a meal at the Lyceum. He attributes
the fragment to Chrysippus (ca. 280-207 B.C.), but the date of
the event to which it refers is unknown.

---

[57]Cf. George Boas, "Ancient Testimony to Secret Doctrines," *Philo-
sophical Review*, LXII (1953), 92:
". . . we have no reason to believe that Plato and Aristotle, or even
Pythagoras--if there was such a person--had any doctrines which were
secret or which they felt it necessary to conceal from the public."
Boas is correct with respect to Plato and Aristotle, but the case of
Pythagoras is more complex. Clearly, secrecy was attached to some
Pythagorean doctrines. See above, p. 50.

[58]Düring, *Biographical Tradition*, pp. 337-38; Field, *Plato and His
Contemporaries*, p. 47.

[59]Kenyon, *Books and Readers in Ancient Greece and Rome*, pp. 24-25.

[60]XIII. i. 54.

[61]D. L. V. 52; Strabo XIII. i. 54. See below, p. 96.

[62]D. L. V. 4: . . . ἀλλὰ καὶ ἐν τῇ σχολῇ νομοθετεῖν μιμούμενον
Ξενοκράτην, ὥστε κατὰ δέκα ἡμέρας ἄρχοντα ποιεῖν. Cf. Athenaeus V. 186b.

[63]See below, p. 98.

At the Lyceum, again, the cook who had brought in some salt
meat which he had made over in imitation of salt-fish was
flogged for playing the impostor with his over-refinement.[64]

In the above description an attempt has been made to separate
what can be said about the school during Aristotle's life from
later developments. In the following section these developments are discussed. It is possible, however, that some of the
things that are said about the Lyceum under Aristotle's successors may have been true of the school at an earlier time
also.

The history of the Lyceum

When Aristotle withdrew to Chalcis because he did not want
the Athenians ". . . to sin twice against philosophy,"[65]
Theophrastus (*ca.* 370-288/85 B.C.) became head of the Lyceum.[66]
Theophrastus continued the full spectrum of research initiated
by Aristotle. In addition, he entered into closer relations
with contemporary schools of medicine.[67] He also became a very
popular lecturer:

> Hermippus says that Theophrastus used to appear at the
> School [περίπατον] at the regular hour glistening with oil
> and exquisitely dressed, and after seating himself he gave
> free play to every motion and gesture in delivering his
> discourse. On one occasion, while portraying an epicure, he
> thrust forth his tongue and licked his lips.[68]

These antics undoubtedly helped to attract the two thousand
students who are alleged to have attended his lectures.[69]
Like Aristotle, Theophrastus was a metic and not able to
acquire property, but Demetrius of Phalerum appears to have
given him special permission to buy a garden and control the
school's property.[70] Jaeger conjectures that the property ". . .

---

[64]Athenaeus IV. 137f:

τὸν δ' ἐν τῷ Λυκείῳ κρέας ταριχηρὸν εἰς τάριχος διασκευάσαντα μαστιγωθῆναι
ὡς παρασοφιζόμενον πονηρῶς.

[65]Cf. Düring, *Biographical Tradition*, pp. 341-42. Jaeger, *Aristotle*,
p. 314, observes that some Athenians ". . . saw in Aristotle's school a
Macedonian secret-service bureau."

[66]D. L. V. 36.

[67]Cf. Jaeger, *Aristotle*, pp. 336, 424.

[68]Athenaeus I. 21ab:

Ἕρμιππος δέ φησι Θεόφραστον παραγίνεσθαι εἰς τὸν περίπατον καθ' ὥραν
λαμπρὸν καὶ ἐξησκημένον, εἶτα καθίσαντα διατίθεσθαι τὸν λόγον οὐδεμιᾶς
ἀπεχόμενον κινήσεως οὐδὲ σχήματος ἑνός. καί ποτε ὀψοφάγον μιμούμενον
ἐξείραντα τὴν γλῶσσαν περιλείχειν τὰ χείλη.

[69]D. L. V. 37.

[70]D. L. V. 39; cf. William Scott Ferguson, *Hellenistic Athens: An
Historical Essay* (London: Macmillan and Co., Limited, 1911), p. 60; Clarke,

was precisely that on which Aristotle himself had taught."[71]
It appears that the school acquired legal status as a θίασος
under Theophrastus.

When Demetrius Poliorcetes (336-283 B.C.) took over
Athens, the school was threatened. Sophocles of Sunium proposed a law in 307 ". . . that no philosopher should preside
over a school except by permission of the Senate and the
people, under penalty of death."[72] Theophrastus and other
philosophers withdrew from Athens.[73] The following year Philo
successfully challenged the law and forced its repeal.

> A law of Solon had laid down that any ordinances made by the
> members of a *thiasos* and other such bodies with regard to
> their own members were valid unless they were contrary to
> the laws of the state, [*Digest* 47. 22. 4.] and it has
> been suggested that it was on the basis of this law that
> Philo made his case against Sophocles, and that as a philo-
> sophical school had the status of a *thiasos*, to infringe on
> its rights was to be guilty of impiety, *asebeia*. But a
> *graphe paranomon* was not necessarily based on purely legal
> considerations. . . . Clearly this was primarily a politi-
> cal case, and it is unlikely that much consideration was
> given to such nice questions as the rights of corporations.[74]

This was the last serious challenge to the philosophical
schools in Athens. Soon after the repeal of Sophocles' law
Theophrastus returned to the Lyceum, Epicurus established his
Garden, and Zeno began to teach in the Stoa.[75]

Theophrastus' will is one of the most important documents
for the study of ancient schools. He refers to ". . . trust
funds at the disposal of Hipparchus. . ." from which he
requests that expenditures be made for rebuilding the Museum

Higher Education, p. 61. For discussion of the legal status of the Lyceum
the following work is still valuable: U[lrich] v[on] Wilamowitz-
Moellendorff, "Excurs 2: Die rechtliche Stellung der Philosophischen-
schulen," in *Antigonos von Karystos*, Philologische Untersuchungen, Heft IV
(Berlin: Weidmannsche Buchhandlung, 1881), pp. 263-91. See above, p. 91
n. 46.

[71]*Aristotle*, p. 315.

[72]D. L. V. 38: . . . μηδένα τῶν φιλοσόφων σχολῆς ἀφηγεῖσθαι, ἀν μὴ
τῇ βουλῇ καὶ τῷ δήμῳ δόξῃ· εἰ δὲ μή, θάνατον εἶναι τὴν ζημίαν. Cf.
Athenaeus XIII. 610ef; Pollux IX. 42. For the text of Pollux see: Ericus
Bethe, ed., *Pollucis Onomasticon*, Lexicographi Graeci, Vol. IX (Leipzig:
B. G. Teubneri, 1931). Cf. Clarke, *Higher Education*, pp. 61-62; Ferguson,
Hellenistic Athens, pp. 104-07.

[73]D. L. V. 38.

[74]Clarke, *Higher Education*, p. 62. Cf. J. Walter Jones, *The Law and
Legal Theory of the Greeks: An Introduction* (Oxford: At the Clarendon
Press, 1956), pp. 161-65.

[75]See below, pp. 103-04, 126-27.

and the small cloister adjoining it.[76] The bust of Aristotle
is to be replaced and properly dedicated, and ". . . the
tablets containing maps of the countries traversed by explorers
should be replaced in the lower cloister [τὴν κάτω στοάν].[77]
The statue of Nicomachus must be completed, and the temple
offering should be cared for. The garden, the *peripatos*, and
the adjoining buildings he leaves to:

> . . . such of my friends hereinafter named as may wish to
> study literature and philosophy there in common [συσχολάζειν
> since it is not possible for all men to be always in resi-
> dence, on condition that no one alienates the property or
> devotes it to his private use, but so that they hold it like
> a temple in joint possession and live, as is right and
> proper, on terms of familiarity and friendship.[78]

He then names the community [κοινωνοῦντες] of ten men, charges
the elder men [πρεσβυτάτους] to teach philosophy, and asks to
be buried in the garden. His library, which presumably included Aristotle's writings, he leaves to Neleus. This will
thus indicates that by the time of Theophrastus' death the
school was well organized and possessed a considerable amount
of property. The difference between the wills of Aristotle and
Theophrastus reflects a tremendous change in the nature of the
school. So influential was Theophrastus that Kerferd suggests:
"Indeed, in a sense the school of Aristotle might more correctl
be called the school of Theophrastus."[79]

Strabo (64/63 B.C.-A.D. 21 at least), a student of
Tyrannion, records that Theophrastus bequeathed his library
(including Aristotle's writings) to Neleus, who bequeathed
it to his heirs.[80] The manuscripts were then stored care-
lessly in a damp cellar in Scepsis for fear that the Attalids
would confiscate them and place them in the library at
Pergamum. Much later the damaged manuscripts were sold to
Apellicon of Teos, a bibliophile who published a faulty edition

---

[76]D. L. V. 51: τῶν παρ' Ἱππάρχου συμβεβλημένων . . . . Clarke,
Higher Education, p. 61, suggests that the school was damaged in the siege
of Athens in 196-94 B.C.

[77]D. L. V. 51: . . . ἀναθεῖναι δὲ καὶ τοὺς πίνακας, ἐν οἷς αἱ τῆς
γῆς περίοδοί εἰσιν, εἰς τὴν κάτω στοάν.

[78]D. L. V. 52-53:

. . . τῶν γεγραμμένων φίλων ἀεὶ τοῖς βουλομένοις συσχολάζειν καὶ
συμφιλοσοφεῖν ἐν αὐταῖς, ἐπειδήπερ οὐ δυνατὸν πᾶσιν ἀνθρώποις ἀεὶ
ἐπιδημεῖν, μήτ' ἐξαλλοτριοῦσι μήτ' ἐξιδιαζομένου μηδενός, ἀλλ' ὡς ἂν
ἱερὸν κοινῇ κεκτημένοις, καὶ τὰ πρὸς ἀλλήλους οἰκείως καὶ φιλικῶς
χρωμένοις, ὥσπερ προσῆκον καὶ δίκαιον.

[79]"Peripatetics," *EncPhilos*, VI, 92.

[80]XIII. i. 54; cf. Plutarch *Sulla* 26; Athenaeus V. 214de.

of the books. Strabo then adds that these manuscripts were the
only extant copy of Aristotle's work and that for all these
years the Peripatetic school was deprived of all but the published works, i.e., the dialogues. When Sulla conquered Athens
he seized Apellicon's library and sent it to Rome where it was
bought by Tyrannion (early 1st c. B.C.), Strabo's teacher.
Shortly thereafter Andronicus of Rhodes produced the edition of
Aristotle's work on which all subsequent editions rest, and
there was a revival of interest among the Peripatetics in
Aristotelian philosophy. The most questionable and crucial
part of Strabo's account is his assertion that the manuscripts
hidden in Scepsis were the only copy of Aristotle's work. This
assertion has been discounted by most scholars since Eduard
Zeller, who gathered scraps of evidence which demonstrate that
most of the writings were known during the centuries in question.[81] The story may even be a fabrication invented to add
prestige to the new edition produced by Tyrannion and
Andronicus.[82] Furthermore, the revival of interest in
Aristotle came in the heyday of Neo-Pythagoreanism when reports
of secret doctrines were rampant.[83]

Strato, one of the ten to whom Theophrastus willed the
Lyceum, became its head (ca. 287-269 B.C.) even though he was
not specifically appointed to the office by the will. He was
the last strong head of the Lyceum, and Diogenes Laertius
states that he taught Ptolemy Philadelphus.[84] Nevertheless,
the school began to decline. Strato willed the school
[διατριβὴν] to Lyco, ". . . since of the rest some are too old
and others too busy,"[85] and named nine executors (one of whom
was Lyco). He also left to Lyco his books (except those of
which he was the author) and ". . . all the furniture in the

---

[81]*Aristotle and the Earlier Peripatetics*, trans by B. F. C. Costelloe
and J. H. Muirhead (2 vols.; London: Longmans, Green, and Co., 1897), I,
143-52; cf. Felix Grayeff, "The Problem of the Genesis of Aristotle's Text,"
pp. 105-22; Wheelwright, *Aristotle*, pp. xxi-xxiii; Kerferd, "Peripatetics,"
EncPhilos, VI, 92. Edward Alexander Parsons, *The Alexandrian Library:
Glory of the Hellenic World, Its Rise, Antiquities, and Destructions*
(London: Cleaver-Hume Press, 1952), p. 14, cites a tradition that some of
Aristotle's writings went to Ptolemy II for the library at Alexandria.

[82]Grayeff, "The Problem of the Genesis of Aristotle's Text," p. 106.

[83]Jaeger, *Aristotle*, p. 33 n. 1.

[84]V. 58.

[85]D. L. V. 62: . . . , ἐπειδὴ τῶν ἄλλων οἱ μέν εἰσι πρεσβύτεροι, οἱ
δὲ ἄσχολοι.

dining-hall, the cushions and the drinking cups."[86] These last items were probably used for the communal symposia.

Under Lyco (*ca*. 302/298-*ca*. 228/24 B.C.) the Peripatetic school continued to decline. The school turned its attention to the pursuit of the good life, and the members ". . . devoted themselves to literary criticism, gossipy biography, and unimportant moralizing."[87] Gradually the Peripatetics were superseded by the Stoics and Epicureans. Lyco still participated in Athenian politics, but the schools soon began to pursue a higher ideal of life in retreat from public affairs.[88] Lyco may also be charged with corrupting the school's symposia. His dinners were ostentatious, expensive affairs, the expense of which frightened many away from the school:

> For they were obliged to assume the regular administration of the school for a period of thirty days, which meant that they were in charge of the good behaviour of the new students; then on the last day of the month they received ninepence from each of the new students, and on that sum they had to entertain at dinner not only those who had paid the fee, but any others whom Lycon invited, besides all those among the older men who made a business of visiting the school; consequently the money collected was not enough even to pay for the perfumery and the wreaths; he also had charge of the sacrifices, and was administrator of the rites in honour of the Muses.[89]

This passage reflects a striking development of the office of *archon*. On the basis of the wills, Clarke suggests that there were nine senior members in the school who had to fill the office of *archon*; each held it for a month and there was a long three-month vacation.[90] Still, there was a sad departure from the original purpose of the symposia, which Athenaeus describes as:

---

[86]D. L. V. 62: . . . τὰ σκεύη πάντα κατὰ τὸ συσσίτιον καὶ τὰ στρώματα καὶ τὰ ποτήρια.

[87]David Furley, "Peripatetic School," *OCD*, p. 802.

[88]Ferguson, *Hellenistic Athens*, p. 214.

[89]Athenaeus XII. 547ef:
ἔδει γὰρ ἄρξαι τε τὴν νομιζομένην ἐν τῷ περιπάτῳ ἀρχὴν (αὕτη δ' ἦν ἐπὶ τῆς εὐκοσμίας τῶν ἐπιχειρούντων) τριάκονθ' ἡμέρας, εἶτα τῇ ἔνῃ καὶ νέα λαβόντα ἀφ' ἑκάστου τῶν ἐπιχειρούντων ἐννέα ὀβολοὺς ὑποδέξασθαι μὴ μόνον αὐτοὺς τοὺς τὴν συμβολὴν εἰσενεγκόντας, ἀλλὰ καὶ οὓς παρακαλέσειεν ὁ Λύκων, ἔτι δὲ καὶ τοὺς ἐπιμελῶς συναντῶντας τῶν πρεσβυτέρων εἰς τὴν σχολήν, ὥστε γίνεσθαι μηδὲ εἰς τὸν μυρισμὸν καὶ τοὺς στεφάνους ἱκανὸν τὸ ἐκλεγόμενον ἀργύριον· ἱεροποιῆσαί τε καὶ τῶν Μουσείων ἐπιμελητὴν γενέσθαι

[90]*Higher Education*, p. 65.

. . . to show that they revered the gods and consorted with one another as cultivated persons should; and chief of all, to gain relaxation and take part in learned discussions.[91]

In a brief sentence in his will, Lyco leaves the περίπατον to ". . . such of my friends as choose to make use of it. . . ." He then names ten men and charges them to: ". . . put over it any such person as in their opinion will persevere in the work of the school and will be most capable of extending it."[92] The rest are to cooperate for love of him (Lyco) and of the spot [τοῦ τόπου]. Thus, he relinquishes his right to name his successor. Later in his will he leaves his published manuscripts to one of the above-named ten to edit.[93]

Ariston of Ceos was chosen to succeed Lyco,[94] and probably during his tenure the Lyceum was destroyed by Philip (200 B.C.).[95] The Lyceum was again ravaged by Sulla in 86 B.C.,[96] but seems to have maintained a continuous existence until that time.[97] Although the Peripatetic tradition survived, the destruction of the Lyceum by Sulla and the removal of its library to Rome marked the end of the Lyceum as a school which could trace its history to Aristotle.[98] Following the publication of Aristotle's works by Andronicus of Rhodes (1st c. B.C.), the writing of commentaries on the Aristotelian corpus occupied most of the energy of the Peripatetics.[99] Gradually, Neo-Platonism absorbed Aristotelian and Stoic thought.

---

[91]Athenaeus XII. 548a: . . . ἵνα φαίνωνται καὶ τὸ θεῖον τιμῶντες καὶ μουσικῶς ἀλλήλοις συμπεριφερόμενοι, καὶ τὸ πλεῖστον, ἕνεκεν ἀνέσεως καὶ φιλολογίας.

[92]D. L. V. 70: . . . τῶν γνωρίμων τοῖς βουλομένοις, ... προστησάσθωσαν δ᾽ αὐτοῦ ὃν ἂν ὑπολαμβάνωσι διαμενεῖν ἐπὶ τοῦ πράγματος καὶ συναύξειν μάλιστα δυνήσεσθαι.

[93]D. L. V. 73.

[94]See above, p. 85.

[95]Livy XXXI. xxiv. 18.

[96]Plutarch *Sulla* XII. 3.

[97]Cicero *De Finibus* V. iv. 9-10.

[98]For this conclusion I am indebted to John Patrick Lynch, *Aristotle's School: A Study of a Greek Educational Institution* (Berkeley: University of California Press, 1972), pp. 206-207. This work, which did not come to my attention until after I had finished the dissertation, is now the most complete study of the school to date. It offers a fresh assessment of the location, legal status, and later history of the Lyceum. Compare the following regarding the later history of the Lyceum: Clarke, *Higher Education*, p. 82; Kerferd, "Peripatetics," *EncPhilos*, VI, 92; Furley, "Peripatetic School," *OCD*, p. 802.

[99]Regarding Andronicus of Rhodes, see above, p. 97.

The influence of the Lyceum

Even though the brilliance and power of Aristotle's thought was soon obscured and not recovered for centuries, the Lyceum had a powerful influence on the development of ancient schools. Aristotle had freed the various branches of science from the domination of philosophy.[100] This feat made it possible for schools to pursue inquiries in these areas with relative freedom, as we see in the Museum at Alexandria. The students of the Lyceum dispersed all over the Hellenistic world, and it is through them that we can trace the influence of the Lyceum on the libraries at Alexandria, Pergamum, and Rhodes.[101] The dynamic power of the Lyceum was not carried by Aristotle's writings but by his pupils and their pupils; such men as Dicaearchus, Eudemus, Aristoxenus, and Demetrius of Phalerum. In a real sense the philosophical schools which began to appear in various cities could look to Aristotle and Theophrastus as their founders, and the legal battle won by the Lyceum made it possible for Epicurus and Zeno to establish their schools.

---

[100]Lesky, *A History of Greek Literature*, p. 575.

[101]Grayeff, "The Problem of the Genesis of Aristotle's Text," p. 109.

Chapter V

THE GARDEN

The importance of the Garden

Epicurus' Garden was probably the first philosophical school intentionally established by its founder. The Garden also placed more emphasis on community and friendship than any other philosophical school. Life in the school was guided primarily by the ethical principles of Epicurus' philosophy, and consequently a strong tradition of orthodoxy developed. In addition, Epicureanism was the first missionary philosophy, and its spread through the Hellenistic world was predictably more rapid than that of any of its predecessors. Epicurus required commitment to his way of life, required that his tenets be memorized, and wrote epitomes of his works so that students could grasp the outlines of his philosophy more easily. In many respects Epicureanism formed a link between Greek philosophy and Christianity and prepared the way for the latter: ". . . Epicureanism was primarily a cult of the founder and his way of life and only secondarily a system of thought."[1]

The sources for the study of the Garden

Nothing comparable to Düring's *Aristotle in the Ancient Biographical Tradition* exists for the study of Epicurus. The most complete treatment to date is Norman W. DeWitt's *Epicurus and His Philosophy*.[2] This is a full and helpful work, but one which is somewhat vitiated by the author's eagerness to show similarities between Epicureanism and Christianity.

Epicurus is reputed to have written more than any previous philosopher.[3] Many of his writings were destroyed by later opponents,[4] and only a fraction of them have survived.[5]

---

[1]Norman W. DeWitt, "Organization and Procedure in Epicurean Groups," *CP*, XXXI (1936), 205.

[2]Minneapolis: University of Minnesota Press, 1954). Cf. Kurt von Fritz, Review of *Epicurus and His Philosophy*, by Norman W. DeWitt, *CP*, L (1955), 262-66. For additional bibliography see: P. De Lacy, "Some Recent Publications on Epicurus and Epicureanism (1937-1954)," *CW*, XLVIII (1955), 169-77.

[3]D. L. X. 26.

[4]Cf. for example Lucian *Alexander* 47.

[5]For the texts see: Hermann Usener, ed., *Epicurea* (Leipzig: B. G.

The fragments, however, are noticeably more relevant for the study of his school than was the case with the writings of Plato and Aristotle. Epicurus wrote maxims, epitomes, and letters with the apparent purpose of establishing principles for the conduct of his school; and since we know that his teachings were followed rigorously by his disciples, we may use his writings to characterize the school.

The biographical tradition also transmits information about his school. This tradition, however, is relatively less important than Epicurus' writings for two reasons: as stated above, the nature of his own writings allows us to make more use of them; and secondly, much of the biographical tradition is given over to the abuse of Epicurus by his opponents. Diogenes Laertius nevertheless remains one of our best secondary sources: ". . . he was abundantly supplied with books and he exhibited better judgment in excerpting the material bearing upon Epicurus than in any other part of his work."[6] The papyrus texts found at Herculaneum contain writings by Philodemus and other Epicureans and are helpful for reconstructing the history of Epicureanism.[7] There are also surprisingly frequent references to Epicurus and Epicureanism in various classical writers and in Jewish and Christian sources.

The origin of the Garden

The pronounced differences between the Garden and the other philosophical schools prompts the investigator to review the life of Epicurus in an attempt to discover the factors which led to this new kind of philosophical school. Diogenes Laertius preserved the chronology of Epicurus' life established by Apollodorus,[8] and this tradition is the basis for our understanding of the life of Epicurus. Although he was born at Samos in 341, Epicurus was an Athenian citizen.[9] His father, Neocles, was a schoolmaster. His early experience, however,

Teubneri, 1887); for an English translation see: Whitney J. Oates, ed., *The Stoic and Epicurean Philosophers: The Complete Extant Writings of Epicurus, Epictetus, Lucretius, Marcus Aurelius* (New York: The Modern Library, 1940), pp. 3-66.

[6]DeWitt, *Epicurus and His Philosophy*, p. 38.

[7]For the texts see: Achilles Vogliano, ed., *Epicuri et Epicureorum scripta: In Herculanensibus papyris servata* (Berlin: Weidmann, 1928).

[8]D. L. X. 15.

[9]D. L. X. 1. The following works provide full discussions of the life of Epicurus: DeWitt, *Epicurus and His Philosophy*, pp. 36-105, esp. pp. 37-38; Horst Steckel, "Epikur," *RE*, Suppl. XI, 579-87.

seems to have turned him against the contemporary form of
education, for he is alleged to have written: "Hoist all sail,
my dear boy, and steer clear of all culture [παιδείαν]."[10] We
are told that Epicurus began his study of philosophy under the
Platonist Pamphilus at the age of twelve or fourteen.[11]

In 323 Epicurus went to Athens to serve as an *ephebe*, and
it is possible that he heard some of the public lectures of
Theophrastus and Xenocrates[12] and met Menander[13] during these
two years. It has even been suggested that the camaraderie
which Epicurus experienced as an *ephebe* was the source of his
emphasis on friendship in the Garden.[14] Following his cadet-
ship, Epicurus joined his family in Colophon where for the next
ten years he developed the essential elements of his philosophy. He studied for a while under Praxiphanes and then was a
pupil of Nausiphanes.[15] Following a quarrel with his teacher,
Epicurus moved to Mytilene (311-310) and then to Lampsacus
(310-306). He established schools in both cities.[16] Epicurus
was highly regarded in Lampsacus and soon attracted a group of
followers who were later to become the nucleus of his Garden in
Athens.[17] DeWitt assigns the development of the organization
of the Epicurean school to the Lampsacene period.[18] When
Epicurus moved to Athens some of his followers remained in
Lampsacus. That he kept in touch with this part of his school
is indicated by the letter he wrote years later *To the Friends
in Lampsacus*.[19]

When Epicurus and his friends arrived in Athens in 306,
they established a philosophical school very different from the
Academy or the Lyceum. They probably came with the basic
organization and purpose of the school already in mind.
Epicurus had no intention of competing with other schools in

---

[10]D. L. X. 6: παιδείαν δὲ πᾶσαν, μακάριε, φεῦγε τἀκάτιον ἀράμενος.

[11]D. L. X. 2, 14.

[12]D. L. X. 13.

[13]Strabo XIV. i. 18.

[14]Wolfgang Schmid, "Epikur," *RAC*, V, 682.

[15]D. L. X. 7, 8, 12, 14.

[16]D. L. X. 15.

[17]Strabo XIII. i. 19.

[18]*Epicurus and His Philosophy*, p. 88.

[19]DeWitt, *Epicurus and His Philosophy*, p. 84, dates this letter in
293/92 B.C., and claims: "Such letters were forerunners of the epistles
of the apostles to the various churches."

educating the youth of Athens.[20] To some extent Epicurus may
have used the model of the Lyceum, but DeWitt suggests that his
real model was ". . . the hippocratic medical fraternity."[21]
Whatever his model, he departed from the pattern of the other
philosophical schools. Instead of establishing himself in a
public gymnasium he bought a house and garden and confined his
activities to his own property. The law of Sophocles had been
repealed, but since he did not offer instruction in a public
place he probably would not have been affected by it.[22]

Since he was an Athenian citizen and entitled to own
property, Epicurus was able to purchase his garden. Its diminutive size may be inferred from the price--only eighty minae.[23]
The house and garden thrived with the activity of a large community; space must have been at a premium and privacy for work
and study at a minimum.[24] Plato's *Protagoras*[25] provides us
with a description of a similar household and is evidence for
R. E. Wycherley's observation: "The Greek philosophical school
was essentially an extension of the Greek household."[26]

Was the garden within or outside the city? Were the house
and garden a single unit, or separated by some distance? These
are questions which have been debated recently. On the basis
of Epicurus' will and a reference in Cicero,[27] DeWitt proposes
that they were separate.

> The house was situated within the city walls in a respect-
> able district known as Melite, and the garden was not far
> distant, outside the old Dipylon Gate on the same road that
> led to the Academy.[28]

---

[20]Ibid., p. 29.

[21]Ibid., p. 27.

[22]Ibid., p. 90.

[23]D. L. X. 10.

[24]Cf. Cicero *De Finibus* I. 65:
"Yet Epicurus in a single house and that a small one maintained a whole
company of friends, united by the closest sympathy and affection; and
this still goes on in the Epicurean school."
At vero Epicurus una in domo, et ea quidem angusta, quam magnos quantaque
amoris conspiratione consentientes tenuit amicorum greges! quod fit
etiam nunc ab Epicureis.

[25]314e-316a.

[26]"The Garden of Epicurus," *The Phoenix*, XIII (1959), 73.

[27]*De Finibus* V. 3; for a summary of Epicurus' will see below, p. 115.

[28]*Epicurus and His Philosophy*, p. 92. Benjamin Farrington, *The Faith
of Epicurus* (New York: Basic Books, Inc., 1967), pp. 11-12, agrees that
the house and garden were separated by some distance.

DeWitt further suggests that the enigmatic word τρικύλιστος means "a three-wheeled chair," which Epicurus used to commute between house and garden.[29] Since Epicurus' health seems to have been a handicap, there is some plausibility to this suggestion. Wycherley, however, argues that Kolonus was not a deme separating the deme Melite from Dipylon, but rather that the Melite included the Dipylon. Hence he concludes that the house and garden were ". . . near to one another, possibly adjacent, forming a close unit, like the Master's residence closely linked to a college court.[30] The spirited fight of the Epicureans during the time of Cicero to preserve the house and a reference in Pliny (A.D. 23/24-79) both lend additional weight to his case:

> Nowadays indeed under the name of gardens people possess the luxury of regular farms and country houses actually within the city. This practice was first introduced at Athens by that connoisseur of luxurious ease, Epicurus; down to his day the custom had not existed of having country dwellings in towns.[31]

Since Wycherley is probably correct, we are forced to the realization that the Garden was not located in a quiet, secluded suburb.

> If the garden, with the house nearby, was on our proposed site, then it was not only within the city, but in a well-populated and busy quarter. In fact the peace and quiet which Epicurus and his friends knew would then be something like what one experiences in a college court adjoining a busy street, or that extraordinary sense of withdrawal and

---

[29]Norman W. DeWitt, "Epicurus' Three-wheeled Chair," *CP*, XXXV (1940), 183-85. D. L. X. 5:

πρὸς δὲ Θεμίσταν τὴν Λεοντέως γυναῖκα Οἵός τε φησίν εἰμί, ἐὰν μὴ ὑμεῖς πρός με ἀφίκησθε, αὐτὸς τρικύλιστος, ὅπου ἂν ὑμεῖς καὶ Θεμίστα παρακαλῆτε, ὠθεῖσθαι.

Compare the translation given by Oates, *The Stoic and Epicurean Philosophers*, p. 47: "If you two don't come to me, I am capable of arriving with a hop, skip, and jump, wherever you and Themista summon me." R. D. Hicks, trans., *Diogenes Laertius*, The Loeb Classical Library (Cambridge, Mass.: Harvard University Press, 1925), translates the saying as follows: "I am ready, if you do not come to see me, to spin thrice on my own axis and be propelled to any place that you, including Themista, agree upon."

[30]Wycherley, "The Garden of Epicurus," p. 75; Clarke, *Higher Education*, p. 62, agrees: "The garden was a small one within the city boundaries, and there was of course a house attached to it, or not far distant."

[31]Pliny *Natural History* XIX. xix. 50-51:

iam quidem hortorum nomine in ipsa urbe delicias agros villasque possident. primus hoc instituit Athenis Epicurus otii magister; usque ad eum moris non fuerat in oppidis habitari rura.

Wycherley, "The Garden of Epicurus," p. 76, cites inscriptions which indicate that Pliny was mistaken; Epicurus was not the first to have a garden in the city. For discussion of Cicero see below, p. 118.

detachment which one feels when buried in a library in the heart of a teeming city.[32]

In this unusual retreat was carved this motto: "Stranger, here you will do well to tarry; here our highest good is pleasure."[33]

The nature of the Garden

In order to understand the school of Epicurus one must realize the way in which Epicurus dominated it. He was its founder, its organizer, its model for life and wisdom, and the sole source of its doctrine. Epicurus required a kind of allegiance which was unknown in other philosophical schools. The words "sect," or "cult" describe some aspects of the Garden more accurately than "school."[34]

The role of Epicurus in the Garden can be elucidated by a survey of the titles applied to him. It is possible that Epicurus was called ἡγεμών,[35] which Cicero translated as *dux*.[36] This is the title which Epicurus used in his will when referring to his successor. A more strongly attested title is ὁ σοφός.[37] Epicurus shared this title only with his closest associate.

And you have no reason to be ashamed of sharing the opinions of a Wise Man--who stands alone, so far as I am aware, in venturing to arrogate to himself that title. For I do not suppose that Metrodorus himself claimed to be a Wise Man,

---

[32]Wycherley, "The Garden of Epicurus," p. 77.

[33]Seneca *Epistles* XXI. 10: Hospes, hic bene manebis, hic summum bonum voluptas est, ...

[34]See the discussion of the terms below, pp. 258-59.

[35]D. L. X. 20; cf. DeWitt, *Epicurus and His Philosophy*, p. 93; J[ohn] M. Rist, *Epicurus: An Introduction* (Cambridge: At the University Press, 1972), p. 10. In the New Testament this word occurs with the following frequency: Matt. 10x, Mk. 1x, Lk. 2x, Acts 6x, and I Peter 1x. These and all subsequent statistics of word usage in the New Testament are taken from: Robert Morgenthaler, *Statistik des neutestamentlichen Wortschatzes* (Zurich: Gotthelf-Verlag, 1958). If this term came to have a special usage in later schools, it is interesting that it occurs so frequently in Matthew but never in the Johannine writings.

[36]*Tusculan Disputations* III. xvii. 37.

[37]For discussion of its use in the fragments of Philodemus, see DeWitt, "Organization and Procedure in Epicurean Groups," p. 208. The application of this title to Epicurus is found frequently in later sources: Baton *The Fellow-Cheat* (Middle of the third c. B.C.) in Edmonds, *Fragments of Attic Comedy*, IIIA, p. 263; Damoxenus *The Foster-Brothers* (dated by Edmonds *ca*. 269 B.C.) in Edmonds, *Fragments of Attic Comedy*, IIIA, p. 211; Plutarch *Moralia* 1117F; Athenaeus VII. 279d. In the New Testament σοφός is found almost exclusively in the Pauline writings: Matt. 2x, Lk. 1x, Paul 16x, James 1x. The word is found 11 times in I Cor.

though he did not care to refuse the compliment when the name was bestowed upon him by Epicurus; . . . .[38]

As ὁ σοφός, Epicurus was the source or revealer of the school's wisdom.

The title "father" was also applied to Epicurus. Lucretius (*ca.* 94-55 B.C.) writes in an address to Epicurus:

Thou, father, art the discoverer of truths, from thy pages, illustrious man, as bees in the flowery glades sip all the sweets, so we likewise feed on all thy golden words, thy words of gold, ever most worthy of life eternal.[39]

DeWitt concludes that Epicurus applied this title to himself: "He thought of himself as standing in the relation of father to his adherents, who upon the same principle were counted his children."[40] As evidence for this conclusion he cites a fragment of a letter to Idomeneus which he translates as follows: "Send us therefore your first fruits for the sustenance of my sacred person for its own sake and for that of my children, for so it occurs to me to express it."[41] The text of this problematic fragment is as follows:

πέμπε οὖν ἀπαρχὰς ἡμῖν εἰς τὴν τοῦ ἱεροῦ σώματος θεραπείαν ὑπέρ τε αὐτοῦ καὶ τέκνων· οὕτω γάρ μοι λέγειν ἐπέρχεται.[42]

Two problems concern us here. Do the words τοῦ ἱεροῦ σώματος refer to the person or to the school of Epicurus, and do the words τε αὐτοῦ καὶ τέκνων refer to Idomeneus and his children or to the students of Epicurus?[43] The final phrase, ". . . for

---

[38]Cicero *De Finibus* II. 7:
. . . , nec est quod te pudeat sapienti assentiri qui se unus, quod sciam, sapientem profiteri sit ausus. Nam Metrodorum non puto ipsum professum, sed, cum appellaretur ab Epicuro, repudiare tantum beneficium noluisse; . . . .

[39]Lucretius *De Rerum Natura* III. 9:
tu, pater, es rerum inventor, tu patria nobis suppeditas praecepta, tuisque ex, inclute, chartis, floriferis ut apes in saltibus omnia libant, omnia nos itidem depascimur aurea dicta, aurea, perpetua semper dignissima vita.

[40]*Epicurus and His Philosophy*, p. 97.

[41]Ibid., p. 99.

[42]Usener, *Epicurea*, fr. 130; Plutarch *Moralia* 1117E.

[43]Compare the translation by Benedict Einarson and Phillip H. de Lacy, *Plutarch's Moralia*, The Loeb Classical Library, Vol. XIV (Cambridge, Mass.: Harvard University Press, 1959), p. 251: "So send us for the care of our sacred person an offering of first-fruits on behalf of yourself and your children--for thus I am moved to speak."
'Απαρχή occurs 9 times in the New Testament; 7 of these occurrences are in Paul. The expression τοῦ ἱεροῦ σώματος is not found in the New Testament, but is close to the Pauline metaphor of the Church as the Body of Christ. The closest Johannine parallel is found in John 2:21. The idea of adherents as children, however, appears strikingly in the Johannine epistles: II John 1, 4, 13; III John 4.

thus I am moved to speak," lends credence to the view that what precedes it is analogical language. Although the fragment may be interpreted in other ways, it is possible that Epicurus refers to his school as "my holy body" and to his adherents as his "children." This fragment also suggests that Idomeneus (and probably others) made annual contributions for the support of the Garden.

As these titles suggest, Epicurus was venerated by his school. Philodemus records that every disciple took an oath of obedience to Epicurus,[44] and one of the fragments from Epicurus endorses this allegiance: "The veneration of the wise man is a great blessing to those who venerate him."[45] A remarkable act of worship is recounted by Plutarch (before A.D. 50 - after 120):

> Colotes himself, for another, while hearing a lecture of
> Epicurus on natural philosophy, suddenly cast himself down
> before him and embraced his knees; . . . .[46]

This veneration, fostered by Epicurus himself, involved rigid adherence to his teaching. Cicero parenthetically mentions that Epicurean doctrines were memorized.

> . . . (for every good Epicurean has got by heart the mas-
> ter's *Kuriai Doxai* or Authoritative Doctrines, since these
> brief aphorisms or maxims are held to be of sovereign effi-
> cacy for happiness).[47]

In this regard the school honored the tradition of the last words of Epicurus, which are said to have been as follows:

> . . . , and then, having bidden his friends remember his
> doctrines, breathed his last.
> Here is something of my own about him:
> Farewell, my friends; the truths I taught hold fast:
> Thus Epicurus spake, and breathed his last.[48]

---

[44]Philodemus, ΠΕΡΙ ΠΑΡΡΗΣΙΑΣ, ed. by Alexander Olivieri (Leipzig: B. G. Teubneri, 1914), fr. 45, 8-11.

[45]Oates, *The Stoic and Epicurean Philosophers*, p. 41, fr. XXXII.

[46]*Moralia* 1117B:
Κωλώτης δὲ αὐτὸς ἀκροώμενος 'Επικούρου φυσιολογοῦντος ἄφνω τοῖς γόνασιν αὐτοῦ προσέπεσε, ...
Cf. Usener, *Epicurea*, fr. 141.

[47]*De Finibus* II. 20: . . . (quis enim vestrum non edidict Epicuri κυρίας δόξας, id est quasi maxime ratas, quia gravissimae sint ad beate vivendum breviter enuntiatae sententiae?) Cf. Karl Heinrich Rengstorf, "μαθητής," *TDNT*, IV, 424-25.

[48]D. L. X. 16:
. . . τοῖς τε φίλοις παραγγείλαντα τῶν δογμάτων μεμνῆσθαι, οὕτω τελευτῆσαι.
Καὶ ἔστιν ἡμῶν εἰς αὐτὸν οὕτω·
χαίρετε, καὶ μέμνησθε τὰ δόγματα· τοῦτ' 'Επίκουρος ὕστατον εἶπε φίλοις τοὖπος ἀποφθίμενος.
Cf. John 15:14-15:

As a result, the Epicurean school was marked by an absence of
dissension unparalleled in the other philosophical schools.[49]
At least by the first century B.C., Epicurus was worshipped by
his followers as a god who had revealed wisdom.[50] Icons were a
part of this worship.

Still I could not forget Epicurus, even if I wanted; the
members of our body not only have pictures of him, but even
have his likeness on their drinking-cups and rings.[51]

On the basis of the various titles applied to other members
of the school during the lifetime of Epicurus and in the writ-

---

ὑμεῖς φίλοι μού ἐστε ἐὰν ποιῆτε ἃ ἐγὼ ἐντέλλομαι ὑμῖν. οὐκέτι λέγω
ὑμᾶς δούλους, ὅτι ὁ δοῦλος οὐκ οἶδεν τί ποιεῖ αὐτοῦ ὁ κύριος· ὑμᾶς δὲ
εἴρηκα φίλους, ὅτι πάντα ἃ ἤκουσα παρὰ τοῦ πατρός μου ἐγνώρισα ὑμῖν.
Cf. Luke 12:4. Another Epicurean saying is similar to John 15:13. D. L. X.
120:
   "And he [the wise man] will on occasion die for a friend."
   καὶ ὑπὲρ φίλου ποτὲ τεθνήξεσθαι.
John 15:13:
   μείζονα ταύτης ἀγάπην οὐδεὶς ἔχει, ἵνα τις τὴν ψυχὴν αὐτοῦ θῇ ὑπὲρ
   τῶν φίλων αὐτοῦ.
Cf. Rom. 5:7. Compare also Aristotle *Nicomachean Ethics* IX. viii. 9:
   "But it is also true that the virtuous man's conduct is often guided by
   the interests of his friends and of his country, and that he will if
   necessary lay down his life in their behalf."
   ἀληθὲς δὲ περὶ τοῦ σπουδαίου καὶ τὸ τῶν φίλων ἕνεκα πολλὰ πράττειν καὶ
   τῆς παρτίδος, κἂν δέῃ ὑπεραποθνήσκειν·
Nicomachean Ethics VIII and IX contain an extensive discussion of "friendship" (φιλία) — see the discussion of friendship in the Epicurean school below, p. 111. Φίλος occurs more often in Luke than in John (Matt. 1x, Lk. 15x,
Jn. 6x, Acts 3x, James 2x, III Jn. 2x), but the use of the term in John and
III John probably indicates that φίλος had a special meaning with the
Johannine community. Note its use with the article in III John 15:
   ἀσπάζονταί σε οἱ φίλοι.
   ἀσπάζου τοὺς φίλους κατ' ὄνομα.
The verb φιλεῖν also occurs most frequently in John: Matt. 5x, Mk. 1x,
Lk. 2x, Jn. 13x, Cor. 1x, Titus 1x, Rev. 2x. Cf. Gustav Stählin, "φίλος,"
TWNT, IX, 164: "Zweifellos hat hier die Bezeichnung φίλοι in Verbindung mit
dem Grüssen Anteil an der Exklusivität der johanneischen Gemeinden."

   [49]Cf. Rist, *Epicurus*, p. 9; Clarke, *Higher Education*, p. 70:
"Nowhere else was there so rigid an orthodoxy. As a non-Epicurean of the
second century after Christ put it, the Epicureans 'never speak in opposition to one another or to Epicurus in any respect worth mentioning, but
innovation to them is an act of lawlessness, or rather impiety, and is
condemned, and for that reason no one even ventures on it. Their doctrines rest unchanged in perfect peace as a result of the harmony they
maintain with one another. Epicurus's school is like a city wholly un-
disturbed by faction, with one mind and one opinion.'" [Numenius, *ap.*
Eusebius, *Praeparationis Evangelicae*, ed. by Guilielmus Dindorfius
(Leipzig: B. G. Teubneri, 1867), XIV. 5].

   [50]Cf. Cicero *Tusculan Disputations* I. 48; Lucretius *De Rerum Natura*
V. 8-10; Plutarch *Moralia* 1117B; Lucian *Alexander* 61.

   [51]Cicero *De Finibus* V. 3:
. . . nec tamen Epicuri licet oblivisci, si cupiam, cuius imaginem non
modo in tabulis nostri familiares sed etiam in poculis et in anulis habent.
Cf. Pliny *Natural History* XXXV. 5.

ings of Philodemus (*ca.* 110 - *ca.* 40/35 B.C.), DeWitt finds a
well-developed hierarchy in the school. Beneath Epicurus
ranked his "associate leaders" [καθηγεμόνες], i.e., Metrodorus,
Hermarchus, and Polyaenus. These three apparently also shared
the title φιλόσοφοι and were thus distinguished from Epicurus,
ὁ σοφός. Next in rank came the instructors or "assistant
leaders" [καθηγηταί], who may also have been known as φιλόλογοι.
The συνηθεῖς were advanced students, while the κατασκευαζόμενοι
were the novices "in course of preparation."[52]   Each instructor
had a group of students for whom he was responsible, and members of every rank looked not only to the next higher rank but
on to Epicurus for their model. Finally DeWitt finds in
Diogenes Laertius the following "two grades of adherents":

> . . . first, the friends, *philoi*, associate members of the
> sect, as it were, and second, the devotees, *gnorimoi*, the
> members of the inner circle in the lifetime of Epicurus, or
> of any Epicurean circle anywhere in later times.[53]

This elaborate hierarchical organization proposed by
DeWitt has met with reservations on the part of other scholars.
Clarke states that it is ". . . not altogether convincing."[54]
Steckel acknowledges that there were differences of advancement
among the adherents but rejects DeWitt's scheme.[55]   Rist, however, is more positive in his judgment.[56]   Even though DeWitt
may have exaggerated the importance of these titles and proposed a hierarchical organization which never existed at any
time in a particular school, the general picture of teachers
lower in rank than Epicurus teaching groups of students of
varying stages of advancement is probably accurate at least for
the period of Philodemus' life. Some of the students may have
been very young.[57]

The presence of women among the adherents at the Garden
was the source of much abuse and gossip. Since the Garden had

---

[52]For full discussion of these titles see DeWitt, "Organization and
Procedure in Epicurean Groups," pp. 205-11; and DeWitt, *Epicurus and His
Philosophy*, pp. 94-100. Most of these titles either do not occur in the
New Testament or are not used there as titles. The notable exception is the
occurrence of καθηγητής twice in Matthew 23:10. Κατασκευάζειν from which
"catechumen" is derived occurs most frequently (6 times) in Hebrews, but
never as a title. None of these titles appears in the Johannine writings.

[53]DeWitt, *Epicurus and His Philosophy*, p. 102. Cf. D. L. X. 9.

[54]*Higher Education*, p. 168 n. 90.

[55]"Epikur," *RE*, Suppl. XI, 587.

[56]*Epicurus*, p. 10 n. 2.

[57]Cf. Clarke, *Higher Education*, p. 3; DeWitt, *Epicurus and His Philosophy*, pp. 68, 93.

abandoned the goal of producing politicians and counsellors-of-state, the way was open for the admission of women to their corporate pursuit of pleasure and wisdom.[58] While it is probably correct to say that women were treated with unusual status in the Garden, one should not imagine that Epicurus was an ascetic who abstained from intercourse with the *hetairae*.[59] Athenaeus quotes Epicurus as follows:

> As for myself, I cannot conceive of the Good if I exclude the pleasures derived from taste, or those derived from sexual intercourse, or those derived from entertainments to which we listen, or those derived from the motions of a figure delightful to the eye.[60]

Cicero, on the other hand, provides evidence that Leontion, one of the *hetairae*, wrote an attack on Theophrastus which was both clever and skillfully written.[61]

Festugière emphasizes the role of "friendship" in the philosophical schools: "In general terms it could be said that all the philosophic schools of the ancient world have the appearance of groups of friends."[62] He then immediately draws the reader's attention to the difference between friendship at the Academy and Epicurean friendship. At the Academy friendship was regarded as a catalyst or means to the love of wisdom; for the Epicureans, however, friendship was an end in itself. It was wisdom itself.[63] Cicero describes the Epicurean teaching as follows:

> Now Epicurus's pronouncement about friendship is that of all the means to happiness that wisdom has devised, none is greater, none more fruitful, none more delightful than this. Nor did he only commend this doctrine by his eloquence, but far more by the example of his life and conduct.[64]

---

[58]A. J. Festugière, *Epicurus and His Gods*, trans by. C. W. Chilton (Oxford: Basil Blackwell, 1955), p. 29.

[59]Cf. Rist, *Epicurus*, p. 11.

[60]Athenaeus VII. 280ab:
οὐ γὰρ ἔγωγε δύναμαι νοῆσαι τἀγαθὸν ἀφαιρῶν μὲν τὰς διὰ χυλῶν ἡδονάς, ἀφαιρῶν δὲ τὰς δι' ἀφροδισίων, ἀφαιρῶν δὲ τὰς δι' ἀκροαμάτων, ἀφαιρῶν δὲ τὰς διὰ μορφῆς κατ' ὄψιν ἡδείας κινήσεις.
Cf. XII. 546f; Usener, *Epicurea*, p. 120.

[61]*De Natura Deorum* I. xxxiii. 93.

[62]*Epicurus and His Gods*, p. 27. See above, p. 108 n. 48.

[63]Ibid., pp. 30-31; cf. Schmid, "Epikur," *RAC*, V, 724. Farrington, *The Faith of Epicurus*, pp. 27-30, notes the ways in which Epicurus was indebted to Aristotle for his doctrine of friendship.

[64]*De Finibus* I. 65:
de qua Epicurus quidem ita dicit, omnium rerum quas ad beate vivendum sapientia comparaverit nihil esse maius amicitia, nihil uberius, nihil

In spite of his emphasis on friendship, we learn that Epicurus
would not allow the school's goods to be held in common according to the tradition of the Pythagoreans because he thought
that such a practice implied mistrust.[65] Consequently, the
Epicureans lived a simple and frugal life and relied on volun-
tary contributions from their wealthier adherents,[66] ". . . and
it seems that the communities outside Athens may have paid some
kind of dues to the central organization."[67] The friends lived
together in Epicurus' house,[68] and as a result of their teaching and practice of friendship the concept spread across the
Hellenistic world.[69]

Epicurus and his followers used the Garden as a retreat
from the swirl of public affairs in Athens.[70] Upon admission
to the school the young student would be taught to spurn the
customary forms of education and to be submissive to his instructors.[71] Classes were probably conducted simultaneously in
various parts of the garden and house. As the student pro-
gressed toward wisdom he moved upward within the membership of
the school.[72] Some of the teachings of Epicurus may have been
esoteric in the sense that they could be grasped only by the
advanced Epicureans, but there is no evidence that he attempted
to keep any of his doctrines secret.[73]

In addition to its other activities the school met on the
twentieth of each month for a sumptuous dinner in honor of

---

iucundius. Nec vero hoc oratione solum sed multo magis vita et factis
et moribus comprobavit.
Cf. I. 66; Oates, *The Stoic and Epicurean Philosophers*, p. 41, fr. XXIII;
p. 37, fr. XXVII.

[65]D. L. X. 11.

[66]See above, p. 107.

[67]Rist, *Epicurus*, p. 12.

[68]See above, p. 104 n. 24.

[69]Norman W. DeWitt, "Notes on the History of Epicureanism," *TAPA*,
LXIII (1932), 173-74, traces the development of "the cult of friendship"
from the Pythagoreans through Plato and Aristotle to the Epicureans and
Cicero.

[70]Cf. D. L. X. 120; Oates, *The Stoic and Epicurean Philosophers*, p.
43, fr. LVIII: "We must release ourselves from the prison of affairs and
politics."

[71]DeWitt, "Organization and Procedure in Epicurean Groups," p. 207.

[72]DeWitt, *Epicurus and His Philosophy*, pp. 99-100.

[73]Steckel, "Epikur," *RE*, Suppl. XI, 587. Note, however, the reference in D. L. X. 5, to τὰ κρύφια. Steckel (col. 586) also states: "Die
Haltung der Schule erinnert hier an die der Mysterienreligionen, ..."

Metrodorus and Epicurus. This practice probably began prior to
Epicurus' death and continued for centuries. In his will
Epicurus stipulates that revenues be used for funeral offerings
for members of his family and:

> . . . for the customary celebration of my birthday on the
> tenth day of Gamelion in each year, and for the meeting of
> all my School held every month on the twentieth day to com-
> memorate Metrodorus and myself according to the rules now in
> force.[74]

He also requests that commemorations be held for his brothers
and Polyaenus, ". . . as I have done hitherto." Several later
writers refer to these dinners,[75] and according to Plutarch the
mysteries were celebrated on the twentieth of Boëdromion.[76]
It is difficult to decide whether the Garden departed sharply
from the customary constitution of a philosophical school as a
cult of the Muses. In contrast to the Academy and Lyceum, the
Garden was a private organization on private property.[77]
Nevertheless, Epicurus may have used the model of a religious
brotherhood to secure perpetuity for his school.[78] Did Epicurus
take the place of the gods in the worship of his school?[79] The
veneration accorded him by the school makes this likely.[80]

Writing was another important activity at the Garden.
Reference has already been made to the tradition that Epicurus
was a prolific writer.[81] DeWitt divides the writings into
three classes: dogmatic, refutative, and memorial. The dogmatic works were textbooks on various subjects. The refutative
works were aimed at belittling the doctrines of other schools,

---

[74]D. L. X. 18:
. . . καὶ ἡμῖν εἰς τὴν εἰθισμένην ἄγεσθαι γενέθλιον ἡμέραν ἑκάστου ἔτους
τῇ προτέρᾳ δεκάτῃ τοῦ Γαμηλιῶνος, ὥσπερ καὶ εἰς τὴν γινομένην σύνοδον
ἑκάστου μηνὸς ταῖς εἰκάσι τῶν συμφιλοσοφούντων ἡμῖν εἰς τὴν ἡμῶν τε καὶ
Μητροδώρου [μνήμην] κατατεταγμένην.
Cf. Joachim Jeremias, *The Eucharistic Words of Jesus*, trans. by N. Perrin
(New York: Charles Scribner's Sons, 1966), pp. 238-43.

[75]Cf. Cicero *De Finibus* II. 101; Plutarch *Moralia* 1089C.

[76]*Phocion* XXVIII. 1; for further discussion of the significance of the
twentieth day of the month see DeWitt, *Epicurus and His Philosophy*, pp. 104-
05.

[77]Cf. Steckel, "Epikur," *RE*, Suppl. XI, 584-85.

[78]DeWitt, *Epicurus and His Philosophy*, p. 104.

[79]For reference to the worship of the Muses at the time of Philodemus
see: *Anthologia Graeca: Epigrammatum Palatina cum Planudea*, ed. by Hugo
Stadtmueller (Leipzig: B. G. Teubner, 1899), II, 44. 2.

[80]For contrasting viewpoints on this question see: Boyancé, *Culte*,
pp. 322-27; and Schmid, "Epikur," *RAC*, V, 747-48.

[81]See above, p. 101 n. 3.

and the memorial writings recount the lives of deceased members
of the school.[82] Epitomes of these works were also written by
Epicurus and others so that the beginner could grasp an overview of each subject before pursuing it further.[83] There may
also have been a prescribed order in which the student was to
study the texts.[84] Finally, there were the basic doctrines or
Kuriai Doxai which every Epicurean was to know by heart.[85]

Cyril Bailey suggests that ". . . perhaps we should
recognize an exoteric and an esoteric style in Epicurus'
writings."[86] The basis for his suggestion is that the *Letter
to Menoeceus* is clearer in style than other writings of Epicurus.
Epicurus probably did use a clearer style in writings for
general audiences and recent converts than in treatises for
advanced students, but this does not imply that the "esoteric"
writings contained secret teachings. A by-product of the
school's writing must have been the presence of ". . . a number
of literate slaves to serve as secretaries and copyists" at the
Garden.[87] One of these slaves, Mys, was manumitted by Epicurus
in his will.[88] The picture of the house and garden that emerges
is one of industrious activity rather than tranquility. Classes
on various levels were taught probably simultaneously by
instructors in various parts of the garden, Epicurus and others
were engaged in writing, copyists poured over manuscripts,
lectures were given, and memorial banquets were celebrated
regularly.

No description of the Garden would be complete without an
indication of the missionary activity which emerged from it.
Although there is no missionary command in Epicurus' will, his
writings are clearly composed for the purpose of facilitating
the spread of his philosophy and way of life. Nock explains
the popularity of the philosophical schools by noting that they

---

[82]DeWitt, *Epicurus and His Philosophy*, p. 113.

[83]Cf. D. L. X. 35-37; Epicurus' *Letter to Herodotus* explains why he
is writing an epitome and stresses the need for memorizing the main points
of his system.

[84]Cf. DeWitt, *Epicurus and His Philosophy*, p. 26.

[85]Cicero *De Finibus* II. 20; see above, p. 108 n. 47.

[86]*The Greek Atomists and Epicurus* (Oxford: At the Clarendon Press,
1928), pp. 227-28.

[87]DeWitt, *Epicurus and His Philosophy*, p. 95; cf. p. 93.

[88]D. L. X. 3, 21.

offered intelligible explanations for phenomena and a way of life:[89]

> So again Epicureanism gave to its ideal of the calm life the driving force of a joy rooted in deliverance from fears of capricious divine action and of supernatural terrors, the joy we may say of a great simplification of life which others must be enabled to share. . . . The real note of Epicurus and his followers is a simple evangelical fervour.[90]

Epicureans became missionaries bearing the epitomes of Epicurus' teachings to distant cities with the objective of awakening men ". . . to the blessedness of the Epicurean way of life."[91]   The phenomenal spread of Epicureanism will be traced below, but first the history of the parent school must be surveyed.

The history of the Garden

Epicurus' will shows that he was aware of having established a school and that he intended for it to continue after his death. He left his property to Amynomachus and Timocrates on the condition that they place the garden at the disposal of Hermarchus and the rest of the school.[92]   Hermarchus was then to leave it to his successors. The school was to continue the common life [διατριβὴν] in the garden, and Hermarchus and his fellow-philosophers were to live in the house in Melite. The instructions for the meals in honor of Epicurus and Metrodorus have been discussed above.[93]   Hermarchus was made trustee of the funds [κύριον τῶν προσόδων] and given Epicurus' books. These provisions for the future of the school indicate that Epicurus was more aware of having founded a school than any of his predecessors had been.

Little is known about the Garden during the third and second centuries B.C. Successors followed Hermarchus, but their importance was secondary to the spread of Epicureanism to other cities.[94]   The Garden probably became less isolated from society and attracted converts from foreign cities, especially

---

[89]Nock, *Conversion*, p. 167.

[90]Ibid., pp. 171-72.

[91]DeWitt, *Epicurus and His Philosophy*, p. 30.

[92]For the text of Epicurus' will see D. L. X. 16-21.

[93]See above, p. 113.

[94]Cf. D. L. X. 25; *IG*, II^2, 1099; P. H. De Lacy, "Epicureanism and the Epicurean School," *EncPhilos*, III, 2-3; DeWitt, *Epicurus and His Philosophy*, pp. 331-32.

116

from Syria:[95] "Die weitaus originellsten und für die weitere
Entwicklung der Schule fruchtbarsten Epikureer stammten seit
dem 2. Jhdt. aus Syrien."[96] During this period the doctrines
and writings of the Epicureans underwent some slight but significant developments. Due to their reverence for Epicurus,
the Epicureans held more firmly to the teaching of their
founder than any other philosophical school. Nevertheless,
new elements developed, and De Lacy articulates the following
principle for their development.

> New elements in the Epicurean school are more easily
> discerned in the refutation of opponents than in the for-
> mulation of orthodox doctrine. The Epicureans were con-
> stantly attacked, and they in their turn felt obliged to
> refute all rival philosophies. This interchange with other
> schools required occasional innovations, as new schools
> arose and old schools underwent changes.[97]

At first their chief rivals were the Platonists and Peripatetics, then the Stoics. During the first centuries B.C. and
A.D. the process of syncretism accelerated, and during the
second century A.D. Christianity emerged as their foremost
adversary.[98] One of the innovations was the use of popular
half-literary, half-philosophical essays ". . . as a means of
presenting their philosophy to a broader audience."[99] This
type of popular literature did not stem from Epicurus but was
common among the philosophical schools in the third and second
centuries B.C.

References to Epicurus' house and garden appear in the
writings of Cicero about 51 B.C.[100] The garden was apparently
still being used, and the house still belonged to Epicureans
even though it was in ruins. Memmius wanted to erect some
buildings on the site but was opposed by Patro, who was then

---

[95]Cf. Steckel, "Epikur," *RE*, Suppl. XI, 641; Ferguson, *Hellenistic Athens*, p. 215.

[96]Steckel, "Epikur," *RE*, Suppl. XI, 643; DeWitt, "Notes on the History of Epicureanism," pp. 175-76, comments: "Noticeable in the last phase of Epicurean propaganda in Rome is the presence of teachers from obscure schools in Asia, and especially Palestine."

[97]P. H. De Lacy, "Lucretius and the History of Epicureanism," *TAPA*, LXXIX (1948), 13. This principle is probably applicable to the development of other traditions which derive from a revered teacher whose doctrines were memorized and cherished by his followers. In particular it may provide a useful perspective from which to study the development of Johannine Chris-tianity.

[98]DeWitt, *Epicurus and His Philosophy*, p. 328.

[99]De Lacy, "Lucretius and the History of Epicureanism," pp. 20-21.

[100]Cicero *Letters to Atticus* V. 11, 19; *Letters to Friends* XIII. 3; cf

head of the school. Cicero, who had once been an Epicurean, wrote to Memmius in an attempt to persuade him to change his plans. We do not know whether he succeeded or not.

In A.D. 121, an appeal was made and granted to rescind the requirement that the head of the school must be a Roman citizen.[101] Later, Marcus Aurelius ordered that proper heads be chosen for the four Athenian schools of philosophy and that each receive ten thousand drachmae per annum.[102] The schools were no longer free to choose their heads; "Independence was now lost."[103] The last noteworthy Epicurean was Diogenes of Oenoanda of the second century A.D.[104] The lists of the successors stop at the time of Augustus,[105] but Diogenes Laertius claims: ". . . the School itself which, while nearly all the others died out, continues for ever without interruption through numberless reigns of one scholarch after another; . . . ."[106] Steckel concludes that ". . . eine intakte epikureische Schulorganisation. . ." existed as late as Porphyry.[107] By the fourth century A.D., if not earlier, however, the Epicurean school had succumbed to Christianity and Neo-Platonism.[108]

The influence of the Garden

The activities and influence of the Epicureans extended far beyond the confines of their garden. Riding the tide of the spread of Hellenism in the wake of Alexander's conquests, Epicureans carried their doctrine through the Hellenistic world. Epicureanism was a missionary philosophy, and its adherents were well equipped with the epitomes written by Epicurus and his closest associates.[109] Prior to the founder's death there were Epicurean communities at Mytilene and

---

Clarke, *Higher Education*, p. 63.

[101]*IG*, II^2, 1099; cf. DeWitt, *Epicurus and His Philosophy*, p. 332.

[102]Dio Cassius *Roman History* LXXII. 31. 3; Lucian *The Eunuch* 3.

[103]Clarke, *Higher Education*, p. 79.

[104]Cf. De Lacy, "Epicureanism and the Epicurean School," *EncPhilos*, III, 2.

[105]Usener, *Epicurea*, p. 373; cf. Clarke, *Higher Education*, p. 78.

[106]D. L. X. 9: . . . ἥ τε διαδοχή, πασῶν σχεδὸν ἐκλιπουσῶν τῶν ἄλλων ἐσαεὶ διαμένουσα καὶ νηρίθμους ἀρχὰς ἀπολύουσα ἄλλην ἐξ ἄλλης τῶν γνωρίμων·

[107]Steckel, "Epikur," *RE*, Suppl. XI, 647.

[108]Clarke, *Higher Education*, p. 82.

[109]DeWitt, *Epicurus and His Philosophy*, pp. 28-30.

118

Lampsacus.[110] Cicero remarks that Epicurus' influence ". . .
has spread not only over Greece and Italy but throughout all
barbarian lands as well, ..."[111] Diogenes Laertius adds
that his friends were ". . . so many in number that they could
hardly be counted by whole cities, ..."[112] The success of
Epicureanism in winning converts was satirically explained by
Arcesilaus (316/5-242/1 B.C.), who said that men desert from
other schools but not from the Epicureans, "because men may
become eunuchs, but a eunuch never becomes a man."[113]

The establishment of Epicurean schools in the eastern part
of the Hellenistic world is more important for this study than
the spread of Epicureanism to Italy. Nevertheless, this
westward movement provides the context for understanding the
influence of Epicureanism. In 173 B.C., two Epicureans were
banished from Rome, and Epicureans did not emerge there in
great numbers until the first century B.C.[114] They seem to
have been quite numerous, however, by the time of Cicero, who
in response to Lucretius' *On the Nature of Things* began to
write a ". . . stream of anti-Epicurean propaganda."[115]
Largely as a result of Cicero's writings Epicureanism was
discredited in Italy.

At an early date Epicureanism began to spread through Asia
Minor. Plutarch informs us that the ruler of Cilicia kept some
Epicureans about him.[116] Epicurean groups probably formed in
Pontus, Lycia, Rhodes, Alexandria, and Tarsus prior to the turn
of the era.[117]

---

[110]See above, p. 103.

[111]*De Finibus* II. xv. 49: . . . , a quo non solum Graecia et Italia
sed etiam omnis barbaria commota est, ...

[112]D. L. X. 9: . . . οἵ τε φίλοι τοσοῦτοι τὸ πλῆθος ὡς μηδ' ἂν
πόλεσιν ὅλαις μετρεῖσθαι δύνασθαι·

[113]D. L. IV. 43: ἐκ μὲν γὰρ ἀνδρῶν γάλλοι γίνονται, ἐκ δὲ γάλλων
ἄνδρες οὐ γίνονται.

[114]Athenaeus XII. 547a; cf. Clarke, *Higher Education*, pp. 72-74;
Clayton M. Hall, "Some Epicureans at Rome," *CW*, XXVIII (1935), 113-15.

[115]DeWitt, *Epicurus and His Philosophy*, pp. 344-45.

[116]*Moralia* 434D.

[117]Cf. Lucian *Alexander* 25, 45-47; Strabo XIV. v. 13; D. L. X. 25-26;
Clarke, *Higher Education*, p. 81; Steckel, "Epikur," *RE*, Suppl. XI, 647.

The career of Philonides provides one of the most exciting glimpses of the spread of Epicureanism into Palestine.[118] Philonides appears in Antioch during the reign of Antiochus IV.[119] Although he did not succeed in converting Antiochus, he did convert his successor, Demetrius, and establish an Epicurean school at Antioch. Twice Philonides made trips to visit the parent school in Athens, and later he opened a school in Laodicea.[120] Another Epicurean, Diogenes, taught at the court of Alexander Balas but was executed by Antiochus VI.[121]

Even though our evidence is meager, the influence of the Epicurean school in Antioch was probably significant during the Hellenization of Palestine. Although the Hellenizers may have embraced Epicurean doctrines, and the influence of this philosophy may be evident in the book of Ecclesiastes; DeWitt's contention that the school probably ". . . served as a base of operations for the forcible introduction of Epicureanism into Judaea, . . ." is an over-statement.[122] Nevertheless, Josephus instructs that all who read of Daniel should learn how mistaken are the Epicureans.[123] The association of Epicureanism with the Hellenizers may also explain why the term "Epicurean" is used in the Rabbinic literature to denote an unbeliever.[124] Again, one encounters Strabo's (64/3 B.C. – A.D. 21 at least) statement about Gadara:

> Antiochus the philosopher, who was born a little before my time, was a native of this place. Philodemus, the Epicu-

---

[118]For the text of the papyrus which is our primary source on Philonides see: Wilhelm Crönert, "Der Epikureer Philonides," *SBBerl*, XLI, 2 (1900), 942-59; for discussion see: Ulrich Köhler, "Ein Nachtrag zum Lebenslauf des Epikureers Philonides," *SBBerl*, XLI, 2 (1900), 999-1001; Hermann Usener, "Philonides," in *Kleine Schriften* (Osnabrück: Otto Zeller, 1964), III, 188-92; R. Philippson, "Philonides," *RE*, XX[1], 63-73.

[119]For texts which show that there was a public library at Antioch as early as Antiochus the Great see: Jenö Platthy, *Sources on the Earliest Greek Libraries: With the Testimonia* (Amsterdam: Adolf M. Hakkert, 1968), pp. 170-73. Cf. Cicero *Pro Archia Poeta* III. 4.

[120]Cf. esp. Philippson, "Philonides," *RE*, XX[1], 67-68.

[121]Athenaeus V. 211ad, XII. 547ab; cf. Clarke, *Higher Education*, pp. 71-72.

[122]*Epicurus and His Philosophy*, p. 334.

[123]*Ant.* X. 277.

[124]See for example: M. Aboth 2:14; M. Sanhedrin 10:1. Cf. Schmid, "Epikur," *RAC*, V, 802-03. For discussion of the influence of Epicureanism upon rabbinism see Henry A. Fischel, "Epicureanism," *EncJud*, VI, 817; see also below, p. 185.

120

rean, and Meleager and Menippus, the satirist, and Theodorus, the rhetorician of my own time, were natives of Gadaris.[125] Philodemus later became the center of an Epicurean school in Naples.[126] There were also philosophical and literary schools in Tyre and Sidon.[127] In addition to the men from Gadara, the following philosophers may be mentioned: Basilideides of Tyre, Heliodorus of Antioch, Lysias of Tarsus, Zenon of Sidon (b. *ca.* 150 B.C.), Diogenes of Tarsus (probably fl. *ca.* 150-100 B.C.), and Nicolaus of Damascus (b. *ca.* 64 B.C.).[128] Suetonius (b. *ca.* A.D. 69) contributes the name of another Epicurean:

Marcus Pompilius Andronicus, a native of Syria, because of his devotion to the Epicurean sect was considered somewhat indolent in his work as a grammarian and not qualified to conduct a school.[129]

All of these men cannot accurately be called Epicureans, however, because by the second century B.C. the philosophy which thrived in the various schools in Palestine was very eclectic.[130] Still, the evidence here cited for the influence of Epicureanism in Palestine prior to the turn of the era makes it at least plausible that the Epicurean schools influenced the development of Jewish schools during this period.

DeWitt argues with great enthusiasm that Epicureanism also ". . . functioned as a bridge of transition from Greek philosophy to the Christian religion."[131] His thesis would be more acceptable had he not carried it to the extreme. He insists,

---

[125]Strabo XVI. ii. 29:

ἐντεῦθεν ἦν 'Αντίοχος ὁ φιλόσοφος, μικρὸν πρὸ ἡμῶν γεγονώς, ἐκ δὲ τῶν Γαδάρων Φιλόδημος τε ὁ 'Επικούρειος καὶ Μελέαγρος καὶ Μένιππος ὁ σπουδογέλοιος καὶ Θεόδωρος ὁ καθ' ἡμᾶς ῥήτωρ.
Cf. Moses Hadas, "Gadarenes in Pagan Literature," *CW*, XXV (1931), 25-30.

[126]Cf. Wilhelm Crönert, "Die Epikureer in Syrien," *JOAI*, X (1907), 145-52; Robert Philippson, "Philodemos," *RE*, XIX², 2444-82; Jane I. M. Tait, *Philodemus' Influence on the Latin Poets* (Bryn Mawr, Pa.: Bryn Mawr, 1941), pp. 1-23; Philip H. De Lacy and Estelle A. De Lacy, *Philodemus: On the Methods of Inference, A Study in Ancient Empiricism*, Philological Monographs No. X (Philadelphia: American Philological Association, 1941), pp. 1-9.

[127]Cf. Hengel, *Judentum und Hellenismus*, p. 161: "Zumindest in Sidon und Tyrus gab es auch eine Dichter- und Philosophenschule."

[128]Cf. Crönert, "Die Epikureer in Syrien," pp. 145-52.

[129]Suetonius *De Grammaticis* VIII:
M. Pompilius Andronicus, natione Syrus, studio Epicureae sectae desidiosior in professione grammatica habebatur minusque idoneus ad tuendam scholam.

[130]Cf. Hengel, *Judentum und Hellenismus*, p. 159.

[131]Norman Wentworth DeWitt, *St. Paul and Epicurus* (Minneapolis: University of Minnesota Press, 1954), p. v; cf. DeWitt, *Epicurus and His Philosophy*, pp. 31-32, 338-40.

however, that allusions to Epicureanism can be found in Paul's
use of terms like "flesh," "faith, hope, and charity," "corrup-
tion," and "incorruption"; and he characterizes Paul as ". . .
a Jew by birth, by early education an Epicurean, and by conversion a Christian."[132] Steckel similarly suggests that:

> Es ist nicht ausgeschlossen, dass Paulus Einzelheiten seiner
> Missionstechnik einer epikureischen Schulgemeinde in Tarsos
> abgesehen hat.[133]

Both DeWitt and Steckel exaggerate the effect of Epicurean influence on Paul.[134] On the other hand, it is probable that Epicureanism had a significant influence on the development of
Jewish schools and on the general intellectual climate of most
of the major cities in the first century. If so, it is conceivable that there was indirect influence from these sources
on early Christianity. This indirect influence may account for
the similarity between the use of φίλος in the Epicurean and
Johannine literature.

During the second century A.D., the Epicureans and
Christians were occasionally mentioned together.[135] Adelaide
D. Simpson traces the similarities between Epicureanism and
Christianity in the second century and attempts to show why
they were both persecuted.[136] One also finds numerous refer-
ences to Epicureans in the patristic literature, but Richard
Jungkuntz demonstrates that

> . . . in certain contexts at least 'Epicureanism' had
> acquired the force of a *Schimpfwort* and that in theological
> controversy especially it served as a convenient label of
> disparagement to pin on any sort of opponent whatsoever.[137]

Nevertheless, the use of the term even for general abuse indicates that the influence of the Epicurean school on the milieu
of early Christianity was profound. In spite of DeWitt's over-
enthusiasm in this direction, perhaps Epicureanism should be
examined more seriously (and critically) for its influence on
early Christianity.

---

[132]DeWitt, *St. Paul and Epicurus*, p. 168.

[133]"Epikur," *RE*, Suppl. XI, 647.

[134]Compare the influences on Paul discussed by W. D. Davies, *Paul and Rabbinic Judaism: Some Rabbinic Elements in Pauline Theology* (3rd ed.; London: S. P. C. K. Press, 1970); see esp. p. 16.

[135]Cf. Lucian *Alexander* 25, 38.

[136]"Epicureans, Christians, Atheists in the Second Century," *TAPA*, LXXII (1941), 372-81.

[137]"Fathers, Heretics and Epicureans," *JEH*, XVII (1966), 10.

Chapter VI

THE STOA

The importance of the Stoa

The Stoic school was very different from the other philosophical schools. Indeed, one probably ought not to speak of
"the Stoic school" in the same sense as the Platonic, Aristotelian, and Epicurean schools. The Stoics had no organization or
community spirit comparable to that of the other schools.
Their founder, Zeno, taught in a public colonnade and to our
knowledge left no will or provision for the perpetuity of his
school.[1] After the founder's death his followers dispersed,
and had it not been for Chrysippus, its "second founder," the
Stoic school would have died with Zeno.[2] Yet, the school survived through a succession of heads, which suggests that it
developed some organization.[3] It is probably best to think of
the Stoic school as a succession of philosophers who proclaimed
the same principles. At the same time, one can study various
Stoic schools. The school of Epictetus, for example, is extremely important. Finally, the Stoic school is significant
because it illustrates how a tradition could be passed on
through various schools with little or no continuity of organization.[4]

The sources for the study of the Stoa

Since information about each of the philosophers and
schools surveyed in this chapter comes to us from various
ancient sources and has been collected by several different
scholars, there will be less repetition if the sources are
treated separately at various points below. The most comprehensive study of the Stoics, however, is still probably that by
Max Pohlenz.[5]

---

[1]See Clarke, *Higher Education*, pp. 63, 70.

[2]D. L. VII. 183: εἰ μὴ γὰρ ἦν Χρύσιππος, οὐκ ἂν ἦν στοά.

[3]Cicero *De Divinatione* I. iii. 6, gives the succession of Stoics.

[4]The implication of this observation for Johannine studies is that it
may be wrong to think in terms of a Johannine school in a particular community which had a continuous existence for a period of time. The Johannine
tradition may have emerged and survived in several communities which had no
organizational ties with each other. For further discussion of this possibility see below, p. 286.

[5]*Die Stoa: Geschichte einer geistigen Bewegung* (2 vols.; 4th ed.;

124

For information about Zeno and his immediate successors
we are dependent upon fragments collected by Pearson[6] and von
Arnim[7] and upon the biographical tradition preserved by Diogenes
Laertius.[8] The biographical tradition is less useful as a
source for a study of the school under Zeno than it has been
for the other philosophical schools; it transmits only a few
glimpses of activities in the Stoa. There are probably two
reasons for this lack of attention to the school under the
founder: 1) the school in its earliest period had little or no
organization, and 2) Zeno exerted less influence on his school
than the founders of the earlier schools had. Moreover, the
continuity of succession was at least partially broken after
Zeno, and the Stoic school was re-organized by its "second
founder."

The origin of the Stoa

Zeno's philosophy emerged from the blending of powerful
forces in his life. He was born into a Semitic family, studied
under Greek teachers, and was profoundly influenced by Crates
the Cynic. The effect of each of these influences must be
assessed by anyone attempting to trace the development of Zeno's
thought, but they probably also influenced the way in which he
related to his disciples.

Although the date of Zeno's death (262/61 B.C.) can be
established with much more certainty than any other point in
his life, he was probably born about 335 B.C.[9] His father,
Mnaseas, was a Phoenician merchant at Citium in Cyprus.[10] Our
sources are unanimous in affirming that Zeno was "Vollblut-

Göttingen: Vandenhoeck & Ruprecht, 1970-72). Regarding sources, see:
Pohlenz, "Die Überlieferung über die Stoa," *Die Stoa*, II, 9-12. Cf. Pohlenz,
Stoa und Stoiker: Die Gründer, Panaitios, Poseidonios (Zürich: Artemis-
Verlag, 1950); Paul Barth and Albert Goedeckemeyer, *Die Stoa* (Stuttgart: Fr.
Frommanns Verlag, 1946).

[6]A. C. Pearson, *The Fragments of Zeno and Cleanthes* (London: C. J.
Clay, and Sons, 1891).

[7]Ioannes ab Arnim, *Stoicorum veterum fragmenta* (4 vols.; Leipzig: B. G.
Teubneri, 1921-24). See also: August Traversa, ed., *Index Stoicorum
Herculanensis*, Pubblicazioni dell'Istituto di Filologia Classica, I (Genova:
Istituto di Filologia Classica, [1952]).

[8]Book VII.

[9]For full discussion of the problems of chronology, see: Kurt von
Fritz, "Zenon von Kition," *RE*, Reihe 2, Bd. Xa (1972), 83-84; cf. von Fritz,
"Zeno (2)," *OCD*, p. 1145.

[10]D. L. VII. 1.

semit,"[11] and he is described as having been ". . . a mere foreigner and an obscure coiner of phrases, [who] seems to have wormed his way into ancient philosophy, ..."[12] Citium was a Greek *polis* but had a mixed population.[13] The question of whether his Semitic origin was a significant influence on his life and thought has been widely discussed. The strongest advocate of Semitic influence has been Pohlenz, who reasons as follows:

> Zenon war Semit, und wenn er auch schon in der Heimat griechischer Bücher las, so hat er doch seine ganze Jugend in semitischer Kultur zugebracht, bis er, zweiundzwanzigjährig, 312 nach Athen kam. Ist es da psychologisch überhaupt denkbar, dass die Weltanschauung eines solchen Mannes von semitischen Elementen gänzlich unbeeinflusst ist?[14]

Citing the work of Wolfgang Schmid,[15] Lesky contends that "Contrary to Pohlenz it is now assumed that the importance of such [Semitic] elements is slight; . . . ."[16] Lesky proceeds to list Zeno's Greek teachers, the Megarian Stilpon, the Academic Polemon, and the Cynic Crates, and to observe that Zeno ". . . occupied himself thoroughly with the older philosophers."[17] The question cannot be settled here,[18] but Lesky is probably correct; there is no solid evidence for any significant Semitic influence on Zeno.

In approximately 312/11 B.C., Zeno came to Athens.[19] Several traditions about the circumstances of his arrival and

---

[11]Pohlenz, *Die Stoa*, I, 22.

[12]Cicero *Tusculan Disputations* V. xii. 34: ". . . , advena quidam et ignobilis verborum opifex, insinuasse se in antiquam philosophiam videtur, ..." Cf. Cicero *De Finibus* IV. xx. 56.

[13]von Fritz, "Zenon von Kition," *RE*, Reihe 2, Bd. Xa, 85.

[14]Max Pohlenz, "Stoa und Semitismus," *Neue Jahrbücher für Wissenschaft und Jugendbildung*, II (1926), 258.

[15]"Philosophie," in *Der Hellenismus in der deutschen Forschung 1938-1948*, ed. by E. Kiessling (Wiesbaden: Otto Harrassowitz, 1956), p. 83.

[16]*A History of Greek Literature*, p. 672.

[17]Ibid.

[18]Edwyn Bevan, *Stoics and Sceptics: Four Lectures Delivered in Oxford during Hilary Term 1913 for the Common University Fund* (Oxford: At the University Press, 1913), p. 20, doubts ". . . that the question can ever be answered, for the simple reason that we do not know anything about the wisdom of the Phoenicians." Hengel, however, who has considerably advanced our knowledge of Phoenician thought and culture during this period, follows Pohlenz: "Diese Anleihen waren um so eher möglich, weil die Stoa aus semitischem Boden herausgewachsen war und mit der Gedankenwelt des A.T. manches Gemeinsame besass: . . ." (*Judentum und Hellenismus*, p. 268.).

[19]von Fritz, "Zenon von Kition," *RE*, Reihe 2, Bd. Xa, 83.

initial meeting with Crates are preserved by Diogenes Laertius.
According to Demetrius the Magnesian (fl. 50 B.C.),[20] Zeno's
father went to Athens often and brought many books about
Socrates back to Zeno. Thus, Zeno was acquainted with writings
of the earlier philosophers before he left Citium. In another
passage, Diogenes Laertius records that Zeno came to Athens as
a result of a shipwreck.[21] He is alleged to have been introduced to Crates the Cynic while browsing at a bookstall.[22]
Thereafter he spent some time as Crates' student,[23] and one
tradition claims that he studied under others as well:

> He was a pupil of Crates, as stated above. Next they
> say he attended the lectures of Stilpo and Xenocrates for
> ten years--so Timocrates says in his *Dion*--and Polemo as
> well.[24]

The influence of Crates on Zeno is probably most significant for
this study because of the lack of organization among the Cynics.
Clarke characterizes them as follows:

> Marked out by staff and wallet in addition to the usual beard
> and worn cloak of the philosopher, they were to be seen
> throughout the Greek-speaking world in the imperial period,
> at once admired and scorned by their fellow-men. They had
> no organization or central direction. There was some conti-
> nuity throughout the ages from the time of Diogenes and
> Crates, and no doubt in any period a leading figure among
> the Cynics would attract disciples and to some extent assume
> their direction, as Peregrinus did in the second century.
> Cynics, however, were essentially independent, and normally
> each of them would go his own way as free from direction and
> organization as he was from other ties.[25]

The date at which Zeno began to teach in the Stoa Poikile is
unknown, but was probably about 301/300 B.C.[26] The Stoa was
located on the north side of the Agora in Athens[27] and had been

---

[20]Cited by D. L. VII. 31.

[21]D. L. VII. 2; cf. VII. 5, 13.

[22]D. L. VII. 2.

[23]D. L. VII. 3, 5. Cf. Donald R. Dudley, *A History of Cynicism:
From Diogenes to the 6th Century A.D.* (London: Methuen & Co. Ltd., 1937),
pp. 96-99.

[24]D. L. VII. 2:

Διήκουσε δέ, καθὰ προείρηται, Κράτητος· εἶτα καὶ Στίλπωνος ἀκοῦσαί
φασιν αὐτὸν καὶ Ξενοκράτους ἔτη δέκα, ὡς Τιμοκράτης ἐν τῷ Δίωνι· ἀλλὰ
καὶ Πολέμωνος.
Cf. D. L. VII. 16, 24.

[25]Clarke, *Higher Education*, p. 84. See Epictetus' description of a
Cynic-Stoic quoted below, p. 224.

[26]Pohlenz, *Die Stoa*, I, 24.

[27]R. E. Wycherley, "The Painted Stoa," *The Phoenix*, VII (1953), 22;

a gathering place for philosophers prior to Zeno's activity
there.[28] Although the stoa was famous for its paintings, they
were added as an after-thought by one Polygnotus (fl. *ca.* 475-
447 B.C.). Originally the Stoa was called the Peisianacteum,
and only later did it come to be known as the Stoa Poikile, i.e.,
"Painted Porch."[29]

> Like other public buildings at Athens the Poikile must
> have had its religious associations, but we do not know
> whether it was dedicated to any particular deity or what
> sacred rites were performed in or before it, . . . An
> Altar stood in the stoa, but whose it was we do not know.[30]

Even if the building had religious associations, there is no
evidence that they were adopted by Zeno and his adherents.
What is clear is that in the Stoa Poikile ". . . high art and
high thought rubbed shoulders, almost literally, with vulgar
everyday life."[31] Zeno may have chosen to teach in the Stoa
for this very reason, or it may be that he had no alternative
since as a foreigner he could not buy property.[32] The Stoa
Poikile gave Zeno's school its name,[33] but it is not possible
to say how long the school remained in the Stoa.[34]

The nature of the Stoa

The problems involved in describing Zeno and his disciples
as a school have been mentioned above.[35] In spite of these
problems, it does appear that Zeno was the founder both of a
local school (σχολή)[36] and a philosophical tradition or school

---

Homer A. Thompson, "Excavations in the Athenian Agora: 1949," *Hesperia*, XIX
(1950), 327-29.

[28]Cf. Alciphron *Letters* I. 3. 2; D. L. VII. 5; LSJ, "λέσχ-η," p. 1040;
Wycherley, "The Painted Stoa," p. 30.

[29]Plutarch *Cimon* IV. 5-6; Pausanias *Attica* xv. 1-4; for a description
of the paintings, see: Wycherley, "The Painted Stoa," pp. 24-30; Thompson,
"Excavations in the Athenian Agora: 1949," p. 329. For further discussion
see: Hobein, "Stoa," *RE*, Reihe 2, Bd. 4-A-1 (1931), 1-47.

[30]Wycherley, "The Painted Stoa," pp. 30-31.

[31]Ibid., p. 20.

[32]Cf. von Fritz, "Zenon von Kition," *RE*, Reihe 2, Bd. Xa, 86.

[33]The Stoics were commonly referred to as "those in the stoa" [οἱ δ'
ἐν τῇ στοᾷ]. Cf. Edmonds, *Fragments of Attic Comedy*, IIIA, 16, 214; see
also p. 226 [τῶν γὰρ ἐκ τῆς ποικίλης στοᾶς λογαρίων]; D. L. VII. 5.

[34]Cf. Wycherley, "Peripatos: The Athenian Philosophical Scene," p.
17.

[35]See above, p. 123.

[36]Cf. D. L. VII. 28; LSJ, p. 1747, defines "σχολή" as follows: "a
group to whom lectures were given, school."

128

in a more general sense (αἵρεσις).[37] We have very little evidence regarding the nature of Zeno's σχολή, but it seems to have had little organization or community spirit, a factor which may be due both to Zeno's association with the Cynics and the location of the school in the Stoa Poikile.

One may attempt first to understand Zeno's position at the Stoa. He discoursed while pacing up and down in the Stoa.[38] When large crowds gathered he drove off those whom he deemed unfit. On one occasion he asked a rich Rhodian to sit on a dusty bench by the beggars.[39] He is also said to have begged for coins in an attempt to drive people away[40] and even to have resorted to direct request:

> When several persons stood about him in the Colonnade he pointed to the wooden railing at the top round the altar and said, "This was once open to all, but because it was found to be a hindrance it was railed off. If you then will take yourselves out of the way you will be the less annoyance to us."[41]

Zeno's graceless actions provoked a mixed response. There are some indications that he was sought after and held in high esteem by the Athenians and even invited to the court of Antigonus Gonatas.[42] At the same time, Zeno remained a barbarian in the eyes of his contemporaries. Pohlenz contrasts him with Epicurus as follows:

> Von Zenons Persönlichkeit ging auch nicht ein Zauber aus wie von der Epikurs, das in seiner Gemeinde schwärmerisch geliebt und als Gott verehrt wurde. . . . Die Einfachheit, mit der er als Schulhaupt die unumgänglichen Repräsentationspflichten erfüllte, wurde ihm als 'barbarische knauserigkeit' ausgelegt.[43]

This judgment on Zeno may account for the fact that he was never regarded by his followers as the ideal wise man. While the

---

[37] Cf. D. L. VII. 38: ". . . διὰ τὸ τοῦτον κτίστην γενέσθαι τῆς αἱρέσεως." LSJ, p. 41, defines "αἵρεσις" as follows: "system of philosophic principles, or those who profess such principles, sect, school." Cf. D. L. VII. 30.

[38] D. L. VII. 5.

[39] D. L. VII. 22.

[40] D. L. VII. 14; cf. Wycherley, "The Painted Stoa," p. 33.

[41] D. L. VII. 14:
πλειόνων τε περιστάντων αὐτόν, δείξας ἐν τῇ στοᾷ κατ' ἄκρου τὸ ξύλινον περιφερὲς τοῦ βωμοῦ ἔφη, "τοῦτό ποτ' ἐν μέσῳ ἔκειτο, διὰ δὲ τὸ ἐμποδίζειν ἰδίᾳ ἐτέθη· καὶ ὑμεῖς οὖν ἐκ τοῦ μέσου Βαστάσαντες αὐτοὺς ἧττον ἡμῖν ἐνοχλήσετε."
Note the reference to the altar in the Stoa.

[42] Cf. D. L. VII. 6.

[43] Pohlenz, *Die Stoa*, I, 24.

Stoics spoke of "the wise man," they did not believe that the ideal had ever been realized.[44] In this regard they were different from both Epicureanism and Christianity.[45]

The Stoics constituted more of an intellectual and philosophical movement than a community organized as a school. In fact, it would have been contrary to their philosophy for them to have drawn together as a closely-knit or exclusive community.[46] Zeno proposed, for example, that the existing cities and towns be replaced by one universal society under natural law. Margaret E. Reesor cites a fragment of Zeno's *Republic* in this connection:

> As one very important fragment states, the *Republic* of Zeno was organized with one purpose in view, "that we may not live by cities and demes, severally divided according to our own ideas of what is just, but may consider all men our demesmen and fellow citizens, and that there may be one life and one world just as a herd feeding together, nurtured by common law."[47]

The disciples of Zeno, therefore, had little community spirit; nor did they feel it necessary to follow Zeno's teaching as though it were a binding orthodoxy. Various branches of Stoicism developed soon after Zeno's death.[48] It is amazing that the Stoic school developed basic principles and rules for conduct in view of the absence of a community to foster or enforce the Stoic way of life.[49]

In contrast to the Epicurean school, women were not admitted to the Stoic school; nor do we hear of any slaves among Zeno's adherents.[50] On the contrary, Zeno advocated that women in his ideal society should be held as common property of the community.[51] Every man would then view all children as his own.

---

[44]Cf. Bevan, *Stoics and Sceptics*, pp. 70-71.

[45]Tiede, *The Charismatic Figure as Miracle Worker*, p. 52, observes: "Although the Stoa regarded its founder as an exemplary σοφός, the figure of Zeno never exerted the kind of singular personal force on subsequent traditions as has been observed for Socrates, Diogenes, and Epicurus."

[46]Cf. Eleuterio Elorduy, "Die Sozialphilosophie der Stoa," *Philologus*, Supplementband XXVIII, Heft 3 (1936), 136.

[47]*The Political Theory of the Old and Middle Stoa* (New York: J. J. Augustin Publisher, 1951), p. 10; cf. von Arnim, *Stoicorum veterum fragmenta*, I, fr. 262.

[48]Cf. von Fritz, "Zenon von Kition," *RE*, Reihe 2, Bd. Xa, 86-87; Pohlenz, *Die Stoa*, I, 27.

[49]Cf. Bevan, *Stoics and Sceptics*, p. 96.

[50]Cf. Pohlenz, *Die Stoa*, I, 24.

[51]Cf. Reesor, *The Political Theory of the Old and Middle Stoa*, p. 11; von Arnim, *Stoicorum veterum fragmenta*, I, fr. 269.

Preaching and debating were activities in which the Stoics engaged enthusiastically. They included rhetoric as part of philosophy; ". . . they claimed it as an integral part of their logic, which was the first of the three stages into which they divided philosophy."[52] Lucian (b. *ca.* A.D. 120), for example, recounts an amusing tale about how Zeus witnessed a debate between a Stoic and an Epicurean in the Stoa Poikile concerning the existence of the gods and called a meeting of the gods to decide what to do about the course of the debate.[53] While Zeno is known to have done some writing,[54] it is unlikely that the Stoics kept a library in the Poikile.[55] Moreover, as Simon and Simon conclude, we know little about the way in which the Stoic school was supported financially.[56]

Diogenes Laertius reports traditions that Zeno was a temperate man who lived a long life.[57] The disciples who gathered around him were men ". . . of practical and speculative capacity, not unworthy of comparison with the companions of Socrates."[58] His death broke the tie between them, however, and they moved into independent occupations. Some became counsellors-of-state, as had some of the pupils at the Academy earlier;[59] while others (e.g., Ariston of Chios[60] and Herillus

---

[52]Marrou, *A History of Education in Antiquity*, p. 289; cf. D. L. VII. 4

[53]Lucian *Zeus Rants* 16ff.

[54]D. L. VII. 4, 34.

[55]Wycherley, "The Painted Stoa," p. 33 n. 57; cf. DeWitt, *Epicurus and His Philosophy*, p. 92.

[56]Heinrich Simon and Marie Simon, *Die alte Stoa und ihr Naturbegriff: Ein Beitrag zur Philosophiegeschichte des Hellenismus* (Berlin: Aufbau-Verlag, 1956), p. 24.

[57]Cf. D. L. VII. 27-28. There is tradition to the contrary, however, if Alciphron *Letters* 28. 1-3, means for his readers to understand that he is describing Zeno when he tells of ". . . that austere old fellow who never smiles, the one in the Painted Porch, . . ." At night this teacher ". . . wrapped his head in a mantle and went the round of the brothels."
. . . τὸν αὐστηρὸν πρεσβύτην καὶ ἀμειδῆ, τὸν ἐκ τῆς Ποικίλης, ...
νύκτωρ δὲ περικαλύπτοντα τὴν κεφαλὴν τριβωνίω καὶ περὶ χαμαιτυπεῖα
εἰλούμενον, ...

[58]E. Vernon Arnold, *Roman Stoicism: Being Lectures on the History of the Stoic Philosophy with Special Reference to Its Development within the Roman Empire* (Cambridge: At the University Press, 1911), p. 78.

[59]D. L. VII. 6-9; von Arnim, *Stoicorum veterum fragmenta*, I, frs. 435-45; Plutarch *Cleomenes* II. 2, XI. 2; cf. Marrou, *A History of Education in Antiquity*, p. 101.

[60]Simon and Simon, *Die alte Stoa und ihr Naturbegriff*, p. 34; D. L. VII. 161; von Arnim, *Stoicorum veterum fragmenta*, I, pp. 75-90; Dudley, *A History of Cynicism*, pp. 100-03.

of Carthage[61]) founded independent schools. We have no evidence
that Zeno left a will appointing a successor. The Stoic school
could have died with Zeno: "Zeno's work had not yet been
exposed to the test of time, and another century was to pass
before it could be seen that the Stoic school was to be of
permanent importance."[62]

The history of the Stoa

Although we know very little about the school after Zeno's
death, Stoicism did survive. It spread slowly during the third
century and more rapidly during the second.[63] Stoics became
wandering preachers who addressed their diatribes to the masses
in the market places.[64] Gradually groups of Stoics formed in
various cities. Arnold suggests that at this point the school
became a sect.

> Fathers handed down its doctrine to their sons, and teachers
> to their pupils. Groups of men united by a common respect
> for the school and its founders began to associate together,
> not only at Athens, but also (. . .) at such centres as Perga-
> mus, Babylon, Seleucia, Tarsus, Sidon, and even Alexandria.
> Thus out of the school there grew up the 'sect' (*secta*); that
> is, a society of men drawn from different nations and ranks,
> but sharing the same convictions, united by a bond of brother-
> hood, and feeling their way towards mutual consolation and
> support; a company going through life on the same path, and
> prepared to submit to a common authority.[65]

While the philosophy was being spread by individual philosophers, the school at Athens survived under a succession of
heads.

Cleanthes of Assos (331-232 B.C.) succeeded Zeno and
headed the school until his own death. He seems to have followed Zeno's teachings closely but introduced a religious

---

[61]Simon and Simon, *Die alte Stoa und ihr Naturbegriff*, p. 34; von
Arnim, *Stoicorum veterum fragmenta*, I, pp. 91-93.

[62]Arnold, *Roman Stoicism*, p. 78.

[63]D. L. VII. 5 states: τὸν λόγον ἐπὶ πλεῖον ηὔξησαν· R. D. Hicks
(Loeb) interprets τὸν λόγον as referring to "the name Stoic" rather than
the Stoic philosophy. Still, the phrase is similar to some found in the
New Testament:

Acts 6:7   καὶ ὁ λόγος τοῦ θεοῦ ηὔξανεν, . . .
Acts 12:24   ὁ δὲ λόγος τοῦ κυρίου ηὔξανεν . . .
Acts 19:20   . . . ὁ λόγος ηὔξανεν . . .

[64]For a classic study of the diatribe style see: Rud[olf] Bultmann,
Der Stil der paulinischen Predigt und die kynisch-stoische Diatribe, FRLANT,
13. Heft (Göttingen: Vandenhoeck & Ruprecht, 1910); cf. [Johannes] v[on]
Arnim, "Epiktetos," *RE*, VI, 129.

[65]Arnold, *Roman Stoicism*, p. 99. See the discussion of the terms
"school" and "sect" below, p. 258-259.

fervour into the school which it had not previously known. He
is best known for his *Hymn to Zeus*, however, and was not particularly able as a head of the school. Simon and Simon characterize his administration as follows: "Allerdings zeigte
sich Kleanthes als Schulleiter nicht besonders fähig; die
Schüler verliefen sich, und die Schule begann ihren Einfluss
zu verlieren."[66] Politically, Cleanthes turned away from the
lower classes and from the school's association with Macedonian
influence and alligned the school with the ruling authorities.[67]

Chrysippus (*ca.* 280-207 B.C.) was the most important of
Zeno's successors. Prior to his conversion to Stoicism under
Cleanthes he studied with Arcesilaus. Later he defended
Stoicism against the attacks of the Academy and the Garden.[68]
We know very little about his work as head of the school except
that his following was so large he gave open-air lectures at
the Lyceum.[69] He also lectured at the Odeum. He was a
prodigious writer, but Diogenes Laertius, who records that 705
books were attributed to him, also preserves the following
charge against him: "If one were to strip the books of
Chrysippus of all extraneous quotations, his pages would be
left bare."[70]

How should Chrysippus' work be understood in relation to
that of his predecessors? Chrysippus did not entirely replace
Zeno and Cleanthes. Rather, Dörrie concludes from the way in
which Chrysippus treated his predecessors that the traditions
of the school had already become fixed.[71] Pohlenz likens
Chrysippus' role to that of an apostle content merely to
expound the teaching of the founder (*Schulgründer*) correctly.[72]
Chrysippus' contribution to the Stoic school has recently been

----

[66]Simon and Simon, *Die alte Stoa und ihr Naturbegriff*, p. 35; cf.
D. L. VII. 168-76; Pohlenz, *Die Stoa*, I, 27.

[67]Simon and Simon, *Die alte Stoa und ihr Naturbegriff*, p. 36.

[68]Cf. Pohlenz, *Die Stoa*, I, 28-29; Athenaeus III. 104b. See above,
p. 123 n. 2.

[69]D. L. VII. 184-85; cf. Edmonds, *Fragments of Attic Comedy*, II, 387.

[70]D. L. VII. 181:
εἰ γὰρ τις ἀφέλοι τῶν Χρυσίππου βιβλίων ὅσ' ἀλλότρια παρατέθειται, κενὸς
αὐτῷ ὁ χάρτης καταλελείψεται.
Cf. VII. 180.

[71]Heinrich Dörrie, "Chrysippos," *RE*, Suppl. XII (1970), 151; cf.
Rengstorf, "μαθητής," *TDNT*, IV, 425.

[72]*Die Stoa*, I, 30.

re-evaluated, however, by J. B. Gould, whose study basically
confirms the following four points:

> (i) Chrysippus systematizes and strengthens Stoic doctrine;
> (ii) Chrysippus is more or less original: . . . ; (iii)
> Chrysippus argues more acutely than his predecessors and
> was responsible for the importance logic assumed in the
> Stoa; (iv) Chrysippus' works remained for centuries the
> recognized standard of orthodoxy.[73]

By the first century A.D., at least, Chrysippus' works were
the most widely known Stoic writings, and were used as texts
in Epictetus' school.[74] Chrysippus was popular among the
Athenians because of his democratic sentiments; he never dedicated a book to a king.[75] In one of his writings, however, he
stated that one of the three ways of life open to a wise man
was to live at the court of a king. The alternatives were
either to live with friends or to teach students for fees.[76]
Later Stoics are found in all three positions.

Chrysippus was followed by two heads about whom little is
known: Zeno of Tarsus and Diogenes of Babylon (ca. 240-152 B.C.).
Many of Diogenes' students also came from the east: Antipater
of Tarsus, Archedemus of Tarsus and Boethus of Sidon. But, his
influence extended westward also.[77] In 156-55 B.C. Diogenes
visited Rome along with Carneades the Academic and Critolaus
the Peripatetic on an embassy. They gave lectures and were
well received in Rome.[78] Thereafter Stoicism rapidly became
the most popular philosophy among the Romans.

Diogenes was followed by Antipater of Tarsus (2nd c. B.C.),
who was succeeded by Panaetius of Rhodes (ca. 185-109 B.C.).
Panaetius softened the asceticism of his philosophy and made it
more attractive.[79] He was a friend of Scipio Aemilanus (185/4-

---

[73]Josiah B. Gould, *The Philosophy of Chrysippus* (Albany: State
University of New York Press, 1970), p. 14; cf. pp. 206-07. Other important works on Chrysippus include: Émile Bréhier, *Chrysippe et l'ancien
Stoïcisme*, Nouvelle édition revue (Paris: Presses Universitaires de France,
1951); Heinrich Dörrie, "Chrysippos," *RE*, Suppl. XII, 148-55.

[74]Cf. Gould, *The Philosophy of Chrysippus*, pp. 12-14.

[75]D. L. VII. 185; Pohlenz, *Die Stoa*, I, 29.

[76]von Arnim, *Stoicorum veterum fragmenta*, III, fr. 693; Reesor, *The
Political Theory of the Old and Middle Stoa*, p. 23.

[77]Hadas, *Hellenistic Culture*, p. 107.

[78]Plutarch *Marcus Cato* XXII; cf. Clarke, *Higher Education*, p. 72;
Suetonius *On Rhetoricians* I.

[79]Reesor, *The Political Theory of the Old and Middle Stoa*, p. 26,
indicates that Cicero's *De Officiis* is our main source for the study of
Panaetius. For further discussion, see: Max Pohlenz, *Antikes Führertum:*

129 B.C.) and Polybius (*ca.* 200 - after 118 B.C.) and may have established a school in Rome prior to becoming head of the Stoa (129-109 B.C.).[80] Although we are adequately informed about Stoic doctrine during this period of the school's history, we have little information about its organization.[81]

One of Panaetius' pupils, Posidonius of Apamea [in Syria] (*ca.* 135-51/50 B.C.), carried forward the succession of Stoic philosophers, though he was never head of the school in Athens.[82] After studying with Panaetius in Athens, Posidonius settled in Rhodes; and it was there that Cicero studied with him briefly.[83] Posidonius is important within the history of schools and their influence because as a Syrian trained in Athens he illustrates the way in which the Greek philosophical schools influenced the eastern part of the Hellenistic world and how this influence was reciprocal.[84]

During the first century B.C., one encounters the emergence of a new status for philosophers. Rather than students seeking out teachers in schools, one finds philosophers joining the households of prominent citizens. Cicero was taught by Diodotus, who remained in his household and (although he was a Stoic) practiced Pythagorean disciplines.[85] Cato the Younger

---

Cicero De Officiis und das Lebensideal des Panaitios, Neue Wege zur Antike, II Reihe; Interpretationen, Heft 3 (Leipzig: B. G. Teubner, 1934); Modestus van Straaten, *Panêtius: sa vie, ses écrits et sa doctrine avec une édition des fragments* (Amsterdam: Uitgeverij H. J. Paris, 1946); Fritz-Arthur Steinmetz, *Die Freundschaftslehre des Panaitios: Nach einer Analyse von Ciceros 'Laelius de Amicita'*, Palingenesia: Monographien und Texte zur klassischen Altertumswissenschaft, Bd. III (Wiesbaden: Franz Steiner Verlag GMBH, 1967).

[80]Cicero *De Republica* I. xxi. 34.

[81]Clarke, *Higher Education*, p. 71.

[82]Cf. Marie Laffranque, *Poseidonios d'Apamée: Essai de mise au point*, Publications de la faculté des lettres et sciences humaines de Paris, Série "Recherches," Tome XIII (Paris: Presses Universitaires de France, 1964); Lesky, *A History of Greek Literature*, pp. 678-81; L. Edelstein and I. G. Kidd, eds., *Posidonius*, Vol. I: *The Fragments*, Cambridge Classical Texts and Commentaries, 13 (Cambridge: At the University Press, 1972).

[83]Plutarch *Cicero* IV. 4; Cicero *De Natura Deorum* I. iii. 6; II. xxxiv. 88; *De Divinatione* I. iii. 6; II. xxi. 47.

[84]Cf. Hadas, *Hellenistic Culture*, p. 108. See also Paul Schubert, *Die Eschatologie des Posidonius*, Veröffentlichungen des Forschungsinstituts für vergleichende Religionsgeschichte an der Universität Leipzig, II Reihe, Heft 4 (Leipzig: Verlag von Eduard Pfeiffer, 1927). Regarding the possibility that Posidonius influenced Philo, see below, p. 200 n. 14.

[85]Cicero *De Natura Deorum* I. iii. 6; *Brutus* XC. 309; *Academica* II. 115; *Epistulae ad Familiares* XIII. xvi; *Tusculan Disputations* V. xxxix. 113.

(95-46 B.C.) also kept Stoic philosophers in his house; he was a companion of Antipater of Tyre (d. before 44 B.C.) and brought Athenodorus into his household from Pergamum.[86] In view of this development it is not surprising that we know little about the Stoic school in Athens during this period.[87]

The writings of Seneca (4 B.C./A.D. 1 - 65) provide evidence concerning developments within Stoicism during the first century A.D. Seneca studied with Sotion, an eclectic Pythagorean philosopher whose example Seneca followed for a while by refraining from animal food and engaging in self-examination every night.[88] Seneca later attended the lectures of Attalus, a Stoic philosopher who paced up and down while lecturing and engaged in discussion with his students.[89] Attalus was such an effective speaker that Seneca often desired to leave his lecture room a poor man when he had been lecturing on the blessings of poverty.[90] This apparent emphasis on moral exhortation in Attalus' teaching carried over into Seneca's own works,[91] but we also learn that many students came to the lectures merely to be entertained and to take down witty phrases.[92]

The school of Epictetus (*ca.* A.D. 55 - *ca.* 135) deserves special attention both because its date is so close to that of the Gospel of John and because our sources provide such a complete picture of the school. Epictetus may properly be treated in this chapter because he is commonly regarded as a Stoic. Nevertheless, he was at times critical of the Stoics, and there is no evidence of any contact between him and Athens.[93]

Epictetus himself wrote nothing, but one of his students, Flavius Arrian, recorded many of his diatribes and conversations.

---

[86]Plutarch *Cato the Younger* IV. 1; X. 1; XVI. 1.

[87]Cicero *De Oratore* III. xi. 43, states that Athenians had long ago ceased to enjoy erudition and the city merely provided lodging for foreign students.

[88]Seneca *Epistles* CVIII. 17, 22; *On Anger* III. xxxvi. 1.

[89]Seneca *Epistles* CVIII. 3.

[90]Seneca *Epistles* CVIII. 13-14.

[91]The instructions Seneca gives in *Epistles* CVIII. 12 about speaking could have been addressed to a class of students aspiring to become evangelists.

[92]Seneca *Epistles* CVIII. 6-7, 23.

[93]Epictetus I. xxix. 56; II. xix. 22; cf. Iason Xenakis, *Epictetus: Philosopher-Therapist* (The Hague: Martinus Nijhoff, 1969), p. 4; Benjamin L. Hijmans, Jr., "ΑΣΚΗΣΙΣ: *Notes on Epictetus' Educational System* (Assen: Van Gorcum & Comp. N.V., [1959]), p. 2.

136

In his introduction Arrian describes the nature of his work:

> . . . , I acknowledge that I have not "composed" them at
> all. But whatever I heard him say I used to write down,
> word for word, as best I could, endeavouring to preserve it
> as a memorial, for my own future use, of his way of think-
> ing and the frankness of his speech.[94]

The discourses are not formal lectures. Nor are they the basic curriculum; they are Epictetus' comments and conversations in the classroom which followed the formal instruction.[95] They provide us, however, with an astonishingly detailed picture of life at Epictetus' school.[96]

Epictetus' early life undoubtedly influenced the develop-ment of his thought and interest in education. He was born a slave in Phrygia about the middle of the first century A.D. After he gained his freedom when his master, Epaphroditus, died, he became a student of Musonius Rufus (before A.D. 30 - before 101/2), a prominent Stoic.[97] Epictetus acquired his basic philosophical orientation from Musonius, and, as an interesting detail, Clarke suggests that it was from Musonius that Epictetus acquired the habit of calling his pupils "slave."[98]

Most Roman philosophers during the first century were associated with those Roman nobles who opposed the emperors:

> A few turncoats supported Domitian. But, leaving them
> aside, there seems to be no prominent philosopher from the

---

[94]Epictetus I. 1-2:

. . . , ὅς γε οὐδὲ συγγράψαι φημί. ὅσα δὲ ἤκουον αὐτοῦ λέγοντος, ταῦτα αὐτὰ ἐπειράθην αὐτοῖς ὀνόμασιν ὡς οἷόν τε ἦν γραψάμενος ὑπομνήματα εἰς ὕστερον ἐμαυτῷ διαφυλάξαι τῆς ἐκείνου διανοίας καὶ παρρησίας. (Citations referring to "Epictetus" designate the Discourses of Epictetus as reported by Arrian.)

[95]Cf. W. A. Oldfather, trans., *Epictetus: The Discourses as Reported by Arrian, The Manual, and Fragments*, The Loeb Classical Library (2 vols.; Cambridge, Mass.: Harvard University Press, 1967), I, xv.

[96]Oldfather, *Epictetus*, I, xiii, describes Arrian's work as ". . . really unique in literature, the actual words of an extraordinarily gifted teacher upon scores, not to say hundreds of occasions in his own class-room, ..." Similarly, von Arnim, "Epiktetos," *RE*, VI, 128, character-izes the discourses as: ". . . ein photographisch treues Bild von der Lehrweise und von den einzelnen Vorträgen E.s." For bibliographical information on editions of Epictetus' discourses see: W. A. Oldfather, *Contributions Toward a Bibliography of Epictetus*, University of Illinois Bulletin, Vol. XXV, No. 12 (Urbana, Ill.: The University of Illinois, 1927), and the *Supplement*, edited by M. Harman (Urbana, Ill.: The University of Illinois Press, 1952).

[97]Cf. A. C. van Geytenbeek, *Musonius Rufus and Greek Diatribe*, trans. by B. L. Hijmans, Jr., Wijsgerige Teksten en Studies, 8 (Rev. ed.; Assen: Van Gorcum & Comp. N.V., 1963).

[98]Clarke, *Higher Education*, p. 90; cf. Epictetus I. vii. 31, 32. The word used by Epictetus is ἀνδράποδον, but it is still interesting to recall that Jesus addressed his disciples as δούλους according to John 15:15.

death of Athenodorus to the reign of Trajan who sided with
the emperors against the large number of 'opposition'
philosophers.[99]

Hence it is not surprising that Domitian banned the philosophers from Rome about A.D. 92-94.[100] Epictetus was already
well known when he left Rome and established a school at
Nicopolis where he settled for the rest of his life.

Nicopolis is located on the coast of the Adriatic Sea in
Northern Greece. The city is mentioned in the New Testament;
according to Titus 3:12, Paul planned to spend the winter
there.[101] Moreover, two passages from the discourses
indicate that there were probably Christians in Nicopolis when
Epictetus taught there.[102] These passages have been the basis
for wild speculation about Christian influence on Epictetus,
but these speculations were deflated by the sober work of
Adolf Bonhoeffer.[103] Although Epictetus probably knew of

---

[99]Ramsay MacMullen, *Enemies of the Roman Order: Treason, Unrest, and Alienation in the Empire* (Cambridge, Mass.: Harvard University Press, 1966), pp. 48-49.

[100]Cf. Xenakis, *Epictetus*, p. 5; Hijmans, "ΑΣΚΗΣΙΣ, p. 8. Aulus Gellius *The Attic Nights* XV. xi. 3-5:
". . . , but even in the reign of Domitian by a decree of the senate they were driven from the city and forbidden Italy. And it was at that time that the philosopher Epictetus also withdrew from Rome to Nicopolis because of that senatorial decree."
. . . , verum etiam Domitiano imperante senatusconsulto eiecti atque urbe et Italia interdicti sunt. Qua tempestate Epictetus quoque philoso-phus propter id senatusconsultum Nicopolim Roma decessit.

[101]Martin Dibelius and Hans Conzelmann, *The Pastoral Epistles*, trans. by P. Buttolph and A. Yarbro, ed. by H. Koester, Hermeneia (Philadelphia: Fortress Press, 1972), pp. 152-53, agrees that the reference in Titus 3:12 is to the same Nicopolis in which Epictetus settled.

[102]Epictetus II. ix. 19-21 (a difficult passage in which Epictetus speaks of "Jew" and "counterfeit 'baptists'" [παραβαπτισταί]); IV. vii. 6 (where Epictetus refers to "the Galileans"); cf. Hijmans, "ΑΣΚΗΣΙΣ, p. 1.

[103]*Epiktet und das Neue Testament*, Religionsgeschichtliche Versuche und Vorarbeiten, Bd. X (Giessen: Verlag von Alfred Töpelmann, 1911); cf. Rudolf Bultmann, "Das religiöse Moment in der ethischen Unterweisung des Epiktet und das Neue Testament," *ZNW*, XIII (1912), 97-110, 177-91; Adolf Bonhoeffer, "Epiktet und das Neue Testament," *ZNW*, XIII (1912), 281-92; Douglas S. Sharp, *Epictetus and the New Testament* (London: Charles H. Kelly, 1914); J. N. Sevenster, "Education or Conversion: Epictetus and the Gospels," *NovT*, VIII (1966), 247-62. Also of interest is the study by Ernest C. Colwell, *The Greek of the Fourth Gospel: A Study of Its Aramaisms in the Light of Hellenistic Greek* (Chicago: University of Chicago Press, 1931), in which the author compares John's Greek with that of Epictetus. After the studies by Bonhoeffer, Bultmann, and Sharp, interest in Epictetus faded for New Testament scholars. Perhaps it is time for the question of Epictetus and the New Testament to be raised again: what can the discourses tell us about the religious attitudes of a Hellenistic school during the New Testament period? The hymn of praise in Epictetus I. xvi. 16-17, and the prayer in II. xvi. 41-42 are especially illuminating.

138

Christians in Nicopolis [Had he learned of them while in Rome?],
it is doubtful that he had read their literature.

Whether Epictetus taught in a local gymnasium or in his
own house is not clear,[104] but he apparently owned some books
and may have had access to a public library.[105] Many of his
students came from other cities, some no doubt from well-to-do
families in Rome.[106] Epictetus was probably paid by his students, but we have no information on this point.[107] The students do not seem to have lived at the school, however.[108]
The school was also visited frequently by men seeking the philosopher's advice, and Arrian records many of these conversations.[109] Although the size of the school is difficult to
estimate, it was sufficiently large for Epictetus to use his
more advanced students as instructors for the younger ones. On
one occasion Epictetus rebuked a tutor for laughing at his
student when he read poorly.[110] Some of the advanced students
aspired to teaching careers,[111] while others intended to go
into court life and public service.[112] Another passage records
Epictetus' exhortation to a student to become an exegete of the
laws sent to him (by God).[113]

---

[104]Cf. Hijmans, "ΑΣΚΗΣΙΣ, pp. 2-3; Seneca *Epistles* LXXVI. 1-4, suggests that Metronax lectured in his own house.

[105]Epictetus IV. x. 26; cf. Hijmans, "ΑΣΚΗΣΙΣ, p. 3.

[106]Epictetus II. xxi. 12, indicates that the students depended on
supplies from home.

[107]Cf. Hijmans, "ΑΣΚΗΣΙΣ, p. 3.

[108]Epictetus II. xxi. 14.

[109]Cf. Epictetus I. x. 2; I. xi. 1; II. iv. 1; II. xiv. 1; III. iv. 1;
III. vii. 1.

[110]Epictetus I. xxvi. 13.

[111]Epictetus I. xxi; cf. Hijmans, "ΑΣΚΗΣΙΣ, p. 43.

[112]Epictetus II. xix. 17ff; and I. xxx. The reference to God as
"Another [who] looks from above on what is taking place," (ἄλλος ἄνωθεν
βλέπει τὰ γιγνόμενα) provides interesting background for the use of ἄνωθεν
in John and in James.

[113]Epictetus IV. iii. 12:
"These are the laws that have been sent you from God, these are His
ordinances; it is of these you ought to become an interpreter, to these
you ought to subject yourself, not the laws of Masurius and Cassius."
οὗτοί εἰσιν οἱ ἐκεῖθεν ἀπεσταλμένοι νόμοι, ταῦτα τὰ διατάγματα· τούτων
ἐξηγητὴν δεῖ γενέσθαι, τούτοις ὑποτεταγμένον, οὐ τοῖς Μασουρίου καὶ Κασσίου.
Similar examples of the use of the passive to denote the activity of God may
be found in the New Testament (cf. John 3:28).

From the discourses one may also reconstruct an impression of the curriculum and daily activity of the school. The reading and interpretation of philosophical works (especially the writings of Chrysippus) were the primary classroom exercises. The students read at home, and while they occasionally gave interpretations in class, most of the work of interpreting fell to Epictetus.[114] He prepared carefully for this task and appears to have depended chiefly upon the earlier Stoics for his own philosophical position.[115] The diatribes preserved by Arrian probably grew out of his comments on the readings. The students also wrote essays which were read by their tutors.[116] The tutors were responsible for supervising the students' progress in their ability to work problems in logic.[117] Whether the main sessions were held in the morning or afternoon is not clear, but after a day at school most of the students lit their lamps and worked some in the evening.[118]

In order to perceive Epictetus' basic interest in education one must look behind the daily routine of readings and interpretations. Epictetus states his attitude toward this activity clearly:

> If, however, I admire the mere act of interpretation, what have I done but turned into a grammarian instead of a philosopher? The only difference, indeed, is that I interpret Chrysippus instead of Homer.[119]

For Epictetus education was more than merely learning the history of philosophy;[120] the end of education was the acquisition of virtue through disciplining one's rational abilities.[121] One of his favorite analogies appears to have been that ". . .

---

[114]Cf. Epictetus I. x. 8; III. xxi. 7; Oldfather, *Epictetus*, p. xiv.

[115]von Arnim, "Epiktetos," *RE*, VI, 129.

[116]Epictetus II. i. 34-35; III. xxvi. 3; IV. v. 36.

[117]Epictetus I. vii. 1-4; I. vii. 32; II. xiii. 21; II. xvii. 27.

[118]Epictetus II. xxi. 19. For further discussion of the curriculum and exercises see: Hijmans, "ΑΣΚΗΣΙΣ, pp. 41-48; Clarke, *Higher Education*, pp. 88-91.

[119]Epictetus *Encheiridion* 49:
ἂν δὲ αὐτὸ τοῦτο τὸ ἐξηγεῖσθαι θαυμάσω, τί ἄλλο ἢ γραμματικὸς ἀπετελέσθην ἀντὶ φιλοσόφου; πλήν γε δὴ ὅτι ἀντὶ Ὁμήρου Χρύσιππον ἐξηγούμενος.

[120]Cf. Epictetus II. vi. 23; II. xxi. 10; II. xvii. 24; Dudley, *A History of Cynicism*, pp. 190-99.

[121]Epictetus III. xxi. 8-9; cf. Hijmans, "ΑΣΚΗΣΙΣ, p. 36: "To the old and famous question whether virtue could be learnt Epictetus unhesitatingly would answer: 'Yes'."

140

the lecture-room of the philosopher is a hospital; . . ."[122]
He viewed his students as men who had come to a clinic in
order to cure their souls.[123] Moral training was thus more
important than the mere acquisition of theoretical knowledge.
Socrates appears to have become for Epictetus the exemplary
Wise Man whose attributes he and his students emulated.[124]
Fellowship within the school provided the context for this
growth of character, and the prayers and hymns quoted by
Epictetus may have been used in the context of worship at the
school.[125] This emphasis on the acquisition of virtue, the
cure of the soul, and one's duties to God makes the school of
Epictetus extremely important for the study of the development
of Christian schools.[126]

Epictetus was a friend of Hadrian and was studied by
Marcus Aurelius.[127] Paradoxically, however, he seems to have
had no worthy successors at his school:

> No outstanding pupils, that we know of, . . . were trained
> by Epictetus' school. Nor, if we may believe Epictetus
> himself, did he manage to exercise any of his pupils to
> virtue with really outstanding results.[128]

Nor is there any record of the school after his death.

During Epictetus' life, Stoicism was very popular both
among the Romans and in the Greek-speaking areas of the

---

[122]Epictetus III. xxiii. 30: Ἰατρεῖόν ἐστιν, . . . , τὸ τοῦ
φιλοσόφου σχολεῖον·

[123]Epictetus II. xxi. 15-22; II. xix. 29.

[124]Hijmans, "ΑΣΚΗΣΙΣ, p. 76; cf. Oldfather, *Epictetus*, index, *s.v.*
Socrates.

[125]The prayer in Epictetus II. xvi. 41-42, and the hymn of praise in
I. xvi. 16-17, may have been used regularly. Regarding the hymn, Epictetus
states: "This is what we ought to sing on every occasion, and above all to
sing the greatest and divinest hymn, that God has given us the faculty to
comprehend these things and to follow the path of reason."
ταῦτα ἐφ' ἑκάστου ἐφυμνεῖν ἔδει καὶ τὸν μέγιστον καὶ θειότατον ὕμνον
ἐφυμνεῖν, ὅτι τὴν δύναμιν ἔδωκεν τὴν παρακολουθητικὴν τούτοις καὶ ὁδῷ
χρηστικήν.
Cf. Epictetus II. xvii. 29.

[126]Cf. Plutarch *Moralia* 7DF. Clarke's comment on this passage is
equally applicable to some aspects of Epictetus' curriculum:
"This hardly suggests the syllabus of a philosophy department in a modern university; much of it reminds one rather of what the Church
catechism teaches about man's duty towards his neighbour. A philosopher's school indeed had something of the character of a Confirmation
class." (*Higher Education*, p. 96.)

[127]Cf. Oldfather, *Epictetus*, p. xxvii; Xenakis, *Epictetus*, pp. 10-11.

[128]Hijmans, "ΑΣΚΗΣΙΣ, p. 48.

Empire.[129] Lucian (b. *ca.* A.D. 120) claimed that the Stoics were the most numerous of the philosophers.[130] During the second century, however, Stoicism began to decline and was soon absorbed by Neo-Platonism.

The influence of the Stoa

Stoicism did not die before it left a profound impression on the culture within which Christianity emerged and spread. The influence of this philosophy can perhaps be traced most clearly at Tarsus. Strabo's testimony may not be exaggerated;

> The people of Tarsus have devoted themselves so eagerly, not only to philosophy, but also to the whole of education in general, that they have surpassed Athens, Alexandria, or any other place that can be named where there have been schools and lectures of philosophers.[131]

Strabo adds that most of those who studied there were natives, and even they had a tendency to finish their education elsewhere. He lists the famous Stoics who were natives of Tarsus: Antipater (2nd c. B.C.), Archedemus, Nestor, and the two Athenodoruses.[132] Juvenal (A.D. 50/65 - after 127) mentions a Stoic named Barea who was born at Tarsus,[133] and Philostratus (*ca.* A.D. 170 - 244/9) claims that Apollonius of Tyana studied at Aegae, a town near Tarsus where there was a more serious school of study and where he could meet philosophers of every stripe.[134]

A disproportionately large number of Stoic philosophers came from Semitic backgrounds. These philosophers probably indicate both the ease with which certain Stoic doctrines could be assimilated to Jewish thought and the rising popularity which Stoic thought enjoyed in Syria and Palestine during the third and second centuries B.C. Hengel calls the popularity of Stoic thought from Ben-Sira and Aristobulus to Philo an "orientalische Rückinterpretation" of Stoicism.[135] Specific

---

[129]Cf. Clarke, *Higher Education*, p. 81-82.

[130]Lucian *Hermotimus* 16.

[131]Strabo XIV. v. 13:

Τοσαύτη δὲ τοῖς ἐνθάδε ἀνθρώποις σπουδὴ πρός τε φιλοσοφίαν καὶ τὴν ἄλλην παιδείαν ἐγκύκλιον ἅπασαν γέγονεν, ὥσθ' ὑπερβέβληνται καὶ Ἀθήνας καὶ Ἀλεξάνδρειαν καὶ εἴ τινα ἄλλον τόπον δυνατὸν εἰπεῖν, ἐν ᾧ σχολαὶ καὶ διατριβαὶ φιλοσόφων γεγόνασι.

[132]Strabo XIV. v. 14.

[133]Juvenal *Satire* III. 116-17.

[134]Philostratus *VA* I. vii.

[135]Hengel, *Judentum und Hellenismus*, p. 268.

142

points of contact can be observed. Athenaeus preserves the
tradition that Alexander Balas, the pretender who ruled Syria
from 150 to 145 B.C., ". . . delighted in the doctrines of the
Stoics,"[136] and recent work has sought to clarify traces of
Stoic thought in Ben-Sira. Hengel discusses conceptual parallels between the Stoics and Ben-Sira and concludes that
Ben-Sira's opponents and students were Palestinian Jews for
whom Hellenistic thought and culture were a danger.[137] Raymond
Pautrel reaches a similar conclusion: "L'influence de
l'hellénisme, sous la forme du stoïcisme, est vraisemblable
dans son oeuvre."[138] That Stoicism exercised some influence
on Jewish thought during the third and second centuries B.C.
appears highly probable. It is likely, however, that while
many elements of Stoic thought were more useful to Jewish
teachers than Epicurean doctrines, Stoicism probably had less
influence on the development and organization of Jewish schools
than did Epicureanism.[139]

To the extent that the Jewish milieu which influenced
John had made use of Stoic thought one might argue for an
indirect influence of Stoicism on the Gospel of John. Attempts
to argue for a more direct and significant influence have
usually focused on the *logos* concept in the prologue. J. Rendel
Harris, for example, found Stoic influence on the prologue by
tracing Stoic influence on the seventh chapter of the Wisdom
of Solomon and then noting the similarities between this chapter and the prologue to John.[140] Nevertheless, arguments for
anything more than a superficial resemblance to Stoic thought
have found little acceptance.[141] This study does not seek to
re-open the question of the influence of Stoic thought on the
Gospel of John, but asks: what role did the Stoa play in the
development of ancient schools which may have been models for
the Johannine community? This chapter concludes the study of

---

[136]Athenaeus V. 211b: . . . τοῖς ἀπὸ τῆς στοᾶς λόγοις χαίρουντι.

[137]Hengel, *Judentum und Hellenismus*, p. 270; cf. pp. 160, 265-70.

[138]"Ben Sira et le Stoïcisme," *RSR*, LI (1963), 548.

[139]Cf. Henry A. Fischel, "Stoicism," *EncJud*, XV, 410. See also above
pp. 118-20, and below p. 185 for discussion of the influence of Stoicism and
Epicureanism on Jewish schools.

[140]"Stoic Origins of the Prologue of St. John's Gospel," *BJRL*, VI
(1922), 439-51.

[141]Cf. Barrett, *The Gospel According to St. John*, pp. 28-30; Brown,
The Gospel According to John, I, lvii, 519-24.

the philosophical schools and opens the way for an investigation of a selection of Jewish schools founded by individual teachers.

Chapter VII

THE SCHOOL AT QUMRAN

The importance of the
school at Qumran

A subtle shift occurs when one moves from an examination
of the philosophical schools to the Jewish school at Qumran.
The change in the atmosphere of the primary documents is
unmistakable. Moreover, one moves from the study of schools
long recognized as such to the study of a recently-discovered
community not usually regarded as a school. Thus the question
arises: In what sense may one speak of "the school at Qumran"?
This chapter seeks to demonstrate that we should view the settlement at Qumran as a community organized around a school.

The school at Qumran is important because the documents
it produced shed light on what a sectarian, Jewish school was
like during the period immediately preceding the composition
of the Gospel of John. The literary and conceptual similarities between John and Qumran have received more attention than
the institutional similarities,[1] but this investigation focuses
on the latter. The similarities between the role and functions
of the Teacher of Righteousness (hereafter referred to as TR)
and the Beloved Disciple are particularly striking and provoc-
ative. Both figures occupied places of leadership in their
communities, both were mediators and interpreters of a tradition, both drew about them adherents who followed their teachings, both were venerated by their followers, and the teachings
(and writings?) of each were cherished after their deaths.[2]
Other similarities between the Qumran and Johannine communities
will become apparent below.

While the influence of Qumran on other Jewish schools and
on Christian communities is still being assessed its significance cannot be denied. The Qumran community was the center of

---

[1]J. T. Milik, *Ten Years of Discovery in the Wilderness of Judaea*,
trans. by J. Strugnell, SBT, No. 26 (London: SCM Press, Ltd., 1959), p. 142,
classifies the similarities as follows: "The relations between Essenism and
early Christianity can be considered under three heads: we find literary,
institutional, and doctrinal similarities." (Hereinafter referred to as
Ten Years.) For studies of the literary and doctrinal similarities see esp.:
James H. Charlesworth, ed., *John and Qumran* (London: Geoffrey Chapman,
1972), and the full bibliography therein on pp. 195-204.

[2]Cf. Jürgen Roloff, "Der johanneische 'Lieblingsjünger' und der Lehrer
der Gerechtigkeit," *NTS*, XV (1968), 129-51.

a sect whose literature refers to related camps and settlements in the Judean villages.[3] The Qumran scrolls, therefore, are also an important source for the study of a larger phenomenon --sectarian Judaism.

The sources for the study
of the school at Qumran

The primary sources for this study are the so-called Dead Sea Scrolls, which we may now assume were used by the community at Qumran.[4] Some of the scrolls now published were secret documents, so we know more about the organization and activities of the community than contemporary writers who did not have access to these scrolls.[5] Cave 4 yielded what has been called "the great library" of the community, and the scrolls found in some of the minor caves may have been lent out from it for private use.[6]

The writings of the community provide information about the TR, who was probably the founder of the school and the author of parts of the scrolls.[7] Other scrolls were composed after his death and indicate the way in which the tradition of his teachings continued to shape the life of the community. As was the case with each of the philosophical schools, so with the school at Qumran the traditions about the founder also incidentally inform us about the school. The tradition about the TR is different from that about the philosophers, however, in that our only knowledge of it comes from writings produced by the school itself, and these show little interest in biographical information. There is no identifiable tradition about the TR in sources outside of the school, and aside from his honorific title he is anonymous.

---

[3]CD 14:3ff.; cf. Frank M. Cross, Jr., *The Ancient Library of Qumran and Modern Biblical Studies: The Haskell Lectures 1956-1957* (Rev. ed.; Garden City, N.Y.: Doubleday & Company, 1961), p. 73 n. 33. (Hereinafter referred to as *Ancient Library*.)

[4]See below, p. 160. Unless otherwise indicated the English translation used is that of A. Dupont-Sommer, *The Essene Writings from Qumran*, trans. by G. Vermes (Cleveland: The World Publishing Company, 1961), (Hereinafter referred to as *Essene Writings*) and the Hebrew text cited is that of Eduard Lohse, trans. and ed., *Die Texte aus Qumran: Hebräisch und deutsch* (Munich: Kösel-Verlag, 1964). Volumes of DJD are also referred to concerning the text of crucial passages.

[5]Dupont-Sommer, *Essene Writings*, p. 369.

[6]Cross, *Ancient Library*, pp. 20, 25.

[7]For further discussion of the TR and the writings attributed to him see below, pp. 153-56.

The approximate dates and provenance to which one assigns the various scrolls determine in large measure his understanding of the development and history of the Qumran community. Hence, it is necessary to discuss briefly each of the main sources and note the recent source and form-critical work on them. Because of the scope of the present investigation the work of others in this area will be used to guide our interpretation of the sources.

The Rule of the Community (1QS) is the most important scroll for any study of the community's organization. Two copies of it date from 100-75 B.C.[8] The work is composite in character, and the extant text reflects two early text-types.[9] Hence, the composition of this scroll must date back into the second century B.C. Since the TR is never mentioned, some have suggested that he is the author of 1QS.[10] It is probably better, however, to associate the TR with only the earliest sections of the work. J. Murphy-O'Connor has attempted to demonstrate that the writing evolved through four main stages of development: 1) 1QS 8:1-16a and 9:3-10:8a--the Manifesto for the community written prior to the foundation of Qumran, probably by the TR; 2) 1QS 8:16b-19 and 8:20-9:2--written after the foundation of the community; 3) 1QS 5:1-13a and 5:15b-7:25--sections which reflect the life of a well-developed community; and 4) additions to the basic document: 1QS 1-4, then the final hymn (1QS 9:9-11:22), and finally two interpolations (5:13b-15a and 10:4b and 6a).[11] Even though he assigns the important section 1QS 3:13-4:26 to a late stage of the composition, Murphy-O'Connor agrees with Peter von der Osten-Sacken's conclusion that it is composite and has a long composition-history of its own.[12] Murphy-O'Connor's work is important for this study

---

[8]Cross, *Ancient Library*, p. 119.

[9]Ibid., p. 121.

[10]Ibid.; Milik, *Ten Years*, p. 37; Dupont-Sommer, *Essene Writings*, p. 72.

[11]Jerome Murphy-O'Connor, "La genèse littéraire de la Règle de la Communauté," *RB*, LXXVI (1969), 528-49. One may argue that Murphy-O'Connor has forced the composition-history of 1QS to conform to the history of the community as reconstructed by Cross and R. de Vaux, but his identification of the Manifesto for the community as the earliest part of the scroll is still probably correct.

[12]Cf. Peter von der Osten-Sacken, *Gott und Belial: Traditionsgeschichtliche Untersuchungen zum Dualismus in den Texten aus Qumran*, SUNT, Bd. VI (Göttingen: Vandenhoeck & Ruprecht, 1969), pp. 168-69.

148

because if he is correct in separating Stage 1 from the later
stages, then 1QS contains both the Manifesto written prior to
foundation of the community and sections reflecting various
stages of the community's development.[13]

The problems relating to the interpretation of the
Damascus Document (CD) are so complex that no attempt can be
made here to resolve them. Nevertheless, some indication must
be given of the recent work on this perplexing document so
that assumptions can be made regarding the general provenance
and date of the passages cited below. Seven manuscripts of CD
were found in cave 4 and one in cave 6.[14] The oldest copy dates
from *ca.* 75-50 B.C., and Cross dates the composition of CD at
the end of the second or early in the first century B.C.[15]

A helpful reconstruction of the composition-history of CD
has recently been provided by several form and source-critical
studies by Murphy-O'Connor.[16] His work has not yet been tested
by scholarly cross-examination but can at least be used to
identify the way in which passages important for the present
study relate to other sections of the document. The
composition-history of CD reconstructed by Murphy-O'Connor may
be divided into the following five stages. Early in the
Maccabean period a group of exiles returned to Judah.[17] This
group's return was prompted by the promising developments of
the Maccabean revolt. From this group derive two independent
writings (Stage I of the composition of CD): an Essene Mission-

[13]Jürgen Becker, *Das Heil Gottes: Heils- und Sündenbegriffe in den
Qumrantexten und im Neuen Testament*, SUNT, Bd. III (Göttingen: Vandenhoeck
& Ruprecht, 1964), p. 42, similarly finds various stages of the development
of the community reflected in 1QS 5:1-9:11 (10:8): ". . . hier verschiedene
Stadien innerhalb der Entwicklung der Sekte ihren Niederschlag gefunden
haben."

[14]Cross, *Ancient Library*, p. 82.

[15]Ibid., pp. 82-83, 120; cf. Milik, *Ten Years*, p. 58; Géza Vermès,
Discovery in the Judean Desert (New York: Desclee Company, 1956), p. 84.

[16]Jerome Murphy-O'Connor, "An Essene Missionary Document? CD II, 14-
VI, 1," *RB*, LXXVII (1970), 201-29; "A Literary Analysis of Damascus Docu-
ment VI, 2 - VIII, 3," *RB*, LXXVIII (1971), 210-32, "The Original Text of
CD 7:9 - 8:2 = 19:5-14," *HTR*, LXIV (1971), 379-86; "The Critique of the
Princes of Judah (CD VIII, 3-19)," *RB*, LXXIX (1972), 200-16; "The Transla-
tion of Damascus Document VI, 11-14," *RQ*, VII (1971), 553-56; "A Literary
Analysis of Damascus Document XIX, 33 - XX, 34," *RB*, LXXIX (1972), 544-64.
Jerome Murphy-O'Connor, "The Essenes and Their History," *RB*, LXXXI (1974),
215-45, was published after the present work was completed.

[17]At this point Murphy-O'Connor endorses the work of Samuel Iwry,
"Was there a Migration to Damascus? The Problem of שבי ישראל," *Eretz-
Israel*, IX [W. F. Albright Volume, ed. by A. Malamat] (1969), 80-88.

ary Document (CD 2:14-6:1), and a Memorandum setting forth the
group's ordinances (CD 6:11b-8:3a). These writings pre-date
the Manifesto in 1QS. After a period of some disillusionment
in Jerusalem the TR emerged. During this period (Stage II)--
probably in the reign of Jonathan--a Critique of the Princes
of Judah (CD 8:3-18) was written by the TR or one of his
followers.[18] After the foundation of the Qumran community
but still during the lifetime of the TR (Stage III), a section
concerning the reintegration of deliberate sinners (CD 20:1c-
8a) was composed.[19] The date of this pericope corresponds to
that of Stage II of the composition of 1QS. Early in the first
century B.C. (Stage IV), the *Grundschrift* of CD 19:33-20:34
[19:33b-20:1b plus 20:8b-13 plus 20:17b-22b] was written to
defuse discontent and rebellion in the community. The date of
this writing corresponds to that of Stage IV in the composition
of 1QS. Subsequently--in the first quarter of the first century B.C. (Stage V)--a compiler added the introductions (1:1-
2:1 and 2:1-13), an allegorical *pesher* on Numbers 21:18 (CD
6:2-11a) which may have existed as an independent document, and
the conclusion of the Admonition (CD 20:22c-34). The compiler
also added the interpolations (3:15b-16a; 6:10b; 8:19; 19:10a;
20:13c-17a; and 4:19; 8:13). The purpose of the compilation
was to combat defections from the community and bolster its
morale.[20] This reconstruction has the advantage of allowing
for a Babylonian (or at least exilic) origin of Essenism.
"The land of Damascus" may then be interpreted figuratively as
Babylon, the place of exile, or Qumran, the place of withdrawal.[21] Moreover, the discrepancies between the orders of 1QS
and CD are accounted for by relating them to different groups

---

[18]"The Critique of the Princes of Judah (CD VIII, 3-19)," pp. 214-15.

[19]"A Literary Analysis of Damascus Document XIX, 33 - XX, 34," p. 555.

[20]For discussion of this last point see: Murphy-O'Connor, "An Essene
Missionary Document? CD II, 14 - VI, 1," pp. 225-26; "The Critique of the
Princes of Judah (CD VIII, 3-19)," p. 216; "A Literary Analysis of Damascus
Document XIX, 33 - XX, 34," p. 563.

[21]Cf. Charlesworth, *John and Qumran*, p. 104 n. 125; W. D. Davies,
The Gospel and the Land: Early Christianity and Jewish Territorial Doctrine
(Berkeley: University of California Press, 1974), pp. 100, 223 n. 9. Both
writers endorse the latter interpretation of "the land of Damascus" which
was proposed by Cross, *Ancient Library*, pp. 82-83 n. 46; and A. Jaubert,
"Le Pays de Damas," *RB*, LXV (1958), 214-48. Murphy-O'Connor, "The Essenes
and Their History," pp. 221-22, claims that "Damascus" originally meant
Babylon but later was applied also to Qumran.

150

and stages within the movement's history.[22] Ultimately, however, the weight of the literary and linguistic analyses which
buttress Murphy-O'Connor's conclusions can only be appreciated
by firsthand acquaintance with his work.

The next scroll which is important for the study of the
TR and his school is the hymn scroll (1QH). Very early it was
recognized that at least some of the hymns are probably the
work of the TR,[23] and detailed form-critical studies by German
scholars have resulted in an emerging consensus regarding the
hymns which derive from the TR. With only minor differences
concerning the proper beginning or ending of individual hymns,
Gert Jeremias,[24] Jürgen Becker,[25] and Heinz-Wolfgang Kuhn[26]
agree in attributing the following hymns to the TR: 1QH 2:1-
19; 2:31-39; (3:1-18); 4:5-5:4; 5:5-19; 5:20-7:5; 7:6-25; and
8:4-40. Some doubt remains about the inclusion of 3:1-18 in
this group. Becker includes the following also but with reservations: 2:20-30; 3:37-4:4 and 7:1-5.[27]

While the TR's hymns contain no biographical information
beyond what we learn from CD and the commentaries, "Sie liessen
uns teilnehmen am geistlichen Leben des Lehrers."[28] The hymns
which do not derive from the TR are characterized by Jeremias
as "Schülerpsalmen,"[29] and by Kuhn as "Bekenntnislieder des
Frommen" or more simply as "Gemeindelieder."[30] With the hymns
of the community Kuhn includes the hymn at the conclusion of
1QS (10:9-11:22),[31] and postulates that they were first used in

[22]Cf. Cross, *Ancient Library*, p. 83 n. 46. For comparison of the
similarities and differences between the ordinances of 1QS and CD see:
Vermès, *Discovery in the Judean Desert*, pp. 43-48.

[23]See for example: Milik, *Ten Years*, p. 40; Dupont-Sommer, *Essene Writings*, p. 200.

[24]*Der Lehrer der Gerechtigkeit*, SUNT, Bd. II (Göttingen: Vandenhoeck & Ruprecht, 1963), esp. p. 171.

[25]*Das Heil Gottes*, pp. 50-56.

[26]*Enderwartung und gegenwärtiges Heil: Untersuchungen zu den Gemeindeliedern von Qumran*, SUNT, Bd. IV (Göttingen: Vandenhoeck & Ruprecht, 1966), esp. p. 23.

[27]*Das Heil Gottes*, pp. 53-54.

[28]Jeremias, *Der Lehrer der Gerechtigkeit*, p. 266.

[29]Ibid., p. 171.

[30]*Enderwartung und gegenwärtiges Heil*, pp. 24-25.

[31]Ibid., p. 11.

connection with admission into the community at the yearly
covenant-renewal celebration ("Bundeserneuerungsfest") and
then were carried over into use at "die täglichen Gebets-
zeiten."[32] These observations regarding the authorship and
use of the hymns in 1QH provide additional help in classifying
and dating passages which illuminate the school at Qumran.

The Biblical commentaries, *pesharim*, also provide important information. They show that members of the community
searched the Scriptures and related their interpretation to
the life and teachings of the TR. This method of exegesis,
pesher, is distinctively Qumranic, and the commentaries contain ". . . a body of traditional exegesis, . . ." which
developed within the community and was committed to writing
only late in its history.[33] The commentaries also reflect a
great reverence for the TR and the tradition of his teachings.[34]
The earliest commentary is 4Q Testimonia. Cross claims that it
was written by the same scribe who copied 1QS in the first
quarter of the first century B.C. and that most of the other
commentaries are autographs dating from 50 B.C. to A.D. 50.[35]
Cross's conclusions have been contested, however, and the
important Habakkuk commentary in particular has been assigned
various dates.[36] For the purposes of the present study it is
sufficient to regard the commentaries (with the exception of
4Q Testimonia) as late but containing a body of traditional
exegesis and reflecting a high regard for the place of the TR
in the sect's history.

---

[32]Ibid., pp. 31-32.

[33]Cross, *Ancient Library*, pp. 94, 115; F. M. Cross, "The Early History
of the Qumran Community," in *New Directions in Biblical Archaeology*, ed. by
D. N. Freedman and J. C. Jonas (Garden City, N. Y.: Doubleday & Company,
Inc., 1971), p. 79.

[34]Cf. Jeremias, *Der Lehrer der Gerechtigkeit*, p. 151; Dupont-Sommer,
Essene Writings, p. 258.

[35]*Ancient Library*, p. 114; cf. Milik, *Ten Years*, p. 61, who also
dates 4Q Testimonia between 100 and 75 B.C.

[36]E. Hammershaimb, "On the Method Applied in the Copying of Manuscripts in Qumran," *VT*, IX (1959), 417, finds it "difficult to imagine"
the commentaries (and specifically 1QpHab) to be autographs. Some of the
dates proposed for the composition of 1QpHab are: Vermès, *Discovery in
the Judean Desert*, p. 84--between 65 and 63 B.C.; Kurt Schubert, *The Dead
Sea Community: Its Origin and Teachings* (New York: Harper and Brothers,
1959), p. 96--before 63 B.C.; Becker, *Das Heil Gottes*, p. 39--after 63 B.C.;
Dupont-Sommer, *Essene Writings*, p. 349--about 40 B.C.; Milik, *Ten Years*,
p. 64--"On the whole, the script appears to be of the first half of the
first century A.D."

Philo, Josephus, Pliny the Elder, and Hippolytus also provide descriptions of the Essenes.[37] These sources supplement our knowledge of the school at Qumran in only a few instances and must be regarded as secondary to the Qumran scrolls. Still, the classical sources may be used on the assumption that the Qumran community was Essene. This assumption may now be made without further argument.[38]

The origin of the school at Qumran

Many dates have been proposed for the life of the TR and the establishment of the community at Qumran. The arguments usually proceed by attempting to identify the Wicked Priest as one or another known figure and fixing the date of his contemporary, the TR, accordingly. The importance of the archaeological and paleographic controls emphasized by Cross have further enhanced our ability to fix the date of the foundation of the Qumran community.[39] Theories regarding the identity of the Wicked Priest still abound, however.[40] Two considerations allow us to skirt the complexities of this issue: 1) The identification of the Wicked Priest as Jonathan corresponds best with the literary evidence, the archaeological and paleographic controls, and our understanding of the historical events of the period;[41] and 2) neither the identity of the Wicked Priest nor the exact date of the foundation of the community are crucial for the study of the nature of the school at Qumran. Suffice it to say that the Wicked Priest is here understood to be Jonathan (152-143 B.C.) and that the conflict with the TR took place during these years with the foundation of the community at Qumran following shortly thereafter.

---

[37]Cf. Alfred Adam, ed., *Antike Berichte über die Essener*, Kleine Texte für Vorlesungen und Übungen, 182 (Berlin: Verlag Walter de Gruyter & Co., 1961).

[38]Cf. Cross, *Ancient Library*, pp. 51, 57; Cross, "The Early History of the Qumran Community," p. 77; Dupont-Sommer, *Essene Writings*, pp. 11-14.

[39]"The Early History of the Qumran Community," pp. 70-75.

[40]For a convenient overview of the most viable theories see: Géza Vermès, *The Dead Sea Scrolls in English* (Baltimore: Penguin Books, 1962), pp. 57-58.

[41]Cf. Milik, *Ten Years*, p. 85; Vermès, *Discovery in the Judean Desert*, pp. 90-91; Jeremias, *Der Lehrer der Gerechtigkeit*, pp. 75-76; Murphy-O'Connor, "The Critique of the Princes of Judah (CD VIII, 3-19)," p. 214. Cross identifies the Wicked Priest as Jonathan and the persecutor as Simon; *Ancient Library*, p. 134; "The Early History of the Qumran Community," pp. 86-87.

The origin of the school is closely related to the career of the elusive figure known to us only as the Teacher of Righteousness. The title (מורה הצדק[42]), which may also by translated "Righteous Teacher,"[43] was probably derived from Hosea 10:12 and Joel 2:23,[44] and its application to this otherwise anonymous figure reflects the esteem and veneration accorded him by the community.[45] Some scholars[46] have held that this title denotes an office and was applied to various persons, but the convergence of three lines of evidence indicates that the TR was a particular individual who exercised great influence on the community: 1) expressions of an individual teacher in 1QH, 2) the community's veneration of the TR as the individual through whom the secrets of the scriptures are disclosed,[47] and 3) clues to the TR's career in 1QpHab and CD.

The TR was a priest from the Zadokite lineage,[48] and his conflicts with the Wicked Priest concerned the temple cult.[49] The function of the TR as teacher is discussed below,[50] but it is relevant here to note that teaching was a "priestly function."[51]

We have no information about the first contact of the TR with the Essene movement. The movement could trace its history

---

[42]1QpHab 1:13; 2:2; 5:10; 7:4; 8:3; 9:9; 11:5; 4QpPs37 2:15(?); CD 1:11; 20:32.

[43]Cf. Jeremias, *Der Lehrer der Gerechtigkeit*, pp. 308-18, esp. p. 315.

[44]Cf. ibid., pp. 312, 315; Cross, "The Early History of the Qumran Community," p. 80.

[45]Jeremias, *Der Lehrer der Gerechtigkeit*, p. 166. The anonymity of the TR is particularly interesting because of the parallel with the anonymity of the Beloved Disciple in John and the similar practice among the Pythagoreans of refraining from using their teacher's name. See Dupont-Sommer, *Essene Writings*, pp. 358, 372. The contrast between this practice and the free use of the name of other venerated teachers (Jesus) is striking.

[46]Theodor H. Gaster, *The Dead Sea Scriptures* (Rev. ed.; Garden City, N. Y.: Doubleday & Company, Inc., 1964), pp. vi, 6, 30-31; George W. Buchanan, "The Priestly Teacher of Righteousness," *RQ*, VI (1969), 558.

[47]1QpHab 7:4-5; cf. Geza Vermes, "The Qumran Interpretation of Scripture in its Historical Setting," *ALUOS*, VI, (1966-1968), 87 and 91.

[48]1QpHab 2:8; 4QpPs37 2:15.

[49]Cf. Georg Klinzing, *Die Umdeutung des Kultus in der Qumrangemeinde und im Neuen Testament*, SUNT, Bd. VII (Göttingen: Vandenhoeck & Ruprecht, 1971), p. 11: "In Jerusalem und am Tempel müssen die ersten Auseinandersetzung zwischen dem Lehrer der Gerechtigkeit und seinem Gegenspieler, dem Frevelpriester, stattgefunden haben."

[50]See below, pp. 154, 162, 163, 169.

[51]Cross, *Ancient Library*, p. 225.

for at least twenty years prior to the emergence of the TR,[52] and the "former ordinances" have been interpreted as those precepts which guided the movement prior to his ministry.[53] One may conjecture that the TR was a priestly teacher in Jerusalem before he (and his students?) joined the (Essene) returnees.

> We may take it for granted that a school of copyists, or several schools, were connected with the centre of post-Exilic Judaism, the Jerusalem Temple.[1] . . . However, we know very little about the way in which these priestly and levitical schools functioned during the period of the Temple. It is possible that the Qumran scriptorium can be taken as a smaller version of the comparative phenomenon in the Jerusalem Temple.

> _____
> [1]Cf. Jer. 36,10, 20f., Josephus, *Ant.* 11.5.1: γραμματεῖς τοῦ ἱεροῦ [Cf. Josephus *Ant.* XII. 142; I Esdras 8:22].[54]

His teaching eventually provoked a conflict with the Wicked Priest, the following lines from the Essene Missionary Document (CD 2:14-6:1) may summarize the issues involved:

> . . . His holy Sabbaths and His glorious feasts, His testimony of righteousness, and his ways of Truth, and the desires of His will which man must fulfill that he may live by them.[55]

Eventually the conflict grew so intense that the TR and his followers withdrew from the temple in Jerusalem. At this point there was a schism among the followers of the TR; a group led by the Man of Lies (cf. 1QpHab 2:1ff. איש הכזב) could not reconcile separation from the temple with their obedience to the

_____

[52]CD 1:10; cf. Milik, *Ten Years*, p. 74.

[53]CD 20:31; cf. Murphy-O'Connor, "La genèse littéraire de la Règle de la Communauté," p. 531; "A Literary Analysis of Damascus Document XIX, 33 - XX, 34," p. 548.

[54]Gerhardsson, *Memory and Manuscript*, p. 50. See the references to the *bet hammidrash* at the temple in Tosefta Sanhedrin 7:1 and Tosefta Baba Batra 21a. Cf. Jeremias, *Jerusalem in the Time of Jesus*, p. 233: "In Jerusalem before AD 70 we can prove the existence of a large number of priests who were scribes (pp. 207, 243 n. 32)." See also Hengel, *Judentum und Hellenismus*, p. 144 n. 155; and the contributions of Iwry and Murphy-O'Connor discussed above, pp. 147-49. That the TR taught and wrote after his association with the Essene movement is clear; it is conceivable that he also engaged in these activities earlier in his career in Jerusalem.

[55]CD 3:14-16:

שבחות קדשו ומועדי כבודו עידות צדקו ודרכי אמתו וחפצי רצונו אשר יעשה האדם וחיה בהם

(Translation adapted from Dupont-Sommer; cf. above p. 146 n. 4). Cf. Jeremias, *Der Lehrer der Gerechtigkeit*, p. 166.

Law.[56] In order to study Torah and escape persecution, the TR
led his followers into the wilderness and established the settlement at Qumran.[57] Assuming that the TR or one of his
followers wrote the Manifesto (1QS 8:1-16a and 9:3-10:8a),[58]
it is possible that the training period of two years was
observed by the TR and his followers. The following statement
by Edmund F. Sutcliffe offers a plausible interpretation of the
first part of the Manifesto:

> These texts take the reader back to the time before the
> settlement at Qumran. Before a commencement could be made
> there (at least) fifteen men had to be trained to the new
> manner of life for two years, the period fixed for the dura-
> tion of the noviceship of future candidates. The Congrega-
> tion as a whole already existed consisting mainly, in all
> probability, of married men. Now within the framework of
> the larger society a stricter form of life was to be intro-
> duced for volunteers willing to undertake it. The leader
> of this group of pioneers would be the founder, the person-
> age commonly known today as the Teacher of Righteousness or,
> more accurately, the Authorized Teacher.[59]

Thus, the TR moved his followers (and school?) to the wilderness and founded there the Qumran community.

---

[56]Jeremias, *Der Lehrer der Gerechtigkeit*, p. 126. This reconstruction
of the schism between the followers of the Man of Lies and the followers
of the TR is similar to that proposed by Hartmut Stegemann, *Die Entstehung
der Qumrangemeinde* (Bonn: Rheinische Friedrich-Wilhelms-Universität, 1971),
pp. 225-26. Murphy-O'Connor, "The Essenes and Their History," pp. 233-38,
responds that the Essenes had already separated from the temple; the issue
between the TR and the Man of Lies was the TR's demand for rigorism and
withdrawal to the wilderness.

[57]Although Vermès, *Discovery in the Judean Desert*, p. 100, proposes
an alternative reconstruction of these events, Cross, *Ancient Library*, p.
122, confidently concludes: "All evidence points to the assumption that
the Teacher led his flock into the desert, ..." See, for example, CD
20:22-23; note the references to the TR in the same context in CD 20:14,
28, 32. Shemaryahu Talmon, "The 'Desert Motif' in the Bible and in Qumran
Literature," in *Biblical Motifs: Origins and Transformations*, ed. by A.
Altmann, P. W. Lown Institute of Advanced Judaic Studies, Brandeis University, Studies and Texts, Vol. III (Cambridge, Mass.: Harvard University
Press, 1966), pp. 62-63, concludes that the original purpose of the flight
to the desert was to escape persecution; later the desert became a place of
purification and preparation for the goal of taking Jerusalem and reestab-
lishing the temple cult. However, see the discussion of 1QS 8:10c-16a
(below, p. 161), which emphasizes that the community went to the desert to
study Torah.

[58]See above, p. 147.

[59]"The First Fifteen Members of the Qumran Community: A Note on 1QS
8:1ff," *JSS*, IV (1959), 137-38. This interpretation is endorsed by Murphy-
O'Connor, "La genèse littéraire de la Règle de la Communauté," p. 529.
William S. LaSor, *The Dead Sea Scrolls and the New Testament* (Grand Rapids,
Mich.: William B. Eerdmans Publishing Company, 1972), p. 217, asserts that
there is no indication that the "council of Twelve (1QS 8:1)" received
"special instruction." The twelve (probably fifteen) did receive "special
instruction"; see below, p. 162 and CD 4:8.

Before undertaking an examination of the evidence which suggests that the community was organized around a school, it may be well to consider how the TR compares with the founders of the philosophical schools. Both the philosophers considered above and Jesus founded their movements (or sects) as well as their schools. The TR founded only the latter;[60] he was the founder of the Qumran community,[61] but he was not the founder of the Essene movement.[62]

The nature of the
school at Qumran

Three independent lines of evidence support the conclusion that there was a school at Qumran: the archaeological, scribal, and literary data. The archaeological evidence provides a context for the other data. Hence, it will be considered first.

The settlement at Qumran was no ordinary village. Cross describes it as follows:

> Khirbet Qumran proved to be the hub of a Hellenistic-Roman occupation spreading nearly two miles north along the cliffs, and some two miles south to the agricultural complex at 'En Feskhah. The people of this broad settlement lived in caves, tents, and solid constructions, but shared pottery made in a common kiln, read common biblical and sectarian scrolls, operated a common irrigation system, and, as we shall see, depended on common stores of food and water furnished by the installations of the community center.[63]

The scrolls discovered in the nearby caves are now generally associated with the ruins at Qumran.[64]

---

[60]See the discussion of the terms "sect" and "school" below, pp. 258-59. The position taken here is substantially in agreement with that of W. D. Davies, *The Setting of the Sermon on the Mount* (Cambridge: At the University Press, 1966), pp. 216-17. (Hereinafter referred to as *Setting*.) Note that the parallel between the TR and the Beloved Disciple is closer than that between the TR and Jesus; both probably founded their schools but not the movements to which their schools belonged.

[61]Cf. Cross, *Ancient Library*, pp. 113, 122; Pierre Benoit, "Qumran and the New Testament," in *Paul and Qumran: Studies in New Testament Exegesis*, ed. by J. Murphy-O'Connor (Chicago: The Priory Press, 1968), p. 11; Krister Stendahl, "The Scrolls and the New Testament: An Introduction and a Perspective," in *The Scrolls and the New Testament*, ed. by K. Stendahl (New York: Harper & Brothers, 1957), p. 12; Jeremias, *Der Lehrer der Gerechtigkeit*, p. 148; and Becker, *Das Heil Gottes*, p. 56 n. 1, cites 1QH 3:7ff.; 5:8f.; 5:23-26; 6:19; 7:10, 17-24; 8:10ff. as evidence.

[62]See above, p. 154.

[63]*Ancient Library*, p. 57.

[64]Malachi Martin, *The Scribal Character of the Dead Sea Scrolls*, Bibliothèque de Muséon, vols. XLIV and XLV (Louvain: Université de Louvain Institut Orientaliste, 1958), I, 385, summarizes the evidence for this association.

The identification of the so-called "scriptorium" is especially important for this study. In 1953, a long "table" and one or two smaller "tables" with "benches" and two inkpots were discovered. Roland de Vaux proposed that the room in which these items were found was a scriptorium--perhaps the scriptorium in which the scrolls were copied.[65] While this identification is widely accepted,[66] there has been some discussion of the function of the furniture[67] and the methods of copying.[68] G. R. Driver rejected the identification of the scriptorium proposing that the tables were refectory tables, not writing tables.[69] D. Winton Thomas has also rejected the conclusion that the scrolls were penned in the scriptorium, but his argument founders under the weight of the evidence:

> The three ink wells found in the room have seemed to some to support the belief that the room was a *scriptorium*. Many other ink wells may, of course, have perished, but three are hardly impressive testimony to so great literary activity as is attested by the scrolls. *The fact that the traces of ink in them show that the ink is the same as that used in the scrolls* proves nothing, for the ink was probably of a kind in common use at the time.[70]

For the present the burden of proof is on those who reject the designation "scriptorium." In addition to the "tables" and ink wells, an ostracon bearing the letters of an inexperienced hand was found. Probably it is the work of an apprentice being trained at Qumran.[71] Such a conjecture is not unreasonable in view of the unlikelihood that secular scribes were used to copy the secret scrolls of the sect. Apprentices were probably trained to take over this work from their elders. In short,

---

[65]R. de Vaux, "Fouilles au Khirbet Qumrân," *RB*, LXI (1954), 212; R. P. de Vaux, "La seconde saison de fouilles a Khirbet Qumrân," *CRAI*, (1953), 319, concludes that there was "un collège de scribes" at Qumran; cf. R. de Vaux, *Archaeology and The Dead Sea Scrolls* (London: Oxford University Press, 1973), pp. 30-33.

[66]Cf. Cross, *Ancient Library*, p. 67; Milik, *Ten Years*, p. 22; Dupont-Sommer, *Essene Writings*, p. 63.

[67]Bruce M. Metzger, "The Furniture in the Scriptorium at Qumran," *RQ*, I (1958-59), 509-15, suggests that the "tables" were really benches on which the scribes sat. The "benches" were footrests used to raise their knees to a better position for supporting a writing tablet.

[68]Hammershaimb, "On the Method Applied in the Copying of Manuscripts in Qumran," pp. 415-18. See below, p. 158.

[69]"Myths of Qumran," *ALUOS*, VI (1966-1968), 23-27.

[70]"The Dead Sea Scrolls: What May We Believe?" *ALUOS*, VI (1966-1968), 10. My italics.

[71]Cf. Dupont-Sommer, *Essene Writings*, p. 63; Milik, *Ten Years*, p. 23.

158

the archaeological evidence, while not conclusive, supports
the hypothesis that there was a scriptorium at Qumran in which
the scrolls were written.[72]

Analysis of the scribal character of the scrolls provides
an independent line of evidence for a school at Qumran. M.
Martin's ground-breaking work studies the scribal character of
six scrolls from cave 1 (1QIs[a], 1QIs[b], 1QS, 1QM, 1QH, and
1QpHab).[73] The author carefully analyzes the handwriting,
methods of presentation, use of *wau*, orthography, and methods of
scribal revision. He finds that thirteen scribes participated
in the production of the six scrolls, and several collaborated
with one another on individual scrolls.[74] Some of the scrolls,
for example 1QH, appear to be scribal exercises.[75] Each scribe
displays individual characteristics, but the similarity of their
methods of presentation ". . . leads to the general conclusions
that all thirteen scribes are tributary to some specific school
of scribal activity, ..."[76] Martin further finds that the
scribes worked as compilers[77]--a conclusion which raises the
question of whether the scribal evidence can be correlated with
the literary analyses of 1QS and CD discussed above. Significantly, Martin finds "a strict unity of scribal tradition" only
among the "organizational texts" (e.g., 1QS and 1QM).[78]

Does Martin's work support the hypothesis that a scribal
school at Qumran produced the scrolls? Martin is very cautious
at this point, claiming that there are difficulties with this
position and that other explanations may account for the scribal
characteristics equally well. The evidence against the scribal-
school-at-Qumran hypothesis is presented as follows:

1. A scribal school, if it existed at Qumran and produced
the Scrolls which we now possess, would have no common and
imposed handwriting style, especially among the primary
scribes of the documents.

---

[72]Cross, *Ancient Library*, p. 67, further suggests that the library of
the community was normally housed near the scriptorium.

[73]*The Scribal Character of the Dead Sea Scrolls*; see I, 30.

[74]Ibid., I, 392, 406.

[75]Ibid., I, 64.

[76]Ibid., I, 406.

[77]Ibid., I, 386-87.

[78]Ibid., I, 394, 407.

2. No specifically sectarian orthography was utilized.
. . . One would, *a priori*, expect a tightly knit group
such as the proposed Community to have their own specific
style.
3. An additional reflection on the last point is provided by the fact that documents like 1QS, 1QM and 1QH are
compilations. No general levelling of orthography is
noticeable. . . .
4. The scribal methods of presentation (. . .) and the
use of such para-textual elements as diacritic points, while
similar in principle, offer no strict unity in practice. . . .
In sum, if a scribal school existed there, it had neither
an imposed and accepted style of presentation nor normative
rules of orthography nor official and fixed methods of
textual indication.[79]

These objections may be answered by adopting an image of the

school with which these observations are compatible. In partic-

ular, the *a priori* expectation referred to in the second point

above may not be correct.

Martin, however, adds three observations which favor the

existence of a school at Qumran:

1. We find that identically the same methods of correc-
tion are used in all manuscripts, ... Now this unity
of revision technique can be taken as a sign of a common
scribal outlook and methodology; we would spontaneously
ascribe the latter to a organized scribal school of some
sort.
2. We find that the scribal history of 1QS (together with
1QS^a and 1QS^b) and 1QH is a complicated one, and that 1QIs^a
has had a very long one. 1QS (1QS^a and 1QS^b) was written
by two scribes who worked alternatively and collaborated
mutually and successively and the final form of the document
was fixed by a third hand which we have tentatively identified with Hand B of 1QpHab. 1QH is the work of three scribes
who worked near each other in time and space, and Hand B can
be regarded as some sort of master-scribe or general censor
and revisor. . . . And the proposed historical framework
of the Qumran settlement allows for such a considerable
lapse of time.
3. It is a noticeable fact that *official phonetic* is practically confined to the 'organizational' texts, to certain
hymns and to the second half 1QI^a [sic]. . . . It is, then,
possible to conclude that this heterogeneity of the texts
corresponds more or less to the historical evolution through
which they passed.[80]

Martin's reticence to conclude that there was a scribal school

at Qumran should be tempered by the following considerations:

1) Martin is overly influenced by Del Medico's "depository

theory"[81] and hence does not allow sufficiently for what we

----

[79]Ibid., II, 709-10.

[80]Ibid., II, 710-11.

[81]H. E. Del Medico, *L'énigme des manuscrits de la Mer morte* (Paris:
Librairie Plon, 1957), pp. 23-27, suggests that the caves served merely as a

know of the historical development of the community; 2) the
founding group probably brought scrolls with them from various
scribal traditions; 3) the earliest scribes at Qumran were
probably not all trained at the same school; 4) if there was
not a school at Qumran, a comparable school must be postulated
to account for the complex relationship of the scribes whose
work in 1QS and 1QH demands the continuous existence of a group
of scribes over a period of time; 5) Martin deals with only
six scrolls from cave 1--a small percentage of the scrolls
found in the area; and 6) further study may provide significant correlations between Martin's work and that of Murphy-
O'Connor, Jeremias, Becker, and Kuhn regarding the compilatory
work reflected in 1QS, 1QH, and CD.[82] The best way to account
for the scribal evidence is to postulate a school of scribes
drawn from different scribal traditions, possibly through the
merging of the followers of the TR with the returnees and by
influxes of new members.[83] These scribes probably brought
master scrolls of Biblical books[84] and early writings now contained in 1QS and CD and worked for a period of time at Qumran.
Thus, the evidence provided by the scribal character of the
scrolls indicates there was a school at Qumran, one in which
the scrolls were transcribed by a heterogeneous group of
scribes whose work contains a variety of scribal styles and
procedures.

Significant support for a school can also be drawn from
several passages in the scrolls. Three passages have been
chosen for analysis. Each contains many problems which lie
beyond the scope of this study; only the relevant issues can be
dealt with here. Our analysis of the literary evidence can
logically begin with a few lines from the Manifesto:

---

geniza or depository for heterodox scrolls which were not associated with
Qumran. See Dupont-Sommer's devastating critique of Del Medico's position
in his *Essene Writings*, pp. 408-12.

[82]Cf. Stanislav Segert, Review of *The Scribal Character of the Dead
Sea Scrolls*, by Malachi Martin, *RQ*, I, (1958-59), 517-33; II (1959-60), 99-
111. Segert responds (p. 111) that Martin's conclusion regarding the
school at Qumran is "dürftig" and blames Martin's hesitance to embrace the
conclusion that there was a school at Qumran on his "unbegründete Reserve"
regarding the identification of the Qumran community with the Essenes (pp.
700, 708 n. 57).

[83]See below, p. 169 n. 125, regarding the influx of new members (probably Pharisees) following John Hyrcanus' persecution of the Pharisees.

[84]Cf. Cross, *Ancient Library*, p. 42.

When they have established them in the Institution of the Community, in perfection of way, for two years day for day, (11) they shall be set apart (as) holy (persons) within the Council of the members of the Community; and let nothing of that which was hidden from Israel, but found by the Man (12) who sought [or "but which the seeker finds"], be hidden from them out of fear of the spirit of apostasy.

And when these things come to pass for the Community in Israel (13) at these appointed times, they shall be separated from the midst of the habitation of perverse men to go into the desert to prepare the way of 'Him': (14) as it is written,

In the wilderness prepare the way of . . . . Make straight in the desert a highway for our God.

(15) This (way) is the study of the Law which He has promulgated by the hand of Moses, that they may act according to all that is revealed, season by season, and (16) according to that which the Prophets have revealed by His Holy Spirit.[85]

From this section one learns that the purpose of the withdrawal to the desert (Qumran) was to study (דרש) Torah. "They" in lines 10 and 11 refer to the fifteen men mentioned in line 1 who were to be experts on the Law.[86] They are to be set apart from the rest of the community and nothing that is found by the Seeker (הדורש) is to be withheld from them. What was "hidden from Israel"? The answer depends in part on the meaning of "Israel" here. It is important to note that ליחד is written immediately above "Israel,"[87] making it probable that "Israel" here refers to the community rather than to all the people of Israel.[88] "That which is hidden from Israel" may refer either to those portions of scripture normally withheld from the masses of the people[89] or to the secret meaning of scripture found by

---

[85]1QS 8:10c-16a:

בהכין אלה ביסוד היחד שנתים ימים בתמים דרך   11 יבדלו קודש
בתוך עצת אנשי היחד וכול דבר הנסתר מישראל ונמצאו לאיש
12 הדורש אל יסתרהו מאלה מיראת רוח נסוגה ובהיות אלה ליחד
בישראל   13 בתכונים האלה יבדלו מתוך מושב חנשי העול ללכת
למדבר לפנות שם את דרך הואהאא   14 כאשר כתוב במדבר פנו דרך
....יושרו בערבה מסלה לאלוהינו   15 היאה מדרש התורה [אשר]
צוה ביד מושה לעשות ככול הנגלה עת בעת   16 וכאשר גלו הנביאים
ברוח קודשו

[86]Cf. A. R. C. Leaney, *The Rule of Qumran and Its Meaning: Introduction, Translation, and Commentary*, The New Testament Library (Philadelphia: The Westminster Press, 1966), p. 212.

[87]Cf. Millar Burrows, ed., *The Dead Sea Scrolls of St. Mark's Monastery*, Vol. II, Fascicle 2: *Plates and Transcription of the Manual of Discipline* (New Haven: The American Schools of Oriental Research, 1951), *ad loc.*

[88]Cf. W. D. Davies, "'Knowledge' in the Dead Sea Scrolls and Matthew 11:25-30," *HTR*, XLVI (1953), pp. 117-18, esp. n. 17.

[89]Cf. Leaney, *The Rule of Qumran and Its Meaning*, p. 220; Otto Betz, *Offenbarung und Schriftforschung in der Qumransekte*, WUNT, VI (Tübingen: J. C. B. Mohr, 1960), p. 21.

162

the Seeker. The latter is probably the intended meaning,[90] and "the Seeker" probably referred, originally at least, to the TR.[91] The verb "to find" (מצא) refers to discovering the true meaning of the Torah through study (דרש) and revelation (גלה).[92] The TR is the Seeker and Interpreter of Torah par excellence, and all that is "found" by him is to be made known to the inner circle (school) of the community.[93]

Further light is shed upon the nature of the school by CD 6:2-11a:

> And God remembered the Covenant of the Patriarchs
> and raised out of Aaron men of understanding
> and out of Israel (3) sages,
> and He caused them to hear (His voice) and they dug [חפר] the well:
> *The well which the princes dug* [חפר],
> *which* (4) *the nobles of the people delved* [כרה] *with a rod* [Num. 21:18].
> The well is the Law,
> and those who dug [חפר] it (5) are the returnees of Israel
> who had gone out from the land of Judah
> and were exiled in the Land of Damascus;
> (6) all of whom God called princes,
> for they sought [דרש] Him
> and their [glory] is denied (7) by the mouth of no man.
> And the rod (the Lawgiver) is the Seeker of the Law;
> as (8) Isaiah said, *He has made a tool for His work.* [Isa. 54:16]
> And the nobles of the people are they (9) that come to dig [כרה] the well
> with the help of the Lawgiver's precepts,
> (10) that they may walk in them during all the time of wickedness,
> and without which they shall not succeed
> until the coming (11) of the Teacher of Righteousness at the end of days.[94]

---

[90]Cf. Chaim Rabin, *Qumran Studies*, Scripta Judaica, II (Oxford: University Press, 1957), p. 99.

[91]Cf. Betz, *Offenbarung und Schriftforschung in der Qumransekte*, pp. 23-25. See also the discussion of CD 6:2-11 below.

[92]Ibid., pp. 36-37; Rabin, *Qumran Studies*, p. 100. Note the use of the passive of גלה, "to reveal or uncover" in 1QS 5:9, 12; *8:1, 15*; 9:13, 19; CD 3:13.

[93]Cf. Dupont-Sommer, *Essene Writings*, p. 306.

[94]CD 6:2-11a:
ויזכר אל ברית ראשנים ויקם מאהרן נבונים ומישראל 3 חכמים
וישמיעם ויחפורו את הבאר באר חפרוה שרים כרוה 4 נדיבי העם
במחוקק הבאר היא התורה וחופריה הם 5 שבי ישראל היוצאים מארץ
יהודה ויגורו בארץ דמשק 6 אשר קרא אל את כולם שרים כי דרשוהו
ולא הושבה 7 פארתם בפי אחד והמחוקק הוא דורש התורה אשר
8 אמר ישעיה מוציא כלי למעשיהו ונדיבי העם הם 9 הבאים לכרות
את הבאר במחוקקות אשר חקק המחוקק 10 להתהלך במה בכל קץ הרשיע
וזולתם לא ישיגו עד עמד 11 יורה הצדק באחרית הימים

(Translation adapted from Dupont-Sommer.)

This *midrash* on Numbers 21:18 was included in CD by the compiler. It may have been written by the compiler to fit its
present context, or it may have had an independent existence
prior to its inclusion in CD.[95] In either case, it was probably written during the first quarter of the first century B.C.
Numbers 21:18 is here related allegorically to the origins of
the community, but the problems which this *midrash* presents
are numerous and complex.

The principal problem for this study is whether the
"princes" and the "nobles of the people" are synonymous or
refer to different groups. Jeremias claims that they are
synonymous and mean "die Gemeindeglieder."[96] Dupont-Sommer
distinguishes between the two, claiming that the "princes" are
". . . the first disciples of the Teacher, . . ." while the
"nobles of the people" are ". . . those who have continued to
rally to the sect since the Teacher's death and the Damascus
exile."[97] Betz offers a third interpretation: the "nobles of
the people" (from Israel) are the laymen of the sect; the
"princes" (from Aaron) are the priests.[98] This distinction is
supported by the occurrence of the phrase הם שבי ישראל היוצאים
מארץ יהודה in both CD 6:5 and 4:2-3. In the former it refers
to the "princes"; in the latter to the priests (CD 4:2).

Although Betz does not mention it, his position is strengthened by the observation that the only other occurrence of the
verb חפר in CD is in 3:16, and again the subject of the verb
appears to be the priests (4:2). Thus, only the "princes" or
priests חפר the well = Torah. According to this distinction,
only the "princes" study (דרש). The "nobles of the people"
merely keep the Torah according to the teachings of the Seeker.
Again, the Seeker is understood to be the TR.[99] The strongest

---

[95]See above, p. 149.

[96]*Der Lehrer der Gerechtigkeit*, p. 271. Jeremias weakens his case by
citing passages which refer to the "Princes of Judah" (CD 8:3; 19:15), who
are clearly not the "princes" in question here. His strongest support comes
from 1QH 6:14.

[97]*Essene Writings*, p. 131 n. 5.

[98]*Offenbarung und Schriftforschung in der Qumransekte*, p. 26:
"Das Graben der Edlen des Volkes, d. h. der Laien der Sekte, meint das
eifrige Bemühen, die Tora nach der Weisung des Lehrers zu erfüllen. . . .
Der Ausleger interpretiert das Brunnengraben der "Fürsten" als Gottsuche
(דרשוהו Z. 6) und bemerkt dazu, Gott habe alle diese Männer um ihres
frommen Strebens willen "Fürsten" genannt (Z. 6f)."

[99]Jeremias, *Der Lehrer der Gerechtigkeit*, p. 292.

challenge which can be raised against Betz's interpretation
is that line six states that God called "all of them" princes.
This appears to mean that the "nobles of the people" were also
called "princes." Does this mean that there was no difference
in their rank and function within the community? Probably not
(cf. 1QS 2:19-23). By joining with the priests, the "nobles of
the people" also became seekers of God and sons of the "Prince
of Lights" (CD 5:18 and 1QS 3:20). Nevertheless, while they
could be called "princes," they did not share in the rank and
work of the princes = priests; they merely כרה the well (6:9).

The image of the Torah as a well occurs elsewhere,[100] and
the play on בְּאֵר (well) and בָּאֵר (to explain) is clear.[101] The
images hold together beautifully. The "princes" dig (חפר and
דרש) the well (Torah) with the help of the *Mehoqeq's* (Rod or
Lawgiver) precepts (his hermeneutical method?[102]), and from other
passages we learn that "living water" then flows from the well
(cf. Gen. 26:19 and Jub. 24:24-25) and waters (gives life to)
the "eternal plantation,"[103] which is the Qumran community. The
"princes" (members of the school), guided by the Seeker (the
head of the school?), thus interpreted the Law for the rest of
the community. The precepts and interpretations were to remain
binding until the coming of another Teacher at the end of
days.[104] If this interpretation of CD 6:2-11a is correct, it
provides significant evidence for, and of, the role of the
school at Qumran.

1QS 6:6-8a provides further evidence for the distinction
between the school and the rest of the community:

> (6) And in the place where the ten are, let there not lack
> a man who studies the Torah night and day, (7) continually,
> concerning the duties of each towards his friend.

---

[100]Cf. CD 3:16; 19:34; and the discussion and references to this image
in N. Wieder, "The 'Law-Interpreter' of the Sect of the Dead Sea Scrolls:
The Second Moses," *JJS*, IV (1953), 159-61.

[101]Cf. לבאר in 1Q22 2:8 (DJD, I, 93); Betz, *Offenbarung und Schriftforschung in der Qumransekte*, p. 28.

[102]Cf. CD 4:8, and Roloff, "Der johanneische 'Lieblingsjünger' und der
Lehrer der Gerechtigkeit," pp. 147-48.

[103]Cf. 1QH 2:18; and esp. 8:4, 16 *passim*. These references are to
hymns of the TR. See above, p. 150. See also J. H. Charlesworth, "Les Odes
de Salomon et les manuscrits de la Mer Morte," *RB*, LXXVII (1970), 534-38.

[104]The interpretations of CD 6:11 need not detain us here; see the
discussions of the problem by Jeremias, *Der Lehrer der Gerechtigkeit*, pp.
268-307; and A. S. van der Woude, *Die messianischen Vorstellungen der
Gemeinde von Qumrân*, Studia Semitica Neerlandica, III (Assen: Van Gorcum
& Comp. N. V., 1957), pp. 67-74.

> And let the Many watch in common for a third of all the
> nights of the year, to read the Book and study the judgment
> [*mishpat*] (8) and bless in common.[105]

Murphy-O'Connor assigns this section to Stage III in the composition of 1QS--the stage which reflects the life of a well-
developed community.[106] These lines emphasize two features of
the community: 1) that it stressed study, and 2) that study
of the Torah was the duty of a particular group. Only one man
out of the ten studies Torah (דורש בתורה line 6); the others
meditate, read the Torah, and study *mishpat* (the judgments or
rulings made by the school?).[107] Betz clarifies the distinction:

> In Jos. 1,8 und Ps. 1,2 wird die Beschäftigung mit der Tora
> als 'Murmeln, Meditieren' (הגה) angegeben, in 1QS 6,6 steht
> dafür das 'Forschen' (דרש). Diese Änderung ist nicht ohne
> Absicht geschehen; sie liegt darin begründet, dass die
> Begriffe הגה und דרש schaf voneinanderunterschieden werden
> und im Schulbetrieb der Sekte technische Bedeutung erlangt
> haben. הגה bezeichnet den Umgang mit einem Buch, bei dem
> man dessen Inhalt einübt und dem Gedächtnis einprägt, דרש
> meint dagegen das Forschen, das die Deutung der Schrift und
> die Eröffnung der darin verborgenen Geheimnisse zum Ziel
> hat. Das Lernen ist Aufgabe aller, das Forschen Amt eines
> Einzelnen.[108]

It is not clear just how this one man out of ten was related
to the fifteen original experts in the Law or the "princes"
referred to in the above passages. It is improbable, however,
that they worked independently, i.e., with no contact with one
another. The literary evidence clearly points to an emphasis
on serious study of scripture by a few members of the Qumran
community. These interpreters of scripture were guided by the

---

[105]1QS 6:8a:

ואל ימש במקום אשר יהיו שם העשרה איש דורש בתורה יומם ולילה
7 תמיד על יפות איש לרעהו והרבים ישקודו ביחד את שלישית כול לילות
השנה לקרוא בספר ולדרוש משפט   8 ולברך ביחד

(Translation adapted from Dupont-Sommer.) Is רעה in 1QS 6:7 an echo of
the use of φίλος in the Hellenistic school traditions?

[106]See above, p. 147.

[107]Gerhardsson, *Memory and Manuscript*, maintains that there was a
"doctrinal *collegia*" at Qumran (p. 36 n. 82), and that the members of the
sect were required to memorize its rulings (p. 87):
> "Furthermore, the sect had its own strict interpretation of the Law and
> its fixed halakah, [1QS, 1QSa and CD] which was partly laid down in writ-
> ing. We may take it that the members of the sect were compelled to know
> this halakah off by heart." [1QS V.21,23; VI. 18.]
That the school at Qumran functioned as a "doctrinal *collegia*," interpreting
the scripture for the community is probable; but the evidence for claiming
that members of the sect were required to memorize the school's rulings is
not compelling.

[108]*Offenbarung und Schriftforschung in der Qumransekte*, p. 21; cf.
Rabin, *Qumran Studies*, pp. 43-44; and Appendix I below.

principles set forth by the TR. Thus, the literary evidence, while open to other interpretations, also supports the school hypothesis.

Do the conclusions reached independently from the archaeological, scribal, and literary data agree in supporting the school hypothesis? Tentatively one may answer affirmatively. The problem is that one cannot be sure that the archaeological and scribal evidence for the activity of scribes at Qumran is related to the literary evidence of serious Torah study by certain members of the community. The Biblical commentaries, some of which are generally held to be autographs, are the primary link between the lines of evidence. These scrolls reflect advanced scribal activity and a highly-developed interpretation of scripture; both are best accounted for as the work of a school. Thus, we may conclude that the three lines of evidence converge in support of the existence of a school at Qumran. Further research into the linguistic affinities of the writings produced by the school in its early period (the Manifesto, the Hymns of the TR, the Critique of the Princes of Judah, and possibly CD 20:1c-8a) may confirm this conclusion.

Precisely how the school was related to the community as a whole still lies beyond our vision. As suggested above, however, it probably had the responsibility of establishing and preserving the proper interpretations of scripture for the rest of the community. The frequency of references to teaching and the variety of persons charged with this responsibility indicate the significance of this activity at Qumran: the TR (e.g. 1QH 2:18), the *Maskil* (e.g. 1QS 3:13), the council of the community (e.g. 1QS 3:6), the *Mebaqqer* (e.g. CD 13:7-8; 16:1), and the *Paqid* (e.g. 1QS 6:15).[109] The difficulty in sorting out how the duties of each differed may be due in part at least to changes in organization as the community developed. These

---

[109]The *Mebaqqer* and the *Paqid* may have been synonymous; cf. Cross, *Ancient Library*, p. 233; Bo Reicke, "The Constitution of the Primitive Church in the Light of Jewish Documents," in *The Scrolls and the New Testament*, ed. by K. Stendahl (New York: Harper & Brothers, 1957), pp. 154-55; Raymond E. Brown, *New Testament Essays* (Garden City, N.Y.: Image Books, 1968), p. 157; Jeremias, *Der Lehrer der Gerechtigkeit*, p. 175. The number of verbs for teaching is also indicative of the importance of this activity at Qumran: למד (e.g. 1QS 3:13), יסר (e.g. 1QS 3:1), להבין (e.g. 1QS 3:13), ירה (e.g. 1QH 8:16; CD 3:8), להשכיל (e.g. 1QS 9:18). Further research is needed before judgments can be made concerning the precise use of these verbs and their correlations with the officials of the sect mentioned above.

changes were probably most frequent during the early period.[110]
There was also a ten-year period of instruction for the youths
of the community,[111] and instruction in the secret knowledge
of the sect was an integral part of the initiation of new
members.[112]

The designation היחד, moreover, may be associated with the
Hellenistic school-tradition. B. W. Dombrowski has persuasively
argued that היחד is the equivalent of the Greek τὸ κοινὸν--a
customary designation for religious associations.[113] His conclusion is supported by the references in Philo and Josephus to
the κοινωνία of the Essenes.[114] Dombrowski, however, does not
take into account the use of τὸ κοινὸν and derivative terms in

---

[110]Cf. Milik, *Ten Years*, p. 80; and Peter von der Osten-Sacken,
"Bemerkungen zur Stellung des MEBAQQER in der Sektenschrift," *ZNW*, LV (1964),
18-26, who finds that a comparison of 1QS 5:6 and CD shows a steady decline
of the *rabbim* and a constant growth of the powers of the *Mebaqqer*.

[111]1QSa 1:7-8. Cf. Gerhardsson, *Memory and Manuscript*, p. 58 n. 6:
"The ten year instruction mentioned in 1QSa I.1 ff. (7 f.) must refer to a
form of organized teaching process, probably taken over from priestly circles in Jerusalem. Cf. Ab. V. 21." See also the report by Josephus *War* II.
12. 159:
"There are some among them who profess to foretell the future, being
versed from their early years in the holy books, various forms of purification and apophthegms of prophets; and seldom, if ever, do they err in
their predictions."
Εἰσὶν δ' ἐν αὐτοῖς οἳ καὶ τὰ μέλλοντα προγινώσκειν ὑπισχνοῦνται, βίβλοις
ἱεραῖς καὶ διαφόροις ἁγνείαις καὶ προφητῶν ἀποφθέγμασιν ἐμπαιδοτριβού-
μενοι· σπάνιον δ' εἴ ποτε ἐν ταῖς προαγορεύσεσιν ἀστοχοῦσιν.
The verb ἐμπαιδοτριβέομαι means "to be brought up or educated in." (LSJ, p.
543.)

[112]Cf. Kuhn, *Endererwartung und gegenwärtiges Heil*, pp. 155-63, for discussion of the disclosure of knowledge during initiation into the sect.

[113]Bruno W. Dombrowski, "HYHD in 1QS and *to koinon*. An Instance of
Early Greek and Jewish Synthesis," *HTR*, LIX (1966), 293-307; cf. Johann Maier,
"Zum Begriff יחד in den Texten von Qumran," *ZAW*, LXXII (1960), 148-66.

[114]See Philo *Quod Omnis Probus Liber sit* 84-91; *Hypothetica* 11. 1ff.;
Josephus *War* II. 122, 139; *Ant*. XVIII. 20; compare these references with 1QS
1:11-12; 6:2-3; and 1QH 3:22 where יחד means "fellowship." Cf. Ralph
Marcus, "Philo, Josephus and the Dead Sea YAḤAD," *JBL*, LXXI (1952), 207-09,
who suggests that Philo and Josephus translate יחד as ὅμιλος. See also
Friedrich Hauck, "κοινός," *TDNT*, III, 789-809. George R. Edwards, "The
Qumran Sect and the New Testament Church" (unpublished Ph.D. dissertation,
Duke University, 1955), p. 137, concludes that in the New Testament κοινωνία
does not emphasize the idea of "association," as יחד does in the Qumran
Scrolls. He finds, however, that I John 1:3-7 is an exception:
"It is of interest that the I John i, 3-7 passage could be connected with
the sectarian concept of community, since 'walking in the light' as a
condition of κοινωνία implies separation from the world. 'Cleansing,'
furthermore, is introduced in the same context (καὶ τὸ αἷμα τοῦ υἱοῦ
καθαρίζει ἡμᾶς ἀπὸ πάσης ἁμαρτίας).
See below, p. 280.

168

the literature related to the philosophical schools, particularly the Pythagorean.[115] The similarities between the יחד
and the Pharisaic *ḥaburoth* were first pointed out by Saul
Lieberman.[116] Chaim Rabin then proposed that the Qumran community preserved the form of the *ḥaburah* of the first century
B.C. more purely than did the Rabbinic *ḥaburoth*.[117] Rabin's
proposal has generally been rejected,[118] but the problem of explaining the similarities between the two institutions remains
and is complicated by the limitations of our evidence regarding the origin of the *ḥaburah*. At least it can be said that
the historical conditions which led to the development of the
ḥaburah also influenced the community at Qumran.[119]

A similarity between Qumran and the philosophical schools
may also be seen in the communal meal. Again, there is no
evidence of dependence. The communal meal at Qumran was
observed in an entirely different context and for purposes
different from those of the philosophical schools. At Qumran
the eschatological dimensions of the meal were important, and
great emphasis was placed on the observance of rank.[120] On
both counts the meal at Qumran differs from that of the philosophical schools. Whether members of the school at Qumran
occupied a particular place at the communal meal is not known.

---

[115]For discussion of the similarities between the Pythagoreans and the
Essenes see above, pp. 58-60.

[116]"The Discipline in the So-called Dead Sea Manual of Discipline,"
JBL, LXXI (1952), 199-206; cf. Vermès, *Discovery in the Judean Desert*, pp.
48-52.

[117]*Qumran Studies*, esp. p. viii. Rabin also suggested (p. 1) that
rules concerning admission or initiation into an organization may be used
as a "tracer element" independent of the ideology and purpose of the organization to investigate the origins of documents. This methodology might
yield significant results if applied to the rules for admission to the
various ranks within ancient schools and to the kind of κατήχησις received
by candidates for admission to the philosophical schools, Qumran, the
ḥaburoth, and the early Church.

[118]Cf. Dupont-Sommer, *Essene Writings*, pp. 404-08; with the more posi-
tive reactions of Joseph M. Baumgarten, "Qumran Studies," Review of *Qumran
Studies*, by Chaim Rabin, *JBL*, LXXVII (1958), 249-57; and P. Wernberg-Møller,
"The Nature of the *YAḤAD* According to the *Manual of Discipline* and Related
Documents," *ALUOS*, VI (1966-1968), 56-81.

[119]For further discussion of the *ḥaburah* see below, p. 192. See also
Hengel, *Judentum und Hellenismus*, p. 447.

[120]Cf. Cross, *Ancient Library*, pp. 85, 236.

The history of the
school at Qumran

We can only guess what effect the TR's death had on the community. From the passages which refer to his death (CD 19:35-20:1 and 20:14) it appears that it was neither a violent death nor one which had soteriological significance for the community.[121] The teachings of the TR, which guided the school's interpretation of scripture, became part of the tradition of the community and did acquire soteriological significance. This significance is attested by CD 20:27-34 (written during Stage V of the composition of CD)[122] and by the following lines from the Habakkuk commentary:

> [*But the righteous will live by his faith*.] (II, 4b)
> VIII (1) The explanation of this concerns all those who observe the Law in the House of Judah. (2) God will deliver them from the House of Judgement because of their affliction and their faith (3) in the Teacher of Righteousness.[123]

Even here, the tradition of the teachings of the TR is more important than his person:

> . . . 'faith in the Teacher of Righteousness' may here mean no more than faithfulness to his teaching, that is to the Law as interpreted by him. There is no indication that a saving efficacy is ascribed to faith in the person of the Teacher as such.[124]

Developments which affected the community must have also altered the nature of the school, its work, and its relation to the rest of the community. In particular, the influx of new members which probably followed John Hyrcanus' (134-104 B.C.) persecution of the Pharisees, the destruction of the community by earthquake and fire in 31 B.C., and the renewal of its life must have brought about changes in the school.[125] The first part of the first century A.D. appears to have been a period of intense activity in the school; copies were made of old scrolls, and the War scroll may have been written (or completed) at this

---

[121]A. Dupont-Sommer, "Le maître de justice fut-il mis à mort?" *VT*, I (1951), 200-15; *Essene Writings*, p. 360, claims that the TR was martyred. His theory has generally been rejected; cf. Cross, *Ancient Library*, p. 157; Milik, *Ten Years*, pp. 79-80; Vermes, *The Dead Sea Scrolls in English*, p. 67.

[122]See above, p. 149.

[123]1QpHab 7:17-8:3:

17] וצדיק באמונתו יחיה] VIII פשרו על כול עושי התורה
בבית יהודה אשר 2 יצילם אל מבית המשפט בעבור עמלם ואמנתם
3 במורה הצדק

[124]Davies, *Setting*, p. 217.

[125]For surveys of the history of the community see especially: de Vaux, *Archaeology and the Dead Sea Scrolls*, pp. 1-48; Cross, *Ancient Library*, pp. 57-65; and Milik, *Ten Years*, pp. 51-56, 83-98.

time along with most of the commentaries.[126] Finally, when
the destruction of the community (A.D. 68) appeared imminent,
the manuscripts produced by the scribes during the past decades
were hidden in the caves where they were recently discovered.

The influence of the
school at Qumran

The influence of the community at Qumran on the thought
and organization of other Jewish and early-Christian groups
was profound; we are still discovering traces of this influence. The evidence for similarities between Qumran and the
Johannine community is especially substantial: the shared
themes of love for the brother,[127] opposition to the world,[128]
the unity of the community,[129] the witness (teaching) of a
respected figure in the history of the community,[130] and the
authority and life-giving power of the community's "living
water."[131] These shared themes indicate that there were many
affinities between the *Weltanschauungen* of the two communities.
The influences of the school at Qumran on the Johannine community
(or school?) is more difficult to assess. Nevertheless, a clue
to understanding both communities may be the concept of a school
(within each community) which interpreted scripture and tradition according to the precepts of a revered teacher and wrote
down its interpretation in order to guide the life of its
community.

---

[126]Regarding the date of the War Scroll and the scribal activity of
this period see Milik, *Ten Years*, pp. 95-96; Yigael Yadin, *The Scroll of
the War of the Sons of Light Against the Sons of Darkness*, trans. by B. and
C. Rabin (London: Oxford University Press, 1962), pp. 243-46. See the
discussion of the commentaries above, p. 151.

[127]Compare 1QS 1:9-10; 2:24-25; 5:4, 25; and 8:2 with John 13:34-35;
15:12; I John 2:10; 3:11, 14, 23; 4:7-8; II John 5. Cf. esp. R. E. Brown,
"The Qumran Scrolls and the Johannine Gospel and Epistles," in *New Testament
Essays*, pp. 163-67.

[128]Compare 1QS 1:9-10 with John 1:10; 12:31 (cf. CD 4:13-18); 14:17,
30; 15:18-19.

[129]Compare the emphasis on unity in 1QS 5:2, 7 (Cf. Cross, *Ancient
Library*, p. 209 n. 22) with John 11:52; 17:11, 21, 23.

[130]Compare CD 20:27-34 with John 19:35; 21:24.

[131]For discussion of "living water" at Qumran see above, p. 164. In
John, Jesus has replaced the Law as the "well" from which the "living water"
flows (see John 7:37-39 and Rev. 7:17), yet the Beloved Disciple probably
functioned much like the TR as an interpreter of the words of the "well."

Chapter VIII

THE HOUSE OF HILLEL

The importance of the House of Hillel

The House of Hillel, located in Jerusalem, represents a type of Jewish school quite different from that at Qumran.[1] It will be studied as an example of the Pharisaic schools of the first century A.D., even though very little can be said about it with certainty. The school of Johanan ben Zakkai might have been selected instead, but it is not as central in the Rabbinic materials as the House of Hillel; after A.D. 70, most of the Jewish schools traced their traditions to Hillel and his disciples. The choice of the latter also gives us the chance to study the traditions about a school contemporary with Jesus. Finally, the House of Hillel is important because Hillel may well be responsible for effecting changes in Pharisaism which enabled it to survive the reign of Herod and the war of A.D. 66-70.

Almost everything about Hillel and his school, however, is still open to debate. Did Hillel found the school which bears his name, was he merely elected head of an already existing school, or was the school established after his death? What was the relationship between the schools of Hillel and Shammai? How much contact was there between them prior to Yavneh? When and why did the Houses cease to exist as schools?[2] When sure answers can be given to these questions we will understand a great deal more about first-century, Pharisaic Judaism and the milieu of early Christianity.

The sources for the study of the House of Hillel

The Rabbinic materials, the New Testament, and Josephus all provide information about the first-century Pharisees from separate perspectives, but the latter two do not mention Hillel or his school: "The Houses of Shammai and Hillel are never referred to in the other extant contemporary documents, e.g.,

---

[1]"The House of Hillel" is a literal translation of בית הלל. It is used interchangeably with "the school of Hillel," and "Hillel's school."

[2]Similar questions are raised by Alexander Guttmann, *Rabbinic Judaism in the Making: A Chapter in the History of the Halakhah from Ezra to Judah I* (Detroit: Wayne State University Press, 1970), p. 60.

New Testament, Qumranian writings, Apocrypha-Pseudepigrapha, and Josephus."[3] Thus, we are dependent upon the Rabbinic materials for information about the House of Hillel.

The publication of Jacob Neusner's three volumes on *The Rabbinic Traditions about the Pharisees Before 70* probably marks the beginning of a new era in the study of the first-century Pharisees. Nothing can be said about Hillel and his school with confidence until Neusner's work has been assessed.[4] Neusner has attempted to establish procedures for dating the Rabbinic *halakoth*, and in the process has left us with only a few scraps of evidence about Hillel. Accurate traditions may be preserved in other pericopae, but we cannot yet identify them. Since the value of Neusner's contribution cannot be assessed in one chapter of a dissertation, the procedure fol- lowed below is to summarize the most important contributions to the study of the Rabbinic tradition prior to Neusner and then state how Neusner's work has altered our understanding of it. The dating and evaluation of the Rabbinic materials is so crucial to the study of the House of Hillel that an extended discussion of the problem is warranted.

The classical treatment of the origin and development of the (oral) Rabbinic traditions is the essay by Jacob Z. Lauter- bach on "Midrash and Mishnah," written in 1915.[5] Lauterbach begins by asking when and why the Mishnah-form originated, i.e., when were *halakoth* separated from the interpretation of particular texts? Midrash was originally the only form in which *halakoth* were taught, but even before the time of Hillel and Shammai there were ". . . collections of independent Hala- kot in the Mishnah-form."[6] During the period of the *Soferim* (or "the Great Synagogue"), the texts were still fluid enough to be changed in detail so as to allow for the desired inter- pretations. Hence, there was no need to develop independent *halakoth*. Simeon the Just I (about 300-270 B.C.) is described

---

[3]Jacob Neusner, *From Politics to Piety: The Emergence of Pharisaic Judaism* (Englewood Cliffs, N.J.: Prentice-Hall, Inc., 1973), p. 93. This fact is all the more surprising since Gamaliel is mentioned in Acts 5:34 and 22:3.

[4](3 parts; Leiden: E. J. Brill, 1971). (Hereinafter referred to as *Rabbinic Traditions*.)

[5]Published in his *Rabbinic Essays* (Cincinnati: Hebrew Union College Press, 1951), pp. 163-256.

[6]Ibid., p. 170 n. 12.

in Aboth 1:2 as one of ". . . the remnants of the Great Synagogue."[7] The earliest surviving independent *halakoth* are
attributed to Jose ben Joezer (d. about 165 B.C.).[8] Lauterbach
argues that following the *Soferim* there was a break in the
tradition. The next authoritative teacher was Antigonus of
Soko (*ca*. 190 B.C.). Between 270 and 190 many customs and
practices developed which had no firm basis in the Law. The
Law was studied by pious laymen and thereby assumed a fixed
form. Around 190, ". . . an authoritative Council of priests
and laymen was again established" and began to interpret the
Law for the community.[9] This council encountered difficulties
in finding scriptural bases for the customs which had emerged
since the last of the *Soferim*. The lay members of the council
devised new midrashic methods for interpreting the Law and
expanded the concept of the "Law of the Fathers" to include
religious laws transmitted orally. These innovations were
rejected by the priestly members, who later became the Sadducees. Jose ben Joezer formulated decisions on the basis of the
new methods of interpretation.[10] Later teachers accepted the
decisions because they came from Jose but rejected the methods
on which they were based. The decisions (*halakoth*) were,
therefore, taught independently and in Aramaic rather than
Hebrew, the language of the scriptures and *Midrashim*.

Accordingly, it may be stated with certainty that the
Mishnah-form was first used to teach those customs and
practices which originated during the time when there was no
official activitiy of the teachers. Having no scriptural
basis, they could not be taught in connection with the
Scripture, i.e., in the Midrash-form. The Mishnah-form was
further used to teach those traditional laws and decisions
which some teachers attempted to derive from Scripture by
means of new methods of interpretation. While some of their
contemporaries or disciples accepted the new methods, and
therefore taught these decisions in the Midrash-form, others,
and by far the majority, rejecting the new methods, accepted

---

[7]Aboth 1:2: שמעון הצדיק היה משירי כנסת הגדולה The English
translation of the Mishnah used in this chapter is Herbert Danby, trans.,
The Mishnah (Oxford: University Press, 1933); and the Hebrew text is taken
from Chanoch Albeck, ed., *Mishnah* [Hebrew] (Jerusalem and Tel-Aviv: The
Bialik Institute and Dvir Co., 1953).

[8]Cf. M. Eduyoth 8:4.

[9]Lauterbach, "Midrash and Mishnah," p. 200.

[10]The weakness of Lauterbach's argument at this point is indicated by
the following *non sequitur:* "That Jose had scriptural proofs for his
decisions, is evidenced by the fact that the Amoraim in the Talmud endeavor
to find these proofs or reasons." ("Midrash and Mishnah," p. 219.)

only the decisions.[11]

The Mishnah-form did not immediately replace Midrash, but it gained popularity among the Pharisees.[12] Decisions issued in Midrash-form were open to attack from the Sadducees, while *halakoth* associated with the name of a respected teacher were not. Moreover, if all teaching had been given in Midrash-form, the position of the Pharisees as teachers and bearers of the tradition would have been threatened:

> That which was at first but hesitatingly proposed, *viz.*, that there was an Oral Law alongside of the Written Law, was now boldly proclaimed. The Pharisaic teachers were represented as the teachers of tradition who received the Oral Law through a chain of teachers in direct succession from Moses.[13]

Gradually, the number of Mishnaic *halakoth* grew. The number of *halakoth* connected with the Scriptures by means of new exegetical methods also increased. The Mishnah-form improved, and new methods of arrangement made it an efficient way to teach rulings on various issues. R. Akiba advocated both the new Midrashic methods and the topical arrangement of Mishnaic *halakoth*.

Having proposed the date and motives for the development of the Mishnah-form, Lauterbach turns to the question of why the Talmudic sources are silent about this change in the form of the teaching materials. Two reasons are adduced for the silence. First, the change was precipitated by the need to authorize customs and judgments which had arisen apart from any scriptural basis. If this situation had been common knowledge, it would have reflected ". . . unfavorably upon the authority of the traditional Law in general."[14] Second, the Mishnaic form had been used increasingly in order to enhance the authority of the Pharisaic teachers. If it had become known that the Pharisees had to use this device to assert their authority over the Sadducees, it would have weakened the Pharisaic claim to an

---

[11]Ibid., p. 229.

[12]Lauterbach links the origin of the Pharisees to the exclusion of the lay-teachers from the assembly during the reign of John Hyrcanus. These teachers, branded as separatists, *Perushim*, claimed the taunt as a title of honor. "Thus was formed the party of the Pharisees, who were conscious of their separateness and different [sic] from the priestly group that now came to be called the Sadducean party." (Jacob Z. Lauterbach, "The Pharisees and Their Teachings," in *Rabbinic Essays*, p. 110.)

[13]Lauterbach, "Midrash and Mishnah," p. 235.

[14]Ibid., p. 241, cf. p. 251.

unbroken chain of tradition reaching back to Moses. As a
result of the suppression of this knowledge, by the time of the
Amoraim very few teachers knew how the change in form had
occurred. The Sadducees lost power but were not entirely
obliterated by the destruction of the temple; the necessity for
suppression continued. In the period of the *Geonim*, the
Karaites rejected the authority of the Pharisaic tradition.
Again, the origin of the Mishnah-form had to be suppressed.
Thus, throughout the Talmudic period the rabbis remained silent
on this point in order to avoid exposing their tradition to
severe attacks by their critics.

Lauterbach's account of the origin of the Mishnah-form
provided the basis for the assumption that the Rabbinic traditions about the early Pharisees could be used as a source of
historical information. Additional support for this assumption
can be derived from the work of Birger Gerhardsson.[15] In
fairness to Gerhardsson, it must be stated that the purpose of
his investigation is to describe the process and techniques of
the transmission of tradition in Pharisaic-Rabbinic Judaism and
early Christianity. Inferences about the authenticity of
sayings and actions ascribed to early Pharisaic teachers can,
however, be legitimately drawn from his work.

Gerhardsson concentrates on the transmission of oral
tradition. The basic principle which he espouses is that oral
Torah was committed to memory, i.e., drilled by repetition into
the mind of the student, before any attempt was made to interpret it.[16] Extreme care was taken to preserve the *ipsissima
verba* of the masters. The rule that one must state his teacher's exact words is found first in M. Eduyoth 1:3,[17] but
Gerhardsson claims: "It would scarcely be going too far to
maintain that this practice is extremely ancient in Judaism."[18]

---

[14]Ibid., p. 241, cf. p. 251.

[15]*Memory and Manuscript*. (First cited above, p. 26 n. 141.)

[16]See the description of the *bet hammidrash* in *Memory and Manuscript*,
pp. 85-86, 90-91, and 105.

[17]M. Eduyoth 1:3:
"Hillel says: One *hin* of drawn water renders the immersion-pool unfit.
([We speak of *hin*] only because a man must use the manner of speaking of
his teacher.)"
הלל אומר: מלא הין מים שאובין פוסלין את המקוה; אלא שאדם חיב
לומר בלשון רבו.

[18]*Memory and Manuscript*, p. 131.

It was also the duty of the student to remember the actions of his master, and *halakoth* were often based on the practices of a revered teacher.[19] Gerhardsson affirms that this procedure was practiced during the first century:

> How did they transmit the *halakot* which had been valid for centuries, ... It seems extremely improbable that trans- mission before Aqiba can have taken place following entirely different principles from those later observed, though there may be certain differences. The balance of probability is that the basic material in the oral Torah was transmitted and learned in a fixed form as early as during the last century of the Temple; this material was arranged in blocks, grouped on midrashic and mishnaic principles.[20]

A basic premise of Gerhardsson's thesis, therefore, is that there was continuity in the transmission of Pharisaic-Rabbinic tradition before and after 70.

Gerhardsson's reconstruction of the transmission of Pharisaic-Rabbinic tradition was severely criticized by Morton Smith on two basic points: 1) the gross anachronism of reading back ". . . into the period before 70 the developed rabbinic technique of ± 200 . . ." and 2) ". . . imposing rabbinism on the Pharisees," and ". . . Pharisaism on the rest of first- century Judaism."[21]

Gerhardsson responded that Smith missed the main concern of the book: describing the "technique of teaching and trans- mission."[22] Even though revolutionary changes occurred between A.D. 65 and 135, the pedagogical methods of the rabbis remained largely unchanged:

> Pedagogics in Antiquity were generally characterized by a remarkable degree of conservatism. As far as Phari- saism and Rabbinism are concerned we must also remember that it was part of their conscious programme to preserve the words and the customs of the fathers inviolate. . . . We

---

[19]Ibid., pp. 183-89.

[20]Ibid., p. 111.

[21]"A Comparison of Early Christian and Early Rabbinic Tradition," *JBL*, LXXXII (1963), 169 and 172; cf. Jacob Neusner, "The Rabbinic Traditions about the Pharisees before 70 A.D.: The Problem of Oral Tradition," *Kairos*, XIV (1972), 57-70; more positive reviews of the first part of *Memory and Manuscript* include: Pierre Benoit, *RB*, LXX (1963), 269-73; B. Brinkmann, *Scholastik*, XXXVII (1962), 426-30; Joseph A. Fitzmyer, *TS*, XXIII (1962), 442-57; Abraham Goldberg, "Handing down Tradition: Classic Work in the Transmission of Written and Oral Law," in *The Jerusalem Post*, September 18, 1963, p. v.

[22]Birger Gerhardsson, *Tradition and Transmission in Early Christianity*, trans. by E. J. Sharpe, Coniectanea Neotestamentica, XX (Lund: C. W. K. Gleerup, 1964), p. 12.

claim that most of the characteristic features of Rabbinic pedagogics have a long history, *which can be traced far back into Old Testament times.*[23]

The implications of this contention for the study of the early Pharisees are obvious.

Another point raised by Morton Smith may be dealt with before taking up the second criticism listed above. Neusner relates the following from a conversation with Smith:

The large place assigned to memorization in ancient education seems to Gerhardsson similar in Judaism. But what students of classics memorized was the *text*, not the words of the teacher, . . .[24]

The accuracy of Smith's observation is borne out in part by the discussion of the school of Epictetus above (p. 139). The students memorized texts, not Epictetus' interpretation of them. The words of the teacher were memorized, however, in the Pythagorean and Epicurean schools. The Pythagoreans used the formula Ἀυτὸς ἔφα when quoting Pythagoras, and Cicero claimed that every good Epicurean memorized his master's *Kuriai Doxai.*[25]

Gerhardsson responded to the charge that he imposed Rabbinism on Pharisaism and Pharisaism on the rest of first-century Judaism by claiming that the basic pedagogical methods of the rabbis were not unique with them but were practiced by other groups in antiquity. He further argued that the Pharisaic teachers were not "a small sectarian party" as Smith claimed; they were ". . . clearly dominant in Palestine as early as the period of the temple, . . ."[26] There was no great change in their position after 70; they merely grew in power and influence. The Pharisaic teachers were also popular educators, ". . . *representatives of a professional teaching class.*"[27]

The implications of Gerhardsson's work for the credibility of the Rabbinic tradition regarding Hillel's school are clear. If Gerhardsson is right, one may assume that the traditions contain the exact words of the first-century teachers and at least nuclei of historical information about their practices.

The greatest threat to the theses of Lauterbach and Gerhardsson is Neusner's recent study of *The Rabbinic Traditions*

---

[23]Ibid., p. 15 (Gerhardsson's italics).

[24]Neusner, *Rabbinic Traditions,* III, 147.

[25]See above, pp. 51, 108.

[26]Gerhardsson, *Tradition and Transmission in Early Christianity,* p. 20.

[27]Ibid., p. 21. (Gerhardsson's italics).

about the Pharisees before 70. Neusner begins by analyzing
the traditions pertaining to the pre-70 masters and the Houses.
A disproportionately large number of the traditions concern
Hillel:

> Hillel by himself has thirty-three traditions in eighty-
> nine pericopae. Hillel's materials include legal traditions
> and exegeses, exegeses turned into narratives; legal prece-
> dents; biographical traditions; and a huge corpus of moral
> and theological logia, which, except for M. Avot 1:1-18, far
> outweighs all moral and theological logia assigned to all
> other masters put together. The traditions center on the
> theme of Hillel's rise to power, Hillel as paragon of virtue,
> model for legal and moral behavior, and authority in legal
> and exegetical matters, particularly with reference to
> ritual cleanness, tithing, and keeping agricultural rules
> and taboos.[28]

In Part III, Neusner examines the various forms and attempts to
date their development. For post-70 rabbis Neusner's basic
principle for establishing the date of a saying or pericope is
that sayings attributed to particular masters were either
actually said by them or assigned to them by their disciples.[29]
Finally, Neusner attempts to reconstruct the history of the
traditions.

The following picture of the Pharisees and their traditions emerges from Neusner's work. The Rabbinic traditions
". . . may be characterized as self-centered, the internal
records of a party concerning its own life, its own laws, and
its own partisan conflicts"; on the basis of these traditions
one ". . . could not have reconstructed a single significant
public event of the period before 70. . . ."[30] For the external history of the Pharisees one is largely dependent upon
Josephus, who, by contrast, says practically nothing about the
matters of chief interest to the Rabbinic tradents. Instead,
he portrays the Pharisees as both a political party and a
philosophical school. In *The Jewish War* (written shortly after
70), the Pharisees appear as a political party which was active
in the Maccabean state:[31]

> Beside Alexandra, and growing as she grew, arose the Phar-
> isees, a body of Jews with the reputation of excelling the
> rest of their nation in the observances of religion, and as
> exact exponents of the laws. . . . But if she ruled the

---

[28]Neusner, *Rabbinic Traditions*, III, 313.

[29]Ibid., III, 181; Neusner, *From Politics to Piety*, pp. 92-95.

[30]Neusner, *Rabbinic Traditions*, III, 304.

[31]Neusner, *From Politics to Piety*, p. 48.

nation, the Pharisees ruled her.[32]

In the same writing, however, he describes the Pharisees as a school:

> Of the two first-named schools, the Pharisees, who are considered the most accurate interpreters of the laws, and hold the position of the leading sect, attribute everything to Fate and to God; . . .
>
> . . . .
>
> The Pharisees are affectionate to each other and cultivate harmonious relations with the community.[33]

He also mentions two teachers who interpreted the Law and educated the youth.[34] Twenty years later, when he wrote the *Jewish Antiquities*, Josephus aligned himself with the Pharisaic party and claimed that the Pharisees enjoyed the support of the majority of the population.[35] On the basis of his accounts, the Pharisees appear to have ceased to take an active part in politics following the attacks on them by Aristobulus and Herod.[36]

The Pharisees of the Gospels—once the polemic and invective have been stripped aside—emerge as a group strikingly different from that described by Josephus. They are chiefly concerned with matters of tithing, the observance of festivals, ritual purity, and dietary laws; they are a "table-fellowship sect."[37] The differences between Jesus and the Pharisees regarding these matters are the subject of many pericopae in the Gospels. The Christian writings, however, do not mention the Houses and show little concern about the ". . . inner groupings within Pharisaism."[38]

---

[32]Josephus *War* I. 110-12:

Παραφύονται δὲ αὐτῆς εἰς τὴν ἐξουσίαν Φαρισαῖοι, σύνταγμά τι Ἰουδαίων δοκοῦν εὐσεβέστερον εἶναι τῶν ἄλλων καὶ τοὺς νόμους ἀκριβέστερον ἀφηγεῖσθαι. . . . ἐκράτει δὲ τῶν μὲν ἄλλων αὐτή, Φαρισαῖοι δ' αὐτῆς.

[33]Ibid., II. 162, 166:

Δύο δὲ τῶν προτέρων Φαρισαῖοι μὲν οἱ μετ' ἀκριβείας δοκοῦντες ἐξηγεῖσθαι τὰ νόμιμα καὶ τὴν πρώτην ἀπάγοντες αἵρεσιν εἱμαρμένη τε καὶ θεῷ προσάπτουσι πάντα, . . .

. . . .
καὶ Φαρισαῖοι μὲν φιλάλληλοί τε καὶ τὴν εἰς τὸ κοινὸν ὁμόνοιαν ἀσκοῦντες,
. . . .

Note that Josephus uses the term τὸ κοινόν.

[34]Ibid., I. 648; *Ant.* XVII. 149.

[35]Cf. Neusner, *From Politics to Piety*, pp. 54-55. Josephus also notes the Pharisees' claim to ancient traditions; cf. *Ant.* XIII. 297-98, XVIII. 11-15.

[36]Neusner, *From Politics to Piety*, pp. 66.

[37]Ibid., pp. 67, 80.

[38]Neusner, *Rabbinic Traditions*, III, 278. While this interpretation

The picture of the pre-70 Pharisees which Neusner constructs from the Rabbinic traditions corresponds closely to that of the Gospels; the Pharisees were primarily a table-fellowship sect. Very few materials of historical value for the earliest period have survived: "Of a historical nature are the references to Yosi b. Yoeser's uncleanness rulings, and a very few other traditions."[39] The reason for the paucity of traditions about the earliest teachers is that

> . . . the first considerable revision of Pharisaic materials took place in the period of Hillel and the formation of the Houses. Then whatever existed about pre-Hillelite Pharisees was simply obliterated.[40]

Each House formed its own traditions and rules without reference to contrary opinions in the other schools.[41] Shammai's House, however, seems to have predominated prior to 70.[42] The Houses also developed the practice of assigning traditions to named authorities, and these attributions are in the main reliable.[43]

Did the Houses transmit oral traditions, as Gerhardsson claims? Neusner cites TB 'Eruvin 54b as the clearest statement of the Rabbinic procedure for transmitting oral traditions and dates the pericope as Ushan (*ca.* A.D. 140).[44] He agrees that it probably reflects the practice from *ca.* A.D. 100, but sharply rejects Gerhardsson's contention that the procedure remained unchanged from early in the first century and even earlier. Neusner also agrees that the substance of traditions was transmitted orally before 70, but argues that the *ipsissima verba* of earlier teachers were not, unless all they said was "clean," "unclean," "to lay," or "not to lay."[45] The mnemonic patterns

---

of the relationship between early Christians and the Pharisees helps to explain the absence of references to the Houses in the Gospels, a caveat must be inserted at this point. W. D. Davies has demonstrated convincingly that the Matthean community, at least, was aware of, and concerned about, the developments at Yavneh. Cf. *Setting*, pp. 256-315.

[39]Neusner, *From Politics to Piety*, p. 121.

[40]Neusner, *Rabbinic Traditions*, III, 240. See below, p. 193.

[41]Neusner, *From Politics to Piety*, p. 102.

[42]Neusner, *Rabbinic Traditions*, III, 266.

[43]Ibid., III, 91, 230.

[44]Ibid., III, 143-44.

[45]Ibid., III, 147-48.

were introduced at Yavneh and indicate only what the Yavneans
intended for the future transmission:

> What solid evidence do we have that the materials originally
> were oral, that is, never written down at all, but formu-
> lated by a master and taught to disciples through repetition
> of formulae or other means. Not a single story or saying
> before us suggests that a pre-70 Pharisaic master ever did
> any such thing. We do not have tales of how they taught,
> nor do we even have internal evidence that they organized
> circles of disciples. Perhaps they did; we cannot claim
> they 'must have' done so.[46]

We hear of no *Tanna* prior to Akiba; rather, we find scribes.
The New Testament, the Qumran scrolls, and the apocryphal and
pseudepigraphical writings were written--not transmitted orally. There were early Christian traditions, but these were not
reproduced verbatim, and there were no certified memorizers.
Neusner, hence, proposes the following origin for the process
described in TB 'Eruvin 54b. Yoḥanan and his disciples claimed
to have ". . . the *essential content* of the ancient Torah"; the
next generation claimed to have not only the content but ". . .
the *exact words* orally formulated and handed on earlier"; and
finally the attempt was made (between 100 and 150) to ". . .
replicate that mnemonic process in the formulation and transmission of Yavnean materials."[47] So, the Yavneans ritualized
the process of transmitting the law; ". . . what the early
Yavneans did in formulating traditions in mnemonic patterns and
teaching them in the manner described in b. 'Eruv. was to act
out that part of the Torah-myth most pertinent to their political needs."[48] The formalized process enhanced their claim to
ancient tradition and its authority. If this reconstruction is
correct, then Gerhardsson's assumption that there was no great
change in pedagogical methods after 70 is mistaken.

The task of Yavneh was to preserve Jerusalemite Pharisaism
and unite Judaism; its chief contribution to the Rabbinic
traditions was the development of the "Houses-form," i.e., the
form in which the judgments of the Houses of Shammai and Hillel
were concisely stated: "As to . . . , the House of Shammai say
. . . , and the House of Hillel say . . . ." This form originated at a time when the House of Shammai still predominated,

---

[46]Ibid., III, 152. See, however, the discussion of the school of
Jesus below, Chapter X.

[47]Ibid., III, 171.

[48]Ibid., III, 174.

but when the two Houses were nearly equal in power.[49] In the
process of organizing the existing traditions in this pattern,
the Yavneans did not attribute judgments to the Houses regarding matters on which they had made no rulings, but they obliterated the earlier strata of traditions. This is argued on the
assumption that prior to Yavneh the Houses preserved their
traditions in a form (like that of the writings from Qumran)
which did not juxtapose its rulings with those of the other
House(s). The Yavnean materials, therefore, preserve the
themes of the disputes of the Houses but not the form of the
earlier traditions:[50]

> It may now be suggested that the pre-70 Houses handed on
> traditions concerning three areas of law: agricultural
> tithes, offerings, and taboos; Sabbath and festival law; and
> cleanness rules.[51]

In contrast to what we can see of the preceding period, the
Yavneans also stressed the master-disciple relationship. The
sayings of individual Hillelites and Shammaites during the
period of the Houses (A.D. 10-70) were subsumed into the
Houses-form. Shemaiah and Abtalion have no masters, but everyone after them does.[52] Moreover, none of the pre-70 teachers
ever refers to a saying by another named teacher.[53] Even
Yoḥanan ben Zakkai, allegedly Hillel's disciple, never claims
to have received a tradition or saying from Hillel.[54] While
the Houses probably existed prior to Yavneh, they were not as
important as the Yavnean materials make them appear to have

---

[49]Ibid., II, 4; Neusner, *From Politics to Piety*, p. 103.

[50]Neusner, *Rabbinic Traditions*, III, 238.

[51]Ibid., III, 234.

[52]Ibid., III, 256.

[53]Neusner, *From Politics to Piety*, p. 99.

[54]Ibid., p. 100. Cf. Neusner, *Rabbinic Traditions*, III, 278:
"We may take it as fact that Yohanan b. Zakkai lived in Jerusalem before
70 A.D. He should, therefore, have known Hillel and Shammai and their
Houses. Since Hillel, Shammai, and the Houses probably were historical
personalities and institutions, it looks as if Yoḥanan was not associated
either with the early masters (presumably because they came before his
time) or with the Houses, but taught as an independent master within the
Pharisaic group, organized his own circle of disciples, and occupied a
modest place in the life of pre-70 Pharisaic Jerusalem."
Cf. Jacob Neusner, *A Life of Yoḥanan ben Zakkai Ca. 1-80 C.E.*, 2nd ed.,
Studia Post-Biblica (Leiden: E. J. Brill, 1970); *Development of a Legend:
Studies on the Traditions Concerning Yoḥanan ben Zakkai*, Studia Post-Biblica
(Leiden: E. J. Brill, 1970); "The Traditions Concerning Yoḥanan ben Zakkai:
Reconsiderations," *JJS*, XXIV (1973), 65-73.

been.[55] Moreover, the Hillelites probably did not gain pre-dominance until the time of Akiba.[56] At this point attempts were made to conciliate the Shammaites. The Akibans also added exegeses to the Houses-pericopae in order to support the Hillelite rulings.[57]

The Ushans (*ca.* A.D. 140) were interested in developing a history of pre-70 Pharisaism; hence most of the stories about the early Pharisees derive from this period. The patriarchal lineage was traced to Hillel;[58] and this development sparked a vigorous, new interest in Hillel as an individual. He became a central figure in the tradition:

> His migration from Babylonia is taken for granted; his rise to power is the subject of serious historical efforts; his sayings about futures, his ordinances about the redemption of property, his expounding the language of common people, some of his moral sayings--these are materials first attested at Usha.[59]

The problem is that the Ushans probably had no traditions about Hillel which were unknown to the Yavneans: "The silence of two generations of masters--from *ca.* 70 to *ca.* 125--on historical questions ought to be suggestive, if not probative, of the unreliability of the Ushans' stories."[60] This observation casts a heavy cloud of doubt over all the pericopae which contain "biographical" or "historical" information about Hillel and his disciples. The final stage in the development of the tradition, however, is the work of the circle around Judah the Patriarch (*ca.* 170-210). In addition to codifying the Mishnah, this group refined the interpretation of the disputes between the Houses and added glosses to the stories of Hillel's rise to power.[61]

Neusner's work virtually sweeps aside all past accounts of Hillel by questioning the reliability of the traditions on which these were built. The Yavnean traditions about the Houses are earlier than the Ushan traditions about their founders,

---

[55]Neusner, *Rabbinic Traditions*, III, 279.

[56]Ibid., III, 275.

[57]Ibid., III, 99; Neusner, *From Politics to Piety*, pp. 118-19.

[58]Neusner, *From Politics to Piety*, p. 105.

[59]Neusner, *Rabbinic Traditions*, III, 283; cf. III, 319.

[60]Neusner, *From Politics to Piety*, p. 137.

[61]Ibid., p. 138.

so the crucial question for future research is whether the work
of these men can be recovered from the traditions of their
schools. Neusner is hopeful that this may be possible:

> Do Hillel and Shammai stand as historical figures behind the
> Houses and did they found the Houses? And if so, do the
> rulings of the Houses in hundreds of specific legal problems
> follow general principles first laid down by the founders of
> the Houses themselves? Here we have no evidence at all,
> except for the existence of the Houses themselves, but that
> evidence seems to me sufficient to point toward an unequivo-
> cal and affirmative answer. Through the laws we may claim
> to reach legal principles held by the masters who founded
> the Houses. I should be inclined to claim that the histori-
> cal Hillel and Shammai stand behind elements of the Houses'
> traditions. I should not, at this juncture, want to specify
> which ones.[62]

The life and work of Hillel is discussed further below, but
enough has been said at this point to indicate that Neusner's
work represents a watershed in the study of the first-century
Pharisees. A few reservations about Neusner's reconstruction
of the development of the Rabbinic traditions might be stated
at this point but may more profitably be held until later since
Neusner's position is developed further below.[63]

The origin of the
House of Hillel

To what extent did the Hellenistic schools (especially the
philosophical schools) influence the organization, pedagogical
methods, and discussions of the early Pharisaic and Rabbinic
schools? The evidence for such an influence is considerable.
Elias Bickerman asserts that the fundamental Pharisaic tenet
that piety is attained through learning is Hellenic: ". . .
this is a Hellenic, one might say, a Platonic notion, that
education could so transform the individual and the entire
people that the nation would be capable of fulfilling the
divine task set it."[64] Study was a pious exercise because it
meant study of the Torah: this emphasis on study reached its
peak in the decision under Akiba that ". . . study of the Law
is of higher rank than practising it."[65] Many of the Rabbinic

---

[62]Neusner, *Rabbinic Traditions*, III, 280.

[63]The reservations are stated below, pp. 192-94.

[64]*From Ezra to the Last of the Maccabees: Foundations of Postbiblical
Judaism*, Part II trans. by M. Hadas (New York: Schocken Books, 1962), p.
162. See above pp. 68 and 139-40.

[65]Sifre Deuteronomy 41 on 11:13; TB Qiddushin 40b. Cf. K. H. Rengstorf
"μανθάνω," *TDNT*, IV, 403. Rengstorf (p. 403 n. 105) also cites the third-

methods of interpretation probably ". . . derive from Hellenistic rhetoric."[66] Moreover, the Pharisees had a sufficient
knowledge of the Epicureans and Stoics to be concerned with
repudiating their teachings.[67] Judah Goldin has shown that
Aboth 2:9 is strikingly parallel in form to the summary of
Stoic doctrines in Diogenes Laertius VII. 92ff.[68] Even the
practice of citing the chain of tradition through one's teachers is Hellenistic.[69] Morton Smith lists the similarities
between the philosophers and the Pharisees:

> Not only was the theory of the Pharisaic school that of a
> school of Greek philosophy, but so were its practices. Its
> teachers taught without pay, like philosophers; they
> attached to themselves particular disciples who followed
> them around and served them, like philosophers; they looked
> to gifts for support, like philosophers; they were exempt
> from taxation, like philosophers; they were distinguished in
> the street by their walk, speech, and peculiar clothing,
> like philosophers; and they practiced and praised asceti-
> cism, like philosophers; and finally--what is, after all,
> the meat of the matter--they discussed the questions philos-
> ophers discussed and reached the conclusions philosophers
> reached.[70]

Although the differences are obvious and profound, the similarities between the schools of the philosophers and those of the
Pharisees are unquestionably extensive.

---

century tradition (TB 'Avodah Zarah 3b) that ". . . God Himself spends 3
hours each day with the Torah (עוֹסֵק) and is thus the great example for His
people."

[66]David Daube, "Rabbinic Methods of Interpretation and Hellenistic
Rhetoric," *HUCA*, XXII (1949), 240. See also: Saul Lieberman, *Hellenism
in Jewish Palestine*, Texts and Studies of the Jewish Theological Seminary
of America, Vol. XVIII (New York: The Jewish Theological Seminary of America,
1950).

[67]Cf. Judah Goldin, "A Philosophical Session in a Tannaite Academy,"
Traditio, XXI (1965), esp. 5-6; W. D. Davies, "Reflexions on Tradition: The
Aboth Revisited," in *Christian History and Interpretation: Studies Presented
to John Knox*, ed. by W. R. Farmer, C. F. D. Moule, and R. R. Niebuhr
(Cambridge: At the University Press, 1967), pp. 145-46; Henry A. Fischel,
"Epicureanism," *EncJud*, VI, 817; Henry A. Fischel, *Rabbinic Literature and
Greco-Roman Philosophy: A Study of Epicurea and Rhetorica in Early Midrashic
Writings*, Studia Post-Biblica, 21 (Leiden: E. J. Brill, 1973); Saul
Lieberman, "How Much Greek in Jewish Palestine?" in *Biblical and Other
Studies*, ed. by A. Altmann; Philip W. Lown Institute of Advanced Judaic
Studies, Brandeis University; Studies and Texts, Vol. I (Cambridge, Mass.:
Harvard University Press, 1963), p. 130; Armand Kaminka, "Hillel's Life and
Work," *JQR*, N.S., XXX (1939-40), 117-19. See also above, p. 119.

[68]Goldin, "A Philosophical Session in a Tannaite Academy," pp. 16-21.

[69]Cf. Élie Bikerman, "La chaine de la tradition pharisienne," *RB*, LIX
(1952), 44-54.

[70]Morton Smith, "Palestinian Judaism in the First Century," in *Israel:
Its Role in Civilization*, ed. by M. Davis (New York: Harper & Brothers,
1956), p. 80.

186

Do these similarities imply that the Pharisaic schools developed from the Hellenistic schools of rhetoric and philosophy? The question is crucial. K. H. Rengstorf claims that the master-disciple relationship and the "principle of tradition" are absent from the Old Testament.[71] This absence leads him to find the essential features of the Rabbinic schools in Hellenism

> . . . we do not find in the OT even the first beginnings of a school or principle of tradition such as may be seen in Rabbinism. Nor is there conscious Mosaism in the sense of reposing everything on the person of Moses. . . . In developing these views later Judaism was under influences which could come only from Hellenism, where they were firmly established. For here were schools in the sense of fellowships of disciples, and here, too, the principle of tradition was accepted.[72]

Rengstorf further suggests that the influence of the Hellenistic schools was conveyed through two early Pharisaic teachers with Greek names: Antigonus of Soko and Abtalion.[73] He observes, however, that when the Greek form of schools was adopted by the Pharisees it was integrated into Judaism's concern for the Torah.[74]

The evidence for the existence of prophetic schools, however, is stronger than Rengstorf realizes. The best example is the circle which gathered around Isaiah and transmitted his teachings: "Those who belonged to this circle are expressly called 'disciples' (*limmûdîm*) and 'sons' (y^e*lādîm*) of the prophet, whom Yahweh had given him."[75] The most important references in Isaiah are the following:

> Bind up the testimony, seal the teaching among my disciples. . . . Behold, I and the children whom the Lord has given me are signs and portents in Israel from the Lord of Hosts. . . (Isa. 8:16, 18 RSV).

> The Lord God has given me the tongue of those who are taught that I may know how to sustain with a word him that is weary. Morning by morning he wakens, he wakens my ear to hear as those who are taught. (Isa. 50:4 RSV; cf. 54:13).[76]

---

[71]Rengstorf, "μανθάνω," *TDNT*, IV, 427, 429.

[72]Ibid., pp. 438, 439.

[73]Ibid., p. 440. Cf. TB Yoma 71b.

[74]Rengstorf, "μανθάνω," *TDNT*, IV, 440.

[75]J[ohannes] Lindblom, *Prophecy in Ancient Israel* (Oxford: Basil Blackwell, 1963), pp. 160-61.

[76]Isaiah 8:16, 18:

16 צור תצודה חתום תורה בלמדי:
18 הנה אנכי והילדים אשר נתן-לי יהוה לאתות ולמופתים בישראל מעם יהוה צבאות

Lindblom argues that Isaiah 8:16 is spoken figuratively. That
which the prophet could not speak publicly he "sealed" or
entrusted ". . . to his disciples to be preserved by them."[77]
The importance of listening as the primary function of the
disciple is also emphasized.[78] Isaiah 19:11 refers to the
"sons of the wise." William McKane understands this phrase in
a technical sense:

> The claim of these statesmen that they are *ben hᵃkamim* prob-
> ably means that they are accredited and properly qualified
> members of their profession who have come up through the
> recognized schools, although it may allude to the operation
> of the hereditary principle in respect of high offices of
> state.[79]

Jeremiah 8:8 also supports the existence of prophetic schools:

> How can you say, 'We are wise, and the law of the Lord is
> with us? But, behold, the false pen of the scribes has made
> it into a lie.[80]

Here "the wise" are those who have studied the Law (Deuteronomy?)
and commend themselves to the people as instructors.[81] These
passages (and others, e.g., II Kings 2:3, 5, 7; 4:38) indicate
that Isaiah and other prophets had disciples who regarded them
as teachers, memorized their sayings, and transmitted them
orally for some time before collecting and writing the traditions

---

Isaiah 50:4:

4 אדני יהוה נתן לי לשון למודים
לדעת לעות את-יעף דבר יעיר
בבקר בבקר יעיר לי אזן לשמע כלמודים:

For further discussion see Appendix II.

[77]Lindblom, *Prophecy in Ancient Israel*, p. 162. Cf. to the contrary,
Rengstorf, "μανθάνω," *TDNT*, IV, 430; and Georg Fohrer, *Introduction to the
Old Testament*, initiated by Ernst Sellin, trans. by David E. Green (Nashville:
Abingdon Press, 1968), p. 375.

[78]Rengstorf, "μανθάνω," *TDNT*, IV, 435, notes the same emphasis in the
Rabbinic sources: "Learning takes place by listening to what the rabbi says,
and appropriating what is heard. Thus שמע describes the true function of
the תלמיד .

[79]*Prophets and Wise Men*, SBT, No. 44 (Naperville, Ill.: Alec. R.
Allenson, Inc., 1965), p. 69.

[80]Jeremiah 8:8:

8 איכה תאמרו חכמים אנחנו ותורת יהוה אתנו אכן הנה לשקר עשה עט
שקר ספרים:

[81]Johannes Lindblom, "Wisdom in the Old Testament Prophets," in *Wisdom
in Israel and in the Ancient Near East: Presented to Professor Harold Henry
Rowley*, ed. by M. Noth and D. W. Thomas, VTSup, Vol. III (Leiden: E. J.
Brill, 1955), p. 195.

about their master.[82]   There is also evidence for a long history of wisdom and scribal schools in Israel.[83]

The above is by no means intended to be an exhaustive survey of the evidence for schools in the Old Testament, but it obviates the necessity of positing the origin of the Rabbinic schools in Hellenism. Although the schools of philosophy and rhetoric exerted a considerable influence on Rabbinic schools, the basic stimulus to teach and preserve tradition through disciples already had a long history in Judaism.[84]

Nahum N. Glatzer's *Hillel the Elder* raises the question: was Hillel influenced by the Essenes?[85] Glatzer pieces together the following life of Hillel. Hillel was born in Babylonia before the middle of the first-century B.C. Around 50 B.C., he journeyed to Jerusalem to continue his studies[86] and supported himself by manual labor. After a period of study under

---

[82]Cf. Lindblom, *Prophecy in Ancient Israel*, p. 163. Cf. Antonius H. J. Gunneweg, *Mündliche und schriftliche Tradition der vorexilischen Prophetenbücher als Problem der neueren Prophetenforschung*, FRLANT, n.F. LV (Göttingen: Vandenhoeck & Ruprecht, 1959), esp. pp. 7-20; Martin Hengel, *Nachfolge und Charisma: Eine exegetisch-religionsgeschichtliche Studie zu Mt 8.21f. und Jesus Ruf in die Nachfolge*, BZNW, XXXIV (Berlin: Verlag Alfred Töpelmann, 1968), pp. 18-20.

[83]For discussion and bibliography on the wisdom schools see: Fohrer, *Introduction to the Old Testament*, pp. 308, 311-17; McKane, *Prophets and Wise Men*, esp. pp. 37-38; Lindblom, "Wisdom in the Old Testament Prophets," p. 203; Jacob Neusner, "'Pharisaic-Rabbinic' Judaism: A Clarification," *History of Religions*, XII (1973), 265; Hans-Jürgen Hermisson, *Studien zur Israelitischen Spruchweisheit* (Neukirchen-Vluyn: Neukirchener Verlag, 1968); R. N. Whybray, *The Intellectual Tradition in the Old Testament*, ZAW Beiheft 135 (Berlin: Walter de Gruyter, 1974). See also above, p. 142 n. 137. Wisdom schools were often found in the temples in the ancient Near East. This association is probably important for understanding the organization of the early church. When there was no temple near, schools were established in the synagogues. Similarly, Christian schools were probably first organized in the places where the churches met. The association of church and school carried over into the middle ages.

[84]Louis Finkelstein, *New Light from the Prophets* (London: Vallentine, Mitchell, 1969), p. 3, has doubtlessly exaggerated the teaching role of the prophets. For a more extensive survey of education in the Old Testament, see R. Alan Culpepper, "Education," in the forthcoming revised edition of *The International Standard Bible Encyclopedia*.

[85]*Hillel the Elder: The Emergence of Classical Judaism*, rev. ed. (New York: Schocken Books, 1966); see also Nahum N. Glatzer, "Hillel the Elder in the Light of the Dead Sea Scrolls," in *The Scrolls and the New Testament*, ed. by K. Stendahl (New York: Harper & Brothers, 1957), pp. 232-44.

[86]Glatzer, *Hillel the Elder*, p. 24. Kaminka, "Hillel's Life and Work," p. 110, suggests that Hillel came from Alexandria rather than Babylonia. Jeremias, *Jerusalem in the Time of Jesus*, p. 112, observes, regarding TB Yoma 35b Bar., that Hillel did not pay his teachers to attend their lectures; the fee was paid to the caretaker of the school building.

Shemaiah and Abtalion, Hillel withdrew from Jerusalem. Our sources are silent about this period, but Glatzer conjectures that Hillel lived among the sectarians near Jerusalem. In about 30 B.C., Hillel re-appears discussing the Passover ritual with the Elders of Batyra.[87] Hillel first cites *midrashic* arguments for his position but finally says that he received the teaching from Shemaiah and Abtalion. Thereupon, the elders accept his ruling and make him "*nasi*." Glatzer maintains that prior to Hillel Pharisaism had concentrated on the transmission of oral tradition. Hillel introduced the study of Torah--which had already found a place among the sectarians--into Pharisaic Judaism in Jerusalem.

> 'In ancient days when the Torah was forgotten from Israel, Ezra came up from Babylon and reestablished it. Then it was again forgotten until Hillel the Babylonian came up and reestablished it.' [Sukkah 20a] . . . . Hillel aimed at reestablishing in Jerusalem a center for the *forgotten* Torah. To accomplish this, Hillel, we suggest, carefully considered the ways of the Early Hasidim and their followers in the Essene and Covenant communities. Here he found prototypes for a valid concept of Torah and its study, of law and life.[88]

The introduction of the study of Torah into his school in Jerusalem was Hillel's most important achievement.[89] Hillel was usually on the side of the poor and, in contrast to Shammai, favored the more lenient interpretation of the Law.[90] Again, Glatzer finds that these emphases emerge out of Hillel's response to sectarian Judaism.[91] Glatzer's life of Hillel, thus, gives a new meaning to Hillel's saying: "Do not separate yourself from the community."[92]

Neusner, in contrast to Glatzer, rules out any attempt to reconstruct the life of Hillel.[93] Nevertheless, he gathers

---

[87]For a synopsis of the traditions (esp. TP Pesahim 33a) about Hillel's "rise to power" see Neusner, *Rabbinic Traditions*, I, 286-89; for analyses see esp. I, 267; II, 99; and *From Politics to Piety*, pp. 23-35.

[88]Glatzer, *Hillel the Elder*, p. 31. Glatzer also suggests that Hillel's associate, Menahem [M. Hagigah 2:2], was influenced by the Essenes and later joined the sect [TP Hagigah 77d].

[89]Judah Goldin, "Hillel," *IDB*, II, 605, offers a more conventional appraisal of Hillel's work. See also Judah Goldin, "Hillel the Elder," *JR*, XXVI (1946), 263-77.

[90]Cf. Louis Ginzberg, *Students, Scholars and Saints* (New York: Meridian Books, Inc., 1958), p. 89.

[91]Glatzer, *Hillel the Elder*, p. 33; see also p. 89.

[92]Cf. Ibid., p. 32. Aboth 2:4: ‏אל תפרש מן הצבור‎ .

[93]Neusner, *From Politics to Piety*, p. xx.

clues about Hillel's contribution to pre-70 Pharisaism:

> The rabbinic tradition thus begins where Josephus's narra-
> tive leaves off, and the difference between them leads us to
> suspect, that the change in the character of Pharisaism from
> a political party to a sect comes with Hillel. If Hillel
> was responsible for directing the party out of its political
> concerns and into more passive, quietistic paths, then we
> should understand why his figure dominates the subsequent
> rabbinic tradition. . . . As Herod's characteristics became
> clear, therefore, the Pharisees must have found themselves
> out of sympathy alike with the government and the opposition.
> And at this moment Hillel arose to change what had been a
> political party into a table-fellowship-sect, not unlike
> other, publicly harmless and politically neutral groups,
> whatever their private eschatological aspirations.
> All this is more than mere conjecture, but less than
> established fact.[94]

Beyond this, very little can be said about Hillel. The proof
texts attached to Hillel's sayings are secondary additions.[95]
Even the rulings of the House of Hillel cannot always be traced
to Hillel. The traditions of ". . . his teachings on the
festivals, (Passover, Sukkot), on purity laws, and on legal
theory (the ordinances), may go back to him,"[96] but further
study is needed before these can be separated from the rest of
the rulings of the Houses.

The nature of the House of Hillel

The Rabbinic traditions contain very little information
about Hillel's school. Relevant details, however, have been
collected by several scholars. According to Guttmann, Hillel
used the hermeneutical rules in use among non-Jews in order to
keep Judaism abreast with the times. He was elected *nasi* of
the *Beth Din ha-Gadol* and used his hermeneutical rules sparingly until resistance to them diminished.[97] Guttmann further
suggests that both Houses met together in the *Beth Din ha-Gadol*
to discuss, and vote on, particular issues. The agenda for
these meetings was set by the Houses in separate meetings.[98]

---

[94]Neusner, *Rabbinic Traditions*, III, 305-06.

[95]Cf. Neusner, *Rabbinic Traditions*, III, 99. Contrast Guttmann's view, cited in the next paragraph.

[96]Ibid., I, 301.

[97]Guttmann, *Rabbinic Judaism in the Making*, pp. 123-24. For further discussion of Hillel's seven rules see: Hermann L. Strack, *Introduction to the Talmud and Midrash* (New York: Atheneum, 1969), pp. 93-94; Meyer, "Φαρισαῖος," *TWNT*, IX, 35. Meyer (p. 31) agrees with Neusner that Hillel never actually held the position of *nasi*.

[98]Guttmann, *Rabbinic Judaism in the Making*, pp. 65, 100, 102-03.

The views of Hillel and Shammai are recorded with their names only when they disagreed with the ruling of their House.[99] The schools continued to exist after their deaths and grew further apart from each other. Most of the controversies between the Houses occurred, however, prior to A.D. 70, and within a few years thereafter the House of Shammai ceased to exist.[100] Significantly, Guttmann anticipated Neusner's argument that the Houses-form developed at a time when the Houses were approximately equal in power and disputing with each other. Guttmann places this period before 70, while Neusner finds it at Yavneh. The decision one makes on this issue determines to a large extent his conception of the schools in the period prior to 70.

Gerhardsson adds another observation about the Rabbinic schools:

> There was a degree of interplay between the different colleges, thanks to the custom, widespread among the Jews (and in Antiquity generally) by which a pupil, after a period of residence with a teacher or in a college, proceeded to another master or another college[6] in which he was able, if called upon to do so, to transmit items of doctrine from his former teachers.
>
> ----
> [6]b. Ber. 63b; b. Ab. Zar. 19a. . . .[101]

The great allegiance which the masters evoked from their disciples was probably a deterent, however, to frequent movement among schools on the part of the disciples.[102] Moreover, the fellowship among the disciples and their master was an important part of the life of the schools.[103]

Guttmann derives this reconstruction primarily from TB Beẓah 20a and never asks to what extent the picture it furnishes is a retrojection from a later period.

[99]Ibid., p. 70.

[100]Ibid., p. 106. Guttmann observes (p. 100) that no heads of Beth Shammai are mentioned after the time of Hillel and Shammai. See also Alexander Guttmann, "Hillelites and Shammaites--a Clarification," *HUCA*, XXVIII (1957), esp. pp. 115, 125.

[101]Gerhardsson, *Memory and Manuscript*, p. 101. Such interplay among Christian schools or teachers could account for some of the shared material in the synoptic gospels and for some of the similarities between the synoptics and John.

[102]Cf. Davies, *Setting*, p. 455: "It was not enough to learn the words of a rabbi, but necessary to live with him, so as to absorb his thought and copy his every gesture."

[103]Cf. Rengstorf, "μανθάνω," *TDNT*, IV, 434; Jacob Neusner, *Fellowship in Judaism: The First Century and Today* (London: Vallentine, Mitchell, 1963), pp. 43-44.

On the basis of his study of the legal (Yavnean) traditions, Neusner ascertains a different perspective on the House of Hillel. While affirming that the school did exist prior to 70, he observes that none of Hillel's students are known to us by name.[104] From the traditions that Hillel had eighty students and from the allegation that the whole Pharisaic group in Jerusalem could use one trough for purifying their dishes, he concludes that the schools were rather small groups: "The narrative convention in the many stories of the Houses is to have pretty much the whole of the respective Houses, or at least their elders, in the same place at the same time."[105] The absence of rules about the school and the study of Torah, combined with the observation that 67% of the legal pericopae deal with matters of table-fellowship, indicates that the pre-70 Pharisaic schools were more interested in the latter than in the study of Torah for its own sake.[106] Moreover, in contrast to the Essenes and early Christians, the Pharisaic schools

> . . . did not conduct their table-fellowship meals as rituals. The table-fellowship laws pertained not to group life, but to ordinary, daily life lived quite apart from heightened ritual occasions.[107]

Even though the existing Yavnean legal pericopae concentrate heavily on matters related to table-fellowship, one wonders whether this emphasis reflects the central concern of the pre-70 Pharisaic schools or a Yavnean interest in preserving decisions regarding table-fellowship matters. If the latter, i.e., if the Yavneans selected the table-fellowship traditions for preservation while allowing decisions on many other matters to perish, then it may be anachronistic to characterize the pre-70 Pharisaic schools as being primarily interested in matters pertaining to table-fellowship.

---

[104]Neusner, *From Politics to Piety*, p. 42; cf. *Rabbinic Traditions*, I, 375; III, 306.

[105]Neusner, *Rabbinic Traditions*, III, 267; cf. III, 280. For the reference to 80 disciples see TB Sukkah 28a.

[106]Ibid., III, 296-97; cf. Neusner, "'Pharisaic-Rabbinic' Judaism: A Clarification," p. 265: "And one looks in vain in the rabbinic traditions about the Pharisees before 70 for stress on, or even the presence of the ideal of, the study of Torah." Neusner does not deny that the Torah was studied before 70. Rather, he finds that the Rabbinic piety expressed through the study of Torah is a continuation of pre-70 scribism. Still, it is difficult to conceive that the study of the Torah was not an essential part of the life of the early Pharisaic schools.

[107]Neusner, *Rabbinic Traditions*, III, 297; cf. III, 300; *From Politics to Piety*, p. 87; Morton Smith, "The Dead Sea Sect in Relation to Ancient Judaism," *NTS*, VII (1961), 352.

Other reservations about Neusner's reconstruction of the
development of the Rabbinic traditions may now be stated in a
programmatic way. While awaiting further research, they must
remain tentative. 1) Neusner dismisses the references in the
Old Testament which indicate that schools and methods for passing on tradition were developed centuries prior to Yavneh.[108]
Rather, he contends that the method of oral transmission practiced in the second century A.D. was developed by the Yavneans.[109]
The Old Testament references, however, indicate that traditions
concerning at least the essential content of prophetic utterances were being transmitted centuries before Yavneh. As earlier
chapters have indicated, sayings attributed to Pythagoras and
Epicurus were memorized and transmitted to younger members and
new converts to these philosophies before the turn of the era.
Finally as Neusner affirms, Yoḥanan and his disciples claimed
the oral tradition of ". . . the essential content of the ancient Torah."[110] These considerations suggest that the methods
for oral transmission of the sayings of teachers were more highly developed in the pre-70 period than Neusner allows. 2)
Neusner dismisses the *Soferim* and the Men of the Great Assembly
and by doing so breaks the continuity of development from the
earlier practices and traditions to the Rabbis.[111] Even though
Lauterbach's argument from silence concerning the period from
270 to 190 B.C. weakens his theory about the origin of the
Mishnah-form, the motives he suggests for its development and
use are plausible. 3) Neusner claims that the Yavneans obliterated the form and substance of the traditions of the Houses
and that the narratives about Hillel are predominantly Ushan.
Yet, Neusner postulates that the first revision of the Pharisaic
traditions took place during the period of Hillel.[112] Neusner's
guess may well be correct, but granting his presuppositions
about the development of the Rabbinic tradition it is difficult

---

[108]Cf. Neusner, *Rabbinic Traditions*, III, 169; and above, pp. 186-88.

[109]Above, pp. 180-81.

[110]Above, p. 181.

[111]Cf. Judah Goldin, "The End of Ecclesiastes: Literal Exegesis and
Its Transformation," in *Biblical Motifs*, ed. by A. Altmann, Studies and Texts,
Vol. III (Cambridge, Mass.: Harvard University Press, 1966), esp. pp. 149-
50, 157; Sidney B. Hoenig, *The Great Sanhedrin: A Study of the Origin,
Development, Composition and Functions of the Bet Din ha-Gadol during the
Second Jewish Commonwealth* (Philadelphia: The Dropsie College for Hebrew
and Cognate Learning, 1953).

[112]Above, p. 180.

to see how he is able to make this inference. Josephus'
accounts do not provide adequate support for it. Finally, 4)
Neusner probably overemphasizes the Pharisees' change "from
politics to piety." He does so by minimizing Josephus' remarks
about the Pharisees' use of ancient traditions, their fame for
interpreting the Law accurately, and their preoccupation with
ritual purity. While Neusner's perception that the Pharisees
became much less active politically during the early part of
the first-century A.D. is probably correct, he slides over the
association of the early Pharisees with the *Ḥasidim* ("pious
ones") too quickly. Piety was the central concern of the
Pharisees from their earliest period. For a while the pursuit
of piety was thought to entail political activity; later, this
activity was abandoned. These reservations are tentative and
programmatic. A full critique of Neusner's work must await a
re-examination of his detailed analyses of the various pericopae, and nothing can be said about Hillel with confidence until
Neusner's contribution has been carefully tested.

As the above discussion indicates, the nature of the
Pharisaic schools is still very obscure; and this obscurity is
due primarily to the difficulty in using the Rabbinic materials.
Nevertheless, three aspects of pre-70 Pharisaism are discern-
ible: 1) the transmission of oral tradition from master to
disciple, 2) the study of Torah, and 3) the definition and
observance of table-fellowship laws. The importance of each of
these features prior to Yavneh is still subject to debate, and
the relative value assigned to each determines one's image of
pre-70 Pharisaism. Gerhardsson emphasizes the first and second,
while Neusner minimizes these and stresses the third. Further
study of these emphases in the Rabbinic materials is needed
before the early Pharisaic schools can be described adequately.

The history of the
House of Hillel

Due to the complexity of the issues surrounding the development of the Rabbinic materials, most of what would normally
have been included in this section of the chapter was inserted
into the discussion of the sources. The history of the development of the Rabbinic traditions is inseparable from the
history of the House of Hillel. Actually, the school of Hillel
as an independent group probably ceased to exist shortly after

70, but its traditions were adopted by the Yavneans and became a dominating force in post-70 Judaism. Yavneh, thus, represents the end of the period of the Houses and the beginning of a period characterized by interest in unity and the codification of Mishnaic traditions.[113] The key to ascertaining a clearer understanding of the Houses will be further study of the work of Yavneh.

The influence of the House of Hillel

The influence of the school of Hillel on the Johannine community does not appear to have been as direct or as extensive as that of Qumran (or more generally, sectarian Judaism). No firm conclusion can be drawn at this point, however, because of the uncertainty of our understanding of the school of Hillel. If the Pharisaic-Rabbinic tradition did influence the Johannine school, however, this influence would probably appear in passages in John which might indicate that the Johannine community was reacting to the three emphases in pre-70 Pharisaism listed above. Does John attempt to replace the Pharisaic transmission of oral tradition, study of the Torah, and/or table-fellowship laws with a new tradition, the study of a new Torah, and/or new standards for table-fellowship?

---

[113]Cf. Davies, *Setting*, p. 266.

Chapter IX

PHILO'S SCHOOL

The importance of
Philo's school

The corpus of Philo's writings is one of the largest collections of first-century works. Yet, it is difficult to
describe their milieu with precision. Reitzenstein characterized Philo as "die komplizierteste und den verschiedensten
Einflüssen ausgesetzte Persönlichkeit des Altertums . . . ."[1]
Because Philo is such a complex figure, he is important for the
study of a variety of areas: Alexandrian Judaism, Alexandrian
Christianity, the influence of the schools of philosophy, the
development of allegorical exegesis, the development and character of Diaspora synagogues, and his possible influence on
New Testament writings (John and Hebrews especially).

In a paradoxical way, Philo is also important for the
study of ancient schools. As will be indicated below, the
hypothesis that Philo belonged to a school of exegetes in
Alexandria has now been either rejected or carefully qualified
by most Philonists. There is no evidence, at least, that Philo
was the founder of a school in the sense that the heads of the
schools already discussed were founders. Hence, Philo could be
excluded from a study of ancient schools and their founders.
Examination of Philo's writings, however, reveals that his community shared many of the characteristics of the schools discussed above. The general consensus is now that Philo was
associated with a synagogue (or synagogue school) in Alexandria.
Moreover, since the the Gospel of John reflects a community in
conflict with a synagogue, a discussion of Philo's synagogue-
milieu is warranted: 1) it provides a glimpse of another kind
of ancient school, and 2) it illuminates the character of an
Alexandrian synagogue, some features of which may have been
shared by synagogues near the Johannine community.[2]

---

[1] R[ichard] Reitzenstein, *Das iranische Erlösungsmysterium: Religionsgeschichtliche Untersuchungen* (Bonn: A. Marcus & E. Weber's Verlag, 1921),
p. 106 n. 1.

[2] Cf. Martyn, *History and Theology in the Fourth Gospel*, esp. p. 58
n. 94.

The sources for the study
of Philo's school

Although Philo's writings are extensive and well preserved,[3] they provide surprisingly little information about the
community in which he worked. Since Philo nowhere describes
his community, the investigator is limited to the inferences
he can draw from Philo's exposition of scripture, knowledge of
Greek philosophy, references to his predecessors or teachers,
and addresses to his readers.[4] The difficulty of describing
Philo's community is compounded by the absence of any references to it outside of Philo's writings. We hear nothing of
students of Philo, and if there was any biographical tradition
it has not survived.[5] In contrast to the paucity of evidence,
there is a vast body of scholarship on Philo in which hypotheses
about his community are propounded and examined.[6] The most
important of these theories are examined below.

The origin of
Philo's school

The only event in Philo's life which can be dated is his
journey to Rome with the embassy to Gaius in A.D. 40,[7] when he

---

[3]Philo's writings fill twelve volumes in the Loeb edition: *Philo*,
trans. by F. H. Colson, G. H. Whitaker, and R. Marcus, The Loeb Classical
Library (12 vols.; Cambridge, Mass.: Harvard University Press, 1929-53).

[4]Regarding Philo's readers see: Samuel Sandmel, "Philo's Environment
and Philo's Exegesis," *JBR*, XXII (1954), 249. Yehoshua Amir (Neumark),
"Philo Judaeus," *EncJud*, XIII, 411, claims that "Exoteric and esoteric sections can be distinguished in Philo's writings."

[5]The only reference to Philo in contemporary literature occurs in
Josephus *Ant.* XVIII. 259-60:

"Philo, who stood at the head of the delegation of the Jews, a man held in
the highest honour, brother of Alexander the alabarch and no novice in
philosophy, ..."
Φίλων ὁ προεστὼς τῶν Ἰουδαίων τῆς πρεσβείας, ἀνὴρ τὰ πάντα ἔνδοξος
Ἀλεξάνδρου τε τοῦ ἀλαβάρχου ἀδελφὸς ὢν καὶ φιλοσοφίας οὐκ ἄπειρος, . . .

[6]For bibliography see: Howard L. Goodhart and Erwin R. Goodenough, "A
General Bibliography of Philo Judaeus," in Erwin R. Goodenough, *The Politics
of Philo Judaeus* (New Haven: Yale University Press, 1938), pp. 125-348;
Ralph Marcus, "Recent Literature on Philo (1924-1934)," in *Jewish Studies in
Memory of George A. Kohut*, ed. by S. W. Baron and A. Marx (New York: The
Alexander Kohut Memorial Foundation, 1935), pp. 463-91; Louis H. Feldman,
Studies in Judaica: Scholarship on Philo and Josephus (1937-1962)(New York:
Yeshiva University, n.d.); E. Hilgert, "A Bibliography of Philo Studies,
1963-70," *Studia Philonica*, I (1972), 57-71; E. Hilgert, "A Bibliography of
Philo Studies in 1971 with Additions for 1965-70," *Studia Philonica*, II
(1973), 51-54. Leisegang's index to Philo's writings has also been a great
assistance: Ioannes Leisegang, *Philonis Alexandrini opera quae supersunt*,
Vol. VII: *Indices ad Philonis Alexandrini opera* (Berlin: Walter de Gruyter
& Co., 1926).

[7]See n. 5 above, and Philo *De Legatione* 349ff.

was an elderly man. On the basis of this data, his dates are usually fixed at *ca*. 25-20 B.C. to *ca*. A.D. 45-50. Philo's brother, Alexander, was a banker, and Philo himself may have held a significant official position.[8]

Philo was born into a leading Jewish family in Alexandria and given an encyclical education.[9] The nature and extent of his Jewish training, however, can only be conjectured.[10] He also pursued the study of philosophy, and in one of his few autobiographical references he related the following:

> There was a time when I had leisure for philosophy and for the contemplation of the universe and its contents, when I made its spirit my own in all its beauty and loveliness and true blessedness, when my constant companions were divine themes and verities, wherein I rejoiced with a joy that never cloyed or sated.[11]

This passage may refer to a period of time which he spent with the "contemplative" Therapeutae.[12] In another place, Philo refers to a pilgrimage to Jerusalem which he made by way of Ascalon.[13] Beyond these fascinating details very little is known about Philo's life.

The crucial question in the study of Philo concerns not the authenticity or date of the materials he transmits (as it is in the study of the Rabbinic tradition) but the interpretation of his background. What influences were formative for the life of the community in which he worked? Four sources of influence are considered below: Greek philosophy, the Therapeutae,

---

[8]Cf. Erwin R. Goodenough, *An Introduction to Philo Judaeus* (2nd ed.; Oxford: Basil Blackwell, 1962), pp. 6-7, 62-63; *The Politics of Philo Judaeus*, pp. 64-85.

[9]Philo held encyclical education in high regard as a necessary stepping stone to higher knowledge. Cf. Colson, "General Introduction," in *Philo*, The Loeb Classical Library (Cambridge, Mass.: Harvard University Press, 1929), I, xvi; Goodenough, *An Introduction to Philo Judaeus*, p. 135.

[10]Cf. Amir, "Philo Judaeus," *EncJud*, XIII, 409: "Everything that has been inferred as to the sources of his Jewish knowledge remains hypothetical, since the existence of Jewish schools in the Diaspora of that time has not been proved." It is now generally agreed that Philo probably did not know Hebrew; cf. Goodenough, *An Introduction to Philo Judaeus*, p. 9; H. Leisegang, "Philon (41)," *RE*, XX (1941), 4; Amir, "Philo Judaeus," *EncJud*, XIII, 409.

[11]Philo *De Specialibus Legibus* III. 1:
ᵀΗν ποτε χρόνος, ὅτε φιλοσοφία σχολάζων καὶ θεωρία τοῦ κόσμου καὶ τῶν ἐν αὐτῷ τὸν καλὸν καὶ περιπόθητον καὶ μακάριον ὄντως νοῦν ἐκαρπούμην, θείοις ἀεὶ λόγοις συγγινόμενος καὶ δόγμασιν, ὧν ἀπλήστως καὶ ἀκορέστως ἔχων ἐνευφραινόμην, ...

[12]See below, p. 201.

[13]Philo *De Providentia* 64.

an exegetical school or scholastic tradition, and a Jewish
mystery-cult. One's assessment of these possible sources of
influence is crucial to his understanding of Philo's community
and, hence, the interpretation of his writings.

Undeniably, Philo had at least a general knowledge of
Greek philosophy. Earlier scholars attempted to trace the
sources of his understanding of philosophy, and the discussion
often centered on Posidonius.[14] More evidence, however, is
available regarding the school(s) of philosophy which influenced
Philo most. Some phrases which Philo uses are found most frequently in Stoic, Platonic, or Pythagorean writings. While
acknowledging that such phrases are not conclusive evidence
and that our knowledge of the ". . . philosophic atmosphere of
Alexandria in his day . . ." is limited,[15] Goodenough characterizes the philosophic influence on Philo as follows:

> Platonism as it had been elaborated in Pythagorean schools
> or under continued Pythagorean influence seems the system
> which as a whole Philo most closely followed. . . .
> The 'vast amount of Stoicism' which Colson rightly saw in
> Philo seems to me much more a matter of terminology and minor
> detail than anything which seriously affected Philo's main
> position. . . . We keep ourselves in needless confusion in
> reading Philo if, for all our recognition of Stoic elements,
> we do not read him as one whose basic philosophical outlook
> was that of the Platonists and Pythagoreans.[16]

Harry A. Wolfson places Philo squarely in the stream of Greek
philosophy. Although Philo was primarily a preacher, he was
". . . perhaps the greatest philosophic preacher that has ever
lived, ..."[17] He was steeped in the philosophies, but was
a critic, reformer, and original thinker:

> . . . he built up a system of philosophy which is consistent,
> coherent, and free from contradictions, all of it being based
> upon certain fundamental principles. Finally, while indeed
> for various historical and perhaps personal reasons he did
> not found any 'sect' in the sense that the Academicians and
> Peripatetics and Stoics and Epicureans are said to consti-
> tute philosophical sects (αἱρέσεις), it is most remarkable
> that without a group of official disciples his teachings

---

[14]Cf. Wendland, *Die hellenistisch-römische Kultur in ihren Beziehungen
zu Judentum und Christentum*, p. 61; Hartwig Thyen, "Die Probleme der neueren
Philo-Forschung," *ThRu*, n.F., XXIII (1955), 232.

[15]Goodenough, *An Introduction to Philo Judaeus*, p. 92.

[16]Ibid., pp. 110-11; cf. Amir, "Philo Judaeus," *EncJud*, XIII, 411; and
Philo's description of the Pythagorean groups in *Quod Omnis Probus Liber sit*
2-4.

[17]Harry A. Wolfson, *Philo: Foundations of Religious Philosophy in
Judaism, Christianity, and Islam* (2 vols.; Cambridge, Mass.: Harvard University Press, 1947), I, 98.

> became the most dominant influence in European philosophy
> for well-nigh seventeen centuries.[18]

Wolfson's enthusiasm for Philo's originality as a philosopher,
however, has not convinced many other Philonists.[19] Instead,
German scholars especially, while acknowledging that the philosophies influenced Philo, have concluded that because of the
syncretism of the period what he owed to each school of philosophy cannot be clearly distinguished:

> Vorwiegend in der deutschen Forschung der letzten 30 Jahre
> schlug man einen anderen Weg ein, um Philos Werk zu verstehen.
> Er wurde als Teil der gnostischen Bewegung angesehen, deren
> Ursprung man auf mythische, vorchristliche Wurzeln
> zurückführte.[20]

Regardless of what the character of the philosophic influence
on Philo was, his primary interest was not in creating a new
philosophy. Richard A. Baer, Jr. correctly subordinates Philo's
interest in philosophy to his work as an exegete: "He is mainly
an exegete of Scripture who intends to present the Scriptural
truth in terms of the best philosophic thought of his day."[21]

The second possible source of influence on Philo is the
Therapeutae. Philo's lengthy and sympathetic description of
this monastic group has led to the speculation that he spent his
period of contemplation and study of philosophy with them.[22]
If so, they may have been a formative influence on him. Nevertheless, while it is now generally agreed that Philo describes a
historical group and not a product of his own imagination, his

---

[18]Ibid., I, 114-15.

[19]See especially, Erwin R. Goodenough, "Wolfson's Philo," *JBL*, LXVII
(1948), 87-109.

[20]Ursula Früchtel, *Die kosmologischen Vorstellungen bei Philo von
Alexandrien: Ein Beitrag zur Geschichte der Genesisexegese*, Arbeiten zur
Literatur und Geschichte des hellenistischen Judentums, II (Leiden: E. J.
Brill, 1968), p. 3. For discussion of gnostic elements in Philo see the
works cited by Früchtel (p. 3 n. 9) and Hans Jonas, *The Gnostic Religion:
The Message of the Alien God and the Beginnings of Christianity* (2nd ed.;
Boston: Beacon Press, 1963), p. 91; Franz-Norbert Klein, *Die Lichttermino-
logie bei Philon von Alexandrien und in den hermetischen Schriften:
Untersuchungen zur Struktur der religiösen Sprache der hellenistischen
Mystik* (Leiden: E. J. Brill, 1962). See also the recent appraisal of the
question by R. McL. Wilson, "Philo of Alexandria and Gnosticism," *Kairos*,
XIV (1972), 213-19, who concludes that ". . . the Bultmannian inclusion of
Philo in the category of Gnosis is justified, *provided* that we remember that
Gnosis is not yet Gnosticism."

[21]*Philo's Use of the Categories Male and Female*, Arbeiten zur Literatur
und Geschichte des hellenistischen Judentums, III (Leiden: E. J. Brill,
1970), p. 5.

[22]See above, p. 199. Cf. Goodenough, *An Introduction to Philo Judaeus*,
p. 32.

description of the Therapeutae (as well as the Essenes) is probably largely ". . . a projection of his own ideals rather than
an accurate description of a real community."[23] Even if the
Therapeutae as we know them are largely the product of Philo's
ideals and apologetic interests, his description of them is
important for this study because of the similarities and contrasts between them and the schools discussed herein.

Philo uses the Therapeutae as an example of the contemplative life as opposed to the "active" life of the Essenes. The
Therapeutae could be found in many places but were especially
numerous around Alexandria. Philo specifically refers to the
group around the Lake of Marea.[24] The Therapeutae, both male
and female, devoted their lives to the study of scripture and
the pursuit of philosophy:

> They read the Holy Scriptures and seek wisdom from their
> ancestral philosophy by taking it as an allegory, since they
> think that the words of the literal text are symbols of some-
> thing whose hidden nature is revealed by studying the under-
> lying meaning.[25]

They lived in simple houses around a communal sanctuary in which
they met every seventh day.[26] The houses were far enough apart
to allow for solitude but close enough for the κοινωνία which
they cherished.[27] In each house there was a sanctuary
(μοναστήριον), in which they kept the ". . . laws and oracles
delivered through the mouth of prophets, and psalms and anything

---

[23]Baer, *Philo's Use of the Categories Male and Female*, p. 98 n. 2; cf.
Samuel Sandmel, *Philo's Place in Judaism: A Study of Conceptions of Abraham
in Jewish Literature* (Cincinnati: Hebrew Union College Press, 1956), p. 193
n. 389. During the nineteenth century both the authenticity of *De Vita
Contemplativa* and the existence of the Therapeutae were challenged. The
writing was regarded as a later Christian work describing early Christian
ascetics. These positions were abandoned, however, following the work of
I. Heinemann, "Therapeutai," *RE*, V A 2 (1934), 2321-46, esp. 2345-46; cf.
G[eza] Vermes, "Essenes--Therapeutai--Qumran," *Durham University Journal*,
LII (1960), 103. See also the recent work by Francois Daumas, "La 'solitude'
des Thérapeutes et les antécédents Égyptiens du monachisme Chrétien," in
Philon d'Alexandrie: Lyon 11-15 Septembre 1966, ed. by R. Arnaldez, C.
Mondésert, and J. Pouilloux (Paris: Éditions du Centre National de la
Recherche Scientifique, 1967), pp. 347-59.

[24]Philo *De Vita Contemplativa* 21-22.

[25]Ibid., 28:
ἐντυγχάνοντες γὰρ τοῖς ἱεροῖς γράμμασι φιλοσοφοῦσι τὴν πάτριον φιλοσοφίαν
ἀλληγοροῦντες, ἐπειδὴ σύμβολα τὰ τῆς ῥητῆς ἑρμηνείας νομίζουσιν ἀποκεκρυμ-
μένης φύσεως ἐν ὑπονοίαις δηλουμένης.

[26]Ibid., 24, 32.

[27]Ibid., 24. Cf. Philo's accounts of the κοινωνία among the Essenes:
Quod Omnis Probus Liber sit 84, 91; *Hypothetica* 11. 4-5.

else which fosters and perfects knowledge and piety,"[28] and to
which the Therapeutae withdrew for study and initiation ". . .
into the mysteries of the sanctified life."[29] If the Therapeutae were a very large group, they collectively possessed
quite a large library; but Philo does not mention any scribal
activity among them, except that they wrote hymns and psalms.[30]
The Therapeutae also possessed

> . . . writings of men of old, the founders of their way of
> thinking, who left many memorials of the form used in
> allegorical interpretation and these they take as a kind of
> archetype and imitate the method in which this principle is
> carried out.[31]

On the Sabbath and on the eve of the chief feast every seventh
week, they met together in the communal sanctuary. There they
sat according to sex and rank, heard the scripture expounded,
sang, ate, and held a sacred vigil, singing until dawn.[32] Philo
contrasts the temperance of their communal meal with the symposia of the Greeks and refers explicitly to the banquets of
Xenophon and Plato.[33] One recognizes, however, that Philo's
claim that the common meal of the Jewish philosophers is superior to that of the pagan philosophers is characteristic of his
apologetic interests.[34]

This summary of Philo's description of the Therapeutae
suggests similarities between them and other schools, especially
the Essenes at Qumran.[35] Nevertheless, Philo's account contains
no references to transmitting the teachings of a venerated
founder (like the TR). We are told only that they had a

---

[28]Philo *De Vita Contemplativa* 25:
. . . νόμους καὶ λόγια θεσπισθέντα διὰ προφητῶν καὶ ὕμνους καὶ τὰ ἄλλα οἷς
ἐπιστήμη καὶ εὐσέβεια συναύξονται καὶ τελειοῦνται.

[29]*De Vita Contemplativa* 25:
. . . τὰ τοῦ σεμνοῦ βίου μυστήρια τελοῦνται, ...
Cf. ibid., 30.

[30]Ibid., 29.

[31]Ibid.:
. . . συγγράμματα παλαιῶν ἀνδρῶν, οἳ τῆς αἱρέσεως ἀρχηγέται γενόμενοι
πολλὰ μνημεῖα τῆς ἐν τοῖς ἀλληγορουμένοις ἰδέας ἀπέλιπον, οἷς καθάπερ
τισὶν ἀρχετύποις χρώμενοι μιμοῦνται τῆς προαιρέσεως τὸν τρόπον·

[32]Philo *De Vita Contemplativa* 30-32, 64-89. Note the reference to
πρεσβύτεροι in section 67. Regarding the exposition of scripture see
Appendix I.

[33]Ibid., esp. 57, 59.

[34]Cf. Vermes, "Essenes--Therapeutai--Qumran," p. 103.

[35]Cf. ibid., *passim*; and below, Chapter XI.

president (πρόεδρος)[36] and that they were "disciples of Moses."[37] There is little evidence, other than this glowing account of their way of life, to show that they were influential in Philo's life; he either viewed them as an ideal community or described them as such for apologetic reasons.

The third possible source of influence on Philo is a Jewish exegetical school in Alexandria. This view was championed by Bousset, who advanced his thesis by attempting to identify Philo's sources.[38] Bousset concluded that Philo relied upon a body of oral and written traditions which were influenced by Hellenistic culture and philosophy.[39] The Hellenistic traditions, however, were mediated to Philo by a Jewish exegetical school. Philo then skillfully adapted his sources to his own ends:

> Alles drängt auch hier zu dem Schluss, der ja auch bei allem Kommentarbetrieb besonders nahe liegt: Philo gibt die ὑπομνήματα und ὑποσημειώσεις, die er der Schule zu verdanken hat, in seinem grossen Kommentarwerk weiter. Unter diesen Umständen begreift man auch besser, wie Philo, der durchaus ein Mann eigener Überzeugungen ist, so widersprechende Traditionen hat verarbeiten können; sie waren für ihn geschützt durch die Ehrfurcht vor der älteren exegetischen Generation, den Nimbus der Schule, vielleicht durch die eigene Vergangenheit Philos.[40]

For Bousset, therefore, Philo is to be seen as a tradent who both preserves and re-mints the tradition of an exegetical school.

In spite of his contributions to the source-critical study of Philo, Bousset's theory of Philo's dependence on a school has not been widely accepted. Bousset's position was endorsed

---

[36]Philo *De Vita Contemplativa* 75, 79.

[37]Cf. ibid., 64: . . . οἱ Μωυσέως γνώριμοι, μεμαθηκότες ἐκ πρώτης ἡλικίας ἐρᾶν ἀληθείας, ...
While Philo uses γνώριμοι, John 9:28 uses μαθηταί when referring to the disciples of Moses. For further references to the phrase in Philo see Wayne A. Meeks, *The Prophet-King: Moses Traditions and the Johannine Christology*, NovTSup, Vol. XIV (Leiden: E. J. Brill, 1967), p. 103 n. 2; cf. Meeks' interpretation (p. 103): "The true Jews in turn, that is, those who are capable of 'clearly understanding' the symbolic meaning of the Torah, are 'Moses' disciples.'"

[38]*Jüdisch-Christlicher Schulbetrieb in Alexandria und Rom*, pp. 1-2, 45, 109, 153; Bousset's thesis was anticipated by James Drummond, *Philo Judaeus or, The Jewish-Alexandrian Philosophy in Its Development and Completion* (2 vols.; London: Williams and Norgate, 1888), I, 20.

[39]Bousset, *Jüdisch-Christlicher Schulbetrieb in Alexandria und Rom*, pp. 43-44. Bousset (p. 153) regards Philo's early writings as an exception.

[40]Ibid., p. 83.

by Hans Lietzmann[41] but rejected by most Philonists.[42] The chief obstacle to Bousset's hypothesis is stated by Thyen:

> Auch die Theorie, dass Philo Lehrbücher oder eigene Nach-schriften aus dem Schulbetrieb einer alexandrinischen Exegetenschule benutzt haben soll, die W. Bousset zu beweisen versuchte, ist nicht sehr wahrscheinlich. Es fehlt in den philonischen Schriften auch jegliche Anspielung auf einen derartigen Schulbetrieb in Alexandria.[43]

Nevertheless, although Philo never explicitly refers to a school, he frequently states that he is working with a tradition he has received. These references are an important clue to Philo's background; and a reappraisal of them may show that while Bousset's position must be qualified, he was correct in viewing Philo as standing within a scholastic tradition. Philo's most important references to this tradition are the following:

> But I will disregard their malice, and tell the story of Moses as I have learned it, both from the sacred books, the wonderful monuments of his wisdom which he has left behind him, and from some of the elders [πρεσβυτέρων] of the nation; for I always interwove what I was told with what I read, and thus believed myself to have gained a closer knowledge than others of his life's history.[44]

> These are the explanations handed down to us from the old-time studies of divinely gifted men who made deep research into the writings of Moses.[45]

> This is the explanation commonly and widely stated, but I have heard another from highly gifted men who think that

---

[41]*The Beginnings of the Christian Church*, trans. by B. L. Woolf (New York: Charles Scribner's Sons, 1937), p. 117. See also: Émile Bréhier, *Les idées philosophiques et religieuses de Philon d'Alexandrie*, Études de philosophie médiévale, VIII (Paris: Librairie Philosophique J. Vrin, 1950), pp. 45-61.

[42]For critiques and rejections of Bousset's position see: Leopold Cohn, *et al.*, *Philo von Alexandria: Die Werke in deutscher Übersetzung* (6 vols.; Berlin: Walter de Gruyter & Co., 1962), III, 6 n. 1; Leisegang, "Philon," *RE*, XX, 6, 11, 13; Walther Völker, *Fortschritt und Vollendung bei Philo von Alexandrien: Eine Studie zur Geschichte der Frömmigkeit*, TU, Bd. IL (Leipzig: J. C. Hinrichs Verlag, 1938), pp. 3 n. 1, 10; Harald Hegermann, *Die Vorstellung vom Schöpfungsmittler im hellenistischen Judentum und Urchristentum*, TU, Bd. LXXXII (Berlin: Akademie-Verlag, 1961), pp. 8-9.

[43]Hartwig Thyen, *Der Stil der Jüdisch-Hellenistischen Homilie*, FRLANT, N.F., 47 Heft (Göttingen: Vandenhoeck & Ruprecht, 1955), p. 79; cf. Thyen, "Die Probleme der neueren Philo-Forschung," p. 234.

[44]Philo *De Vita Mosis* I. 4:
τούτων βασκανίαν ὑπερβὰς τὰ περὶ τὸν ἄνδρα μηνύσω μαθὼν αὐτὰ κἀκ βίβλων τῶν ἱερῶν, ἃς θαυμάσια μνημεῖα τῆς αὐτοῦ σοφίας ἀπολέλοιπε, καὶ παρά τινων ἀπὸ τοῦ ἔθνους πρεσβυτέρων· τὰ γὰρ λεγόμενα τοῖς ἀναγινωσκομένοις ἀεὶ συνύφαινον καὶ διὰ τοῦτ' ἔδοξα μᾶλλον ἑτέρων τὰ περὶ τὸν βίον ἀκριβῶσαι.

[45]Philo *De Specialibus Legibus* I. 8:
Ταῦτα μὲν οὖν εἰς ἀκοὰς ἦλθε τὰς ἡμετέρας, ἀρχαιολογούμενα παρὰ θεσπεσίοις ἀνδράσιν, οἳ τὰ Μωυσέως οὐ παρέργως διηρεύνησαν.

most of the contents of the law-book are outward symbols of
hidden truths, expressing in words what had been left
unsaid.[46]

I have also heard some natural philosophers who took the
passage allegorically, not without good reason.[47]

I have heard, however, some scholars give an allegorical
exposition of this part of the story in a different form.[48]
The pattern which emerges from these references is that the
traditions to which Philo refers: 1) relate to the interpretation of scripture (usually the Law); 2) concern allegorical
interpretation; 3) are esoteric in the sense that they are not
the widely-known interpretation; 4) derive from scholars, philosophers, or gifted men; and 5) were transmitted to Philo
orally [ἤκουσα]. These references, thus, place Philo within a
scholastic tradition, but are not conclusive evidence that he
was a member of a school of exegetes. Sandmel embraces this
modification of Bousset's position:

> The notion commends itself if one will not press 'school'
> too rigidly,[44] as Bousset does infelicitously.

———
44 . . . . The divisive word here is 'school,' with its
overtones of formality and channeled transmission. Perhaps
'scholastic tradition' expresses the idea more properly; I
see no reason to deny the continuity of transmission of
materials.[49]

Before probing the nature of the community which mediated this
"scholastic tradition" to Philo, one further possible source
of influence on him must be considered.

———

[46]Ibid., III. 178:
'Ἤδε μὲν αἰτία ἣ παρὰ πολλοῖς εἴωθε λέγεσθαι· ἑτέραν δὲ ἤκουσα θεσπεσίων
ἀνδρῶν τὰ πλεῖστα τῶν ἐν τοῖς νόμοις ὑπολαμβανόντων εἶναι σύμβολα φανερὰ
ἀφανῶν καὶ ῥητὰ ἀρρήτων.

[47]Philo De Abrahamo 99:
'Ἤκουσα μέντοι καὶ φυσικῶν ἀνδρῶν οὐκ ἀπὸ σκοποῦ τὰ περὶ τὸν τόπον
ἀλληγορούντων, ...

[48]Philo De Iosepho 151:
'Ἤκουσα μέντοι καθ' ἑτέραν ἰδέαν τροπικώτερον τὰ περὶ τὸν τόπον
ἀκριβούντων.
For other passages where Philo refers to tradition see: Carl Siegfried,
Philo von Alexandria als Ausleger des Alten Testaments (Amsterdam: Philo
Press, 1970 [originally published in 1875]), pp. 26-27; Sidney G. Sowers,
The Hermeneutics of Philo and Hebrews, Basel Studies of Theology, No. I
(Zürich: EVZ-Verlag, 1965), p. 18.

[49]Sandmel, Philo's Place in Judaism, p. 17. Cf. Sowers, The Hermeneutics of Philo and Hebrews, p. 43.

Goodenough proposes that Philo must be understood against the background of a Jewish mystery-cult (θίασος).[50] By the first century, he contends, Judaism at least for some Jews in the Diaspora had become a mystery:

> It is quite possible and probable, then, that for two cen-
> turies or more before Philo the Jews in Egypt, especially
> in Alexandria, found in their environment that type of
> thought ready made which we can only describe by an extend-
> ed hyphenization, a Persian-Isiac-Platonic-Pythagorean
> mystery. . . . In Philo the Mystery is not only fully dev-
> eloped, but ripe with the ripeness of very many years. So
> mature is the Mystery that it may well have lost all local-
> ism and been quite as familiar among the Jews of Rome and
> Tarsus as in Alexandria itself.[51]

This mystery was developed by Philo and his predecessors by studying the scriptures and interpreting them allegorically in the light of Greek philosophy. According to this view, the purpose of Philo's allegory was to guide the initiate out of the material world and into the eternal:

> Did Philo think that he was presenting men with a literal or
> real mystery in that he was showing them a literal path to
> the immaterial, one which, if followed, would result in the
> true achievement of the goal? The answer can only be that
> he certainly and passionately did think so, did believe that
> the Patriarchs and Moses uniquely revealed that path and by
> intercession with God and help to man led human beings along
> it.[52]

Philo holds his mystery over against all others as the true mystery. As Goodenough's work attests, Philo uses the language of the mysteries in numerous passages. The following are mere-ly a sample:

> These thoughts, ye initiated, whose ears are purified,
> receive into your souls as holy mysteries indeed and babble
> not of them to any of the profane.[53]

> I myself was initiated under Moses the God-beloved into his
> greater mysteries, yet when I saw the prophet Jeremiah and
> knew him to be not only himself enlightened, but a worthy
> minister of the holy secrets, I was not slow to become his
> disciple.[54]

---

[50]Erwin R. Goodenough, *By Light, Light: The Mystic Gospel of Hellen-istic Judaism* (New Haven: Yale University Press, 1935), p. 5.

[51]Ibid., p. 237.

[52]Goodenough, *An Introduction to Philo Judaeus*, p. 155.

[53]Philo *De Cherubim* 48:
ταῦτα, ὦ μύσται κεκαθαρμένοι τὰ ὦτα, ὡς ἱερὰ ὄντως μυστήρια ψυχαῖς ταῖς ἑαυτῶν παραδέχεσθε καὶ μηδενὶ τῶν ἀμυήτων ἐκλαλήσητε, ...

[54]Ibid., 49:
καὶ γὰρ ἐγὼ παρὰ Μωυσεῖ τῷ θεοφιλεῖ μυηθεὶς τὰ μεγάλα μυστήρια ὅμως αὖθις Ἱερεμίαν τὸν προφήτην ἰδὼν καὶ γνούς, ὅτι οὐ μόνον μύστης ἐστὶν ἀλλὰ καὶ ἱεροφάντης ἱκανός, οὐκ ὤκνησα φοιτῆσαι πρὸς αὐτόν·

Then only does he begin to worship God and entering the darkness, the invisible region, abides there while he learns the secrets of the most holy mysteries. There he becomes not only one of the congregation of the initiated, but also the hierophant and teacher of divine rites, which he will impart to those whose ears are purified.[55]

The holy secrets of the mystery, moreover, are not to be shared with the literalists, who cannot grasp the true meaning of scripture.[56]

Goodenough's contention that there was a widespread Jewish mystery has not been widely accepted;[57] but the language of the mysteries on which he focused attention must be dealt with in any attempt to understand Philo's background. Wolfson claims that "mystery" had by that time acquired a broad range of meanings,[58] and Früchtel responds to Goodenough by claiming that Philo's mystery was not a cult but a "Schreibtischmysterium."[59] Früchtel argues that Philo, using Moses as the model hierophant, attained the vision of the meaning of the scriptures. Having experienced this vision, Philo felt he was able to guide his readers to it:

> Er erkannte seine Umgebung nicht mehr, während ihm eine hermeneutische εὕρεσις geschenkt wurde, ein Lichtgenuss, eine scharfblickende Schau, eine durchsichtige Klarheit der Dinge selbst. Das hat seine Denkkraft schöpferisch und produktiv gemacht. Das Mysterium bei Philo ist daher kein Kultakt, sondern ein Geschehen, das sich am Schreibtisch und im Studierzimmer abspielt.[60]

---

[55]Philo *De Gigantibus* 54:

προσκυνεῖν τὸν θεὸν ἄρχεται καὶ εἰς τὸν γνόφον, τὸν ἀειδῆ χῶρον, εἰσελθὼν αὐτοῦ καταμένει τελούμενος τὰς ἱερωτάτας τελετάς. γίνεται δὲ οὐ μόνον μύστης, ἀλλὰ καὶ ἱεροφάντης ὀργίων καὶ διδάσκαλος θείων, ἃ τοῖς ὦτα κεκαθαρμένοις ὑφηγήσεται.

[56]Cf. Sowers, *The Hermeneutics of Philo and Hebrews*, p. 43.

[57]Cf. Arthur Darby Nock, review of *By Light, Light*, by Erwin R. Goodenough, *Gnomon*, XIII (1937), 156-65; and the response by Goodenough, "Literal Mystery in Hellenistic Judaism," in *Quantalacumque: Studies Presented to Kirsopp Lake by Pupils, Colleagues and Friends*, ed. by R. P. Casey, S. Lake, and A. K. Lake (London: Christophers, 1937), pp. 226-41. See also the reservations expressed by C. H. Dodd, *The Interpretation of the Fourth Gospel* (Cambridge: At the University Press, 1958), p. 59; and the summary of subsequent discussions in Hegermann, *Die Vorstellung vom Schöpfungsmittler im hellenistischen Judentum und Urchristentum*, pp. 6-9.

[58]Wolfson, *Philo*, I, 49.

[59]Früchtel, *Die kosmologischen Vorstellungen bei Philo von Alexandrien*, pp. 112-15, 151.

[60]Ibid., p. 113. Cf. esp. Philo *De Somniis* I. 164. Regarding εὕρεσις, see Appendix I.

For Philo, therefore, ascent into the higher levels of the
mystery meant penetration into the deeper meaning of scripture
through allegorical exegesis. This perception of Philo's writings leads to the following conclusions:

> 1.   Philo steht nicht in einer kultischen, sondern in einer
> hermeneutischen Tradition. In diesem Punkt hat er von der
> Mysterien- und Mythen-exegese gelernt. 2. Die Weihegrade
> haben--wie schon erwähnt--kein reales, sondern ein literar-
> isches Vorbild.[61]

By applying the language of the mysteries to the interpretation
of the Old Testament, Philo attempted to distinguish the Jewish
cult from pagan mysteries. By entering into the mysteries of
the scriptures, the Jews, like Moses, could attain to true virtue and instruct the other religions in the same.[62]

Früchtel's interpretation of the language of the mysteries
in Philo avoids the difficulties of establishing that there was
a widespread Jewish mystery-cult and is supported by the probability that Jews in Alexandria had to make some response to
the popular mystery cults.[63] If Früchtel is correct, Philo
may now be seen as working within a scholastic, hermeneutical
tradition, and using both the language of Greek philosophy and
that of the mysteries in his allegorical interpretation of the
Jewish scriptures in order to demonstrate that Judaism was the
highest philosophy and the truest mystery. The question of the
nature of the community which mediated this tradition to Philo
may now be approached directly.

The nature of
Philo's school

Each of the proposed influences on Philo discussed above
contribute to understanding the community in which he lived.
In recent scholarship it has become axiomatic that Philo was
associated with a synagogue in Alexandria. The warrants for
this conclusion are drawn from several lines of reasoning.

---

[61]Früchtel, *Die kosmologischen Vorstellungen bei Philo von Alexandrien*, p. 114.

[62]Ibid., p. 115; on Moses as hierophant see Meeks, *The Prophet-King*,
pp. 120-25.

[63]On the influence of the mysteries among the Jews see Hengel,
Judentum und Hellenismus, pp. 368-69, and 287. See also Hans Conzelmann,
"The Mother of Wisdom," in *The Future of Our Religious Past: Essays in
Honour of Rudolf Bultmann*, ed. by J. M. Robinson, trans. by C. E. Carlston
and R. P. Scharlemann (New York: Harper & Row, Publishers, 1971), pp. 230-
43.

First Philo was widely known and respected. Josephus praises his brilliance, and he was chosen by the Jewish community to lead the delegation to Gaius.[64] These bits of evidence make it unlikely that Philo worked in a small, sectarian school or community like the Therapeutae.[65]

Secondly, Philo's purpose throughout is to instruct and edify his readers. This purpose may, however, have overly influenced those who maintain that Philo was a teacher or homilist in a synagogue.[66] Instruction and edification were common to all the schools discussed above and hence cannot be made to support the case for Philo's association with a synagogue rather than a separate school of exegetes.

The most important evidence, however, is the homiletic form of Philo's writings and his references to the synagogues. Thyen maintains that Philo's commentary on Genesis is the most important witness to the form of the homily in Alexandrian synagogues of the first century,[67] and Peder Borgen has identified homilies in other Philonic writings.[68] Feldman summarizes Thyen's contributions and offers his own conclusion:

> . . . [Thyen] finds that P. used Hellenistic diatribes as a source for his homilies just as he used Greek philosophy as a source for his theology; P.'s allegorical commentaries, he conjectures, were preached in the Alexandrian synagogues, for they have several of the traits of oral homilies--repetitions, ethical content, and the familiar sayings; a more likely conclusion, we may suggest, is that P. was influenced in his written style (for there is no evidence that he was a preacher) by the homilies that he heard in the streets and synagogues of Alexandria.[69]

Feldman's suggestion is perceptive. For all the similarities between certain passages in Philo's writings and what can be inferred (largely on the basis of these passages) about the homilies, the fact remains that Philo's works are longer than

---

[64]See above, p. 198; cf. Egon Brandenburger, *Fleisch und Geist: Paulus und die dualistische Weisheit*, WMANT, Bd. XXIX (Neukirchen-Vluyn: Neukirchener Verlag, 1968), pp. 120-21.

[65]Philo's influence should not be overestimated, however. See below, pp. 213-14.

[66] Cf. Völker, *Fortschritt und Vollendung bei Philo von Alexandrien*, p. 10. See also Thyen, *Der Stil der Jüdisch-Hellenistischen Homilie*, p. 80; and "Die Probleme der neueren Philo-Forschung," p. 236: "Danach muss man sich Philo als den Homileten in seiner Gemeinde vorstellen, der seine Hörer um jeden Preis erbaut wissen will."

[67]Thyen, *Der Stil der Jüdisch-Hellenistischen Homilie*, p. 11.

[68]Borgen, *Bread From Heaven*, esp. chaps. II, IV, and V.

[69]Feldman, *Studies in Judaica*, p. 24.

the homilies isolated by Borgen, and they were intended to be *read* by a select group. Philo warns against attempting to lead the uninitiated into the mysteries of allegorical exegesis. These observations indicate that while Philo was probably associated with a synagogue, his writings were probably used in a synagogue-school where Philo taught the higher vision of scripture to a select group of initiates whose ears were purified. This solution fits the evidence and offers the balance which our data requires between Philo's public reputation and his esoteric instruction. Philo gives evidence of this *Sitz im Leben* in his apologetically motivated descriptions of the synagogues:

> . . . ; for it was customary on every day when opportunity offered, and pre-eminently on the seventh day, as I have explained above, to pursue the study of wisdom with the ruler expounding and instructing the people what they should say and do, while they received edification and betterment in moral principles and conduct. Even now this practice is retained, and the Jews every seventh day occupy themselves with the philosophy of their fathers, dedicating that time to the acquiring of knowledge and the study of the truths of nature. For what are our places of prayer throughout the cities but schools of prudence and courage and temperance and justice and also of piety, holiness and every virtue by which duties to God and men are discerned and rightly performed?[70]

> So each seventh day there stand wide open in every city thousands of schools of good sense, temperance, courage, justice and the other virtues in which the scholars sit in order quietly with ears alert and with full attention, so much do they thirst for the draught which the teacher's words supply, ...[71]

Philo also supplies evidence that these "schools" were not just open assemblies in which instruction was given. At least for some, more structured training was available:

---

[70]Philo *De Vita Mosis* II. 215-16:
ἔθος γὰρ ἦν, ἀεὶ μὲν κατὰ τὸ παρεῖκον, προηγουμένως δὲ ταῖς ἑβδόμαις, ὡς ἐδήλωσα καὶ πρόσθεν, φιλοσοφεῖν, τοῦ μὲν ἡγεμόνος ὑφηγουμένου καὶ διδάσκοντος ἅ τε χρὴ πράττειν καὶ λέγειν, τῶν δ' εἰς καλοκἀγαθίαν ἐπιδιδόντων καὶ βελτιουμένων τά τε ἤθη καὶ τὸν βίον. ἀφ' οὗ καὶ εἰσέτι νῦν φιλοσοφοῦσι ταῖς ἑβδόμαις Ἰουδαῖοι τὴν πάτριον φιλοσοφίαν τὸν χρόνον ἐκεῖνον ἀναθέντες ἐπιστήμῃ καὶ θεωρίᾳ τῶν περὶ φύσιν· τὰ γὰρ κατὰ πόλεις προσευκτήρια τί ἔτερόν ἐστιν ἢ διδασκαλεῖα φρονήσεως καὶ ἀνδρείας καὶ σωφροσύνης καὶ δικαιοσύνης εὐσεβείας τε καὶ ὁσιότητος καὶ συμπάσης ἀρετῆς, ᾗ κατανοεῖται καὶ κατορθοῦται τά τε ἀνθρώπεια καὶ θεῖα;

[71]Philo *De Specialibus Legibus* II. 62:
ἀναπέπταται γοῦν ταῖς ἑβδόμαις μυρία κατὰ πᾶσαν πόλιν διδασκαλεῖα φρονήσεως καὶ σωφροσύνης καὶ ἀνδρείας καὶ δικαιοσύνης καὶ τῶν ἄλλων ἀρετῶν, ἐν οἷς οἱ μὲν ἐν κόσμῳ καθέζονται σὺν ἡσυχίᾳ τὰ ὦτα ἀνωρθιακότες μετὰ προσοχῆς πάσης ἕνεκα τοῦ διψῆν λόγων ποτίμων, ...

The law tells us that we must set the rules of justice in
the heart and fasten them for a sign upon the hand and have
them shaking before the eyes. . . . He to whom it is given
to set their image in the eye of the soul, not at rest but
in motion and engaged in their natural activities, must be
placed on record as a perfect man. No longer must he be
ranked among the disciples and pupils but among the teachers
and instructors, and he should provide as from a fountain
to the young who are willing to draw therefrom a plenteous
stream of discourses and doctrines.[72]

Although the aim of the instruction Philo describes is virtue,
scripture is its object and its guide to the true philosophy
and virtue.[73] His synagogue, therefore, apparently maintained
a lively interest in catechetical instruction; ". . . the
Synagogue as Philo knew it in Alexandria was achieving a standing as a school in its own right without losing its usefulness
as a popular institution."[74]

The view of Philo which emerges from the present consideration of his writings is that he was a Jew, well-educated in
Greek philosophy, aware of Jewish traditions, interested in
groups like the neo-Pythagoreans, the Essenes, and the
Therapeutae, and influenced by the appeal of the mysteries.
But, he stood within and contributed to the scholastic tradition of an Alexandrian synagogue in which both Jews and Gentile
"God-fearers" sought the vision of the true philosophy, which
was attainable only through the proper (allegorical) interpretation of scripture.[75]

---

[72]Ibid., IV. 137, 140:

τὰ δίκαια, φησὶν ὁ νόμος, ἐντιθέναι δεῖ τῇ καρδίᾳ καὶ ἐξάπτειν εἰς
σημεῖον ἐπὶ τῆς χειρὸς καὶ εἶναι σειόμενα πρὸ ὀφθαλμῶν, ... ὅτῳ δ'
ἐξεγένετο τυπώσασθαι ἐν τῷ τῆς ψυχῆς ὄμματι μὴ ἡσυχάζοντα ἀλλὰ κινού-
μενα καὶ ταῖς κατὰ φύσιν ἐνεργείαις χρώμενα, τέλειος ἀνὴρ ἀναγεγράφθω,
μηκέτι ἐν τοῖς γνωρίμοις καὶ μαθηταῖς ἐξεταζόμενος, ἀλλ' ἐν διδασκάλοις
καὶ ὑφηγηταῖς, καὶ παρεχέτω τοῖς ἐθέλουσιν ἀρύεσθαι τῶν νέων ὥσπερ ἀπὸ
πηγῆς τῶν λόγων καὶ δογμάτων ἄφθονον νᾶμα·
Cf. Wolfson, *Philo*, II, 260-61. Philo frequently refers to disciples
(μαθηταί), e.g., *De Specialibus Legibus* II. 227; *De Posteritate Caini* 136,
146, 151; *De Sacrificiis Abelis et Caini* 64, 79; and to rival teachers,
e.g., *De Somniis* I. 102. For the image of the "well" or "spring" in Philo,
see *De Fuga et Inventione* 178, 195, 197, 198; cf. CD 6:2-11 (discussed
above, p. 163); and Dodd, *The Interpretation of the Fourth Gospel*, p. 56.

[73]Cf. Wolfson, *Philo*, II, 259-60, 266.

[74]Jesse Scott Boughton, *The Idea of Progress in Philo Judaeus* (New
York: [Columbia University], 1932), p. 36; cf. pp. 37, 80, 94.

[75]Hegermann, *Die Vorstellung vom Schöpfungsmittler im hellenistischen
Judentum und Urchristentum*, p. 25, reaches a similar conclusion:
"Philo will bei aller philosophischen Ausdrucksweise letztlich kein
Philosoph und er will trotz aller Mysterienausdrücke kein Mystagoge
sein. Er will als Lehrer seine Hörer dahin führen, dass sie 'geprägt
nach Lehren der Frömmigkeit und Heiligkeit ein seliges und glückliches
Leben führen.'"

The history of
Philo's school

Nothing is known of the history of the synagogue-school
in which Philo worked, and none of the names of his students
has survived. The inference that his writings continued to
be studied arises from the use made of them by the later Christian school in Alexandria and the evident popularity of allegorical exegesis there.

The influence of
Philo's school

Perhaps the reason for the complete silence of our sources
on the history of Philo's school is that he actually exerted
little influence on his community. Recent scholarship has
steadily diminished earlier estimates of Philo's influence.
Hegermann speculates that ". . . er war vielleicht in seiner
Zeit ein Einzelgänger ohne grosse Resonanz,"[76] and R. M. Grant
agrees.[77] In spite of earlier arguments to the contrary, no
direct link can be forged between Philo and the Christian
school of Pantaenus, Clement, and Origen.[78] Wolfson's claim
that Philo founded a new school of philosophy which exerted a
dominant influence on European philosophy for seventeen centuries exaggerates Philo's influence on the Church fathers and
medieval exegesis.[79] Moreover, recent assessments state that
Philo had no significant influence on John[80] and Hebrews.[81]
The chief value of Philo for this study lies, therefore, not in
his influence on the Jewish and Christian schools of the first

---

[76]Ibid., p. 8.

[77]Robert M. Grant, *A Short History of the Interpretation of the Bible* (rev. ed.; New York: The Macmillan Company, 1963), p. 75.

[78]Compare Boughton, *The Idea of Progress in Philo Judaeus*, p. 13, with the more skeptical stance of Grant, *A Short History of the Interpretation of the Bible*, p. 75.

[79]See above, p. 200. Compare Goodenough's response ("Wolfson's Philo," p. 88): "Even as ardent a Philonist as myself must blink at so great a claim for our hero." Goodenough, however, still attributes a considerable influence on early Christianity and medieval thought to ". . . the Philonic school, or hellenized Judaism, ..."

[80]Compare the high estimate of Philo's influence on John by Dodd, *The Interpretation of the Fourth Gospel*, p. 133, with the more conservative assessment by Brown, *The Gospel According to John*, I, lvii-lviii.

[81]Cf. Ronald Williamson, *Philo and the Epistle to the Hebrews*, Arbeiten zur Literatur und Geschichte des hellenistischen Judentums, IV (Leiden: E. J. Brill, 1970), pp. 8, 579.

century but in what his writings indicate about the nature of
the synagogue-schools in Diaspora (especially Alexandrian)
Judaism.

Chapter X

THE SCHOOL OF JESUS

<u>The importance of</u>
<u>the school of Jesus</u>

By the standards we have already established, Jesus and
his disciples constituted a school. Jesus the teacher gathered
disciples, taught, and was regarded as the founder of a religious tradition which transmitted his teachings and later wrote
gospels about his words and deeds. The study of this school is
important for a variety of reasons: 1) if a clearer perception
of Jesus' relationship to his disciples and the roles to which
he called them can be ascertained, many questions about Jesus
and the origin and development of early Christianity might be
moved one step closer to solutions; 2) the study of the school
of Jesus may provide insights into the nature of the pre-
rabbinic, Jewish schools; and finally 3) this study explores
an essential background of the Johannine community.

This chapter attempts to draw together and assess those
elements within the New Testament which suggest that early
Christian communities viewed Jesus and the disciples as a
school, studied the teachings of Jesus, and/or shared many of
the characteristics of the other schools studied herein.
Recent and important discussions about Jesus as a teacher, the
role of the twelve, and the transmission of Jesus' teachings
in the early Church will be considered.[1] Limitations dictated
by the central focus of this dissertation naturally require a
great deal of selectivity in the materials included in this
chapter and attention to this one perspective on the development of the Christian tradition makes a certain degree of dis-
tortion inevitable, but this chapter is not intended to be a
history of early Christianity.

The significance of the teaching ministry of Jesus and
the role of his disciples as tradents of his teachings has
often been underestimated. Moreover, those who have perceived
the value of seeing Jesus as one who taught in much the same
way as other Hellenistic or Jewish teachers have occasionally

---

[1]Harald Riesenfeld's paper on "The Gospel Tradition and Its Beginnings," (1957), reprinted in his *The Gospel Tradition* (Philadelphia:
Fortress Press, 1970), pp. 1-29, provided the stimulus for vigorous discussion in recent years of this aspect of Jesus' ministry.

overemphasized the implications of this perspective for the transmission and development of the Jesus-tradition.[2] A reassessment of Jesus' teaching ministry against the background of other ancient schools may, therefore, serve to correct some past descriptions of the school of Jesus.

The sources for the study
of the school of Jesus

The primary sources for the study of the school of Jesus are extensive and stand chronologically closer to the founder than those of any other ancient school with the possible exceptions of those of Epictetus and the Teacher of Righteousness. The historian must rely on sources produced by writers who stood within the Christian tradition for most of his data, but the number of writers and communities represented in the New Testament allow one to view the school of Jesus from a greater variety of early perspectives than is possible for most of the other schools. Another comparison may be made in that most of our information about the school of Jesus comes from sources which are quasi-biographical in nature. Most of the data about the schools of the philosophers comes from the biographical traditions about their founders, and these are permeated with legendary materials. Similarly, the gospels, our chief sources, contain legendary materials and are by no means biographies.[3] Nevertheless, they structure the traditions along a chronological framework and purport to tell of occasions on which Jesus taught his disciples. The traditions about Jesus contained in non-Christian sources are sparse; but, significantly, a common element in these traditions is that Jesus was crucified as a false teacher.[4]

Form-critical analyses have indicated that some of the gospel materials derive from communities which shared many of the characteristics and functions of schools. Bultmann identified two forms of dialogues in the synoptics: the controversy

---

[2]As indicated below, both Riesenfeld and Gerhardsson carried their arguments beyond the scope of their evidence.

[3]Cf. Rudolf Bultmann, *Die Geschichte der synoptischen Tradition* (Zweite Aufl.; Göttingen: Vandenhoeck & Ruprecht, 1931), pp. 260-61; Martin Dibelius, *From Tradition to Gospel*, trans. by B. L. Woolf (New York: Charles Scribner's Sons, n.d.), pp. 104-32; Vincent Taylor, *The Formation of the Gospel Tradition* (London: Macmillan & Co. Ltd., 1957), p. 32. Each defines "legend" differently.

[4]See T. W. Manson, "The Life of Jesus: A Study of the Available Materials," *BJRL*, XXVII (1943), esp. 330-31.

dialogues (*Streitgespräche*), and the scholastic dialogues
(*Schulgespräche*).[5] The two are similar in form. The former
appear to have grown out of an originally independent dominical
saying; in an imaginary scene an opponent questions Jesus about
some action or attitude and Jesus responds with an apophthegm
(pronouncement). In the latter, Jesus is questioned by someone
seeking knowledge. According to Bultmann, these apophthegms generally reflect the situation of the Palestinian church as it
interpreted teachings ascribed to Jesus and defined its position
vis-à-vis its opponents.[6] The disputes have Rabbinic parallels,
and the gospels generally portray the opponents as scribes and
Pharisees. While these disputes reflect primarily the situation
of the early Church, they are based on historical recollection:
". . . angesichts des Gesamtbestandes der Überlieferung wird
man kaum bezweifeln, dass Jesus als Rabbi gelehrt, 'Schüler'
gesammelt und disputiert hat."[7] In addition to the apophthegms,
one finds that a large part of the gospels is teaching material:
sayings of Jesus (logia, prophetic and apocalyptic sayings,
legal sayings, "I" sayings, and similitudes), and interpretations of these sayings. The quantity of such materials indicates that they were important to the life of some Christian
communities and that they were collected and interpreted by the
communities or their teachers. The work of the teachers is
probably seen most clearly in the earlier collections of
sayings (logia or Q), tractates (cf. Matt. 10; Mk. 2:1-3:6;
13), and homilies (Jn. 6:51-58).[8]

The obvious work of collecting, adapting, and systematizing materials in Matthew is emphasized by Stendahl as evidence
for a school:

It is at this point that the school may be invoked as a more
natural Sitz im Leben. The systematizing work, the adapta-

[5]Bultmann, *Die Geschichte der synoptischen Tradition*, pp. 39-58.

[6]Ibid., p. 56.

[7]Ibid., p. 52.

[8]Cf. James M. Robinson, "*LOGOI SOPHON*: On the Gattung of Q," in
Trajectories through Early Christianity (Philadelphia: Fortress Press,
1971), pp. 71-113; and Helmut Koester, "One Jesus and Four Primitive Gospels," ibid., pp. 158-87. Cf. also the Gospel of Thomas and P. Oxy. 1 and
654: Bernard P. Grenfell, and Arthur S. Hunt, ed. and trans., *The
Oxyrhynchus Papyri* (London: Egypt Exploration Fund, 1898 and 1904), I, 1-3;
IV, 1-22; and by the same authors, ΛΟΓΙΑ ΙΗΣΟΥ: *Sayings of Our Lord from
an Early Greek Papyrus*, Egypt Exploration Fund (New York: Henry Frowde,
1897); and *New Sayings of Jesus and Fragment of a Lost Gospel from Oxyrhynchus*, Egypt Exploration Fund (New York: Oxford University Press, 1904).

tion towards casuistry instead of broad statements of principles, the reflection on the position of church leaders
and their duties, and many other features, all point to a
milieu of study and instruction.[9]

Stendahl draws support for his thesis primarily from the way
in which Matthew uses quotations from the Hebrew scriptures.
The sophistication evident in the handling and interpretation
of the texts reflects the work of a school, and Stendahl
emphasizes the similarities between the treatment of the
scriptures by the school of Matthew and the school at Qumran.[10]
Other features of the First Gospel favor his thesis also:
Matthew stresses the place of teaching in the ministry of Jesus,
arranges the teachings in five discourses, and enjoins the
importance of all that Jesus commanded (Matt. 28:20).[11] Moreover, Matthew is particularly concerned about explaining the
meaning of discipleship. The disciple is to: live by a new
interpretation of the Law (5:21-48), practice a new kind of
piety (6:1-18), "hear" (ἀκούω = obey) Jesus' words (7:24),
forsake possessions and lesser obligations (8:19-22), heal
and teach (10:8, 14), be like his teacher (10:24-25), be ready
to take up his cross (10:37-39), be trained for the kingdom of
heaven (13:52), hold the word of God above the oral tradition
of the Pharisees (15:1-6), confess Jesus as the Christ (16:13-
17), accept a new standard of fellowship (9:10-13; 18), and be
ready for the eschaton (24-25).[12] Matthew had a special interest in the meaning of discipleship and stressed keeping the
teachings of Jesus. Such a concern would be natural within an
early Christian school.

In view of the claim that a school stands behind Matthew,
the injunctions in Matt. 23:8-10 require explanation:

But you are not to be called rabbi, for you have one teacher,
and you are all brethren. And call no man your father on

---

[9]Stendahl, *School*, p. 29.

[10]Stendahl's *School* must be consulted for its detailed analysis of
quotations in Matthew, but he adumbrates his position on p. 35. See D.
Moody Smith, Jr., "The Use of the Old Testament in the New," in *The Use of
the Old Testament in the New and Other Essays: Studies in Honor of
William Franklin Stinespring*, ed. by J. M. Efird (Durham, N.C.: Duke University Press, 1972), pp. 43-49.

[11]Stendahl, *School*, pp. ix-x.

[12]Cf. Gerhard Barth, "Matthew's Understanding of the Law," in *Tradition and Interpretation in Matthew*, trans. by P. Scott (Philadelphia: The
Westminster Press, 1963), pp. 105-25; Martin H. Franzmann, *Follow Me: Discipleship According to Saint Matthew* (St. Louis: Concordia Publishing
House, 1961).

earth, for you have one Father, who is in heaven. Neither be called masters (καθηγηταί, lit. "instructors"), for you have one master (lit. "instructor"), the Christ.

This saying, peculiar to Matthew, would probably not have been inserted in the Gospel had there not been a problem in the Matthean community of members priding themselves in these titles (cf. James 3:1). In addition, the terms "rabbi" (ῥαββί), "teacher" (διδάσκαλος), "brothers" (ἀδελφοί), "father" (πατήρ), and "instructor" (καθηγητής) all suggest that the community was a school. The verses are set in the context of exhortation to humility (Matt. 23:11-12) and are probably a ". . . side-glance at Jamnia."[13] Stendahl correctly observes that these verses pose no threat to his thesis:

When Jesus is said to have forbidden his disciples to be called rabbi, father or teacher, Mt. 23$_{8-10}$, this is in no way a challenge to the existence of a school. On the contrary, it is only if something similar to the schools of the rabbis existed that the saying has any real significance.[14]

In sum, the cumulative force of the evidence to which Stendahl appeals justifies his thesis; there was a Matthean school which influenced the composition of the Gospel of Matthew. That Matthew is in some sense at least the product of a school does not mean, however, that the Matthean traditions are more authentic, or were more carefully transmitted, than those of Mark or Luke. On the contrary, part of the evidence for the school hypothesis is the interpretative work which can be best explained as the work of a school.[15] Whether or not Jesus viewed himself as the teacher of a school of disciples, Matthew shows that there was at least one early Christian community for which this view was important, and which collected, studied, and taught traditions about Jesus and his sayings. In this respect, the Matthean community had much in common with other schools in antiquity.[16]

---

[13]Davies, *Setting*, pp. 297-98; cf. pp. 94-99.

[14]Stendahl, *School*, p. 30.

[15]When one recognizes that interpretation was as much a concern of Christian teachers as collection and preservation of the traditions, ". . . the false accretions to the tradition (the birth stories, the nature miracles, and so on), . . ." and ". . . the losses which it suffered" [Smith, "A Comparison of Early Christian and Early Rabbinic Tradition," p. 176] no longer pose a problem for the contention that traditions about Jesus were transmitted by teachers and used in schools like that reflected in Matthew.

[16]Although the Gospel of John may contain important information about the school of Jesus, it is used sparingly in this chapter. This approach

Further discussion of the gospels as sources for the study of Jesus would be out of place here. Paradoxically, such a discussion could more profitably follow this chapter since one's assessment of the way in which the traditions about Jesus developed and were transmitted affects his evaluation of what the gospels tell us about Jesus.

The origin of the school of Jesus

As the number, vigor, and diversity of the schools in the Hellenistic world indicate, eclectic, scholastic traditions thrived in the first century. Moreover, their influence was not confined to the upper classes.[17] Philosophers appealed to the common people through popular addresses and exhortations,[18] urging them to convert to their philosophy because it possessed a better knowledge and wiser teachers. Simultaneously, and not unrelated to this phenomenon, Judaism was engaging in missionary activities. The common ground was appeal for conversion on the basis of texts (from Homer, a philosopher, or the Hebrew scriptures), and related ethical exhortations. The use of a common body of ethical materials is clearly attested in Greek philosophical, Jewish, and Christian writings of the first century. Wandering preachers were a common sight in the Hellenistic world. Furthermore, as Davies observed, ". . . the milieu within which Jesus appeared was conditioned for the faithful reception and transmission of tradition."[19] This conditioning was due in part to the influence of the schools. A further implication of their influence is that emerging Christian communities probably adapted some of the features of the organization, teaching, and communal life of the various schools (see the discussion of the Matthean community above) and were seen by outsiders as a new religious-philosophical school.

. . . .

is warranted by the observation that the picture of Jesus presented in John is shaped by the (Johannine) community to a degree unparalleled by the other gospels. The study of Johannine tradition is reserved for the final chapter.

[17]Cf. Willem Cornelius van Unnik, "First Century A.D. Literary Culture and Early Christian Literature," *Nederlands Theologisch Tijdschrift*, XXV (1971), 34.

[18]Cf. Werner Jaeger, *Early Christianity and Greek Paideia* (Cambridge, Mass.: The Belknap Press of Harvard University Press, 1965), p. 10; Hatch, *The Influence of Greek Ideas on Christianity*, p. 108; Nock, *Conversion*.

[19]*Setting*, p. 416.

John the Baptist and his disciples formed the immediate background from which the school of Jesus emerged. John did not attempt to found his own sect but called people to repentance and prepared them through his baptism for that of the coming one.[20] In the course of his ministry, however, he gathered a group of disciples (μαθηταί -- Matt. 9:14; 14:12; Mk. 2:18; 6:29; Lk. 5:33; 7:18, 19; 11:1; Jn. 1:35, 37; 3:25), who addressed him as "teacher" (διδάσκαλε Lk. 3:12; ῥαββί Jn. 3:26). John taught his disciples sobriety and fasting (Matt. 9:14; 11:18; Mk. 2:18; Lk. 5:33) and a fixed form of prayer (Lk. 11:1), and they shared in his ministry and ministered to him (Lk. 7:18, 19; Matt. 14:12; Mk. 6:29). Jesus may have been John's disciple prior to commencing his own ministry (see esp. the technical phrase for coming to a teacher to be his disciple in Matt. 3:14);[21] at least he was baptized by John and drew some of his disciples from the Baptist's movement (Jn. 1:35-40). From the mention of disciples of John the Baptist in Ephesus at a later time (Acts 19:1-7) the following inferences can be drawn: 1) the movement survived John's death; 2) in places it rivaled the Christian movement; and 3) it probably transmitted at least the substance of the Baptist's preaching and teachings (cf. Lk. 3:7-14). His teachings were also preserved in the early Christian communities. While it is likely that the model of Jesus and the disciples colored the traditions about the Baptist and his disciples, it is still instructive to note that our sources record some details about John's disciples and affirm that Jesus and some of his followers emerged from the earlier movement. Thus, John's disciples form the immediate background against which the role of Jesus' disciples must be viewed.[22]

The nature of the school of Jesus

Any discussion of Jesus' teaching and the role of his disciples must be prefaced by the observation that the gospels firmly attest that Jesus was regarded as a teacher and that

---

[20]Walter Wink, *John the Baptist in the Gospel Tradition*, NTSMS, VII (Cambridge: At the University Press, 1968), p. 107.

[21]Cf. Erich Fascher, "Jesus der Lehrer: Ein Beitrag zur Frage nach dem 'Quellort der Kirchenidee,'" *TLZ*, LXXIX (1954), 328.

[22]Cf. Martin Hengel, *Nachfolge und Charisma: Eine exegetisch-religionsgeschichtliche Studie zu Mt 8₂₁f. und Jesus Ruf in die Nachfolge*, BZNW, XXXIV (Berlin: Verlag Alfred Töpelmann, 1968), p. 40.

teaching was an integral part of his ministry. As Dodd observed:

> It is not the least remarkable feature of the Gospels as
> historical documents that although they all--even Mark--are
> written under the influence of a 'high' Christology, yet
> they all--even John--represent Jesus as a teacher with His
> school of disciples.[23]

An investigation of the role of the disciples will shed further
light on the school of Jesus.

The use of μαθητής in Acts reveals that the term came to
refer to any Christian believer. In the gospels it is applied
both to large groups (Lk. 6:17; 19:37; Jn. 6:60, 66) and to a
more defined circle who followed him, who are at times at least
synonymous with "the twelve" (Matt. 11:1) and "the apostles"
(Matt. 10:2). What did it mean to be a μαθητής of Jesus during
his ministry? Our sources are no doubt colored by the later
use of the term to designate believers in general, but the
terms used to describe the activities and duties of the μαθηταί
offer clues to the nature of their role.

In Matt. 22:16 and Mk. 2:18, μαθηταί is used to designate
the disciples of the Pharisees. The question arises: was the
role of the μαθηταί of Jesus the same as that of the μαθηταί
of the Pharisaic teachers? Rengstorf observes that the distinctive mark of the disciples is that they walk with Jesus
(Jn. 6:66).[24] Fascher shows that the terms used for following
Jesus (ἀκολουθεῖν, δεῦτε ὀπίσω, and ὀπίσω ἐλθεῖν) are the same
as those used in the Rabbinic tradition for being a disciple--
הלך אחרי (cf. I Kings 19:21 where Elisha "follows after"
Elijah).[25] Moreover, it is only the disciples (and not the
crowds, cf. Lk. 14:26, 27) who "follow after" (ἔρχεσθαι ὀπίσω)
Jesus. Fascher argues convincingly that these were technical
terms which denoted the relationship of a pupil to his master,
and Davies finds that διακονεῖν may be a translation of שמש,
which in the Rabbinic literature denotes the service which
students perform for their master (cf. Mk. 10:45; 15:41).[26]

....

[23]Charles Harold Dodd, "Jesus as Teacher and Prophet," in *Mysterium
Christi: Christological Studies by British and German Theologians*, ed. by
G. K. A. Bell and D. A. Deissmann (London: Longmans, Green and Co., 1930),
p. 53.

[24]Rengstorf, "μαθητής," *TDNT*, IV, 445.

[25]Fascher, "Jesus der Lehrer," esp. cols. 327-31. See also the works
of Anselm Schulz, who emphasizes the similarities between the disciples of
Jesus and the Rabbinic disciples: *Nachfolgen und Nachahmen: Studien über
das Verhältnis der neutestamentlichen Jüngerschaft zur urchristlichen
Vorbildethik*, StANT, Bd. VI (Munich: Kösel-Verlag, 1962); *Jünger des Herrn:
Nachfolge Christi nach dem Neuen Testament* (Munich: Kösel-Verlag, 1964).

Even though the similarities in terminology form an important link between the school of Jesus and the Pharisaic-Rabbinic school-tradition, the differences between the two cannot be overlooked. First, the μαθηταί of Jesus were called by him. This was a departure from the Pharisaic-Rabbinic practice.[27] Again, the devotion of the disciples to the person of Jesus and the services they rendered him surpassed the customary relationship between master and disciple in the Pharisaic-Rabbinic tradition.[28] Rengstorf finds that ἀκολουθεῖν rather than μανθάνειν (which seldom appears in the gospels) is the primary duty of the μαθηταί of Jesus: "His [Jesus'] concern is not to impart information, nor to deepen an existing attitude, but to awaken unconditional commitment to Himself."[29] This concept of discipleship is radically different from that of the Pharisaic-Rabbinic tradition. Discipleship to Jesus differed from the latter in at least two further respects. Discipleship was not a transitory state in their development; they never ceased to be his disciples. Secondly, Jesus stressed that entry into fellowship with him carried with it the obligation to suffer.[30] Ultimately, the μαθηταί of Jesus were witnesses and participants in his ministry and not bearers of a tradition, as were disciples in the Rabbinic schools. Their witness was based on their personal relationship to Jesus, and after Easter Jesus the teacher was promptly replaced by Jesus the Lord.[31]

Hengel follows Rengstorf in rejecting the Pharisaic-Rabbinic master-pupil relationship as the model against which the μαθηταί of Jesus are to be understood. The theme of eschatological crisis in the ministry of Jesus is emphasized by Hengel, who contrasts it with the rather sedate atmosphere of the scribal-rabbinic houses of instruction.[32] Using Matt. 8:18-22 as the springboard for his study, Hengel turns to other possible models for the role of Jesus' μαθηταί. He discusses the meaning of *nachfolgen* for Elisha and Elijah, the holy-war tradition, the charismatic-prophetic leaders, the apocalyptic

---

[27]Cf. Aboth 1:6; Davies, *Setting*, p. 421.

[28]Rengstorf, "μαθητής," *TDNT*, IV, 447-48.

[29]Rengstorf, "μανθάνω," *TDNT*, IV, 406.

[30]Rengstorf, "μαθητής," *TDNT*, IV, 448-49.

[31]Ibid., pp. 454-55.

[32]Hengel, *Nachfolge und Charisma*, p. 16.

prophets, the popular zealotic leaders, and the Cynic-Stoic philosophers, in addition to the scribal-rabbinic model. He finds the teaching that the μαθηταί of Jesus are to be free from possessions very close to the nature of discipleship described by Epictetus:

> And how is it possible for a man who has nothing, who is naked, without home or hearth, in squalor, without a slave, without a city, to live serenely? Behold, God has sent you the man who will show in practice that it is possible. "Look at me," he says, "I am without a home, without a city, without property, without a slave; I sleep on the ground; I have neither wife nor children, no miserable governor's mansion, but only earth, and sky, and one rough cloak. Yet what do I lack? Am I not free from pain and fear, am I not free? When has anyone among you seen me failing to get what I desire, or falling into what I would avoid? When have I ever found fault with either God or man? When have I ever blamed anyone? Has anyone among you seen me with a gloomy face? And how do I face those persons before whom you stand in fear and awe? Do I not face them as slaves? Who, when he lays eyes upon me, does not feel that he is seeing his king and his master?"
> Lo, these are words that befit a Cynic, this is his character, and his plan of life.[33]

This aspect of discipleship is emphasized by Mark, who writes for a Hellenistic-Christian community (cf. Mk. 1:18, 20; 10:28). In contrast, Hengel finds that the theme of disruption of the family as a consequence of discipleship, which was an offense in Palestine, was a condition expected at the end-time by the followers of the apocalyptic prophets and zealotic leaders. This dimension of discipleship is heightened in the Q-tradition (Matt. 10:34-36; Lk. 12:51-53; and Matt. 8:21-22; Lk. 9:59-60).[34]

These observations lead Hengel to consider the disciples of John the Baptist as the closest analogy to Jesus' disciples and stress the similar tone of the ministries of these two figures: ". . . gerade beim Täufer innerhalb des antiken Judentums die prophetisch-eschatologische Form seines [Jesus]

---

[33]Epictetus III. xxii. 45-50:

Καὶ πῶς ἐνδέχεται μηδὲν ἔχοντα, γυμνόν, ἄοικον, ἀνέστιον, αὐχμῶντα, ἄδουλον, ἄπολιν διεξάγειν εὑρόως; ἰδοὺ ἀπέσταλκεν ὑμῖν ὁ θεὸς τὸν δείξοντα ἔργῳ, ὅτι ἐνδέχεται. "ἴδετέ με, ἄοικός εἰμι, ἄπολις, ἀκτήμων, ἄδουλος· χαμαὶ κοιμῶμαι· οὐ γυνή, οὐ παιδία, οὐ πραιτωρίδιον, ἀλλὰ γῆ μόνον καὶ οὐρανὸς καὶ ἓν τριβωνάριον, καὶ τί μοι λείπε; οὐκ εἰμι ἄλυπος, οὐκ εἰμι ἄφοβος, οὐκ εἰμι ἐλεύθερος; πότε ὑμῶν εἶδέν μέ τις ἐγ ὀρέξει ἀποτυγχάνοντα, πότ᾽ ἐν ἐκκλίσει περιπίπτοντα; πότ᾽ ἐμεμφάμην ἢ θεὸν ἢ ἄνθρωπον, πότ᾽ ἐνεκάλεσά τινι; μή τις ὑμῶν ἐσκυθρωπακότα με εἶδεν; πῶς δ᾽ ἐντυγχάνω τούτοις, οὓς ὑμεῖς φοβεῖσθε καὶ θαυμάζετε; οὐχ ὡς ἀνδραπόδοις; τίς με ἰδὼν οὐχὶ τὸν βασιλέα τὸν ἑαυτοῦ ὁρᾶν οἴεται καὶ δεσπότην;"

῎Ιδε κυνικαὶ φωναί, ἴδε χαρακτήρ, ἴδ᾽ ἐπιβολή.
Cf. Hengel, *Nachfolge und Charisma*, pp. 32-33.

[34]Ibid., pp. 36-37.

Wirkens am reinsten zum Ausdruck kommt."[35] Hengel sharply
rejects the idea that Jesus' disciples functioned as μαθηταί
did in the scribal-rabbinic tradition and then asks why Jesus
called a special group to be his disciples. Jesus did not call
them for any of the reasons for which contemporary figures had
followers. Jesus' unconditional call is to be understood in
the context of the absolute demands of the Old Testament prophets. Jesus called his disciples to share in the service of
the imminent Kingdom of God. Hengel sees in the sending out of
the disciples to heal and proclaim the Kingdom (Mk. 6:7-13) the
clearest expression of Jesus' intentions for the disciples.[36]
Because of their role as participants in the service of the
Kingdom, Hengel argues, the disciples were not an "esoterische
Kerngemeinde,"[37] and they probably did not sustain their roles
for a long period of time: "Auf jeden Fall liess, ... ,
die drängende Nähe der Gottesherrschaft selbst keine Zeit zu
einem Lehrer-Schüler-Verhältnis und zu gelehrten Studien nach
rabbinischer Manier."[38]

Before proceeding to the critical question of whether or
not Hengel and others are correct in denying that Jesus spent
time giving his disciples instruction, other aspects of the
unique role of the μαθηταί of Jesus need to be reviewed. As
noted above, the disciples were called to a personal commitment
to Jesus, which involved the acceptance of suffering (Lk.
14:26).[39] The absolute demand as a condition of discipleship
is unique in ancient scholastic traditions; in no other tradition is the demand for commitment raised to a comparable level.
Secondly, just as other schools had common meals, meals played
a central role in the school of Jesus; but in contrast to the
practice of other schools, the school of Jesus maintained open
table-fellowship, eating with outsiders of all classes. Jesus
probably also taught while at table. It has been suggested
that the Last Supper, later commemorated by the early Church,
was in part at least a celebration of the open fellowship of

---

[35]Ibid., p. 40.

[36]Ibid., pp. 80-81.

[37]Ibid., p. 82.

[38]Ibid., p. 89.

[39]Cf. Fascher, "Jesus der Lehrer," col. 328; Eduard Schweizer, *Lord-
ship and Discipleship*, SBT (London: SCM Press Ltd., 1960), pp. 15-17, 21.

earlier meals during the ministry of Jesus and an anticipation of an eschatological banquet.[40] Finally, one observes that being a μαθητής meant hearing and doing the words of Jesus (Matt. 7:24 and Lk. 6:47) and that the disciples taught as part of their participation in Jesus' ministry (Mk. 6:30).[41]

Do these ascriptions of teaching and learning activity to Jesus and his disciples derive from the early Chruch, or do they reflect the situation of the disciples during the ministry of Jesus? This evokes the central question for the study of the school of Jesus: did Jesus instruct his disciples, or do the passages[42] which indicate that he did so derive from a later period when the need arose to trace the traditions of the Church back to Jesus?

There are significant reasons for thinking that Jesus viewed teaching as an integral part of his ministry and called together and taught a group of disciples. If Jesus is commonly called "Rabbi" (especially in John)[43] by both his disciples and outsiders, it must be remembered that this title meant simply "teacher" and had not yet acquired the technical meaning which it has in later Jewish writings.[44] Moreover, the designation "teacher" occurs in the oldest strata of the gospel traditions and was later superseded by more adequate titles for describing the relationship between Jesus and the believers.[45] As noted above, according to the gospels the disciples followed (ἀκολουθεῖν) Jesus and served him in much the same way as other Jewish teachers were served by their pupils. In addition, the crowds showed Jesus the respect normally accorded to teachers,[46] and Jesus, as the head of a school, was held accountable

---

[40]Joseph C. Weber, "The Meals of the Kingdom: A Key to Jesus' Ministry," a paper presented at the one hundred seventh meeting of the Society of Biblical Literature, October 1971; Norman Perrin, *Rediscovering the Teaching of Jesus*, The New Testament Library (London: SCM Press Ltd., 1967), pp. 104, 107.

[41]Cf. Fascher, "Jesus der Lehrer," col. 331; Rengstorf, "διδάσκω," *TDNT*, II, 144.

[42]See below, p. 229 n. 57.

[43]John 1:38, 49; 3:2; 4:31; 6:25; 9:2; 11:8; and 20:16 (ῥαββουνί).

[44]Cf. C. H. Dodd, *The Founder of Christianity* (London: Collier-Macmillan Ltd., 1970), p. 53.

[45]Cf. Fascher, "Jesus der Lehrer," col. 327; Eduard Lohse, "ῥαββί," *TDNT*, VI, 965.

[46]See Rengstorf, "διδάσκω," *TDNT*, II, 153-54.

for the practices of his students (Mk. 2:18, 23ff.).[47] The
prominence of teaching in Jesus' ministry is underscored, finally, by the references to teaching in summary passages in the
gospels (e.g. Matt. 4:23; 9:35; 11:1) and by the observation
that much of the synoptic tradition about Jesus consists of
teaching material.[48]

According to the gospels, Jesus conducted himself in much
the same way as other teachers. Bultmann states the similarities forcefully:

> But if the gospel record is worthy of credence, it is at
> least clear that *Jesus actually lived as a Jewish rabbi*. As
> such he takes his place as a teacher in the synagogue. As
> such he gathers around him a circle of pupils. As such he
> disputes over questions of the Law with pupils and opponents
> or with people seeking knowledge who turn to him as the
> celebrated rabbi. He disputes along the same lines as Jew-
> ish rabbis, uses the same methods of argument, the same
> turns of speech; like them he coins proverbs and teaches in
> parables. Jesus' teaching shows in content also a close
> relationship with that of the rabbis.[49]

In accord with the practices of Jewish teachers, Jesus sat while
he taught (Matt. 5:1; Lk. 4:20-21) and taught in synagogues, in
the temple, and at his home in Capernaum (Mk. 2:1; 9:33).[50]
Jesus also taught "by the sea," "on the mountain," and while
walking with his disciples. Such itinerant or peripatetic
teaching may have been unusual among Jewish teachers, but it
was not among the wandering Cynic-Stoic preachers. Jesus'
practice of teaching crowds wherever he found them rather than
confining his teaching to his circle of followers was also
closer to that of the Cynic-Stoic preachers than to the practices of the later rabbis.[51] One wonders, however, whether
Jesus' teaching practices in this regard did not also resemble
those of the prophets, who made public demonstrations by their
prophetic signs, sang songs [Isa. 5:1-2], and prophesied in the
streets and market places of Jerusalem.[52]

---

[47]Cf. Rengstorf, "μαθητής," *TDNT*, IV, 441-42; David Daube, "Respon-
sibilities of Master and Disciples in the Gospels," *NTS*, XIX (1972), 1-15.

[48]See above, p. 217.

[49]Rudolf Bultmann, *Jesus and the Word*, trans. by L. P. Smith and
E. H. Lantero (New York: Charles Scribner's Sons, 1958), p. 58.

[50]Davies, *Setting*, p. 421 n. 2; and *The Gospel and the Land*, p. 419,
suggests that perhaps οἶκος in Mark sometimes means "school." In the former
he asks: "Was there a 'beth Joshua' as well as a 'beth Hillel'?"

[51]Cf. Fascher, "Jesus der Lehrer," cols. 331-32.

[52]Cf. Dodd, "Jesus as Teacher and Prophet," p. 64; Jesus went to

In spite of the similarities between Jesus and other teachers of his milieu, Jesus' teaching was unique. The point at which his distinctiveness comes most clearly into focus is his relation to the Law. Jesus disputed points of interpretation with the scribes and Pharisees, but he also placed his personal authority above that of the Law and used the Law to defend his actions and buttress his teachings in a way unheard of among the rabbis.[53] According to Matthew, Jesus did not dismiss the Law (Matt. 5:17-19); rather, he promised that one who obeyed and taught the Law would be rewarded (Matt. 5:19).[54] The gospels provide little substantial evidence, however, for the claim that ". . . much of his time with his disciples went into the exposition of the Law."[55] Apart from the Sermon on the Mount, all of Jesus' pronouncements about the Law are made when he is speaking publicly (in a synagogue; Lk. 4:18-22) or in response to an outsider (Lk. 10:25-26; Mk. 12:28-34).[56] On

Jerusalem to appeal to the nation at its center. "When the appeal failed, He pronounced the doom of the Temple and of Jerusalem, quite in the spirit of the earlier prophets, and then, like Isaiah (viii. 16-18), separated His disciples, as the 'Remnant' of Israel." See the discussion of Isa. 8:16, 18 above, p. 187, and in Appendix II.

[53]For discussion of the ways in which Jesus' teaching differed from that of the Rabbis see Davies, *Setting*, p. 420.

[54]Cf. Bultmann, *Die Geschichte der synoptischen Tradition*, pp. 146-47; Barth, "Matthew's Understanding of the Law," in *Tradition and Interpretation in Matthew*, pp. 64-73, 147-48; W. D. Davies, "Matthew 5:17, 18," in *Christian Origins and Judaism* (Philadelphia: The Westminster Press, 1962), esp. pp. 31-37, 65-66. The former two maintain that the verses derive from the Matthean *Gemeindetheologie*; the latter demonstrates that a *Sitz im Leben Jesu* is also plausible.

[55]Davies, *Setting*, p. 423. The strongest support for this claim comes from teachings contained in the Sermon on the Mount (esp. Matt. 5:21-48), and these are peculiarly Matthean. In a letter to the writer (October 1, 1973), Dr. Davies offered further insights concerning Jesus' regard for the Law:

"Here the fact that *his opponents* tackled Jesus on points of Law is important: they assumed that he was concerned with these things. The silence on actual teaching by Jesus should not be allowed to counter this fact nor to compel us to go in the face of historical probabilities. I am now more convinced than ever after some work in Jerusalem this summer that the real question confronting Jesus and the early Christians was: 'What is the true meaning of the Torah?' This was a boiling question in the first century. . . . The problem of how we know God--by ecstasy, by interpretation, by the Spirit, etc. was *the* problem facing Judaism. Within this complex of attempts (frowned upon by the Pharisees) to come to God Jesus is to be placed. This means that the interpretation of Torah must, I think, have occupied him. . . . The section on Jesus and Qumran in *SSM* also implies that Jesus *was* occupied with the understanding of the Law and must therefore have discussed this with his own."

[56]Hengel, *Nachfolge und Charisma*, p. 50.

the occasions when Jesus is said to have taught his disciples in private (κατ' ἰδίαν),[57] his teaching concerns discipleship, the kingdom, and the Son of Man--never the Law. This observation is especially significant, since questions about the proper interpretation of the Law were critical for the early Church as it attempted to define its relation to Judaism. Nevertheless, while Hengel's observation that ". . . das Alte Testament nicht mehr im eigentlichen Mittelpunkt seiner Botschaft steht"[58] may be correct, it would be an exaggeration to say that the interpretation of the Law was merely incidental for Jesus.[59]

In addition to his unique stance toward the Law, Jesus stood apart from the Hellenistic and Rabbinic principle of tradition by claiming no teachers as his authority. He was untrained (Jn. 7:15; Matt. 13:54) and yet taught as one with authority (ἐξουσία) which surpassed that of the scribes (γραμματεῖς; Matt. 7:29). He offered a new teaching (Mk. 1:27) in a milieu in which all knowledge came from the past or was revealed by God.[60] His claim "but I say unto you . . ." (ἐγὼ δὲ λέγω ὑμῖν . . .) in Matt. 5:22-44 surpasses the form of address used by the prophets (e.g. "Thus says the Lord: . . ." [כה אמר יהוה] in Amos 1-2 *passim*) and identifies him with God and the fulfillment of the Law (cf. Matt. 5:17; 7:24).[61] This claim to authority probably arose out of his awareness of his role in the imminent, eschatological crisis. Yet, his awareness of the urgency of this crisis ought not to be exaggerated to the point where one denies that Jesus taught his disciples,[62] nor should it lead to the complete rejection of the title "rabbi" for Jesus.[63] Rather, these observations confirm the

---

[57]Matt. 17:19; 20:17; Mk. 4:34; 6:31; 9:28; Lk. 10:23; see also Mk. 8:31; 9:31; Lk. 11:1.

[58]Hengel, *Nachfolge und Charisma*, p. 50.

[59]Cf. Smith, "The Use of the Old Testament in the New," pp. 20-25.

[60]Cf. Ian A. Muirhead, *Education in the New Testament*, Monographs in Christian Education, No. II (New York: Association Press, 1965), p. 58; Hatch, *The Influence of Greek Ideas on Christianity*, p. 49: ". . . a world whose schools, instead of being the laboratories of the knowledge of the future, were forges in which the chains of the present were fashioned from the knowledge of the past."

[61]Cf. Rengstorf, "διδάσκαλος," *TDNT*, II, 156.

[62]Note the positions of Hengel and Wilder discussed below, p. 230.

[63]Cf. Hengel, *Nachfolge und Charisma*, p. 55: "Man solte darum aus Gründen der Klarheit auf die Bezeichnung Jesus als 'Rabbi' überhaupt

230

uniqueness of Jesus' teaching activity and his independence
from any previous scholastic tradition.[64]

Riesenfeld and Gerhardsson have advanced the theory that,
following the manner of teaching practiced at the time, Jesus
made his disciples memorize his teachings.[65] Riesenfeld adds
that this practice grew out of Jesus' messianic self-
consciousness and that he expected a period of time between his
death and the parousia.[66] Two basic objections have been raised
against the thesis that Jesus instructed his disciples. First,
the claim is made that the heightened sense of eschatological
crisis which characterizes Jesus' ministry makes it absurd to
think that he was concerned about establishing and fixing the
tradition of his teachings. Hengel voices this objection as
follows:

> Nirgendwo findet sich auch die Forderung zum Auswendiglernen
> und Memorieren. Wenn die Gottesherrschaft vor der Tür steht,
> wird alle Traditionsbildung sinnlos. Nicht mehr das Lernen,
> sondern das gehorsame Tun ist dann allein entscheidend.[67]

Wilder reaches a similar conclusion through examining the form
and character of Jesus' utterances: "Our contention is that
the freedom and immediacy of Jesus' teaching in its authentic
elements is such as to exclude conscious concern with mnemonics,
catechetical purpose or halakic procedure."[68] The second objection is that the passages which tell of Jesus giving special
instruction to his disciples are merely the redactorial framework which the evangelists used to present the sayings tradi-
tionally ascribed to Jesus.[69] Moreover, it was in the interest
of the Church to create links between its teaching and its

---

verzichten." Hengel's renunciation of the title derives from his desire
to emphasize the distance between Jesus and the scribal-rabbinic tradition.
His point is well taken, but it remains true that Jesus was a Jewish teacher
(rabbi) of the pre-70 period and that our sources unanimously agree that he
taught his disciples.

[64]Ibid., p. 54.

[65]Riesenfeld, *The Gospel Tradition*, p. 22; Gerhardsson, *Memory and Manuscript*, p. 328.

[66]Riesenfeld, *The Gospel Tradition*, pp. 26, 29.

[67]Hengel, *Nachfolge und Charisma*, p. 90.

[68]Amos N. Wilder, "Form-History and the Oldest Tradition," in
*Neotestamentica et Patristica: Eine Freundesgabe, Herrn Professor Dr. Oscar
Cullmann zu seinem 60. Geburtstag Überreicht*, NovTSup, Vol. VI (Leiden:
E. J. Brill, 1962), p. 8.

[69]Hengel, *Nachfolge und Charisma*, p. 89 n. 158.

founder.[70] Recent discussion regarding Jesus' teaching and his disciples has polarized over the issue of whether he made them memorize his teaching. This polarization is unfortunate since the gospels clearly attest that Jesus taught and that there were significant similarities between his disciples and other contemporary schools.

Perhaps it is best to distinguish first between "memorizing" and "remembering." The claim that the disciples memorized sayings of Jesus is supported by the generally shared view that some of the sayings are authentic and hence must have been remembered by the disciples. This does not necessarily mean, however, that from the beginning they made a systematic effort to memorize his teachings or that they were instructed to do so. But since, as noted above, the unique role of the disciples was to participate in Jesus'ministry, i.e., in the service of the Kingdom, it is highly probable that they received some instruction in the demands of discipleship and the new standards of the Kingdom. Moreover, if the teaching under discussion is confined to these subjects, it is not irreconcilable with the eschatological dimensions of Jesus' ministry. Not surprisingly, some of the sayings most likely to be authentic when judged by the criteria of dissimilarity, multiple attestation, and coherence deal with the demands of discipleship in view of the coming Kingdom:

Matt. 8:22 "Follow (ἀκολούθει) me, and leave the dead to bury their own dead." Lk. 9:60 adds: ". . . ; but as for you, go and proclaim the kingdom of God."

Lk. 9:62 "No one who puts his hand to the plow and looks back is fit for the kingdom of God."

Lk. 14:26 "If any one comes to me (ἔρχεσθαι πρός με) and does not hate his own father and mother and wife and children and brothers and sisters, yes, and even his own life, he cannot be my disciple." (par. Matt. 10:37).

Mk. 10:15 "Truly, I say to you, whoever does not receive the kingdom of God like a child (ὡς παιδίον) shall not enter it." (par. Matt. 18:3; Lk. 18:17; [Jn. 3:3,5]).[71]

---

[70]It is not clear that Jesus intended to "found" the Church, but he was at least the founder of his group of disciples. Cf. Davies, *Setting*, p. 217: ". . . , Jesus called a new group into being from the people at large in Galilee of the Gentiles. He was a founder as the Teacher of Righteousness was not."

[71]See Perrin, *Rediscovering the Teaching of Jesus*, pp. 141, 142, 144, 146. Regarding Q's eschatological emphasis see Howard Clark Kee, *Jesus in History: An Approach to the Study of the Gospels* (New York: Harcourt, Brace & World, Inc., 1970), pp. 76-102. Other sayings might be added.

These sayings could have been remembered easily. They are brief, vivid, and dramatic and could have been used by the disciples when they were sent out to proclaim the Kingdom (cf. Mk. 3:14-16; 6:7-13; Matt 10:5-13). That it is probable that these sayings derive from Jesus and were remembered by his disciples does not imply, however, that Jesus made his disciples memorize the sayings or that the sayings have survived in their original form. The fact remains, nevertheless, that many of the sayings regarding the nature of discipleship are likely to be authentic.[72]

The following conclusions may be stated as a summary of the direction in which the evidence points: 1) we are justified in thinking of Jesus and his disciples as a school; 2) Jesus devoted some of his time to teaching his disciples; and 3) they remembered some of his sayings about discipleship.[73]

The history of the school of Jesus

The purpose of this section is to survey briefly the way in which the traditions of the school of Jesus were collected, interpreted and transmitted. The history of the earliest period of Christianity is so obscure, and appears to have proceeded

---

[72]Cf. Etienne Trocmé, *Jesus and His Contemporaries*, trans. by R. A. Wilson (London: SCM Press, 1973), esp. pp. 25, 37-38; Heinz Schürmann, "Die vorösterlichen Anfänge der Logientradition: Versuch eines formgeschichtlichen Zugangs zum Leben Jesu," in *Der historische Jesus und der kerygmatische Christus: Beiträge zum Christusverständnis in Forschung und Verkündigung*, ed. by H. Ristow and K. Matthiae (Berlin: Evangelische Verlagsanstalt, 1961), pp. 342-70.

[73]Cf. Davies, *Setting*, p. 424:
"Nevertheless, the evidence presented probably justifies us in thinking of the Jesus of history as having a kind of 'school' around him: not a strictly rabbinic school but yet one that had rabbinic traits. Later on there was much in the structure of the Church that recalls the transmission of tradition in Judaism: the impetus to this development was already present in the ministry of Jesus. We need not doubt that those chosen to be with him learnt of him, treasured his words and passed them on."
This writer departs from Davies at the point of seeing the school of Jesus so closely related to the Rabbinic tradition. As the schools discussed in this study and the variety of models for discipleship presented by Hengel in *Nachfolge und Charisma* indicate, the school of Jesus must be viewed against a background much broader than just the Pharisaic-Rabbinic tradition. This tradition provides an illuminating background for the school of Jesus, but so do others, especially the Cynic-Stoic and apocalyptic traditions. See also Davies, *Setting*, pp. 416-17, 468; Dodd, *The Founder of Christianity*, pp. 20-21; Fitzmyer, Review of *Memory and Manuscript*, by Birger Gerhardsson, *TS*, XXIII (1962), 456 n. 19; Stendahl, *School*, pp. ix-x.

in such a variety of ways,[74] that the following caution must be
stated: the development traced below represents only one perspective on that part of early Christianity reflected predominantly in the writings of Paul, Matthew, and Luke. The following statement indicates the direction to be followed below:

> There may therefore be an unbroken line from the School of
> Jesus via the 'teaching of the apostles', the 'ways' of Paul,
> the basic teaching of Mark and other ὑπηρέται τοῦ λόγου, and
> the more mature School of John to the rather more elaborate
> School of Matthew with its ingenious interpretation of the
> O. T. as the crown of its scholarship.[75]

Stendahl later qualified this statement.[76] The most questionable part of it is the term "unbroken." Each of the elements
listed by Stendahl provides insights into the way the traditions
of the early Church were handled, but the connections between
the elements are difficult to establish. How were they actually
related?

The so-called Scandinavian school has presented one answer.
Gerhardsson presents the case for the twelve as guardians of
the tradition of "the word of the Lord" in its most extreme
form. It will be helpful to bear in mind the central points
of his thesis. He finds that Luke consistently applies the
term "apostle" to the twelve only.[77] The apostles stayed in
Jerusalem, the traditional center from which "the word of the
Lord" went out.[78] There they taught and interpreted both the
traditions about Jesus and the scriptures.[79] This work is
designated by the expression "the ministry of the word" (τῆ
διακονία τοῦ λόγου) in Acts 6:4. The twelve were witnesses to
the words and works of Jesus; they were ὑπηρέται τοῦ λόγου (Lk.
1:2; cf. Acts 26:16) and formed an apostolic *collegium*, which
Gerhardsson compares with the general session of the Qumran
community and the rabbinical academies.[80]

The apostles taught both in public (especially in the
temple--Acts 4:18; 5:21, 25) and in private. The classic

---

[74]See esp., Helmut Koester, *"GNOMAI DIAPHOROI*: The Origin and Nature
of Diversification in the History of Early Christianity," in *Trajectories
through Early Christianity*, pp. 114-57.

[75]Stendahl, *School*, p. 34.

[76]Ibid., p. x.

[77]Gerhardsson, *Memory and Manuscript*, p. 220.

[78]Ibid., pp. 216, 244.

[79]Ibid., p. 230.

[80]See Gerhardsson's summary of his position, ibid., p. 331.

reference to their teaching in private occurs at the beginning
of the first summary section in Acts:

> And they devoted themselves to the apostles' teaching (τῇ
> διδαχῇ τῶν ἀποστόλων) and fellowship (κοινωνία), to the
> breaking of bread and the prayers. And fear came upon every
> soul; and many wonders and signs were done through the apos-
> tles. And all who believed were together and had all things
> in common (ἅπαντα κοινά); and they sold their possessions
> and goods and distributed them to all, as any had need. And
> day by day, attending the temple together and breaking bread
> in their homes, they partook of food with glad and generous
> hearts, praising God and having favor with all the people
> (Acts 2:42-47).[81]

Gerhardsson uses this passage to emphasize that the apostles'
teaching was central to the life of the Church and adds that
the διακονία τοῦ λόγου also involved doctrinal discussions
based on both scripture and the traditions of Jesus.[82]

Before evaluating Gerhardsson's image of the apostles,
other features of the summary section should be observed. Acts
2:42-46 presents Luke's idealized conception of the nature of
the earliest Christian community.[83] The factors which influenced Luke's thinking at this point are probably numerous.
Interestingly, the word κοινωνία appears only in Acts 2:42 in
the Lukan corpus but frequently in Paul's epistles; κοινά
occurs in Acts 2:44 and 4:32. The practice of common ownership
recalls the common life of the school of Jesus (cf. Jn. 12:6)
and a host of other associations as well. Common ownership was
practiced by the Pythagoreans[84] and was an ideal in other
schools.[85] Moreover, the common ownership and κοινωνία of the
Essenes and Therapeutae are praised by Philo.[86] When Acts 2:42-
46 is viewed against the background of the Pharisaic-Rabbinic
tradition, one notes the similarity with the ḥaburoth which

---

[81]Note that after "the teaching of the Apostles" D adds "in Jerusalem."

[82]Gerhardsson, *Memory and Manuscript*, pp. 244-45.

[83]Cf. Heinrich Zimmermann, "Die Sammelberichte der Apostelgeschichte,"
BZ, N.F. V (1961), 71-82; Friedrich Hauck, "κοινός," *TDNT*, III, 796; Ernst
Haenchen, *The Acts of the Apostles: A Commentary*, trans. by B. Noble, G.
Shinn, H. Anderson, and R. McL. Wilson (Philadelphia: The Westminster
Press, 1971), pp. 190-96; Werner Georg Kümmel, *Introduction to the New
Testament*, founded by P. Feine and J. Behm, trans. by A. J. Mattill, Jr.
(14th rev. ed.; Nashville: Abingdon Press, 1966), p. 117.

[84]See above, p. 51.

[85]See above, pp. 112, 129; D. L. VIII. 10, X. 11; Iamb. *VP* 167-69;
Plato *Republic* V. 462c.

[86]See above, pp. 167, 202.

also met in homes for fellowship, the breaking of bread, and prayers.[87] From this multiplicity of associations, it appears that κοινωνία was a Hellenistic ideal, discussed and practiced in both Greek and Jewish schools and religious communities. Luke (in Acts 2:42) presents the Christian community with its *agape* meal as the fulfillment of this ideal.[88] Significantly, Luke adds that early Christianity was a αἵρεσις (Acts 24:5, 14; 28:22); the term is also applied to the Sadducees and Pharisees (Acts 5:17; 15:5; 26:5). αἵρεσις normally designated a group which had chosen to follow the principles of a certain philosophical school.[89] The summary section indicates that Luke idealized the earliest Christian community; and while he may have used a source, this section (as illuminating as it is) is of dubious value for reconstructing the role of the teaching of the apostles.

Gerhardsson's contention that the apostles formed a *collegium* in Jerusalem which guarded and interpreted the traditions for fifteen to twenty years has proved to be the least convincing part of his monograph.[90] Davies successfully criticized Gerhardsson's excesses, while maintaining that the twelve did play a significant role during the earliest period.[91] Davies observes that 1) the "apostles" are not always synonymous with "the twelve," 2) ". . . probably the greatest experiment in all the history of the Church, the Mission to the Gentiles, took place without the authority of 'the Twelve,'" and 3) Acts turns away from the twelve, to Paul, too quickly to allow the

---

[87]See above, p. 192.

[88]Cf. Peter Nickels, Review of *Comunione interecclesiale--collegialità, primato, ecumenismo: Acta conventus internationalis de historia sollicitudinis omnium ecclesiarum, Romae 1967*, by Iosepho D'Ercole and Alphonso M. Stickler, in *CBQ*, XXXV (1973), 233:

"The most significant contribution would seem to be J. Dupont's study of *koinonia* in Acts. D.'s attention centers on Acts 2:42; he argues that behind the presentation of Christian unity in this passage (and in 4:32) is the (Lucan) purpose of demonstrating that Christian *agape* fulfills the Greek ideal of friendship."

Dupont's study was unavailable to this writer.

[89]See above, p. 128 n. 37.

[90]Gerhardsson, *Memory and Manuscript*, pp. 329-30.

[91]Davies, *Setting*, pp. 472-80; for recent studies which maintain that the twelve were a later institution thrust back into the ministry of Jesus see: Günter Klein, *Die Zwölf Apostel: Ursprung und Gehalt einer Idee*, FRLANT, N.F. LIX Heft (Göttingen: Vandenhoeck & Ruprecht, 1961); Walter Schmithals, *The Office of Apostle in the Early Church*, trans. by J. E. Steely (Nashville: Abingdon Press, 1969).

"*collegium*" to have played the role Gerhardsson claims for it.[92]
The basic departure which Davies makes from Gerhardsson is, however, that he recognizes much greater fluidity in the transmission of the traditions about Jesus.[93] Davies adds that
Gerhardsson's position is more tenable in regard to Jesus'
moral teaching than the broader *kerygma* and *didache* but emphasizes that Gerhardsson does not sufficiently allow for the
diversity of life and thought in the early Church.[94] While the
twelve may have taught and interpreted the developing traditions
about Jesus, they did not exercise the kind of control over them
which Gerhardsson suggests.

Paul's references to "tradition" provide a much more secure
basis for discussion of the early Church's relationship to the
school of Jesus. Again, however, Paul represents only one
stream within the early Church. The following verses indicate
Paul's use of tradition:

I Cor. 11:2 ". . . maintain the traditions (τὰς παραδόσεις)
even as I have delivered (παρέδωκα) them to you."

I Cor. 11:23 "For I have received (παρέλαβον) from the Lord
what I also delivered (παρέδωκα) to you, ..."

I Cor. 15:3 "For I delivered (παρέδωκα) to you as of first
importance what I also received (παρέλαβον), . . . "

II Thess. 2:15 ". . . . hold to the traditions (τὰς
παραδόσεις) which you were taught (ἐδιδάχθητε) by us, either
by word of mouth or by letter."

II Thess. 3:6 ". . . not in accord with the tradition (τὴν
παράδοσιν) that you received (παρελάβετε) from us."[95]

Paul both received and passed on traditions, and the verbs used
for receiving (παραλαμβάνω) and passing on (παραδίδωμι) the
traditions are the equivalents of the Hebrew terms used for the
transmission of the Pharisaic-Rabbinic tradition with which

---

[92]Davies, *Setting*, p. 472.

[93]Ibid., p. 477. See Gerhardsson's curt response to Davies in *Tradition and Transmission in Early Christianity*, p. 40 n. 91. Cf. Rengstorf,
"διδάσκω," *TDNT*, II, 145 (who probably underestimates the role of scripture
in the teaching of the early Church); Floyd V. Filson, "The Christian
Teacher in the First Century," *JBL*, LX (1941), 326; Wilder, "Form-History
and the Oldest Tradition," p. 7 (who probably underestimates the teaching
activity of the apostles).

[94]Davies, *Setting*, p. 477 n. 2.

[95]Cf. Gerhardsson, *Memory and Manuscript*, p. 290; E. Glenn Hinson,
"Church History 76A: Early Christian Practices," (Louisville, Ky.: The
Southern Baptist Theological Seminary, 1963), p. 122. (Mimeographed.)

Paul was familiar. (cf. M. Aboth 1:1). In the references quoted above, Paul alludes to both "traditions" (I Cor. 11:2; II Thess. 2:15) and "the tradition" (II Thess. 3:6). I Cor. 11:23 and 15:3, while they refer to *a* tradition, are weak support for the theory that Paul is alluding to an "authoritative tradition" from the apostolic *collegium*.

What was the nature or content of the traditions to which Paul appeals, and how important were they for him? These are questions that cannot be dealt with fully here, but it is unlikely either that the traditions consisted mainly of Jesus' words or that they were of central importance for Paul. He appeals to them very infrequently; he is guided by the Spirit (see Romans 8; πνεῦμα occurs 146 times in Paul's writings) rather than tradition (παράδοσις occurs only five times in Paul's writings); and although he at times attempted to restrain the atmosphere of eschatological fervor in his churches (II Thess. 2:1-4; 3:10-12), he was too influenced by it (I Cor. 15; I Thess. 4:13-18) to have been very concerned with establishing or maintaining traditions. When Paul does refer to tradition, it concerns elements of the *kerygma* (I Cor. 15:3; II Thess. 2: 13-15), the eucharist (I Cor. 11:23), or church discipline (I Cor. 11:2; II Thess. 3:6). Beyond this (and Paul's use of a tradition of the words of Jesus),[96] it is difficult to characterize the nature or extent of the traditions at Paul's disposal except by inference from those sections of Paul's letters which probably contain pre-Pauline materials.[97]

From whom did Paul "receive" the traditions? Paul's statement in I Cor. 11:23 that he received a tradition from the Lord calls attention to the fact that Paul regarded the Lord as the ultimate source of the traditions he was using, but it also suggests that the traditions had the same authority as the Lord himself.[98] Gerhardsson observes that the words of the Lord were occasionally referred to simply as "the Lord":

. . . a book or a literary product was often referred to by the name of its originator. The writings of the prophets can be called οἱ προφῆται; the Book of Isaiah may be known

---

[96]See below, p. 239 n. 103.

[97]Archibald M. Hunter, *Paul and His Predecessors* (rev. ed.; Philadelphia: The Westminster Press, 1961).

[98]Oscar Cullmann, "'*Kyrios*' as a Designation for the Oral Tradition Concerning Jesus (*Paradosis* and *Kyrios*)," *SJT*, III (1950), 183, 190-91.

as (ὁ) Ἰσαΐας and--by analogy--the Apostles' writings may
be called οἱ ἀπόστολοι and "the words of the Lord" simply
ὁ κύριος.[99]

Gerhardsson proceeds to emphasize that Paul received "the tradition" for the apostolic *collegium* in Jerusalem and was dependent upon it for decisions on ethical matters also.[100] As the
above passages indicate, however, Paul nowhere says that he
received "the tradition" from the Jerusalem apostles; and in
his defense in Galatians 1-2, Paul emphasizes that he was not
dependent upon them. The reference to receiving a tradition
from the Lord is probably another expression of his feeling that
while he had received traditions (possibly from sources in
Damascus and Antioch), he was not dependent upon the Jerusalem
apostles.

Cullmann observes that the transmission of Christian traditions differed from the Jewish practices in that it did not
proceed mechanically but was associated with the Holy Spirit,
and ". . . the mediator of the tradition is not the teacher,
but the *Apostle* as direct witness; . . . ."[101] Teaching, however, was an important part of the apostle Paul's ministry,
indicating that the roles of apostle and teacher were not clearly distinguished during the early decades of the Church:

> I Cor. 4:17 ". . . to remind (ἀναμνήσει) you of my ways
> (ὁδούς [from Heb. *halakoth*]) in Christ, as I teach (διδάσκω)
> them everywhere in every church."

> Col. 2:7 ". . . just as you were taught (ἐδιδάχθητε),
> . . . ."

See II Thess. 2:15, cited above, and:

> I Thess. 4:6 ". . . concerning all these matters, just as
> we told you before and solemnly testified (διεμαρτυράμεθα)."
> (translation by author).

> Rom. 6:17 ". . . the standard of teaching (διδαχῆς) to
> which you were committed (παρεδόθητε), ..."

> Rom. 16:17 ". . . the doctrine (τὴν διδαχὴν) which you have
> been taught (ἐμάθετε); . . . ."

The importance of teaching in the early Church is underscored
by the references to "remembering" the teachings of Paul (I
Cor. 4:17; II Thess. 2:5) and the apostles (II Peter 3:2; Jude
17), and the words of Jesus (Lk. 24:6, 8; Acts 11:16; 20:35).[102]

[99]Gerhardsson, *Memory and Manuscript*, p. 198.

[100]Ibid., pp. 274, 279, 282, 297.

[101]Cullmann, "'*Kyrios*' as a Designation for the Oral Tradition Concerning Jesus (*Paradosis* and *Kyrios*)," p. 194.

[102]Cf. O. Michel, "μιμνήσκομαι," *TDNT*, IV, 677-78; Muirhead,

A tradition of the words of Jesus was known to Paul and used by him on occasions in the context of moral exhortation.[103] The formula (ἀκριβῶς οἴδατε) associated with the saying in I Thess. 5:2 implies that the words were memorized and transmitted with attention to accuracy: "For you yourselves know well (ἀκριβῶς οἴδατε) that the day of the Lord will come like a thief in the night."[104] The same term (ἀκριβῶς) is used in Acts 18:24-25 to describe the way in which Apollos taught traditions about Jesus:

> Now a Jew named Apollos, a native of Alexandria, came to Ephesus. He was an eloquent man, well versed in the scriptures. He had been instructed in the way of the Lord (ἦν κατηχημένος τὴν ὁδὸν τοῦ κυρίου); and being fervent in spirit, he spoke and taught accurately the things concerning Jesus (ἐδίδασκεν ἀκριβῶς τὰ περὶ τοῦ ʼΙησοῦ), though he knew only the baptism of John.

Apollos was later instructed more accurately by Priscilla and Aquila (Acts 18:26). Although the content of τὴν ὁδὸν τοῦ κυρίου and τὰ περὶ τοῦ ʼΙησοῦ is problematic, these verses illustrate how traditions about Jesus were transmitted independent of catechetical instruction[105] and suggest that Apollos knew a tradition which was independent of the synoptic traditions (cf. the other references to the baptism of John in Acts

---

Education in the New Testament, pp. 39, 81-82. Significantly, Acts 9:25 refers to μαθηταί of Paul.

[103]To what extent Paul knew and used the sayings of Jesus is debatable. Davies, *Paul and Rabbinic Judaism*, pp. 136-44, reduces the number of sayings of Jesus found in the Pauline corpus by Resch but emphasizes their importance for Paul. The number and importance of the sayings is minimized by Victor Paul Furnish, *Theology and Ethics in Paul* (Nashville: Abingdon Press, 1968), pp. 40-42, 56-59, 62-63. See Davies' response to Furnish in "The Moral Teaching of the Early Church," in *The Use of the Old Testament in the New and Other Essays*, ed. by J. M. Efird (Durham, N.C.: Duke University Press, 1972), pp. 324-28. See also David L. Dungan, *The Sayings of Jesus in the Churches of Paul: The Use of the Synoptic Tradition in the Regulation of Early Church Life* (Philadelphia: Fortress Press, 1971), esp. pp. 141-50, in which Dungan discusses "Paul's conservatism regarding the tradition itself," and correlates his results with those of the Scandinavians and the redaction critics. However the evidence is assessed, one finds that Paul appeals to and transmits sayings of Jesus as authoritative.

[104]Cf. Muirhead, *Education in the New Testament*, pp. 22, 29; Edward Gordon Selwyn, *The First Epistle of St. Peter* (London: Macmillan & Co. Ltd., 1949), p. 379.

[105]This observation supports the contention of C. H. Dodd, "The Primitive Catechism and the Sayings of Jesus," in *New Testament Essays: Studies in Memory of Thomas Walter Manson*, ed. by A. J. B. Higgins (Manchester: University Press, 1959), pp. 106-18; and Davies, *Setting*, pp. 386, 461, that the traditions of the words of Jesus were not transmitted primarily through catechetical instruction.

19:1-7 and the attention given to the baptisms of John and Jesus in Jn. 1:24-34; 3:22-30).[106]

The instruction received by Apollos leads to the consideration of another dimension of teaching in the early Church. "Catechesis" denotes the instruction of recent converts in the rudimentary doctrines of the Church.[107] Catechetical instruction, though its content cannot be systematically outlined, probably involved some instruction in the tradition of the words and works of Jesus; but it also employed a common body of traditional, hortatory material drawn from the ethical teachings of the philosophers (especially the Stoics) and from Judaism.[108] One may recall that it is at the point of ethical teachings that there appears to have been the greatest interchange between the

---

[106]Acts 18:24-25 provides significant data in favor of the Ephesian origin of John. Apollos had probably been instructed in the scriptures prior to coming to Ephesus, but the text does not indicate where Apollos received instruction in "the way of the Lord." It states, however, that he taught concerning Jesus, though he knew only the baptism of John. Moreover, when Priscilla and Aquila heard him, they realized that he needed further (more accurate) instruction. I Cor. 3:4-5 indicates further that factions claiming Apollos and Paul as their authorities developed in Corinth. Apollos' teaching of the Jesus-tradition from the perspective of the Baptist movement provides the kind of milieu which the Fourth Gospel, with its polemic against the Baptist tradition, requires. Thus, Acts 18:24-25 supplies information about Ephesus which is favorable to the hypothesis that the Johannine school, conscious of conflict with a Baptist group, later developed there. Cf. Dana, *The Ephesian Tradition*, pp. 120-22.

[107]Dodd, "The Primitive Catechism and the Sayings of Jesus," p. 107, limits catechesis to instruction prior to baptism. Is this limitation justified? During the early decades of Christianity baptism seems to have followed immediately after a confession of faith; further instruction followed baptism. [Cf. W. Robinson, "Historical Survey of the Church's Treatment of New Converts with Reference to Pre- and Post-Baptismal Instruction," *JTS*, XLII (1941), 43-45.] Hinson, "Church History 76A: Early Christian Practices," p. 130, observes: "Acts (2:38, 42; 3:79; 8:12, 37; 9:18; 10:47; 16:14, 15, 32, 33) makes clear that careful indoctrination *followed* Baptism." Moreover, Matt. 28:18:20 supports this sequence: make disciples (by preaching), baptize, and teach. Hinson (p. 131), however, notes that instruction was given to gentile converts prior to baptism in Acts 16:32-33 and suggests that pre-baptismal catechesis was first practiced in gentile areas, while in places where Jewish converts predominated instruction followed baptism. Pre-baptismal instruction is clearly attested by the time of Didache (7:1) and may have been used by the Church as a defense against the gnostic threat.

[108]For further discussion of catechesis see: Alfred Seeberg, *Der Katechismus der Urchristenheit*, Theologische Bücherei, Bd. XXVI (Munich: Chr. Kaiser Verlag, 1966 [originally published in 1903]), esp. the introduction by Ferdinand Hahn, pp. vii-xxxii; G. Klein, *Der älteste christliche Katechismus* (Berlin, 1909); Philip Carrington, *The Primitive Christian Catechism: A Study in the Epistles* (Cambridge: At the University Press, 1940); Selwyn, *The First Epistle of St. Peter*, pp. 363-466; C. F. D. Moule, "The Use of Parables and Sayings as Illustrative Material in Early Christian Catechesis," *JTS*, N.S. III (1952), 75-79; Davies, *Setting*, pp. 366-86.

Jewish and Greek schools.[109] The traditional, ethical, hortatory materials were probably taken over by Christian catechetical teachers and used in much the same way they had been used
in the instruction of converts to a philosophy or Jewish prose-
lytes. Dodd notes that the tradition referred to in I Thessalonians was probably given to the Thessalonians as part of their
catechetical instruction, since Paul wrote the letter shortly
after establishing the church there.[110] The office of teacher,
moreover, probably developed in the early churches largely in
response to the need to instruct recent converts. Gal. 6:6
relates that the catechist should be supported by the catechu-
mens,[111] and Paul seems to place teachers nearest to apostles
in function and rank.[112]

The later writings of the New Testament show that "teacher" increasingly came to denote an office rather than a function (cf. I Cor. 12:28-29; Acts 13:1; Heb. 5:12; Eph. 4:11;
I Tim. 2:7; II Tim. 1:11; 4:3; James 3:1).[113] The progress of
this development cannot be clearly traced, however, and was
certainly not uniform in the various Christian centers. The
activity of teachers during the second half of the first century
was probably not confined to catechetical instruction, though
it may have included such teaching. The following two questions
are worth asking: what influence did catechetical instruction
have on the production of the gospels, and what role did teachers play in the production of the gospels? The questions may
be considered separately.

Catechetical interests have been suggested for Matthew,[114]
but the theory that the principal function of the First Gospel

---

[109]See above, pp. 142, 185.

[110]Dodd, "The Primitive Catechism and the Sayings of Jesus," p. 107;
see also C. H. Dodd, *Gospel and Law: The Relation of Faith and Ethics in
Early Christianity*, Bampton Lectures in America, No. III (New York: Columbia University Press, 1951), pp. 20-24.

[111]Gal. 6:6: Κοινωνείτω δὲ ὁ κατηχούμενος τὸν λόγον τῷ κατηχοῦντι
ἐν πᾶσιν ἀγαθοῖς. (Note the use of the verb κοινωνείτω).

[112]I. Cor. 4:17; II Thess. 2:15; cf. Col. 2:7; Eph. 4:21. W. D.
Davies, *Christian Origins and Judaism*, p. 244.

[113]Cf. Muirhead, *Education in the New Testament*, pp. 30-48; Rengstorf,
"διδάσκαλος," *TDNT*, II, 157-59; and Adolf Harnack, *The Mission and Expansion of Christianity in the First Three Centuries*, trans. by J. Moffatt
(2nd ed.; New York: G. P. Putnam's Sons, 1908), I, 333-68, is still an
instructive discussion of the development of the teaching office.

[114]Ernst von Dobschütz, "Matthäus als Rabbi und Katechet," *ZNW*, XXVII
(1928), 345.

was catechetical is rejected by Kilpatrick and Stendahl because
the Gospel appears to be addressed to a larger audience than the
catechumenate.[115] Dodd, however, suggests that the traditional
order of catechesis determined to some extent the arrangement
of material in the gospels.[116] This suggestion rests on the
assumption that an appeal to the eschatological motives for
Christian conduct was made at the end in catechetical instruction, as it is in the gospels. Although there may be some
truth to Dodd's suggestion, its speculative quality is underscored by Davies' contention that the catechetical materials
should probably not be systematized.[117] It is possible that
future research will indicate that the content, form or arrangement of some gospel traditions was conditioned by catechetical interests; but at the present such conditioning can only
be posited as a possibility.

The second question, i.e., concerning the role of teachers
in the production of the gospels, is more promising. Filson
astutely perceives its importance:

> The part of the teacher in the production of our gospels
> is a subject which deserves consideration. . . . Still more
> probable is the suggestion that the earliest collections
> of pericopes were made by teachers for their convenience in
> teaching and for the aid of those whom they taught. This
> means that the teachers were prominent in selecting, shap-
> ing, and grouping material, and that behind the present
> gospels are intermediate stages, which owe much to the
> teaching group. The earliest written sources may well have
> been their compilations. Indeed, the actual writers of our
> four gospels may be designated as teachers.[118]

As noted above, the work of collecting and interpreting traditions about Jesus and finding and interpreting relevant passages
in the Old Testament is especially clear in Matthew.[119]

The prologue of Luke, however, contributes additional
support for the hypothesis that teachers were instrumental in
collecting, systematizing, and interpreting traditions about
the words and works of Jesus which are now found in the gospels:

---

[115]Cf. G. D. Kilpatrick, *The Origins of the Gospel According to St.
Matthew* (Oxford: At the Clarendon Press, 1946), p. 79; Stendahl, *School*,
pp. 22-23, 29. See the discussion of Matthew as the product of a school,
above, pp. 217-19.

[116]Dodd, "The Primitive Catechism and the Sayings of Jesus," p. 110.

[117]Davies, *Setting*, p. 370.

[118]Filson, "The Christian Teacher in the First Century," p. 327.

[119]See above, pp. 217-19.

Inasmuch as many have undertaken to compile a narrative of the things which have been accomplished among us, just as they were delivered to us by those who from the beginning were eyewitnesses and ministers of the word (καθὼς παρέδοσαν ἡμῖν οἱ ἀπ' ἀρχῆς αὐτόπται καὶ ὑπηρέται γενόμενοι τοῦ λόγου), it seemed good to me also, having followed all things closely (ἀκριβῶς) for some time past, to write an orderly account for you, most excellent Theophilus, that you may know the truth concerning the things (λόγων) of which you have been informed (κατηχήθης; lit "instructed").

Three terms used in the prologue attract special attention.
First, one finds that Luke is writing to confirm or supplement the reader's knowledge of matters in which he had received instruction, perhaps catechetical instruction (cf. Lk. 1:4; κατηχήθης). Secondly, one encounters the term ἀκριβῶς, which, though it occurs only here in Luke and only nine times in the New Testament, has been referred to in connection with other passages dealing with instruction and the traditions of Jesus' words (cf. Acts 18:25, 26; 24:22; Eph. 5:15; I Thess 5:2). Thirdly, Luke refers to the "ministers of the word" (ὑπηρέται τοῦ λόγου) who transmitted (παρέδοσαν) the traditions. It has been persuasively argued that in addition to handing down the tradition the ὑπηρέται τοῦ λόγου also collected and interpreted the reminiscences of the αὐτόπται (Lk. 1:2), thereby forming traditions:

> There existed in the early Christian community a number of persons known as "ministers of the word" whose role it was to form reminiscences into narrative- and saying-units, and to hand them down by recitation. This is equivalent to saying that in the early Church a tradition consisting of narrative- and saying-units concerning the Christ-event existed alongside the kerygmatic formulation of the same. That tradition is the source of the synoptic materials.[120]

Balducelli's interpretation of the role of the ὑπηρέται τοῦ λόγου probably overemphasizes their dependence upon "reminiscences" and their attention to recitation, while neglecting the possibility that they were also interpreters of the traditions. Nevertheless, these elements in Luke's prologue clearly indicate that he was concerned about gathering materials from reliable sources and suggest a close association between teachers and the synoptic traditions in the early churches.

The early patristic writings reveal that teaching in the churches continued; pre-baptismal catechesis was practiced more

---

[120]Roger Balducelli, "Professor Riesenfeld on Synoptic Tradition," *CBQ*, XXII (1960), 420; cf. Stendahl, *School*, pp. 32-33; Gerhardsson, *Memory and Manuscript*, pp. 210-11, 242-45.

widely, the office of the teacher was further institutionalized, and the links of the traditions with the apostles were empha- sized. The Didache implies pre-baptismal instruction (7:1) and instructs the readers to beware of traveling teachers (11:1; cf. II Jn. 10). The true [ἀληθινός occurs 28 times in the New Testament; Jn. 9/I Jn. 4/ Rev. 10] teacher and prophet is worthy of his food (13:1-2; cf. 15:1-2).[121] I Clement 1:3, perhaps a summary of an early *Haustafel*, implies that ". . . some sort of catechism was practiced in Corinth (also persumably Rome) ca. A.D. 100."[122] (Cf. I Clement 42:4). Barnabas explicitly states that he is not writing as a teacher (I. 8; IV. 9).[123] The Shepherd of Hermas ranks teachers with apostles and prophets (*Sim*. IX. xv. 4; IX. xvi. 5; IX. xxv. 2), and its insistence on repentance implies instruction prior to baptism (*Mand*. IV. iii. 1). Ignatius merely mentions that teaching occurred (*Rom*. III. 1). Polycarp writes to the Philippians that Paul taught "the word of truth" accurately (ἀκριβῶς) and exhorts them to study the letters he wrote to them (III. 2). He also urges them to teach themselves "to walk in the commandment of the Lord" and then to teach the children (IV. 1-3). In the Martyrdom of Polycarp the heathen and Jews call Polycarp: ". . . the father of the Christians, the destroyer of our Gods, who teaches many neither to offer sacrifice nor to worship."[124]

Justin Martyr, after having studied the philosophies, con- verted to Christianity as the highest philosophy. He indicates that catechetical instruction occurred prior to baptism (*Apology* I, 61), affirms that he has received a tradition (*Apology* I, 10), and appeals to Jesus' teachings (*Apology* I, 8, 13, 15-17). His description of their weekly worship is especially interesting:

> And we afterwards [after the Eucharist] continually remind
> each other of these things. . . . , and the memoirs of the
> apostles or the writings of the prophets are read, as long
> as time permits; then, when the reader has ceased, the pres-

---

[121]Cf. Koester, *Trajectories through Early Christianity*, pp. 123-24, for discussion of the differences between the offices mentioned in the Didache and those known to Ignatius.

[122]Hinson, "Church History 76A: Early Christian Practices," p. 137.

[123]Cf. Klaus Wengst, *Tradition und Theologie des Barnabasbriefes*, Arbeiten zur Kirchengeschichte, Bd. XLII (Berlin: Walter de Gruyter, 1971), p. 119, who claims that the Epistle of Barnabas came for a school in west- ern Asia Minor during the first third of the second century.

[124]Martyrdom of Polycarp XII. 2: . . . , ὁ πατὴρ τῶν Χριστιανῶν, ὁ τῶν ἡμετέρων θεῶν καθαιρέτης, ὁ πολλοὺς διδάσκων μὴ θύειν μηδὲ προσκυνεῖν. Cf. XVI. 2; XIX. 1.

ident verbally instructs, and exhorts to the imitation of
these good things.[125]

Justin continued to wear the garb of a philosopher as a Christian teacher and established a school of Christian teaching in
Rome (*Martyrdom of Justin*.)[126]

Since Justin taught subsequent to the composition of John
(to which he refers) and foreshadows many of the later developments in the teaching of the Christian tradition (including the
school at Alexandria), the present survey has reached a natural
stopping point. The testimony of Papias and Irenaeus will be
dealt with below in the discussion of the evidence for a Johannine school. Nevertheless, it is relevant to note at this point
that they stressed the continuity of the traditions and traced
them back to the earliest apostles. By the middle of the second century pre-baptismal catechetical instruction is widely
attested, the teaching office was well established, the teacher
was looked upon as a defender of the faith and guarantor of the
traditions reaching back to the teaching of Jesus, Christianity
was confronting the schools of philosophy, and the stage was
set for the subsequent establishment of schools offering Christian education.[127]

The influence of the
school of Jesus

The influence of the school of Jesus on other Jewish and
Greek schools lies beyond the scope of this study. The above
survey of the place of teaching and tradition in early Christianity, however, leads the writer to question Rengstorf's conclusion that ". . . in spite of certain formal analogies, the
first generation and the New Testament are far removed from any
principle of tradition, whether Greek or Rabbinic."[128] Although

---

[125]Justin Martyr *Apology* I, 67; translation from: Alexander Roberts
and James Donaldson, ed., *The Ante-Nicene Fathers: Translations of the
Writings of the Fathers down to A.D. 325* (Grand Rapids, Mich.: Wm. B.
Eerdmans Publishing Company, 1950), I, 185-86. Text from J.-P. Migne, ed.,
Patrologiae cursus completus, Series Graeca (Paris, 1857), VI, 430:

Ἡμεῖς δὲ μετὰ ταῦτα λοιπὸν ἀεὶ τούτων ἀλλήλους ἀναμιμνήσκομεν· . . . . ,
καὶ τὰ ἀπομνημονεύματα τῶν ἀποστόλων, ἢ τὰ συγγράμματα τῶν προφητῶν ἀνα-
γινώσκεται μέχρις ἐγχωρεῖ. Εἶτα παυσαμένου τοῦ ἀναγινώσκοντος, ὁ προεστὼς
διὰ λόγου τὴν νουθεσίαν καὶ πρόκλησιν τῆς τῶν καλῶν τούτων μιμήσεως
ποιεῖται.

Cf. the close parallel in Philo *De Vita Contemplativa* 75, below, p. 291.

[126]Eusebius *Ecclesiastical History* IV. xi. 8.

[127]Hinson, "Church History 76A: Early Christian Practices," p. 140.

[128]Rengstorf, "μαθητής," *TDNT*, IV, 453. Smith, "A Comparison of Early

Jesus' role as teacher was quickly superseded by the confession "Lord," the Church remembered that Jesus had been a teacher, and valued the traditions of his teachings mediated to them by the disciples. The evidence for the strictness of the trans-mission of traditions is not as strong as Gerhardsson contends; but the New Testament provides overwhelming support for the assertion that some early Christian groups labored to collect, interpret, and accurately transmit the traditions concerning Jesus and his teachings.

Christian and Early Rabbinic Tradition," esp. p. 174, probably also under-estimates the influence of the ancient schools on early Christianity.

SUMMARY

Introduction

Before turning to the Johannine community, it will be well
to survey and summarize what has been learned about the schools
of antiquity. Some shared characteristics of schools can be
observed, but the principles by which these schools were selected for study should be recalled first (p. 38):[1] 1) the schools
were all established prior to the composition of John; 2) they
all trace their origin to a founder (except the school of
Philo); and 3) they all have the potential of informing us
about the factors which influenced, or may illuminate for us,
the nature of the Johannine community. These principles insure
that there will be some similarities between the nine schools
studied above, but the extent of these similarities is highly
significant in view of their dissimilarities, i.e., the different milieux in which the schools functioned and the different
purposes for which they were established.

The dissimilarities may be summarized as follows. Pythagoreanism was more a way of life than a philosophy. Plato's
Academy was concerned with training statesmen in the knowledge
of the real world. Aristotle's Lyceum was more research orien-
ted than the other schools. Epicurus' Garden was a community
which withdrew from the world to pursue a better way of life.
The Stoics found their greatest unity in their philosophy, not
in their organization or the succession of philosophers leading back to Zeno. In many ways the school at Qumran was like
the Epicurean school; it was a withdrawal from the world for
the purpose of study and the pursuit of a better, purer way of
life; but it had the added dimensions of the Jewish heritage
and apocalyptic fervor. The school of Hillel stood within a
tradition (the Pharisaic-Rabbinic), like the schools of Plato
and Aristotle stood within the Socratic tradition; but the
school of Hillel was concerned about matters of table-
fellowship, regulations for its way of life, and the strict
transmission of its traditions. Philo worked within a synagogue-
school but did not found a school. Finally, the school of

---

[1]This chapter contains many cross references to earlier discussions.
These are placed in the text and enclosed in parentheses.

Jesus emphasized the disciples' devotion to Jesus and their participation in the coming Kingdom of God. In sum, the dissimilarities between the schools run so deep that the similarities
which can be observed may be used to establish a pattern for
the schools of antiquity (at least those which fit the above
criteria). Moreover, the similarities are so extensive that
the communities which shared these characteristics can safely
be distinguished as schools from other similar organizations
like clubs, secret societies, mysteries, cults, or churches.
Methodologically, however, it is best to refrain from attempting to define the concept of ancient "schools" until the similarities have been assessed.

Summary of the sources for
the study of ancient schools

The principal observation that can be made about the
sources is that much of what we know about the schools comes
from the biographical traditions about the founders. Hence,
Diogenes Laertius, who collected many of these traditions, is
an important source for the study of the schools of the philosophers. The biographical traditions are also usually relatively
late. These traditions, however, are preserved both within
and outside the schools, and it is occasionally possible to recover information about the founder or an earlier period in the
life of the school from later writings produced by the school
or to use the composition-history of a document for information
about the history of the school in which it was produced (as in
the case of using 1QS and CD for information about the school
at Qumran, or the Mishnah for the school of Hillel). When information can be gathered in this way, it is usually the earliest and most reliable evidence available.[2]

Seldom are the writings of the founder of a school extant
and when they are (e.g., Plato and Aristotle) they tell us
little about the school. Occasionally we have the writings of
pupils or disciples of the founder (e.g., Plato's letters,
Arrian's discourses of Epictetus, probably parts of 1QS and CD,
and possibly parts of the gospels). We have not, however, been
able to investigate the degree of similarity (especially linguistic similarity) among the writings produced by each school.

---

[2]For studies of the Johannine community based on the composition-
history of John and I John see below, p. 263 n. 4, p. 279 n. 54 and n. 55.

Such an investigation would lead beyond the scope of this dissertation but could be very valuable.

Summary of the origins
of ancient schools

Only those schools which trace their origins to a founder have been studied. The concept of "founding," however, requires further examination. In a few cases (Epicurus, the TR (?), and Jesus) it is clear that the teacher intentionally established a community of disciples or students. In other cases (Zeno, Hillel) it is more likely that the teacher did not intend to establish a school which would trace its origin to him, the disciples who gathered around him formed a fellowship and preserved his teachings. It is therefore possible to speak of "active" and "passive" founders, those who intended to found a school and those who were later adopted by schools as their hero or "founder." Obviously, there are cases in which we do not know the intention of the founder (Pythagoras, Plato, and Aristotle), and even in the cases of "active" founding the schools developed legends about the founder and traced later traditions to him.[3]

It is useful to distinguish between a philosophy, tradition, or movement (sometimes called a αἵρεσις) and a school (sometimes called a σχολή; above, pp. 127-28). Many of the former trace their origins to a school and its founder; e.g., Platonism traces its origin to the Academy and Plato, and Christianity traces its origin to the twelve and Jesus. While "school" is often used to refer to a philosophy, tradition or movement, it is best to maintain a distinction between these and "schools" in the narrower sense of the term (defined below, p. 258) by using "school" only for the latter. This distinction is especially important when discussing cases in which the founder of a school was not the founder of the tradition or movement in which the school stood; e.g., the TR probably founded the school at Qumran but not the movement known as "Essenism," and John may have founded the Johannine school but not Christianity. In other cases, the active founder of a school (e.g., Jesus) may be the passive founder of a movement or tradition. Or, the founder may have actively founded both a school and a tradition (e.g., Epicurus). Maintaining the distinctions between "active"

---

[3]Cf. Joachim Wach, *Sociology of Religion* (Chicago: The University of Chicago Press, 1944), pp. 130-41.

and "passive" founding and between "schools" and movements or
traditions, therefore, adds greater clarity and precision to
the study of ancient schools and their origins.

Frequently the origin of a school is related to developments within another school or tradition (e.g., the Lyceum
and the Garden originated partly because of developments within
the Academy, and the school at Qumran partly because of developments in other streams of Judaism). Moreover, similarities
in terminology and common ethical teachings suggest that the
schools exerted some influence on one another and shared in
developments which exerted a pervasive influence on Hellenistic
culture. Since it is highly probable that there were such influences (i.e., from other schools and from developments external to the schools), it is also likely that the common pattern
of the schools exercised some influence on later schools so
that they shared many of the characteristics of past and contemporary schools. This would have been likely especially for
the traditions (Epicurean, Stoic, and Christian) which established communities or schools as a result of their missionary
activities. Before the question of the influence of the schools
on each other and other forms of social organization can be
pursued further, however, it is necessary to note the characteristics common to all (or most) of the schools.

Summary of the nature
of ancient schools

The nature of ancient schools can best be summarized by
observing similarities between the schools in the following
areas: the ideal of friendship or fellowship, the role of
tradition, the nature of discipleship, organization, activities,
and their relation to the rest of society. The shared characteristics of ancient schools in these areas can be used to
define what "school" means when it is used to designate social
structures like those studied in this dissertation.

Perhaps the most outstanding characteristic of the schools
is that they all manifest a lively interest in the ideal of
friendship (φιλία) or fellowship (κοινωνία). This interest
first manifests itself in the Pythagorean tradition to which
the maxim "friends have all things in common" (κοινὰ τὰ φίλων)
is traced (p. 50). The Pythagoreans may also have been the
only school to have practiced common ownership of all goods
(pp. 50, 234). At the Academy "friendship" was manifested

primarily through the symposia (p. 78), a practice which was continued at the Lyceum (p. 93). Aristotle, however, also wrote at length on "friendship" (p. 109 n. 48), and Theophrastus willed the school to his "friends" (φίλοι) and named ten κοινωνοῦντες (p. 96). Epicurus' last request is alleged to have been that his "friends" (φίλοι) remember his teachings (p. 108), and the Epicureans viewed "friendship" as an end in itself (p. 111). The earliest Epicureans lived together in Epicurus' house and were probably more instrumental than any other school in spreading the ideal of friendship (pp. 112, 114). In some communities "friend" (φίλος; cf. the frequent occurrence of רע in 1QS and CD [p. 165 n. 105]) probably acquired the technical meaning "fellow member of a school" through its use in the Pythagorean and Epicurean traditions.

The Stoics, on the contrary, had little desire to cultivate a close fellowship within schools; they espoused the ideal of broadening their friendship or fellowship to include the whole society (p. 129). The Essenes are praised by Philo and Josephus for their κοινωνία (p. 167), and the community is referred to as the יחד, which may carry in part the meaning of τὸ κοινὸν (p. 167). The communal meal at Qumran was an important part of the life of the community, but it differed radically in nature from the symposia of the Greek philosophical schools; it was an anticipation of eschatological events, the ranks of the participants were strictly observed, and rather than being an occasion for free discussion (as the symposia were at least originally intended to be) the Essene communal meal centered around the ceremony for its observance. Philo also praised the κοινωνία of the Therapeutae (p. 202) and contrasted the temperance of their communal meal with the excesses of the symposia of the philosophical schools (p. 203). The school of Hillel probably also placed a high value on fellowship. It was in part at least a table-fellowship group (p. 192) and was concerned with finding bases for laws defining the limits of its table-fellowship. Jesus, by contrast, was concerned with including the outcasts in the table-fellowship of his school (p. 225) and proclaimed an inclusive love which (later at least) reached even to the gentiles. Moreover, the school of Matthew was concerned with maintaining its fellowship (Matt. 18), and Luke idealized the early Christian community as a κοινωνία which fulfilled the Hellenistic ideal of friendship and fellow-

ship (p. 235). Φιλία and κοινωνία, therefore, are clearly characteristic of ancient schools and were manifested in their communal meals and in references to members of the same school as
"friends" (φίλοι).

A sense of tradition also characterizes the schools. The
late sources for the study of the Pythagorean school claim that
the teachings of Pythagoras were memorized and the traditions of
the school were kept secret (p. 50). The sense of tradition was
also manifested among the Pythagoreans by adherence to the
taboos and rules for admission (pp. 49-50). At the Academy, the
memory of Socrates was kept alive, and later Socrates and Plato
were venerated as the heroes of the school. As θίασοι, the
philosophical schools were religious societies, i.e., cults of
the Muses and of their founders.[4] Plato's writings were probably preserved by the school (pp. 78-79). There seems to have
been little impulse at the Academy or Lyceum, however, to memorize teachings; rather, the example of the founder was imitated.
The followers of Epicurus, on the contrary, adhered strictly to
the tradition of their founder and memorized his teachings (p.
108). The Stoics traced their origin back to Zeno but did not
regard his teachings as a binding orthodoxy (p. 129). There are
indications that the Qumran community valued the tradition of
the teachings and example of the TR (p. 169), and it is obvious
that they respected the laws and traditions regulating the life
of the community. Moreover, the school at Qumran probably
played an important part in establishing and preserving these
regulations (p. 164). The Pharisaic-Rabbinic schools stressed
the importance of learning, interpreting, and transmitting the
traditions given to them by their teachers (p. 193). Philo
alludes to traditions he received and apparently tells his readers when he is using a tradition in order to give added significance to the interpretation he is about to present (p. 205).
The sayings of Jesus which are generally regarded as authentic
strongly suggest that the disciples remembered and treasured his
teachings (pp. 231-32); and although they may not have been transmitted with great strictness, traditions about the words and works
of Jesus were used, collected, and interpreted by early Christians

---

[4]Cf. Jones, *The Law and Legal Theory of the Greeks*, p. 162: "In this
sense the schools of philosophy were religious associations, and in their
rites of veneration of their founder those later philosophical groups whose
religious attitude was, to say the least, a sceptical one were also not
without this devotional colouring."

(p. 219). In sum, a sense of tradition characterizes the schools and is manifested in their communal meals, worship, veneration of their founders, preservation of the founder's teachings and writings, collection and transmission of biographical traditions, and adherence to taboos and procedures regarding admission and maintenance of membership in the school.[5]

Similarities and differences can also be observed regarding what it meant to be a student or disciple. The schools can be viewed as falling along a line at one end of which the primary concern of the adherent is learning and acquiring knowledge and at the other extreme it is devotion to, or imitation of, the teacher. Between the extremes one finds many blends of the two emphases, and probably in no case does either appear devoid of the other. Nevertheless, the students of the Stoics, Plato, Aristotle, and probably Hillel placed much greater value on acquiring knowledge than on devotion to the person of their teacher. Exceptions certainly occurred. The Pythagoreans, Epicureans, and Christians, on the other hand, valued commitment to the person and principles of their founder over the acquisition of knowledge. The Essenes at Qumran represent a curious blend of the two emphases; they valued the traditions of their righteous teacher, rigorously adhered to their way of life, and emphasized the study of the Law. The nature of discipleship in each of the schools may therefore by judged by the relationship of the adherents to the founder or the tradition of his teachings and is manifested by participation in the fellowship of the school and maintenance of its traditions and regulations.

Progressive degrees of complexity and rigidity of organization among the schools can also be observed. The Pythagorean school probably defined its membership clearly, and two levels of disciples are alleged to have developed (p. 49). Moreover, the school was probably rigidly controlled by Pythagoras while he was alive. The organization of the Academy, at first at least, was much freer. We can discern only a distinction between students and teachers. The Lyceum was also relatively unstructured during its earliest period, but the will of the heads of the school suggest that a more developed structure emerged later; the *archon* was elected and had certain duties

---

[5]Cf. Rengstorf, "μαθητής," *TDNT*, IV, 423-26, 453-55.

(p. 98). Membership among the Epicureans was well-defined from the beginning, and converts probably advanced through successive levels of instruction (pp. 110, 114). There were also various ranks for instructors (p. 110). Among the Stoics, organization, ranks, and titles were disdained because of the ideals of their philosophy. We know very little about the organization of the school at Qumran except that some of the scribes were master scribes while others were apprentices (pp. 158-59). The Essenes at Qumran, however, maintained rigid distinctions between their ranks and strictly observed rules regarding admission to the community and maintenance of membership.[6] The ranks of members were re-evaluated periodically, and there were various officials whose functions are as yet not very clear (p. 166). We know nothing about the organization of Hillel's school, but it is likely that it had rules regarding its membership and may have distinguished between the *talmid* and the *talmid ḥakam*. Among the disciples of Jesus there seems to have been some distinction between the rank of Peter, James, and John and the rest; and John (12:6 and 13:29) suggests that Judas was the "treasurer" for the group. Officials and offices developed in the early churches; and membership was clearly delineated by the believers' participation in baptism, the Eucharist, and the fellowship of the Church (pp. 240-41).

The complexity and rigidity of the organization of the schools were related to the degree of emphasis they placed on fellowship (κοινωνία). The more a school emphasized "fellowship," the more likely it was to have a developed, structured organization and rules governing its communal life. However, there was no linear, evolutionary development toward or away from complexity or rigidity of organization in the schools chosen for study. It is safer to observe that the schools usually developed more organization after the death of their founders. This observation is borne out by the surveys of the history of the schools of Aristotle, Qumran, and Jesus especially.

The distinguishing activities of the schools were teaching, learning, studying, and writing. Other organizations

---

[6]Cf. Göran Forkman, *The Limits of the Religious Community: Expulsion from the Religious Community within the Qumran Sect, within Rabbinic Judaism, and within Primitive Christianity*, trans. by P. Sjölander, Coniectanea Biblica, New Testament Series 5 (Lund: C. W. K. Gleerup, 1972).

shared some of the characteristics of the schools (e.g., fellowship, use of traditions, common meals, and worship) but not
their preoccupation with teaching and learning. Moreover, in
some cases classes were distinguished according to the students'
level of advancement or according to subject matter. Some of
the Pythagoreans were called ἀκουσματικοί (p. 49); among the Epicureans there were κατασκευαζόμενοι (p. 110); the primary duty of
the Rabbinic students was to "hear" (שמע; ἀκούω) (p. 187); Philo
heard the traditions he received (pp. 205-06); and Paul refers to
the κατηχούμενοι (p. 241 n. 111). Oral instruction was clearly
one of the most important activities of the schools. In addition, we find that members of the schools engaged in research
and writing. Plato wrote dialogues which were imitated by his
students, but the Lyceum was the first school to organize itself
for research and may have been the first to assemble a library
(pp. 91, 93). Writing was also a preoccupation at Epicurus'
Garden, and scribes contributed to this work (pp. 113-14). The
Stoics also wrote but did not make as much use of writing as a
means of spreading their philosophy as the Epicureans or place
as much emphasis on research as the Peripatetics. Scribal
activity is also one of our main clues to the existence of a
school at Qumran (pp. 158-60), and the school studied the Law as
well (Appendix I). Moreover, the library at Qumran was extensive. The collection and writing down of the Pharisaic-Rabbinic
traditions did not receive much emphasis until Yavneh and after,
but the study and interpretation of the Law was probably a
central concern of the school of Hillel (p. 194). Philo studied
and interpreted the Law also, but his writing was more an individual activity than a communal one (pp. 208, 211). The school
of Matthew interpreted both the Hebrew scriptures and the words
of Jesus (pp. 217-19) and possibly used several manuscripts of
the scriptures for this activity.[7] Evidence of preoccupation
with teaching or study can, therefore, be used as an indication
that a given community was a school or that a writing which
reflects such concerns was produced within a school.

Some of the most interesting observations about the schools
concern their relation to the rest of society.[8] The Pythagorean

---

[7]Cf. Stendahl, *School*, p. 201.

[8]Cf. Simon and Simon, *Die alte Stoa und ihr Naturbegriff*, pp. 23-25.

school had close ties with the aristocracy and was interested
in political activities during its earliest period (pp. 52-54).
At a later time it probably became more withdrawn from society
and less involved in political activity until finally the Pythagorean groups died out (pp. 54-56). The Academicians were also
concerned with political activity but ironically had little influence on Athenian politics (pp. 72-73). Some lectures at the
Lyceum were open to the public (pp. 92, 94). Although the Garden
was a tightly-knit community, it was still open to strangers
(p. 106); and Epicureanism was a missionary philosophy (p. 114).
The Stoics moved freely in society and opposed withdrawal from it
(p. 129). The Essenes at Qumran, however, withdrew from the
rest of society and maintained their "hatred" for outsiders
(pp. 154-55, 170 n. 128). The Pharisaic *ḥaburoth*, on the contrary, attempted to maintain their purity while remaining within
society (p. 192 n. 107). Philo directed his writings to a select
group of initiates (pp. 207, 211) and admired the sectarian way
of life (p. 212). Most early Christians, like the Pharisees,
remained within society while attempting to follow their way of
life and proclaim their faith. The degree of emphasis placed
upon fellowship within the schools, therefore, had little
relation to the tendency to withdraw from society. In some
cases schools with a marked emphasis on fellowship withdrew
(Pythagoreans, to some extent the Epicureans, the Qumran
Essenes, and the Therapeutae); but others did not (the early
Pythagoreans remained active in politics, the Epicureans worked
to gain converts, some Essenes remained in their villages, and
the Pharisees and most early Christians did not withdraw).

Related to the impulse to withdraw from society is the
control the schools exercised over their teachings. The
Pythagorean teachings were largely esoteric, i.e., confined to
members of the school and withheld from outsiders (p. 50). The
Academy may have had both esoteric and exoteric teachings
(pp. 76-77), and Cicero suggested a similar division among
Aristotle's writings (p. 83). The Epicureans, likewise, dis-
seminated certain teachings and writings to the public while re-
serving others for the advanced students (p. 114). The Qumran
scrolls contain esoteric teachings, and Philo wrote for initiates.
Similarly, at least after Yavneh, certain Rabbinic teachings were
reserved for the advanced students.[9] The early Christians may

---

[9]Jeremias, *Jerusalem in the Time of Jesus*, pp. 235-43.

have had a tendency in this direction; converts were instructed
in more detail (p. 240); and as collections of traditions began
to be compiled (at least in part by teachers), a body of material
became available for those desiring further knowledge of the
Christian faith (pp. 217, 242). There is no indication in Paul's
writings or Matthew, though, that certain doctrines or traditions were revealed only to a select group. Other observations
could be made regarding the movement of students from one school
to another, competition between the schools, and the occasional
persecution of the schools by the rest of society; but these
would not be particularly relevant as characteristics of the
schools.

Summary of the history
of ancient schools

A glance at the similarities between the histories of the
schools will add to the common characteristics which can be
used to define what is meant by a "school." As one would
expect, all of the schools which traced their origins to a
founder underwent significant changes following his death. In
some cases (Pythagoras, Epicurus, and Jesus) the traditions of
the school and the content of its teaching coalesced around the
memory or teaching of the founder. In other cases (Plato,
Qumran, and Hillel) the schools remembered and respected the
teachings of the founder but were not bound so tightly to them.
Finally, some schools (Aristotle, the Stoics, and Philo?) survived with relatively little dependence on the memory of the
founder, but his teachings were still not abandoned.

Following the death of their founders the schools had to
work out (or carry out) some means of passing on authority for
the direction of the school. In some cases the founder may
have given directions for the perpetuity of his school (possibly
Plato, Aristotle, Theophrastus, Epicurus, and the TR); and
whether by request of the founder or by decision of the school,
the schools usually placed the direction of the school in the
hands of the founder's most respected disciple. The philosophical and Pharisaic-Rabbinic schools could therefore trace the
succession of teachers or heads of the school. The head was
chosen either by appointment by the former head of the school
or by election, and the office was usually held for life. In
the Pythagorean, Epicurean, Qumranian, and early Christian
schools the principle of succession was adhered to less rigidly

than in the other schools, but it was very important in these schools that their doctrines could be traced back to the founder. It was also in these schools that the founder was most highly venerated; no one could really succeed him. Later developments in the teachings of these schools often came in response to the need to answer their opponents or rivals (p. 116). Moreover, greater attention was given to the accurate transmission of the founder's teachings in the schools which venerated the founder most highly.

Summary of the influence
of ancient schools

To what extent the schools influenced each other and other forms of social organization is one of the most difficult questions involving the schools. Ultimately, perhaps, the only answer available lies in the degree to which the characteristics of the schools surveyed above are found in other schools, organizations, and groups. Even the widespread appearance of these characteristics, however, would not necessarily indicate influence or borrowing. Nevertheless, it is likely that those schools which appealed to the common people for converts had the greatest impact on other forms of social organization and on other movements which drew their supporters from the same sections of society. The schools of Epicurus, the Stoics, and Christian schools, therefore, are those most likely to have influenced each other and other movements or organizations. Some such influence is confirmed by the polemics against the Epicureans in the Rabbinic literature (p. 185), by the widespread use of the Cynic-Stoic diatribe, and by the emergence and use of a body of traditional, ethical teachings in the schools of these movements (pp. 185, 241). In addition to being spread by missionary activity, the influence or communal characteristics of the schools were probably also spread by the movement of students among the schools and by the general reputation of the schools. Aside from these generalities, however, the influence of the schools is extremely difficult to measure.

Definition of "school"

At this point the essential characteristics of the schools may be summed up, and "school" can be defined. The above summary reveals that the greatest similarities among the schools lie in the following areas: 1) they were groups of disciples which usually emphasized φιλία and κοινωνία; 2) they gathered around, and traced their origins to a founder whom they regarded as an exemplary wise, or good man; 3) they valued the teachings of their founder and the traditions about him; 4) members of the schools were disciples or students of the founder; 5) teaching, learning, studying, and writing were common activities; 6) most schools observed communal meals, often in memory of their founders; 7) they had rules or practices regarding admission, retention of membership, and advancement within the membership; 8) they often maintained some degree of distance or withdrawal from the rest of society; and 9) they developed organizational means of insuring their perpetuity. Since most of the schools studied above share in all of these characteristics, this list of characteristics can be used as a definition of what constituted an ancient "school."

One observes that although they overlap in meaning, there is some difference between "sect" and "school" as it has just been defined. A sect is characterized by its devotion to the person or teachings of a founder or its adherence to a set of principles. Sects, therefore, share many of the characteristics of the schools, and most of the schools studied above were, or were part of, sects. Schools, however, have the additional characteristic of preoccupation with teaching, learning, studying, and writing. Moreover, "sect," as it is normally used, denotes a "tradition" or "movement" (see above, p. 249) more than it does a "school."[10] In this study, "school" refers primarily to a community which may be part of a "sect," "movement," or "tradition" and describes the nature of its communal life.

Conclusion

The fact that the nine characteristics listed above are all found in nearly all of the schools studied indicates that

---

[10]For definitions of "sect" see: Wach, *Sociology of Religion*, pp. 196-205; J. van der Ploeg, *The Excavations at Qumran: A Survey of the Judaean Brotherhood and Its Ideas*, trans. by K. Smyth (London: Longmans, Green and Co., 1958), pp. 90-91; Max Weber, *Grundriss der Sozialökonomik*, III Abt.: *Wirtschaft und Gesellschaft* (Tübingen: Verlag von J. C. B. Mohr, 1922), p. 812; Arnold, *Roman Stoicism*, p. 99; Neusner, *From Politics to Piety*, p. 83; Stendahl, *The Scrolls and the New Testament*, pp. 7-8; Bryan R. Wilson, ed., *Patterns of Sectarianism: Organization and Ideology in Social and Religious Movements* (London: Heinemann, 1967), pp. 1-21; Bryan Wilson, *Religious Sects: A Sociological Study*, World University Library (London: Weidenfeld and Nicolson, 1970), pp. 14-35.

they delineate the distinctive nature of an ancient school and hence can be used in this study as a definition of "school." Therefore, if the Johannine community is found to share all or most of these characteristics and is defined by them as the schools studied above are, it too can then properly be called a school.

Chapter XII

THE JOHANNINE SCHOOL

Introduction

The preceding chapters have provided insights concerning
ancient schools and ways in which they can be studied. The
purpose of this chapter is to apply the perspectives gained
from this study to the problem of determining whether or not
the Johannine community was a school. The survey of the
history of the Johannine-school hypothesis (Chapter I) indicated that it has been supported by three basic arguments:
1) the linguistic and theological similarities and dissimilarities among the Johannine writings can be explained best by
assuming that they were written by several writers working in
one community--hence probably a school; 2) the patristic writings which refer to John and his disciples suggest that there
was a "Johannine" school; and 3) John's use of the Old Testament suggests that the Gospel was composed in a school (similar
to the school of Matthew).[1] These arguments support the
Johannine-school hypothesis, but even taken together they have
not furnished sufficient support to confirm it, nor have they
(with the possible exception of the third argument) cast much
additional light on the nature of the Johannine community. This
writer has chosen to develop a fourth argument in support of
the hypothesis by taking a comparative approach. If the
Johannine community can be shown to share the characteristics
of the ancient schools surveyed above, then it can properly be
regarded as a school; and the Johannine-school hypothesis will
be confirmed. This approach has the additional advantage of
clarifying (and defining) what is meant by the term "school."
All previous attempts to confirm or deny the Johannine-school
hypothesis have been vitiated because they used "school" loosely, imprecisely, or without sufficient evidence for defining
the characteristics of such organizations in antiquity. The
approach taken herein supplies this evidence while bringing a
new perspective--furnished by our study of a variety of ancient
schools--to the study of the Johannine community.

The question which prompted and has guided this dissertation may now be addressed directly: was the Johannine community

---

[1]See above, pp. 217-19.

a school? Having established the most important shared characteristics of ancient schools,[2] it is now immediately apparent
that the Johannine writings reflect a community which shared at
least some of these characteristics. Many of the forms of
address which appear in the Johannine writings were probably
used in the community: οἱ φίλοι, τοὺς ἀδελφοὺς, μαθηταὶ, and
ἀγαπητοί. Moreover, the community's emphasis on fellowship is
probably to be seen in the prominence of κοινωνία in I John and
in the metaphors of the vine and the sheep in the Gospel. Addi-
tionally, the community probably looked to either Jesus or the
Beloved Disciple as its founder. This aspect of the community's
self-understanding will receive special attention below. The
Gospel itself is evidence that the community (or at least some
members of it) were involved in the study of the scriptures and
in reflection upon the significance of their traditions of
Jesus' words and works. The Gospel represents the culmination
of a process of study of scripture and traditions, reflection,
interpretation, compilation, and revision. The peculiar development of metaphors, images, and phrases in John indicates that
it was composed for a readership which was acquainted with its
rather esoteric use of language. In this respect the Johannine
community shared the tendency of ancient schools to develop
esoteric teachings, terminology, and metaphorical systems which
were understood only by members of the school.[3] The community
probably also observed a communal meal, the meaning of which
the writer(s) of the Gospel wished to clarify through the discourses in John 6 and 13-17. Similarly, the Gospel reflects
a distinctive concern for what it meant to be a disciple or
believer, and this concern suggests that attention was given to
the conditions for membership in the community. Finally, the
mere existence of the Johannine epistles is significant evidence
that a community (or several communities) lies behind the
Johannine literature and that it maintained its identity for a
period of time. These clues to the nature of the Johannine
community show that it probably shared the characteristics of
the schools and hence probably was a school. The ways in which
the characteristics of the schools are manifested in the

---

[2]See above, pp. 258-59.

[3]Cf. above, p. 256 and the works of H. Leroy and W. A. Meeks summarized
above, pp. 32 and 33-34.

Johannine literature will occupy our attention for the remainder of this chapter.

The sources for the study
of the Johannine school

The procedure will be to search through the Gospel and epistles of John for clues to the precise nature of the community or communities in which, and to which, they were written. No assumptions are made at the outset regarding whether the epistles were written by more than one person or whether their writer(s) had a part in the composition of John. The Gospel, however, can be regarded as the work of more than one writer without adopting any of the current hypotheses regarding its composition and sources.[4] Moreover, no assumptions are made regarding the location of the Johannine community. Although it is not possible to move beyond the present impasse (in or near Ephesus, Antioch, or Alexandria?),[5] a great deal can be learned about the community even if its location remains problematic. Finally, it should be noted that the question of the relation of the Apocalypse to the rest of the Johannine literature will be left open.[6] That it came from a different author is clear; that it came from the same community is not.

Our study of ancient schools indicates that clues about the following aspects of the Johannine community should be illuminating: the role of its founder or head, its regard for tradition, the role of its members, its activities, and its relation to the rest of society. Study of clues to these aspects of the community has persuaded the writer that the epistles were written later than the Gospel.[7] On this assumption a partial history of the Johannine community may be reconstructed. Much about its origin and later history remains

---

[4]See esp. Smith, *The Composition and Order of the Fourth Gospel*; Robert Tomson Fortna, *The Gospel of Signs: A Reconstruction of the Narrative Source Underlying the Fourth Gospel*, NTSMS, 11 (Cambridge: At the University Press, 1970); James M. Robinson, "The Johannine Trajectory," in *Trajectories through Early Christianity*, pp. 232-52.

[5]Cf. J. H. Charlesworth and R. A. Culpepper, "The Odes of Solomon and the Gospel of John," *CBQ*, XXXV (1973), 320-21.

[6]See the following recent studies: Akira Satake, *Die Gemeindeordnung in der Johannesapokalypse*, WMANT, XXI (Neukirchen-Vluyn: Neukirchener Verlag, 1966); David Hill, "Prophecy and Prophets in the Revelation of St. John," *NTS*, XVIII (1972), 401-18.

[7]Cf. p. 279 n. 55 below.

obscure, however, and no attempt is made here to say all that could be said about the community. Only those aspects of its life which have a bearing on the question at hand can be considered.

From the study of ancient schools one also learns that the traditions about their founders tell a great deal about the schools. If one assumes that the traditions from Papias and Irenaeus are reliable guides to the role of "John" (the Apostle or the Elder) in the Johannine community, "John" could be regarded as the founder of the community. These assumptions have proved difficult, however, and study of the patristic evidence has not resolved the question of the character of the Johannine community. Therefore, it is advisable to consider the Gospel as the primary witness to earlier periods of the community's life, the epistles as the primary witnesses to a later period, and the patristic sources as witnesses to second-century traditions about the community. The result of this approach is that the only traditions about the founder or head of the community which will be considered are those which can be found in the Gospel and epistles.

The origin of the Johannine school

A starting point for the study of the Johannine community is provided by Jaeger's observation about Greek schools:

> Behind the school or little community there always stands an intellectual personality, who is the active force, who speaks with the authority of his own deep knowledge and who gathers around him associates with the same attitude to life.[8]

Our study of the schools confirms Jaeger's observation. Did the Johannine community look back to a founder? On the basis of John 1:17 and 9:28, Klaus Haacker finds that Jesus was regarded as a founder (*Stifter*) opposed to Moses.[9] The success of his thesis indicates that the Johannine community was conversant with the concept of "founder" common in the ancient schools. In view of the Gospel's keen interest in Christology, it would hardly be surprising if the Johannine community regarded

---

[8]Jaeger, *Paideia*, II, 273.

[9]*Die Stiftung des Heils: Untersuchungen zur Struktur der johanneischen Theologie*, Arbeiten zur Theologie, I Reihe, Heft 47 (Stuttgart: Calwer Verlag, 1972), esp. pp. 34-35; see also Josef Kuhl, *Die Sendung Jesu und der Kirche nach dem Johannes-Evangelium*, Studia Instituti Missiologici Societatis Verbi Divini, Nr. XI (St. Augustin: Steyler Verlag, 1967).

Jesus as its founder. According to the distinction made above
between a tradition or movement and a school,[10] however, Jesus
was the founder of the tradition or movement (Christianity)
within which the Johannine community stood, but he can hardly
be regarded as the founder of the Johannine community in anything more than a spiritual sense. The actual founder of the
Johannine community is more likely to be found in the figure of
the Beloved Disciple (hereafter referred to as BD).

Scholars have been divided over the question of whether
the BD represents a historical figure or an ideal, symbolic
one;[11] but recent scholarship has moved beyond this debate to
affirm that the BD probably represents the idealization of a
historical person.[12] The references to the BD at the end of
chapter 21 strongly suggest that the BD was a person who had
played a significant role in the life of the Johannine community
but who had died recently (Jn. 21:23-24). If the BD had been
an ideal form only, the question of his death, which is real
enough, would never have arisen. The BD was regarded as the
ideal disciple of Jesus and the true mediator and interpreter
of his teachings and could therefore be depicted in the Gospel
as having been the disciple closest to Jesus. Whether he was
or not (as is more probable) need not concern us here; the community regarded the BD as its head in much the same way as
ancient schools regarded their founders. The BD may also have
been regarded as the representative of the community; and as
such his authority is held above Peter's, who may at times
serve as the representative of Petrine Christianity. Whether
or not the BD actually established the Johannine community
cannot, of course, be determined. The similarity of function
between the BD and the founders of the schools studied above
strongly suggests that the role of the BD is the key to the
character of the community.[13] If we can perceive more clearly

---

[10]Above, p. 249.

[11]Cf. Thorwald Lorenzen, *Der Lieblingsjünger im Johannesevangelium:
Eine redaktionsgeschichtliche Studie*, SBS, 55 (Stuttgart: Verlag
katholisches Bibelwerk GmbH, 1971), pp. 74-77.

[12]See esp. Jürgen Roloff, "Der johanneische 'Lieblingsjünger' und der
Lehrer der Gerechtigkeit," *NTS*, XV (1968), 150; Schnackenburg, "On the
Origin of the Fourth Gospel," in *Jesus and Man's Hope*, I, 234, and his
thesis on p. 239.

[13]Cf. Günther Baumbach, "Gemeinde und Welt im Johannes-Evangelium,"
Kairos, XIV (1972), 128: "Da diese Aussagen von dem 'Lieblingsjünger'

how the Johannine community understood the role of the BD, we
will be in a much better position to grasp the community's self-
understanding and hence to understand more fully the nature of
the community.

The following texts witness to the community's view of the
role of the BD: 13:21-30; 19:25-27; 19:34b-35; 20:2-10; 21:1-7;
21:18-25. The BD (ὁ μαθητὴς ὃν ἠγάπα [ἐφίλει] ὁ Ἰησοῦς) is
mentioned in all of these passages except 19:34b-35, and here
it is highly probable that the writer is referring to the BD.
John 1:35-42, however, probably does not refer to the BD;
18:15-18 may, but adds little to what the other texts tell us.
Lorenzen's redaction-critical study of these texts reveals that
all of them were added to traditional materials by the evangelist
except the last (21:18-25), which is properly assigned to the
redactor.[14] Assuming that 19:34b-35 refers to the BD and was
written by the evangelist, it reveals that the evangelist was
not the BD but that he looked upon the BD as the guarantor of
his traditions, and it implies that the evangelist was a disciple of the BD.[15]

Of the above texts, John 13:21-30 is probably the most
important witness to the community's understanding of the role
and functions of the BD. The BD reclines in the bosom (ἐν τῷ
κόλπῳ) of Jesus. The word κόλπος occurs elsewhere in John only
in 1:18,[16] where Jesus, the only son (μονογενὴς) of God, is in
the bosom (εἰς τὸν κόλπον) of the Father and hence is able to
reveal, explain, and interpret (ἐκεῖνος ἐξηγήσατο) the Father.
By analogy, the BD is credited with having the same relation to
Jesus that Jesus had to the Father (cf. 3:35; 15:9) and with
performing the same function in the community, i.e., making him
known. Peter asks the BD to ask Jesus who the traitor is
(13:24); hence the BD is viewed as the one who is able to find
out for the disciples (even Peter) what Jesus meant. The BD is

---

nicht den Eindruck einer späteren redaktionellen Einfügung machen, dürfte
sich hierin das Selbstverständnis der johanneischen Gemeinde niederschlagen
haben, ..."

[14]Lorenzen, *Der Lieblingsjünger im Johannesevangelium*, p. 73; cf. the
review of this work by D. Moody Smith, Jr., in *The Outlook*, XXII, 3 (1973),
5.

[15]Cf. Smith, *The Composition and Order of the Fourth Gospel*, p. 233.

[16]Cf. II Clement iv. 5, where the term also occurs.

therefore the authoritative exegete of Jesus' teachings and is able to guide the community in interpreting them.[17] This aspect of the community's understanding of the BD is confirmed by the other relevant texts. The BD is present at the crucifixion (19:26-27, 34b-35) and is the one who perceives (and presumably explained to Peter) the meaning of the empty tomb (20:8). The BD is also said to have borne witness to the things which he saw and heard (19:35), and the community does the same (cf. 3:11 and 32 where the writer speaks in the plural). The community recognizes that his witness is true (21:24). Moreover, to the extent that the Gospel represents the work of the community, the latter must be understood to be guided by the BD because he directed the community's interpretation of the words and signs of Jesus.

From this discussion of the functions of the BD it can be seen that he functioned in the Johannine community precisely as the Gospel's Paraclete sayings predict that the Paraclete would function.[18] The Paraclete will teach the disciples all things and remind them of all that Jesus said (14:26); the BD has borne witness (19:35; 21:24) and made known what Jesus said (13:23; 1:18). That the BD fulfilled the prediction that the Paraclete would remind (ὑπομνήσει) the disciples is suggested by the observation that the evangelist placed the BD closest to Jesus during the last discourse and claimed that he was present at the crucial moments of Jesus' glorification. Because the BD "reminded" the community of these things, the evangelist felt

---

[17]Cf. Roloff, "Der johanneische 'Lieblingsjünger' und der Lehrer der Gerechtigkeit," pp. 134-35, 138; Anton Dauer, *Die Passionsgeschichte im Johannesevangelium: Eine traditionsgeschichtliche und theologische Untersuchung zu Joh 18,1-19,30*, StANT, Bd. XXX (Munich: Kösel-Verlag, 1972), p. 319.

[18]The position about to be set forth was arrived at independently by the writer but will be recognized as a variation of other theories regarding the relationship between the BD and the Paraclete. Cf. Hermann Sasse, "Der Paraklet im Johannesevangelium," *ZNW*, XXIV (1925), esp. 273-77; Kragerud, *Der Lieblingsjünger im Johannesevangelium*, p. 82; Franz Mussner, "Die johanneischen Parakletsprüche und die apostolische Tradition," *BZ*, N.F. V (1961), 65 n. 28; Robert Hoeferkamp, "The Holy Spirit in the Fourth Gospel from the Viewpoint of Christ's Glorification," *CTM*, XXXIII (1962), 528; R. E. Brown, "The Paraclete in the Fourth Gospel," *NTS*, XIII (1966-67), 128-30; Roloff, "Der johanneische 'Lieblingsjünger' und der Lehrer der Gerechtigkeit," p. 148; George Johnston, *The Spirit-Paraclete in the Gospel of John*, NTSMS, 12 (Cambridge: At the University Press, 1970), pp. 131, 134; Brown, *The Gospel According to John*, II, 1142; Birger Olsson, *Structure and Meaning in the Fourth Gospel: A Text-Linguistic Analysis of John 2:1-11 and 4:1-42*, trans. by J. Gray, Coniectanea Biblica, NT Series, 6 (Lund: C. W. K. Gleerup, 1974), pp. 272-74.

it necessary and proper to have him present and closest to
Jesus. Moreover, what he says is true (ἀληθὴς: 19:35; 21:24),
i.e., he has the Spirit of Truth (ἀληθείας: 14:17), and he
guides the community in all truth (16:13) by declaring all he
has received from Jesus (cf. 16:14 and 19:27). He glorifies
Jesus (16:14) because he proclaims to the community what he has
received from Jesus; and just as the BD and Paraclete bear
witness, so the community bears witness (3:11, 32). The BD can
do so because he is understood by the community to have been
with Jesus (cf. 15:27: ἀπ' ἀρχῆς μετ' ἐμοῦ ἐστε) and to have
received the tradition from Jesus (cf. 14:24: ὁ λόγος ὃν
ἀκούετε; and 17:8, 14). In addition, both the BD and the Paraclete are sent by Jesus (cf. 14:26 and 17:18 which must be
understood to apply to the BD as well as the other disciples).[19]
Finally, the BD was probably rejected by the "world";[20] otherwise there would be no need for the community to uphold the
truth of his witness so persistently (19:35; 21:24). The BD
"convicts" (ἐλέγχειν) the world (16:8-11) because he bears Jesus'
λόγος (cf. 5:24; 8:46)[21] and abides in it (15:1-10), but the
world rejects it.

Clearly, the Johannine community felt that the BD fulfilled
for it the role of the Paraclete; both are held to have perform-
ed the same functions. If this be the case, why does the Gospel
maintain a clear separation between the two? The BD was *not*
the Paraclete. At this point Martyn's suggestion that the
Johannine text at times moves on two levels is helpful. At
times it tells us both of events ". . . during Jesus' earthly
lifetime," and of ". . . actual events experienced by the
Johannine church."[22] That we should find the text speaking on
the second level in the last discourse is hardly surprising
since chapters 13-17 deal primarily with Jesus' preparation of

---

[19]Kuhl, *Die Sendung Jesu und der Kirche nach dem Johannes-Evangelium*,
p. 150, observes similarities between the sending of the Spirit (Paraclete)
and the sending of the disciples but does not relate these to the BD.

[20]Since Martyn, *History and Theology in the Fourth Gospel*, has almost
certainly been successful in identifying part of the *Sitz im Leben* of the
Johannine community, one may confidently conclude that as the head of the
Christian (Johannine) community the BD would have been rejected by the
synagogue with which it was in conflict.

[21]Presumably the community thought the BD had also received the πνεῦμα
ἅγιον given by Jesus (20:22) and had the authority to "bind" and "loose"
sins (20:23).

[22]Martyn, *History and Theology in the Fourth Gospel*, pp. 9-10.

his disciples for the period after his death. What event(s), then, would explain the parallels between the functions of the BD and those of the Paraclete? The answer is probably to be found in the death of the BD, which is referred to in 21:23. The community had found its identity in receiving the teachings and following the guidance of the BD. Then, the BD died. Like the original disciples of Jesus, the disciples of the BD knew well what it was like to be left as "orphans" (ὀρφανούς: 14:18) in the world. They found great comfort in the traditions that Jesus had assured his followers that they would have a Paraclete who would take his place and fulfill his functions after he left them. Perhaps the two levels of meaning can be seen most clearly in the expression "another Paraclete" in 14:16. Just as Jesus had been the first Paraclete for the original group of disciples, so the BD had been the first Paraclete for the Johannine community. In the person of the BD the community saw most clearly the activity of the Paraclete in their midst and therefore was influenced in the formulation of its concept of the Paraclete by what the BD did. On the basis of this hypothesis, the Paraclete sayings could be used as further evidence concerning the role of the BD in the community, but they merely confirm and supplement the evidence of the texts which refer explicitly to the BD.

After the BD died, it was necessary for the community to reaffirm that the BD was not the Paraclete, or at least not the only Paraclete, but that the Paraclete was Spirit (14:26) and that he would remain always (14:17). This view of the relationship between the BD and Paraclete also explains why the evangelist combined--apparently for the first time--the concepts of Paraclete and Spirit.[23] The concept of the Paraclete had been so intimately related to the role of the BD within the community that the identification of the Paraclete's work with that of the Holy Spirit reassured the community that although *their* first Paraclete, the BD, had died, the work of the Paraclete would continue.

One also observes that the functions of the BD/Paraclete probably related to the activities most central to the life of

---

[23]Otto Betz, *Der Paraklet: Fürsprecher im häretischen Spätjudentum, im Johannes-Evangelium und in neu gefundenen gnostischen Schriften*, AGSU, II (Leiden: E. J. Brill, 1963), p. 147: "Eine grosse Zahl der neueren Ausleger ist der Ansicht, der Paraklet und der Geist seien ursprünglich zwei *verschiedene* Grössen, die erst der Evangelist oder auch der letzte Bearbeiter seines Werkes einander gleichsetzt hätten."

the community. If so, these activities were teaching, remembering (or reminding), "keeping" what the BD/Paraclete had taught, and witnessing to the "world." All of these activities, undertaken as they were under the guidance of the BD/Paraclete, contributed to (but were probably not limited to) the composition of the Gospel of John. Members of the community probably imitated the BD and hence shared in his functions. The BD, therefore, functioned as founder of the Johannine community, source of its traditions, and authority for its interpretation of the traditions.

The nature of the
Johannine school

Analysis of the terms used to designate ancient schools and their adherents proved in the earlier chapters to be a fruitful way to investigate the nature and organization of each school. This approach may also shed light on the Johannine community.

It is well known, however, that no officials are mentioned in the Gospel of John.[24] Instead, one finds such titles as "disciples," "children," "children of God," "servants," "friends," and "brothers" and metaphors for the community like the sheep (10:1-18) and the vine (15:1-10). Aside from the special position of the BD, no other distinctions of office or rank can be seen among the members of the community. Terms in common use in other communities (e.g., γνώριμοι and ἑταῖροι) do not appear in John or the epistles.[25] Analysis of the terms and images used in John may cast further light on the characteristics and activities of the Johannine community, if one assumes, as is probable, that the way in which they are used in the Gospel reflects their usage in the community. For example, the qualities that distinguish a disciple of Jesus in the Gospel are probably those which were emphasized in the Johannine community.

In the New Testament the term μαθητής occurs only in the first five books and most frequently in John (followed closely

---

[24]Cf. E. Schweizer, "The Concept of the Church in the Gospel and Epistles of St. John," in *New Testament Essays: Studies in Memory of Thomas Walter Manson*, ed. by A. J. B. Higgins (Manchester: University Press, 1959), p. 237; Käsemann, *The Testament of Jesus*, pp. 30-32; Baumbach, "Gemeinde und Welt im Johannes-Evangelium," p. 127.

[25]Rengstorf, "μαθητής," *TDNT*, IV, 449. See Eusebius *Ecclesiastical History*, VI. xiv. 7, which states that John was urged by his γνωρίμων to write the gospel.

by Matt.): 73/46/37/78/28. The frequency of the term's occurrence in these two books reflects the nature of the communities
which produced them; both were concerned with what it meant to
be a μαθητής of Jesus during the period in which the gospels
were composed. What characterizes a μαθητής in John? The
μαθηταί believe in Jesus (2:11) and are distinguished as the
disciples of Jesus in contrast to the Jews who are disciples of
Moses (9:28). Moreover, they are truly Jesus' μαθηταί if they
abide in his word (λόγῳ: 8:31) and his ῥήματα abide in them
(15:7-8). They are recognized by all because of their ἀγάπη
(13:35). In addition, the disciples remember the scriptures
written about Jesus (2:17; 12:16) and the things he said (2:22).
They discuss with one another the meaning of what Jesus said
(16:17); they keep his commandments (ἐντολὰς: 14:15), and the
Paraclete reminds them of Jesus' teachings and teaches them
(14:26). The disciples also baptize (4:2). They are harassed
by the Jews (9:27), and only in John (18:19) does the Chief
Priest question Jesus concerning his disciples (μαθητῶν) and
concerning his teaching (διδαχῆς). The way in which themes
(e.g., λόγος, ῥήματα, ἀγάπη, μένειν, μαρτύρειν) which recur
throughout the Gospel are linked with the μαθηταί suggests that
these lie at the heart of the Johannine community's self-
understanding. As the true μαθηταί of Jesus, members of the
community love one another, follow the guidance of the Paraclete,
keep Jesus' teaching (λόγος and ῥήματα), study the scriptures,
keep Jesus' commandments (ἐντολὰς), and bear witness before the
Jews (who are at times called "the world"). Membership in the
Johannine community, therefore, involved learning, remembering,
obeying, and studying both the traditions about Jesus' words
and signs and the scriptures.

Why is μαθητής not used in the Johannine epistles? Since
the term does not appear in the New Testament outside of the
gospels and Acts, and since it is not used in John 17 (and is
used only for the twelve and the BD in the last discourse), it
is possible that in the Johannine community the term was reserved for the followers of the earthly Jesus. Therefore, the
recipients of the epistles are addressed as ἀγαπητοί and τεκνία
but never μαθηταί.[26] This observation does not mean, however,
that the concept of discipleship developed in John does not

---

[26]See below, p. 281.

reflect the qualities and activities of the members of the
Johannine community; the community probably both viewed itself
as a continuation of the original group of disciples and allowed
its activities and self-image to color its description of the
original disciples.

The other titles for the disciples reinforce the picture
of the community which the study of μαθητής yields. Other
designations occur relatively infrequently in John, but some
of these (τέκνα, ἀδελφός, φίλος) appear prominently in the
epistles. As noted above,[27] φίλος has a rich background in
Greek, Hellenistic sources and was used with special significance by the members of the Epicurean school. Jesus explicitly
calls his disciples his "friends" (Jn. 15:14-15; cf. Lk. 12:4;
Isa. 41:8) because he made known to them what he heard from the
Father, but the title was also dependent upon their doing what
he commanded. III John 15 confirms that we are again in touch
with an aspect of the Johannine community's self-understanding;
members of the community shared the status of "friends," and
the title communicated something about their relationship with
each other and with their Lord. Lazarus is the only individual
in John who is called a φίλος of Jesus and the disciples (11:11).
He appears in John, therefore, as a paradigm of Jesus' relationship with the members of the Johannine community.[28] In Jn. 3:29
the Baptist is said to have referred to himself as the φίλος of
the bridegroom, and, significantly, his role is that of standing
and "hearing" (ἀκούων) the bridegroom. The use of φίλος in John
and III John 15 emphasizes the exclusivity of the Johannine
community (contrast Matt. 5:46f.); Jesus loves "his own" (13:1),
who are to love one another as he has loved them (13:34f.) and
are hated by "the world" which loves "its own" (15:19).[29]

The members of the community are also called τεκνία
(13:33).[30] The association of this title with the new command-

---

[27]See above, p. 108 n. 48.

[28]Cf. Stählin, "φιλέω," *TWNT*, IX, 129, 163.

[29]Cf. Victor Paul Furnish, *The Love Command in the New Testament*
(Nashville: Abingdon Press, 1972), esp. p. 144; Käsemann, *The Testament of
Jesus*, p. 59. Käsemann may restrict the love command too tightly to the
community, but the absence from John of any command to love one's neighbor
or one's enemy further emphasizes the embattled situation of the community.
In the heat of conflict, love for one's friends became so important to the
community that it reduced the ideal of love for those outside the community
to love for "the world" (3:16), not for *individuals* outside the community.

[30]See Appendix II.

ment suggests its importance for the community, which probably also viewed itself as τὰ τέκνα τοῦ θεοῦ (1:12; 11:52). In John there is only one "Son of God," and the believers are never called "sons of God" but τέκνα θεοῦ.[31] Through being disciples of the Son of God, the believers are able to become τέκνα θεοῦ. As noted in Appendix II, the use of τέκνα in the apocryphal literature and the use of its Hebrew equivalents in Old Testament passages reveals that the term was used by teachers for their pupils. That τέκνα carries this meaning, in part at least, in John is indicated by the Old Testament quotation in 6:45: καὶ ἔσονται πάντες διδακτοὶ θεοῦ, which is interpreted in John by the phrase which follows it: πᾶς ὁ ἀκούσας παρὰ τοῦ πατρὸς καὶ μαθὼν ἔρχεται πρὸς ἐμέ. For the Johannine community discipleship involves the ability to "hear," which entails both understanding and obedience and which is given by the Father. In "hearing" the scriptures and the words of Jesus they are διδακτοὶ θεοῦ and hence τέκνα (pupils) of God.[32] Understanding and obeying what Jesus and the scriptures taught must, therefore, have been extremely important for the Johannine community because it was through this that they proved themselves the true τέκνα θεοῦ.

The use of ἀδελφός in John confirms the picture of the community which has already been sketched. In John the term is used only twice (20:17; 21:23) to denote persons other than blood brothers. In these passages "the brothers" are evidently a specific group of believers.[33] In the former (20:17) one assumes that Jesus is referring to his disciples; in the latter (21:23), however, the Johannine community is clearly intended. The importance of this title and similarly φίλος and τέκνα as designations for the members of the community is heightened by their use in the epistles.[34]

In view of the Gospel's interest in the nature of discipleship it is not surprising that one finds a comparable interest in Jesus' role as teacher.[35] Although διδάσκαλος and διδάσκειν

---

[31]Baumbach, "Gemeinde und Welt im Johannes-Evangelium," p. 135.

[32]Cf. Rengstorf, "μανθάνω," *TDNT*, IV, 408.

[33]Cf. Joseph Ratzinger, *The Open Circle: The Meaning of Christian Brotherhood*, trans. by W. A. Glen-Doeple (New York: Sheed and Ward, 1966), pp. 52, 64.

[34]See below, p. 281.

[35]Cf. Rengstorf, "διδάσκω," *TDNT*, II, 143. Compare the view of Jesus as teacher in the synoptics, above pp. 226-32.

occur less frequently in John than in the synoptics, the importance and authority of Jesus' teaching are of special concern
for John.[36]   Nicodemus (3:2) acknowledges that Jesus is a
teacher sent from God; Jesus was taught by the Father (8:28),
and his διδαχή is from God (7:16-17).   The teaching of Jesus,
preserved and proclaimed by the Johannine community, could
therefore claim the highest authority. Moreover, like the
scriptures, the teaching of Jesus in John is revelation because
he made known to his disciples all that he heard from the Father
(15:15), even the name of the Father (17:26). Nor should it be
forgotten that these teachings were mediated to the community
by the BD/Paraclete who had special authority to teach and
remind. It is no wonder then that the Johannine community
viewed itself as διδακτοὶ θεοῦ.

The Johannine concepts of discipleship and Jesus' role as
teacher (both of which are related to the role of the BD)
suggest that the community engaged in study and interpretation
of the teachings of Jesus and the scriptures (2:22).   The
Gospel's reflection of these activities strongly suggests that
the Gospel was written within a school. The Johannine community
studied the scriptures to verify and explain Jesus' words (5:46).
Jesus knew the scriptures even though he had not been trained
in them (7:15),[37] and after his death the disciples "remembered"
many things written in the scriptures (2:17; 12:16; 20:9).
Through studying the scriptures (ἐραυνᾶτε: 5:39; cf. Appendix
I), the Johannine community found that Jesus had fulfilled them;
ἵνα ἡ γραφὴ πληρωθῇ occurs four times in John. Although there
are fewer quotations from the Old Testament in John than in the
synoptic gospels, allusions to the Old Testament abound in
John.[38] John is permeated with Old Testament imagery.[39] It is
also significant that scripture is commonly referred to as "that
which is written." The perfect [participle (γεγραμμένος) or

---

[36]Jesus is addressed as ῥαββί, however, more frequently in John (9
times) than in any of the synoptics.

[37]Cf. Rengstorf, "μανθάνω," *TDNT*, IV, 408: "μανθάνω is also used as a
technical term for academic study of Scripture in Jn. 7:15."

[38]Eighteen quotations are set in bold-face type in John in *The Greek
New Testament*, ed. K. Aland, M. Black, B. M. Metzger, and A. Wikgren (New
York: United Bible Societies, 1966). Cf. Smith, "The Use of the Old
Testament in the New," pp. 53-58.

[39]That the Old Testament is the primary source of John's images has
recently been demonstrated by R. E. Brown's commentary on John.

verb (γέγραπται)] appears eight times in John in reference to
the Old Testament (2:17; 6:31, 45; 8:17; 10:34; 12:14, 16;
15:25).[40] The appearance of the verb "to write" in the perfect
again in John 20:30, 31, therefore, may reflect the understanding of the writer that the community--under the guidance of the
BD/Paraclete--had produced a γραφή equal in authority and
inspiration with the scriptures. The purpose of the Gospel,
like that of the scriptures (for the Johannine community), was
to awaken and strengthen belief in Jesus as the Christ. Writing
the Gospel was an integral part of fulfilling their mission to
witness; hence it is likely that studying and interpreting the
scriptures and words of Jesus were viewed as important communal
activities--activities which witnessed to the truth of Jesus'
ministry. These observations regarding John's use of the Old
Testament support the studies of Lindars, Freed, and Borgen,
which maintain that the Johannine community was (or contained)
an early Christian school in which the Old Testament was
studied.[41]

The community's conflict with the synagogue gave it
further reason to study the scriptures and promulgate its own
interpretations showing how Jesus fulfilled the scriptures of
the Jews. In this confrontation it is unlikely that the evangelist relied on his memory, on testimonia, or on traditional
sources alone.[42] The allusions and quotations in John emerge
from the life and work of a community for which the study and
interpretation of scripture was an integral part of its witness
to the "world."

Even more important than the study of scripture, however,
was the keeping of Jesus' ἐντολάς and his λόγον. The teachings
of Jesus were understood to be a holy tradition (λόγος) given
by the Father through Jesus (14:24) and received by the community (17:8, 14, 17). Τηρέω occurs more frequently in John than

---

[40]Cf. Mussner, "Die johanneischen Parakletsprüche und die apostolische Tradition," p. 68.

[41]See the summaries of the findings of these men above, pp. 26, 29. The sketch of the nature of the Johannine community developed in this dissertation provides the kind of background which Lindars, Freed, and Borgen presuppose. Günter Reim, *Studien zum alttestamentlichen Hintergrund des Johannesevangeliums*, NTSMS, XXII (Cambridge: At the University Press, 1973), on the contrary, argues that John's use of the Old Testament was conditioned more by oral tradition than by the study of written texts.

[42]Cf. Charles Goodwin, "How Did John Treat His Sources?" *JBL*, LXXIII (1954), 61-75, who suggests that John's quotations are cited from memory.

in any other book of the New Testament (18 times) and is used
with both a personal object (the disciples: 17:11, 12, 15) and
impersonal objects (wine: 2:10; the Sabbath: 9:16; ointment:
12:7), but most frequently with Jesus' λόγον (8:51, 52, 55;
14:23; 15:20; 17:6), λόγους (14:24), and his ἐντολάς (14:15, 21;
15:10).[43] Surprisingly, it never has as its object Jesus'
ῥήματα, even though John refers to the ῥήματα twelve times.
Instead, the disciples are to abide (μένειν) in the ῥήματα
(15:7). The parallelism between 15:7 (ἐὰν μείνητε ἐν ἐμοὶ καὶ
τὰ ῥήματά μου ἐν ὑμῖν μείνη, . . .) and 15:10 (ἐὰν τὰς ἐντολάς
μου τηρήσητε, μενεῖτε ἐν τῇ ἀγάπη μου, . . .) indicates, however, that one cannot draw too great a distinction between the
ῥήματα and the ἐντολάς. Like Jesus' διδαχή, the ῥήματα come
from God (3:34; 14:10) and give life (6:68), but those who do
not hear (ἀκούω) and guard (φυλάσσω) will have a judge--ὁ λόγος
ὃν ἐλάλησα--on the last day (12:48). The inter-relationships
in what is said about the λόγος, ῥήματα, ἐντολάς, and διδαχή
of Jesus indicate their importance for the Johannine community,
which was the bearer and defender of Jesus' words and teachings.

The implications of John's use of τηρέω are especially
important. Bultmann interpreted the word as meaning primarily
to obey and believe;[44] Riesenfeld saw in it the meaning "to
preserve, protect, or guard a tradition."[45] Neither meaning
should be denied.[46] Belief and obedience were required, but
more than that, τηρέω probably meant following the guidance of
the BD/Paraclete, i.e., learning, remembering, preserving, and
interpreting the teachings of Jesus which he gave. The teachings had the same authority as the scriptures, and the same
formula is used in John (18:9, 32) for the fulfillment of Jesus'
words and for the fulfillment of the scriptures.[47] Keeping the
teaching of Jesus, however, did not bind the community to a
mechanical reception and transmission of his words. The inter-

---

[43]Cf. Harald Riesenfeld, "τηρέω," *TDNT*, VII, 142-44.

[44]Bultmann, *The Gospel of John*, pp. 301 n. 5, 324 n. 4, 612-14.

[45]Riesenfeld, "τηρέω," *TDNT*, VII, 144.

[46]Cf. Fascher, "Jesus der Lehrer," col. 333; Haacker, *Die Stiftung
des Heils*, pp. 75-78, 87: "Es gibt ein Traditionsdenken, das nicht mit
institutioneller Erstarrung verbunden ist, sondern der Kraft des über-
lieferten Wortes selbst vertraut. An ein solches Traditionsprinzip
scheint Johannes zu denken."

[47]Cf. Meeks, *The Prophet-King*, p. 289; Haacker, *Die Stiftung des
Heils*, p. 35.

pretations of Jesus' teachings found in the Gospel's discourses
are ample testimony to the community's greater concern for the
relevance and proper understanding of the teachings. The
authority for their traditions was important for the community,
but the interpretation and writing of these traditions so that
members of the community (and those caught between it and the
synagogue) might be able to "hear," believe, and have life
(20:30-31) was more important. As a result one finds the teachings of Jesus in new form in John, and one frequently finds the
two levels of meaning suggested by Martyn.[48] The evangelist
(and probably others whose interpretations of the scriptures
and the teaching of Jesus found a place in the Gospel) was most
concerned that the revelation of God in Jesus should be "heard"
clearly in his time.

When John's use of the scriptures and the traditions about
Jesus is set against the historical background of the community,
its significance can be seen more clearly. Much about the historical context is still obscure, but one aspect is especially
promising--the community's conflict with "the Jews."[49] The
community found itself in debate with Jews, and its members were
being excluded from the synagogue (9:22; 12:42; 16:2). The
effect of this conflict on the community is manifested in the
Gospel in a number of ways. "The world" is often used to
represent unbelievers who are hostile to the community;[50] the
community steadfastly maintains that it has the true understanding of the Law and of Jesus because Jesus now manifests himself
only to the disciples, i.e., to the Johannine community, and not
to the world (14:22). The synagogue's practice of excluding
(ἐκβαλλεῖν: 9:34, 35) Johannine Christians is contrasted with
the policy of the Johannine community. Jesus' statement in
6:37, ". . . and him who comes to me I will certainly not cast

---

[48]See above, p. 268 n. 22.

[49]The discussion at this point relies upon the work of Martyn, *History and Theology in the Fourth Gospel.* See also the recent contribution to the study of the background of John by M. de Jonge, "Jewish Expectations and the 'Messiah' according to the Fourth Gospel," *NTS*, XIX (1973), esp. 263-66.

[50]Cf. Baumbach, "Gemeinde und Welt im Johannes-Evangelium," p. 124: "Hinter der Verallgemeinerung dieser Juden zur 'Welt' steht dann offensicht-lich die Erfahrung von Verfolgungen und Leiden durch die Umwelt als Reaktion auf die Verkündigung der Christusbotschaft durch die Gemeinde." Regarding the community's separation from the world see also: Bultmann, *The Gospel of John*, pp. 509-10; Conzelmann, *An Outline of the Theology of the New Testament*, p. 355.

out (ἐκβάλω)," probably reflects the attitude of the community.
This attitude or policy was contrary to that of its opponents.
Membership in the Johannine community was open to any believer,
but he was expected to confess (ὁμολογεῖν: note the use of this
verb in 9:22; 12:42; and 1:20) his faith. Only by confessing
one's faith publicly and entering the community could one have
access to the truth, which was mediated to the community by the
BD/Paraclete and kept (τηρέω) in its communal life and teaching
activities.

The principal purposes of the Gospel appear to have been
to strengthen the community and clarify its beliefs, but also
to encourage those who were in danger of denying (ἄρνεσθαι) the
faith and those who were on the verge of confessing (ὁμολογεῖν).
John's concern for these marginal members of the community may
be seen in his peculiar interest in such characters as the
disciples of John (1:35-51), Nicodemus (3:1-5; 7:50-52; 19:39),
the Samaritan woman (4:1-42), the official (4:46-54), the lame
man (5:1-18), the unbelieving brothers of Jesus (7:5), the man
born blind (9:1-41), the Jewish leaders (12:42), and Thomas
(20:24-29). All of these figures faced the revelation that came
through Jesus and had to decide to confess or deny. There were
probably many who were caught between the Johannine community
and the synagogue and faced a similar decision. For this reason
John brings forth a variety of witnesses. The BD, of course, is
a witness (21:24). The principal function of John the Baptist
in the Gospel is to bear witness, and many others are summoned
especially in 5:30-40 and 8:12-20.[51] Again, one should probably
understand this emphasis in John in terms of the situation of
the community when John was written. Their faith, teaching, and
interpretation of scripture had been rejected. So, with Jesus
as their spokesman they summoned witnesses for the defense of
their faith. They also found great comfort in the traditions
about Jesus. Just as Jesus had been rejected by his own, the
Johannine Christians were rejected by their own—the Jews of
the synagogue. They knew what it meant to be rejected and found
comfort and encouragement in knowing that Jesus too had been
rejected and persecuted (15:18).

---

[51]Cf. David Deeks, "The Structure of the Fourth Gospel," *NTS*, XV
(1968-69), 107-29; James Montgomery Boice, *Witness and Revelation in the
Gospel of John* (Grand Rapids, Mich.: Zondervan Publishing House, 1970).

The picture of the community which emerges from these considerations is one that is characterized by conflict. The conflict led the community to study the scriptures and interpret the traditions about Jesus given to it by the BD so that they could be used in its debate with the Jews. The evangelist urged other members of the community to abide in the love of Jesus by abiding in the teaching and fellowship of the community.

The community probably also celebrated a communal meal like other Christian communities and like the schools of antiquity.[52] Again, the Gospel manifests concern for the proper understanding of this meal. It is to be celebrated in a spirit of love and service to other members of the community (13:1-17),[53] and only those who are "clean" (καθαροί: 13:10, 11) are to participate in it. The word (λόγον) which Jesus spoke, and which the community keeps, makes one clean (15:3), and it is because they have the λόγον that the world hates the community (17:14). Moreover, only those who participate in the meal have life (6:53). In separation from the world the community enjoys *life* and maintains its purity by abiding in its teachings, but its teachings are a witness to the world, a warning, and an invitation to believe.

The history of the Johannine school

The history of the Johannine community will be more fully understood when the composition-history of the Gospel can be traced with more confidence.[54] For the present, however, our best evidence for the history of the community is the Johannine epistles. The mere existence of this group of epistles indicates that there was more than one community of believers which shared the same traditions, vocabulary, doctrines, and ethical principles. I John reflects a later period in the life of the community, but it is difficult to say how much later.[55] Although

---

[52]See the discussion of communal meals in the schools above, pp. 251-52.

[53]Davies, *Setting*, p. 407 n. 4, observes that Jesus performs for the disciples a service which pupils were not expected to perform for their rabbis.

[54]Cf. Martyn, "Source Criticism and *Religionsgeschichte* in the Fourth Gospel," in *Jesus and Man's Hope*, I, 247-73.

[55]Among others, the following have maintained that I John was written after the Gospel: Ernst Haenchen, "Neuere Literatur zu den Johannesbriefen," *ThRu*, N.F. XXVI (1960), 43; Hans Conzelmann, "Was von Anfang war," in *Neutestamentliche Studien für Rudolf Bultmann zu seinem siebzigsten Geburtstag*

it lacks many of the characteristics of a letter,[56] I John does
not have the appearance of a homily or tractate written to a
general audience.[57] It was written to the Johannine community,
or at least a part of it, with the purpose of helping it deal
with certain problems which were well known to both writer and
readers but which we can only infer from the epistle. The writer
refers to "Antichrists" (2:18-19) and "false prophets" (4:1) who
had been members of the community but who left it (2:19; 4:1).
They were not really "from us," however, or they would have
remained (μεμενήκεισαν) "with us" (2:19). The error of their
teaching was that they did not confess (όμολογέομαι) that Jesus
Christ had come in the flesh (4:3). This has generally been
taken to imply that they held a docetic Christology.[58] The
problem for the community was severe because these men had
apparently been leaders or teachers (2:17) in the community,
and after they withdrew from it their teaching was well received
by "the world" (4:5). Their departure, however, was merely the
background of the immediate problem; some who remained in the
community were swayed by the teachings of these false prophets
and had given up the principles of conduct held by the community.[59] I John, therefore, was written to appeal to these members of the community to remain within it and not to disrupt
the fellowship (κοινωνία: 1:3, 6, 7) by letting false doctrines
corrupt their conduct.

---

am 20. August 1954, ed. by W. Eltester, BZNW 21 (Berlin: Alfred Toṗelmann,
1954), p. 198; Conzelmann, *An Outline of the Theology of the New Testament*,
p. 302; Rudolf Bultmann, *The Johannine Epistles*, trans. by R. P. O'Hara with
L. C. McGaughy and R. W. Funk, ed. by R. W. Funk, Hermeneia (Philadelphia:
Fortress Press, 1973), p. 1; Meeks, "The Man from Heaven in Johannine Sec-
tarianism," p. 71; J. A. T. Robinson, "The Destination and Purpose of the
Johannine Epistles," *NTS*, VII (1960-61), 57. See also J. L Houlden, *The
Johannine Epistles*, Harper's New Testament Commentaries (New York: Harper
& Row, 1973).

[56]Regarding the literary character of I John see: Kümmel, *Introduction to the New Testament*, pp. 307-09; Haenchen, "Neuere Literatur zu den
Johannesbriefen," pp. 12-13; Wolfgang Nauck, *Die Tradition und der Charakter
des ersten Johannesbriefes: Zugleich ein Beitrag zur Taufe im Urchristentum
und in der alten Kirche*, WUNT, III (Tübingen: J. C. B. Mohr, 1957), p. 126,
who claims I John is an official letter to the community.

[57]Kümmel, *Introduction to the New Testament*, p. 308, on the contrary,
states: "I John is in no way to be understood as a writing for specific
readers."

[58]Ibid., pp. 309-10; Dodd, *The Johannine Epistles*, pp. xviii-xx.

[59]Frank Stagg, "Orthodoxy and Orthopraxy in the Johannine Epistles,"
RevExp, LXVII (1970), 423-32.

The writer addresses the threatened members of the community as τεκνία (2:1, 12, 28; 3:7, 18; 4:4; 5:21), τέκνα θεοῦ (3:1, 2, 10; 5:2), ἀγαπητοί (2:7; 3:2, 21; 4:1, 7, 11), and ἀδελφοί (3:13, 14, 16 [ἀδελφός occurs in the singular twelve times in I John]). These forms of address underscore the communal relationship between writer and readers.[60] The writer's primary appeal, repeated in countless variations in the course of the epistle, is for his readers to abide (μένειν occurs 24 times in I John)[61] in the love of God (ἀγάπη occurs 18 times in I John) by keeping (τηρεῖν) the commandments (ἐντολὰς; these words appear in conjunction five times in I John), especially the "new commandment" (2:7-8; 3:11, 14, 23; 4:7, 11, 12, 21) and by remembering what they heard (ἀκούω occurs 14 times in I John) "from the beginning" (ἀπ' ἀρχῆς: 2:7, 24; 3:11).

Within the context of fighting false doctrine, the numerous reminders of what the readers had heard strongly suggest that the writer is referring to the instruction the readers had received, i.e., the teaching and traditions of the community. It is no longer a question of abiding in the Spirit but of abiding in the Spirit's teaching.[62] The readers are said to have heard this teaching ἀπ' ἀρχῆς. The phrase (ὁ ἠκούσατε) ἀπ' ἀρχῆς has been understood in a variety of ways,[63] but Conzelmann has made a strong case for interpreting it as follows: ". . . an den Stellen 2^{7.24} 3^{11} II Joh 5f meint ἀπ' ἀρχῆς ohne weitere Erklärung den Anfang der Kirche bzw. das historische Auftreten Jesu (beides ist im Sinne des Verf. nicht zu unterscheiden)."[64]

---

[60]Cf. the discussion of the use of these terms in the Gospel above, pp. 270-73.

[61]Cf. Jürgen Heise, *Bleiben: Menein in den johanneischen Schriften*, Hermeneutische Untersuchungen zur Theologie, VIII (Tübingen: J. C. B. Mohr, 1967), pp. 104-70; Peter Rhea Jones, "A Structural Analysis of I John," *RevExp*, LXVII (1970), 442.

[62]Schweizer, "The Concept of the Church in the Gospel and Epistles of St. John," p. 239; cf. Conzelmann, "Was von Anfang war," pp. 200-01.

[63]Dodd, *The Johannine Epistles*, p. 58, understands it to be a reference to ". . . the fundamental content of the Gospel, . . ."; Brooke, *A Critical and Exegetical Commentary on the Johannine Epistles*, p. 60: ". . . the beginning of their life as Christians. It may, however, include what many of them had heard in the Jewish synagogue"; Haenchen, "Neuere Literatur zu den Johannesbriefen," p. 41, associates the phrase with the "Taufunterricht" which the Christian readers had received; cf. Otto A. Piper, "I John and the Didache of the Primitive Church," *JBL*, LXVI (1947), 437 n. 1.

[64]Conzelmann, "Was von Anfang war," p. 196; Bultmann, *The Johannine Epistles*, p. 9 n. 10, follows Conzelmann.

The references to what *the readers* had heard "from the beginning," (2:7, 24, 3:11; II Jn. 6; cf. Jn. 14:24) suggest, however, that the writer has in mind the earliest period of the
Johannine community. During this period the BD/Paraclete (who
is said to have been one of the disciples who was with Jesus
ἀπ' ἀρχῆς [Jn. 15:27]) taught the community, and the normative
teaching of the community was established. It is to the authority of this teaching that the writer appeals.[65] Since the
community had seen in the BD the working of the Paraclete (cf.
I John 2:1), it is unlikely that it would not have appealed to
his teaching when (some years later) the community was threatened by schism. It is puzzling that there was no direct
appeal to his authority.

Perhaps the reason why the author of I John does not appeal
to the authority of the BD (or the Gospel) directly is that his
opponents, the false teachers, were claiming his authority.
The writer of I John gives a relatively clear picture of his
opponents: 1) they hold a docetic Christology (1:1; 4:2); 2)
they are missionary (4:5); 3) they are false *prophets* (4:1);
4) they do not share the ethical principles or piety of the
community (2:6); and 5) they hold a realized eschatology but
have misunderstood what it means to have crossed from death
into life because they do not love "the brothers" (3:14). The
similarities between the opponents in I John and the Johannine
"conventicle" described by Käsemann in *The Testament of Jesus*
are striking.[66] According to Käsemann, the "conventicle":
1) holds a docetic Christology,[67] 2) is missionary,[68] 3) is
prophetic,[69] 4) is characterized by an enthusiastic piety,[70]
and 5) holds a realized eschatology similar to that of the
opponents in I Cor. 15 and II Timothy 2:18, i.e., they believe
they have crossed from death into life.[71] Taken together, the
similarities between Käsemann's "conventicle," which he recon-
structs on the basis of themes found in the prologue and seven-

---

[65]Cf. Schnackenburg, *Die Johannesbriefe*, pp. 158-59.

[66]I am indebted to Mr. Edward F. Glusman, Jr. for this observation.

[67]Käsemann, *The Testament of Jesus*, pp. 26, 66.

[68]Ibid., pp. 64-65.

[69]Ibid., pp. 38, 49, 77.

[70]Ibid., p. 20.

[71]Ibid., pp. 14-15.

teenth chapter of John, and the false prophets of I John are too extensive to be dismissed.[72]

Nevertheless, one cannot easily attribute the Gospel of John to the opponents of I John. If that were the case, how could one account for the linguistic and theological similarities between the Gospel and I John which have led many to attribute the two writings to the same pen? Moreover, I John regards the opponents' violation of the love command given in the Gospel as a serious offense. It is far more likely that John was written before the departure of the false teachers from the Johannine community. When the false teachers split from the community, they continued to claim the authority of the BD/Paraclete and the Gospel but developed its "naive docetism" into a key element of their faith and missionary preaching. Some members of the community were torn between the two parties. In his appeal to these members, the writer of I John fills his letter with phrases from the Gospel[73] and claims repeatedly that what they had heard "from the beginning" was the full and complete teaching. As Schweizer maintains, in I John ". . . the Spirit cannot teach anything but what existed 'from the beginning.'"[74] Since the BD/Paraclete had taught all things (Jn. 14:26; I Jn. 2:27), any new teaching (e.g., the docetism of the false prophets) could not be from the Spirit. All that was needed was to abide in the teachings given by the BD/Paraclete "from the beginning." This reconstruction of the background of I John suggests why it does not make a more direct appeal to the authority of the BD and why the similarities between I John's false prophets and Käsemann's Johannine conventicle are so extensive. Käsemann has perceived and emphasized precisely those elements in the Fourth Gospel which were emphasized by the opponents of I John as they interpreted John.[75]

---

[72]Käsemann refers to I John only once in *The Testament of Jesus* (p. 60). Wayne A. Meeks, review of *The Testament of Jesus*, by Ernst Käsemann, in *USQR*, XXIV (1969), 418, notes Käsemann's silence about the anti-docetic passages in I and II John.

[73]The words δόξα and δοξάζω, however, do not appear in the epistles.

[74]Schweizer, "The Concept of the Church in the Gospel and Epistles of St. John," p. 239.

[75]Other explanations of why I John never refers to the BD could be offered. This silence could be accounted for on the supposition that either the Presbyter was himself the BD and hence would not apply this title to

Other references in I John suggest developments subsequent
to the writing of the Gospel. The struggle with the synagogue
had either passed or been overshadowed by the community's
internal problems. The admonition to hate the world (2:15) and
love one another (3:11) suggests that the conflict had led the
community to withdraw further from the rest of society ("the
world"). One's love for "the brothers" (3:14) is an indication
that he has already crossed from death into life. In addition
to love, however, the readers are exhorted to hold to the
traditional teachings of the community regarding Jesus as the
Christ who has come in the flesh. These references are an
indication of how the community turned in upon itself and established norms for its orthodoxy and orthopraxy. Even so, one
still does not find any indication of offices or ranks within
the membership of the community.

II John gives the impression of having been composed at
about the same time as I John, because it reflects concern about
the same problems and uses many of the key phrases found in
I John. The writer identifies himself as the presbyter (II Jn.
1)[76] and addresses his letter to "the elect lady and her

---

himself even if others called him the BD, or by supposing that the title was
first used by the evangelist and was not known to the Presbyter. Both of
these explanations, however, require that I John was written before the
Gospel was completed because 21:23 refers to the death of the BD. It is of
course possible that the Johannine epistles were written at some point(s)
during the composition-history of the Fourth Gospel, but the intensity of
the threat of docetism in the epistles, the community's withdrawal from the
world in I John to a degree unmatched in John, and the appeal to what had
been heard ἀπ' ἀρχῆς [which is interpreted above (p. 282) as referring to
the earliest period in the community's history] all suggest that the epistles
were written later than the Gospel.

The Presbyter's address to his readers as ἀγαπητοί may be another
subtle reminder to them of their dependence upon the BD (ὁ μαθητὴς ὃν
ἠγάπα ὁ 'Ιησοῦς) for the true interpretation of the traditions about Jesus.
The use of ἀγαπητοί in I John may be explained by assuming that the Presbyter
was the BD but probably should be explained by assuming that the epistle
was written later than John and reminds the community of its dependence upon
the BD for the authority of its teachings. The absence of any specific
reference to the BD in the Epistles is still a problem, but the best explanation of this silence may be that the opponents of I John were claiming
his authority and that the Presbyter attempted to combat their appeal to his
authority by reminding his readers that they too depended upon the tradition of the community (ὃ ἠκούσατε ἀπ' ἀρχῆς) which had originated with the
BD, and by asserting that the teaching of this tradition was full and complete and that it did not include the docetic Christology of the opponents.
In this way, the Presbyter subtly shifted the appeal to authority away from
the BD to the tradition that derived from him.

[76]Günther Bornkamm, "πρέσβυς," *TDNT*, VI, 671-72, claims the presbyter
was "a specially valued teacher," and ". . . a bearer of tradition, esp. of
the Johannine traditions."

children" (ἐκλεκτῆ κυρία καὶ τοῖς τέκνοις αὐτῆς), and as in
I John the readers are encouraged to hold to the commandment
(ἐντολή) which they heard "from the beginning" (ἠκούσατε ἀπ'
ἀρχῆς) in order that they might love one another (II Jn. 5-6).
In verse seven there is an allusion to the false teachers and
their docetic Christology. The readers are further instructed
to abide in the teaching (διδαχή) and to accept no one into
their οἰκίαν who bears any other teaching or adds to the teaching they have received (II Jn. 9-10). Unlike I John, however,
II John cannot easily be understood as a letter to the community
in which the writer lived; it suggests that there were two
Johannine communities which faced the same problems at about the
same time. The presbyter, who also wrote I John, was known to
both communities and was a defender of the tradition shared by
the two communities. II John may be a summary of I John which
was sent to a sister church.[77]

III John is a private letter from the presbyter (apparently
the same writer as the author of the other two epistles) to
Gaius. Again, the writer regards the members of Gaius' congregation as his children (τὰ ἐμὰ τέκνα: III Jn. 4) and refers to
them as τοὺς φίλους (III Jn. 15). The problem which occasioned
the writing of this letter, however, has little relation to the
problems which prompted the writing of I and II John. This
lack of similarity probably indicates that Gaius was not a
member of the community addressed in II John.[78] Gaius and his
congregation are encouraged to welcome "the brothers" (τοὺς
ἀδελφοὺς: III Jn. 5). Diotrephes may be either an innovator
(cf. II Jn. 9) and false teacher or a representative of orthodox Christianity as Käsemann suggested.[79] The presbyter,
however, does not call Diotrephes an "Antichrist" or "false
prophet," as the opponents are called in the other two epistles.
The dispute, therefore, probably concerned only authority within

---

[77]If II John is a summary of I John which was sent to a sister com-
munity, it is only natural that it appears to be a "secondary work" as
Bultmann asserts; cf. Bultmann, *The Johannine Epistles*, p. 1. See J. L.
Houlden's attractive suggestion (*The Johannine Epistles*, pp. 140-41) that
II John was written prior to I John, which was then written when a personal
visit (cf. II Jn. 12) could not be made.

[78]So also Kümmel, *Introduction to the New Testament*, p. 314.

[79]Käsemann, "Ketzer und Zeuge," in *Exegetische Versuche und Besinnungen*, I, 173; cf. Kümmel, *Introduction to the New Testament*, p. 314; Dodd,
The Johannine Epistles, pp. 162-65; Bultmann, *The Johannine Epistles*, p. 101.

the church and not its doctrine or Christology. For our purposes the most significant thing about the two shorter epistles
is that they show that there were several communities which
shared the Johannine tradition. Probably one ought to think of
a central community in which the BD and later the presbyter
taught (cf. the use of the plural in Jn. 21:24; I Jn. 5:18-20;
III Jn. 12) and satellite communities which shared its influence,
tradition, and doctrine. This concept of the Johannine communities fits well with the problem posed by Diotrephes; Diotrephes
attempted to usurp the leadership of his church and sever relations with the central Johannine community, which was led by the
presbyter. Diotrephes did so by excluding "the brothers" from
his church.

Can this reconstruction of the nature and history of the
Johannine communities be related to the testimony of Papias and
Irenaeus? The principal link between the Johannine community
and the witness of these men is probably to be seen in their use
of titles and phrases which occur prominently in the Johannine
writings. The meaning of πρεσβύτερος in Papias' preface is crucial.[80] As Munck[81] and Bornkamm[82] agree, Papias views the presbyters primarily as teachers and bearers of the traditions about
Jesus. Papias claims to have "learnt well" from the presbyters.
Others followed (παρηκολουθηκώς) the presbyters, and from these
men Papias was able to inquire about the words of the presbyters.
This understanding of the function of the presbyters closely
resembles the above description of the writer of the Johannine
epistles. He was a teacher who opposed the teachings of the
"false prophets" and reminded the community of the teaching of
the BD, their contact with apostolic authority. It is not difficult to imagine how this chain of authority was shortened
(perhaps through ignorance) by Irenaeus or some other later
writer by identifying the BD and the presbyter of the epistles,
who may also been named John, with John the son of Zebedee.[83]

---

[80]Eusebius *Ecclesiastical History* III. xxxix. 3-4. See especially
the discussion of this passage by Barrett, *The Gospel According to St. John*,
pp. 88-92; and Gerhardsson, *Memory and Manuscript*, p. 206.

[81]Johannes Munck, "Presbyters and Disciples of the Lord in Papias,"
HTR, LII (1959), 240.

[82]Günther Bornkamm, "πρέσβυς," *TDNT*, VI, 677-79, claims there was a
"school" of presbyters.

[83]Cf. Richard Heard, "The ΑΠΟΜΝΗΜΟΝΕΥΜΑΤΑ in Papias, Justin, and
Irenaeus," *NTS*, I, (1954-55), 129.

The influence of the
Johannine school

Why do the writings of Papias and Irenaeus contain sketches of the later life of the Apostle John but nothing about the BD or the Johannine community? The answer, of course, is that the Apostle was thought to have been the BD and the head of the Johannine community. Since he probably was not, we have legendary expressions of the interest of the second-century church in the Apostle John but no accounts of the BD or of the Johannine community. This silence suggests that the community did not survive long into the second century and had little immediate influence on other forms of Christianity. The internal evidence of the Johannine writings (treated earlier in this chapter) reveals that the Johannine community was an embattled brotherhood, hard-pressed by conflict with the synagogue, rivalled by a Baptist group, and divided by a docetic Christology. With time the community withdrew further from the world and clung to the teachings and new commandment of its Lord, which were mediated to it by its founder, the BD. The picture is an ironic one; the community probably lost its fight for survival. Wrecked by dissension, it folded. Part of its membership found its way into gnostic communities,[84] while other members were assimilated into other streams of Christianity. The treasured writings of the community were carried into both gnostic (by the false prophets of I John?) and Christian communities; and though their intent was not fully understood, as it is yet only partially known, their beauty and truth were clear. The Johannine community, therefore, probably had little immediate influence on other streams of Christianity. Its writings were its only legacy.

Conclusion

Throughout this discussion of the Johannine community evidence that the community shared the characteristics of ancient schools has been gathered and assessed. In keeping with the methodology proposed above,[85] it can now be shown that the Johannine community shared these characteristics. The following (numbered) characteristics correspond to those of the ancient schools as listed above,[86] 1) The Johannine community

---

[84]The first commentators on John were the Valentinians Ptolemy and Heracleon; cf. Dodd, *The Interpretation of the Fourth Gospel*, p. 102.

[85]Above, pp. 38, 259-61.

[86]Cf. the list of characteristics above, pp. 258-59.

was a fellowship of disciples. Its members were first disciples
of Jesus Christ, but they were also disciples or students of the
BD, who taught and interpreted for them the teachings and traditions about Jesus. The character of the community as a fellowship is confirmed by the way the following terms are used in
its writings: οἱ φίλοι, τοὺς ἀδελφοὺς, μαθηταί, and κοινωνία.
2) The community gathered around, and traced its origins to,
a founder--the BD. References to the BD in the Gospel show that
he was a historical person and the guarantor of the teachings
and doctrine of the community. He is placed in the earliest
circle of disciples by the evangelist. I John also provides
evidence that the community traced its origins to the BD, if,
as argued above,[87] the phrase ἀπ' ἀρχῆς in I John 2:7, 24; 3:11;
and II John 6 refers to the earliest period in the history of
the Johannine community. During this period the BD taught and
guided the community. 3) The community valued the teachings of
its founder and the traditions about him. The teachings of the
BD were held to be the authoritative (true) interpretations of
the words and deeds of Jesus and the meaning of the scriptures.
When these teachings were collected by the evangelist they could
be called a "writing" with the accompanying implication that
the Gospel was equal in authority to the scriptures.[88] As a
result of the BD's importance for the community, traditions
about his relationship to Jesus found expression in various
passages in the Gospel. 4) Members of the community were disciples or students of the founder--the BD. This observation is
warranted by the concept of μαθητής in the Gospel,[89] by the use
of the plural ("we") in John 21:24, by the Gospel's emphasis on
the teaching function of the BD/Paraclete,[90] and by the recur-
rence in I John of the phrase ὃ ἠκούσατε ἀπ' ἀρχῆς.[91] 5) Teaching, learning, studying, and writing were common activities in
the community. Members of the community probably thought of
themselves as διδακτοὶ θεοῦ (Jn. 6:45),[92] and the Gospel itself

[87]Above, pp. 282-83.
[88]Above, pp. 274-76.
[89]Above, pp. 270-72.
[90]Above, pp. 266-68.
[91]Above, pp. 281-82.
[92]Above, p. 273.

is evidence that writing was an important activity. Its references to the scriptures indicate that they were studied along
with the traditions about Jesus.[93] 6) The community observed
a communal meal.[94] 7) The community had rules or practices
regulating admission and retention of membership. The primary
requisites for membership, of course, were belief in Jesus as
the Christ, the Son of God (Jn. 20:21), and baptism (Jn. 3:5;
I Jn. 5:8). Members of the community were also expected to
adhere to the traditions of the community (I Jn. 2:24), and
those who deviated from them eventually had to leave the community (I Jn. 2:19). 8) The community maintained some distance
from the rest of society. Although this withdrawal from "the
world" became more pronounced during the period in which I John
was written, the Gospel (15:18; 16:2; 17:9) also reflects the
community's awareness of its separation from the rest of society.
9) The community developed organizational means of insuring its
perpetuity. Evidence on this point is meager, but the authority
presumed by the author of the epistles (the presbyter) indicates
that the community was not without leadership following the death
of the BD. III John, moreover, addresses one problem which arose
in the course of this development of leadership.

As the previous paragraph shows in summary form, the
Johannine community shared all the essential characteristics of
ancient schools. These characteristics, which describe ancient
schools, also describe the Johannine community. The Johannine
community, therefore, was a school. This conclusion is highly
significant for the interpretation of the Johannine writings,
since they must now be understood against the background of
other ancient schools as well as other streams of early Christianity. Hopefully, a clearer understanding of the school in
which the Johannine writings were composed will lead to a fuller
comprehension of their meaning.

Retrospect

A brief summary of what has been attempted in this dissertation may help to put its various parts in perspective. 1)
The Johannine-school hypothesis was stated.[95] 2) The history

---

[93]Above, pp. 274-75.

[94]Above, p. 279.

[95]Above, p. 1.

of the hypothesis was traced and analyzed.[96] 3) A hitherto
unattempted method of confirming the hypothesis was proposed,
i.e., investigating whether or not the Johannine community
shared the essential characteristics of ancient schools.[97]
4) Nine schools were studied. 5) The essential characteristics
of these schools were stated.[98] 6) The Johannine community was
studied and theses regarding its nature and history were
advanced.[99] 7) The Johannine-school hypothesis was confirmed
by demonstrating that the Johannine community shared the essential characteristics of the ancient schools studied earlier.[100]
The primary conclusion of the dissertation, therefore, is that
the Johannine community was a school.

Prospect

A few avenues for future research suggested by this work
may also be stated. During the course of investigating ancient
schools the need for further study of terms, images, and concepts which assumed special meanings or importance in the schools
became apparent. For example, further study of the following
terms should prove fruitful: the title "friends," the verbs
for "to seek" or "study," and images for the Torah or authoritative teaching (e.g., "well" and "living water"). The metaphors,
images, and terminology of John also need to be analysed in
relation to the tendency of ancient schools to develop esoteric
teachings. Finally, the role and influence of the Johannine
community in early Christianity--in its relation to Qumran,
other streams of Christianity, Revelation, the Odes of Solomon,
Ignatius, and Gnosticism--should be reconsidered in view of the
evidence which indicates that the Johannine community was a
school.

---

[96]Above, pp. 1-37.

[97]Above, pp. 37-38, 259-61.

[98]Above, pp. 258-59.

[99]Above, pp. 263-87.

[100]Above, pp. 287-89.

Appendix I

THE TECHNICAL MEANING OF Ζητέω AND דרש

Otto Betz has noted that in the scrolls the verb דרש has
the technical meaning "to study" or "expound" the meaning of
scripture.[1] Since the article on ζητέω in *TDNT* was written
prior to the discovery of the scrolls,[2] and since Betz does not
relate his insight to the use of ζητέω in the New Testament and
related literature, a re-examination of its use in these writings is needed. This appendix attempts to trace the development
of the technical meaning of ζητέω and דרש and show that it probably influenced John's use of ζητέω.[3]

In 1QS 8:11-12, הדורש refers to the one who studies scripture, and that which is "found" [נמצא] is the hidden meaning of
scripture:

. . . and let every word which is hidden from Israel, but
found [ונמצאו] by the seeker [הדורש], not be hidden from
them out of fear of the spirit of apostasy (1QS 8:11-12).[4]

The technical meaning of דרש is especially clear in references
to the דורש התורה (CD 6:7; 7:18; 4QFlor 1:11; cf. דורש בתורה
in 1QS 6:6).

The technical use of "to seek" [ζητέω] also occurs in
Philo's writings. When the Therapeutae assembled for their
ritual meal and everyone had taken his place according to his
rank, the president waited for silence. Then,

. . . , he discusses [ζητεῖ] some question arising in the
Holy Scriptures or solves one that has been expounded
[προταθὲν; lit "proposed"] by someone else.[5]

_____

[1]*Offenbarung und Schriftforschung in der Qumransekte*, pp. 15-37; cf.
Gerhardsson, *Memory and Manuscript*, pp. 234-35; O. García de la Fuente, "La
búsqueda de Dios en los escritos de Qumrán," *EstBib*, XXXII (1973), 32-36,
M. Gertner, "Terms of Scriptural Interpretation: A Study in Hebrew Seman-
tics," *BSOAS*, XXV (1962), 12.

[2]H. Greeven, "ζητέω," *TDNT*, II, 892-96.

[3]The following concordances have been a great assistance: K. G. Kuhn,
Konkordanz zu den Qumrantexten (Göttingen: Vandenhoeck & Ruprecht, 1960);
I. Leisegang, *Philonis Alexandrini Opera quae Supersunt*, Vol. VII: *Indices
ad Philonis Alexandrini Opera* (Berlin: Walter de Gruyter & Co., 1926); E.
Hatch and H. A. Redpath, *A Concordance to the Septuagint and the Other
Greek Versions of the Old Testament (Including the Apocryphal Books)* (2
vols.; Graz, Austria: Akademisch Druck- u. Verlagsanstalt, 1954); W. F.
Moulton and A. S. Geden, ed., *A Concordance to the Greek Testament* (4th ed.;
Edinburgh: T. & T. Clark, 1963).

[4]The Hebrew text is given above, p. 161 n. 85.

[5]*De Vita Contemplativa* 75:
. . . , ζητεῖ τι τῶν ἐν τοῖς ἱεροῖς γράμμασιν ἢ καὶ ὑπ' ἄλλου προταθὲν
ἐπιλύεται, . . .

292

Here, ζητεῖ means to expound the meaning of scripture; it cannot mean simply "to seek." Philo also uses ζητέω in reference to seeking the meaning of scripture in the following passage:

> When they sought [ζητέω] what it is that nourished the soul (for, as Moses says, "they knew not what it was") (Exod. xvi. 15), they became learners and found it to be a saying of God, that is the Divine Word, from which all kinds of instruction and wisdom flow in perpetual stream.[6]

More specifically, Philo relates ζητέω to finding the hidden, allegorical meaning of scripture:

> And if some allegorical interpretation should appear to underlie them, I shall not fail to state it. For knowledge loves to learn and advance to full understanding and its way is to seek [ζητέω] the hidden meaning rather than the obvious.[7]

These passages in the scrolls and Philo strongly suggest that דרש and ζητέω had acquired the technical meaning of "to search the scriptures in order to find their meaning," and "to expound the meaning of scripture." The use of "to find" or "be found" in reference to the hidden meaning of scripture (as in 1QS 8:11-12) probably derived from the technical meaning of "to seek."

How did "to seek" come to be associated with the study and exposition of scripture? The two words most frequently used for "seeking" in the Old Testament בקש (piel) and דרש. These terms are found in connection with seeking various things and persons, but they are also used to denote religious seeking. In Exod. 33:7 (E tradition), בקש is used in reference to seeking the Lord (MT יהוה; LXX κύριον). In Deut. 4:29-30, both terms are used:

---

[6]*De Fuga et Inventione* 137:

Ζητήσαντες καὶ τί τὸ τρέφον ἐστὶ τὴν ψυχήν--"οὐ γὰρ" ἤ φησι Μωυσῆς "ἤδεισαν τί ἦν"--εὗρον μαθόντες ῥῆμα θεοῦ καὶ λόγον θεῖον, ἀφ' οὗ πᾶσαι παιδεῖαι καὶ σοφίαι ῥέουσιν ἀέννασι.

The possibility of some link between the "stream" metaphor in this passage and the "well" in CD 6:2-11 (above, pp. 162-64) and John 4:4-42, the "river" in John 7:38, and the "stream" and "river" in the Odes of Solomon 6:8 is intriguing. Cf. Charlesworth and Culpepper, "The Odes of Solomon and the Gospel of John," pp. 302, 312-13; Jeremias, *Jerusalem in the Time of Jesus*, pp. 238-39; Sirach 24:30-34; II Esdras 14:45-47; and the passages cited above, pp. 211-12 n. 71 and n. 72. For other instances where Philo uses ζητέω in reference to studying scripture see: *Legum Allegoriae* I. 33, 48, 91, II. 103; *Quod Deus immutabilis sit* 122; *Quis Rerum Divinarum Heres* 1, 101; *De Somniis* I. 41, II. 301; *De Abrahamo* 68.

[7]*De Decalogo* 1:

. . . , εἴ τις ὑποφαίνοιτο τρόπος ἀλληγορίας, τοῦτον παρεὶς ἕνεκα τῆς πρὸς διάνοιαν φιλομαθοῦς ἐπιστήμης, ἤ πρὸ τῶν ἐμφανῶν ἔθος τὰ ἀφανῆ ζητεῖν.

But from there you will seek [MT בקש; LXX ζητέω] the Lord your God, and you will find [MT מצא; LXX εὑρίσκω] him, if you search [MT דרש; LXX ἐκζητέω] after him with all your heart and with all your soul. When you are in tribulation, and all these things [MT הדברים; LXX οἱ λόγοι] come upon [MT מצא; LXX εὑρίσκω; lit. "find"] you in the latter days, you will return to the Lord your God and obey his voice. [8]

בקש is used in other passages for seeking the Lord (e.g., Pss. 27:8; 83:16; 105:3-4 [דרש also appears here]; Prov. 28:5; Isa. 51:1; 65:1; Jer. 50:4; Hos. 3:5; Zeph. 2:3; Zech. 8:22; Mal. 3:1; II Chr. 11:16; 20:4). Mal. 2:7 instructs that men should seek Torah (MT ותורה יבקשו; LXX νόμον ἐκζητήσουσιν) from the mouth of a priest. דרש is used more frequently than בקש, however, in connection with seeking God in Chronicles and other late writings (e.g., I Chr. 10:14; 21:30; 22:19; II Chr. 11:16; 14:4, 7; 15:2, 12, 13; 16:12; 17:4; 18:4, 7; 19:3; 22:9; 26:5; 30:19; 31:21; 34:3, 21, 29 [cf. Wis. 13:6]; 1QS 1:1; 5:9). In the LXX both ζητέω and ἐκζητέω are used to translate דרש in these passages. In the following verses the object of "seeking" and "finding" is the Lord:

Seek [MT דרש; LXX ζητέω] the Lord while he may be found,. . . [9]

If you seek [MT דרש; LXX ζητέω] him [the Lord], he will be found by you; . . . . [10]

He who seeks [ζητέω] the Lord will find [εὑρίσκω] knowledge with righteousness, but those who seek [ζητέω] him in the right way will find [εὑρίσκω] peace. [11]

---

[8]Deut. 4:29-30:

MT: ובקשתם משם את-יהוה אלהיך ומצאת כי תדרשנו בכל-לבבך ובכל-נפשך:
בצר לך ומצאוך כל הדברים האלה באחרית הימים ושבת עד-יהוה
אלהיך ושמעת בקלו

LXX: καὶ ζητήσετε ἐκεῖ κύριον τὸν θεὸν ὑμῶν καὶ εὑρήσετε, ὅταν ἐκζητήσητε αὐτὸν ἐξ ὅλης τῆς καρδίας σου καὶ ἐξ ὅλης τῆς ψυχῆς σου ἐν τῇ θλίψει σου· καὶ εὑρήσουσίν σε πάντες οἱ λόγοι οὗτοι ἐπ' ἐσχάτῳ τῶν ἡμερῶν, καὶ ἐπιστραφήσῃ πρὸς κύριον τὸν θεόν σου καὶ εἰσακούσῃ τῆς φωνῆς αὐτοῦ·

[9]Isa. 55:6:

MT: דרשו יהוה בהמצאו
LXX: Ζητήσατε τὸν θεὸν καὶ ἐν τῷ εὑρίσκειν αὐτὸν . . . .

[10]I Chr. 28:9:

MT: אם-תדרשנו ימצא לך
LXX: ἐὰν ζητήσῃς αὐτόν, εὑρεθήσεταί σοι, ...
Cf. II Chr. 15:2, 4.

[11]Prov. 16:5 (LXX only): ὁ ζητῶν τὸν κύριον εὑρήσει γνῶσιν μετὰ δικαιοσύνης οἱ δὲ ὀρθῶς ζητοῦντες αὐτὸν εὑρήσουσιν εἰρήνην.
Translation by author. This reading is omitted by A. Rahlfs, ed., *Septuaginta* (8th ed.; Stuttgart: Württembergische Bibelanstalt, 1935); see Societatis Litterarum Gottingensis, ed., *Septuaginta: Vetus Testamentum Graecum* (Göttingen: Vandenhoeck & Ruprecht, 1931-), XI, *ad loc*.

294

In the sapiental literature, Wisdom is sought (Prov. 8:17 [MT
שׁחר; LXX ζητέω]; 14:6 [MT בקשׁ; LXX ζητέω]; Eccl. 1:13 [MT דרשׁ;
LXX ἐκζητέω]; Sir. 6:27 [LXX ζητέω]; 51:13 [LXX ζητέω]) and
found (Prov. 3:13 [MT מצא; LXX εὑρίσκω]; Wis. 6:12 [LXX ζητέω,
εὑρίσκω]; cf. Job 28:12 [MT מצא; LXX εὑρίσκω]; 32:13 [MT מצא;
LXX εὑρίσκω]). Wisdom is also sought but not found:

> . . . they will seek [MT שׁחר; LXX ζητέω] me diligently but
> will not find me.[12]

The development toward the technical meaning of "seeking"
as the study and exposition of Torah can be seen in its early
stages in other passages also. In Amos 8:12, the prophet warns
that the time is coming when men will seek [בקשׁ] the word of
the Lord but not find it. In Prov. 2:4-5, the student is told
that if he seeks [בקשׁ] the knowledge of the Lord diligently, he
will find it. In I Chr. 28:8, David tells the people to seek
out [דרשׁ] the commandments [מצות] of the Lord, and the term
מדרשׁ first occurs in II Chr. 13:22; 24:27. Similarly, in Isa.
34:16, the book of the Lord is the object:

> Seek [MT דרשׁ; LXX absent] and read from the book of the
> Lord: . . . .[13]

Not surprisingly, דרשׁ is first used for the study of the Torah
in Ezra:

> For Ezra had set his heart to study [MT דרשׁ; LXX ζητέω] the
> law [MT תורה; LXX τὸν νόμον] of the Lord, and to do it, and
> to teach his statutes and ordinances in Israel.[14]

This is the only place in the Old Testament where תורה is the
object of דרשׁ, and although ζητέω occurs six times in the LXX
translation of Ezra, this is the only place where it translates
דרשׁ. In Neh. 8:13-14, the leaders of the people come to Ezra
to study [להשׁכיל] the words of the Torah and find [מצא] a commandment given by Moses. The foundation for the technical meaning
of דרשׁ is laid in Ezra, but the association is not complete.

Further evidence for the development of the technical meaning is found in Sirach. In 3:21 ζητέω probably refers to study

---

[12]Prov. 1:28:
MT: ישׁחרנני ולא ימצאנני
LXX: . . . ζητήσουσίν με κακοὶ καὶ οὐχ εὑρήσουσιν.

[13]Isa. 34:16:
MT: דרשׁו מעל-ספר יהוה וקראו

[14]Ezra 7:10:
MT: כי עזרא הכין לבבו לדרושׁ את-תורת יהוה ולעשׂת וללמד בישׂראל
                                                                חק ומשׁפט:
LXX: ὅτι Εσδρας ἔδωκεν ἐν καρδία αὐτοῦ ζητῆσαι τὸν νόμον καὶ ποιεῖν καὶ
διδάσκειν ἐν Ισραηλ προστάγματα καὶ κρίματα.

or investigation. In 32:15 it is associated with the study of
the Law:

> He who seeks the law [ὁ ζητῶν νόμον] will be filled with
> it, ...[15]

Νόμον here is probably a translation of תורה, and ζητῶν a
translation of דורש; thus, the Hebrew autograph probably read
דורש התורה--the same phrase found in the scrolls.[16]

The development in the use of the term דרש, as indicated
by the above passages, appears to be as follows. First, דרש
and בקש are both used for seeking the Lord. In Chronicles and
other late works, דרש is used more frequently for seeking with
a religious purpose (i.e., seeking God). דרש is also used for
seeking Wisdom and for searching in writings. Finally, with
Ezra, the first association of דרש with the study of the Torah
occurs. Increasingly, from Ezra on, one probably sought [דרש]
God and Wisdom by studying the Torah. Hence, at Qumran, in
Philo's writings, and probably in the Torah-centric, Jewish
schools generally (e.g. Sirach), דרש assumed the technical meaning of studying, interpreting, and expounding scripture. This
technical meaning also appears in later Jewish (M. Berakoth 1:5;
Sotah 5:1; Hagigah 2:1) and Christian (Barnabas XI. 1) writings.[17]

Is ζητέω used with this technical meaning in the New Testament? The word occurs frequently: 117 times (14/10/25/34/10/
20).[18] In addition to its general usage, one finds that the
"Hellenes" seek wisdom (I Cor. 1:22), men seek signs (Mk. 8:11-
12), God (Acts 17:27; Rom. 3:11), the Kingdom of God (Matt.
6:33; Lk. 12:31), and Jesus (Lk. 2:49; Jn. 6:26; 7:34, 36; 8:21;
13:33), and the Jews seek to kill Jesus (Jn. 5:18; 7:1, 11, 19,
20; 8:37, 40). Moreover, ζητέω appears in the abstract, i.e.,
with no stated object (Matt. 7:7, 8; Lk. 11:9, 10; Jn. 8:50).
The closest verbal parallel to Matt. 7:7 and Lk. 11:9 is found
in the records of the discourses at Epictetus' school:

> ζητεῖτε καὶ εὑρήσετε   (Matt. 7:7; Lk. 11:9)
> ζήτει καὶ εὑρήσεις   (Epictetus I. xxviii. 20; IV. i. 51)

---

[15]Sirach 32:15:
LXX: ὁ ζητῶν νόμον ἐμπλησθήσεται αὐτοῦ, ...
Cf. Sirach 39:1-3 where ἐκζητέω is used in the Greek text.

[16]Cf. Jeremias, *Der Lehrer der Gerechtigkeit*, p. 293.

[17]Cf. Marcus Jastrow, comp., *A Dictionary of the Targumim, the Talmud
Babli and Yerushalmi, and the Midrashic Literature* (New York: Pardes
Publishing House, Inc., 1950), I, 325; G. W. H. Lampe, ed., *A Patristic
Greek Lexicon* (Oxford: Clarendon, 1961), p. 591.

[18]Morgenthaler, *Statistik des neutestamentlichen Wortschatzes*, p. 103.

296

In the synoptics the saying occurs in the context of instruction about prayer, and in the sequence of injunctions ask-seek-knock.[19] In Epictetus, ζητέω refers to philosophical investigation. It is extremely unlikely that there is any dependence in either direction between the synoptics and Epictetus; rather, the parallel suggests that the saying was a proverb known in many milieux. The proverb may also have been used with a technical meaning in Jewish schools where the Torah was studied.

It has already been shown that by the first century B.C. ζητέω had acquired the technical meaning of studying and expounding scripture. Furthermore, מצא appears in the scrolls with a technical meaning probably derived from that of דרש; the hidden meaning of scripture is what the seeker finds. Only in the scrolls, however, do both terms [דרש and מצא] appear with this technical meaning, but the proverb, "Seek and you will find," is not found in the scrolls or in Philo. While no firm conclusions can be drawn, the following probabilities can be stated: 1) the synoptic saying is probably a proverb which circulated independently prior to being incorporated into the teaching on prayer; and 2) because the proverb was known at a philosophical school (Epictetus), and because both key terms are used in a technical sense in passages related to the school at Qumran,[20] the proverb (or a version of it) may have been known and used at Qumran (and possibly other Torah schools) with the technical meaning: "Study the Torah, and you will find its meaning."

Ζητέω is used more often in John (34 times) than in any other book of the New Testament. Can traces of its technical meaning be found in the Fourth Gospel? The repeated use of the term in two ways stands out. First, the question τί [or τίνα] ζητεῖς [or ζητεῖτε] occurs five times (Jn. 1:38); 4:27; 18:4, 7; 20:15 [cf. Gen. 37:15 LXX]). In view of the rich Old Testament background of ζητέω, the question is a profound one, and John is capable of evoking all its profundity. The question is addressed to the two disciples of John, the arrestors, and the women at the tomb. Were they seeking a teacher, the Messiah,

---

[19]In Pesikta 176a, R. Benaiah (*ca.* A.D. 200) applies the proverb "Knock and it shall be opened to you" to the study of the Mishnah. Cf. A. H. McNeile, *The Gospel According to St. Matthew* (London: The Macmillan Co., 1915), p. 92.

[20]See above, pp. 160-66.

Wisdom, or the Lord? The second way in which the term is used
repeatedly is in the saying "You will seek me and you will not
find me":

> . . . ; you will seek [ζητέω] me and you will not find
> [εὑρίσκω] find me; where I am you cannot come." The Jews
> said to one another, "Where does this man intend to go that
> we shall not find him? Does he intend to go to the Disper-
> sion among the Greeks and teach the Greeks? What does he
> mean by saying [τίς ἐστιν ὁ λόγος οὗτος ὃν εἶπεν], 'You will
> seek [ζητέω] me and you will not find me,' and, 'Where I am
> you cannot come'?" (Jn. 7:34-36).

> You will seek [ζητέω] me; and as I said to the Jews so now I
> say to you, 'Where I am going you cannot come.' (Jn. 13:33).

In both places the hearers (the Jews, and the disciples) are
told that they will seek Jesus but not find him. The warning
that they will not find is reminiscent of the use of "seeking"
and "finding" in the wisdom literature (Prov. 1:28; cf. 16:5
LXX; Amos 8:11-12; II Kgs. 17:20).[21] The context of these sayings in John is also significant. In chapter 7, the Jews conjecture that Jesus may be going to the Diaspora to teach the
Hellenes and then ironically ask τίς ἐστιν ὁ λόγος οὗτος ὃν
εἶπεν. This is another case of Johannine irony, the Jews give
the answer to their own question but do not realize it. The key
is that "the Word which he speaks" is "the way" (Jn. 14:6; cf.
14:4) to what they are seeking (God, Wisdom, and the true
meaning of the Torah). The irony in chapter 7 is heightened by
the statements that the Jews, who have the Law (7:19) but do not
seek the glory of God (7:18; cf. 5:44-45), are seeking to kill
Jesus (7:1, 19) because they do not know that his διδαχὴ is from
God (7:16). In John, Jesus (the Word) and his teachings replace
the Torah as the way to the Father, and the members of the
Christian community are to "seek" God through Jesus' words.[22]

Jn. 13:33 appears to present a problem for this interpretation. The disciples are told that they too will seek Jesus, and
like the Jews they will not be able to come where he is going.
But, the saying is preceded by the address τεκνία, a term used
by Jewish teachers for their disciples,[23] and followed by the

---

[21]Cf. Brown, *The Gospel According to John*, I, 318; compare The Gospel
of Thomas, logion 38.

[22]See the discussion of "keeping" Jesus' ἐντολάς and his λόγον, above,
pp. 275-77.

[23]Str-B, II, 559; Cf. Deut. 11:19 LXX; Ps. 33:12 LXX; Isa. 54:13 LXX;
Sir. 2:1; 3:1, 17; 4:1; 6:18, 23, 32; I Jn. 2:1, 12, 28; 3:7, 18; 4:4; 5:21.
Cf. Appendix II.

new commandment, which *will* separate the disciples from the Jews. The future tense in 13:35 stands in contrast to the present tense in 13:33, which is emphasized by ἄρτι. The implication is that even though the disciples could not "seek" Jesus success- fully before the resurrection, subsequently (in the Johannine school), by observing the new commandment and remembering the words of Jesus (Jn. 15:20; 16:4), they were distinguished from the Jews and able to seek (and find) Jesus (the Word).

A second and more serious challenge to the thesis that ζητέω was used with the technical meaning "to study" is posed by the use of ἐραυνάω in Jn. 5:39 (ἐραυνᾶτε τὰς γραφάς) and 7:52 (ἐρεύνησον καὶ ἴδε). Ἐραυνάω (= ἐρευνάω) is generally, but perhaps mistakenly, held to be the equivalent of דרש.[24] Philo uses the term for the study of scripture and possibly to denote the work of the scribes.[25] But, in the LXX neither ἐραυνάω nor ἐξεραυνάω ever translates דרש, and ἐραυνάω never refers to the study of scripture. Ἐξεραυνάω, however, is used in connection with the scriptures (but never τὰς γραφάς) in Ps. 119:2, 34, 69, 115 (129). But, only in this one psalm is it used in this connection, and here (and only here in the LXX) it translates נצר.[26] This lack of correlation in the LXX between ἐραυνάω and דרש or the meaning "to study scripture" suggests that ἐραυνάω was not the equivalent of דרש. Still, it is used by John (and Philo) in connection with scripture. The evidence is there- fore perplexing. The solution to the relation between ἐραυνάω and ζητέω in John may be the following: in both 5:39 (where ἐραυνᾶτε is probably indicative rather than imperative)[27] and 7:52, ἐραυνάω describes the way in which "the Jews" study scripture. They "search" (ἐραυνάω) but do not "seek" (ζητέω) the glory of God (5:44) as do the disciples (and the Johannine community who "seek" the glory of God by studying the Old Testa-

---

[24]For the view that ἐραυνάω is the equivalent of דרש see: Bultmann, *The Gospel of John*, p. 268 n. 1; Barrett, *The Gospel According to St. John*, pp. 222; Brown, *The Gospel According to John*, I, 225; Martyn, *History and Theology in the Fourth Gospel*, p. 92 n. 144. Str-B, II, 467, also maintains that ἐραυνάω is the equivalent of דרש and cites Ezra 7:10, but in the LXX דרש in Ezra 7:10 is translated by ζητέω. Cf. above, p. 294.

[25]*Quod Deterius Potiori insidiari solet* 13, 57; *De Cherubim* 14; cf. Gerhard Delling, "ἐραυνάω," *TDNT*, II, 656.

[26]נצר appears in the Qumran scrolls only in IQH and is always used as a substantive.

[27]So Bultmann, Barrett, and Brown; cf. n. 24. See also M.-E. Boismard, "A propos de Jean V, 39. Essai de critique textuelle," *RB*, LV (1948), 5-34.

ment for its witness to Jesus and by studying the Word (λόγον) of Jesus.

We conclude that John certainly knew the rich background of the term ζητέω, that he probably knew its technical meaning (i.e. "to study"), and that in characteristically Johannine fashion he preserved the profound meaning of the term, while replacing the Torah with the Word of Jesus as the way through which one should "seek" the Lord.

APPENDIX II

Τέκνα AND Τεκνία

Isaiah 8:16, 18 are probably significant for the study of
the Johannine school (cf. above, p. 186). One notices first the
terms "testimony" (μαρτυρία in John) and "signs" (σημεῖα in
John). Moreover, the term "children" (ילדים) in Isaiah 8:18
may refer to his disciples as well as to his sons. בן is used
more frequently in the MT to denote disciples; cf. Deut. 6:7,
20, 21. But, in two significant verses the LXX translates בן
as τέκνα:

Deut. 11:19 (MT): ולמדתם אתם את־בניכם לדבר בם בשבתך בביתך
ובלכתך בדרך ובשכבך ובקומך:

LXX: καὶ διδάξετε αὐτὰ τὰ τέκνα ὑμῶν λαλεῖν αὐτὰ καθημένους
ἐν οἴκῳ καὶ πορευομένους ἐν ὁδῷ καὶ κοιταζομένους καὶ
διανισταμένους·

Ps. 34:12 (MT): לכו־בנים שמעו־לי יראת יהוה אלמדכם:

Ps. 33:12 (LXX): δεῦτε, τέκνα ἀκούσατέ μου· φόβον κυρίου
διδάξω ὑμᾶς.

Isaiah 54:13 strengthens the probability that Isaiah had
disciples and adds a significant link between these Old Testament passages and John.[1] Note that the LXX translates בני once
as υἱούς and once as τέκνα:

Isa. 54:13 (MT): וכל־בניך למודי יהוה ורב שלום בניך:

LXX: καὶ πάντας τοὺς υἱούς σου διδακτοὺς θεοῦ καὶ ἐν πολλῇ
εἰρήνῃ τὰ τέκνα σου.

John 6:45: ἔστιν γεγραμμένον ἐν τοῖς προφήταις· καὶ ἔσονται
πάντες διδακτοὶ θεοῦ· πᾶς ὁ ἀκούσας παρὰ τοῦ πατρὸς καὶ
μαθὼν ἔρχεται πρὸς ἐμέ.

Proverbs (LXX) uses υἱέ throughout to address the student, but
Sirach uses τέκνον and τέκνα (see for example 2:1; 3:1, 17; 4:1;
6:18, 23, 32; 23:7; 41:14; cf. Mk. 10:24). The diminutive form,
τεκνία, does not occur in the LXX.

In John 17:6 the disciples are said to have been given to
Jesus by the Father (cf. Isa. 8:18). Even more significant is
the occurrence of τεκνία in John 13:33 (cf. Str-B, II, 559),
because the verse also instructs the disciples that they will
(should?) seek Jesus. The probability that ζητέω in Matt. 7:7
and parallels and John 7:34, 36 carries the technical meaning
"to study" (דרש), as in 1QS 8:11 and elsewhere in the scrolls
is discussed in Appendix I. In John 13:33-35, τεκνία and ζητέω

---

[1] See Franklin W. Young, "A Study of the Relation of Isaiah to the
Fourth Gospel," ZNW, XLVI (1955), 215-33.

both occur just prior to the giving of the new commandment, which, in addition to the change from the Torah to the "Word" of Jesus as the object of the school's *midrash*, differentiates the Johannine school from the Jewish Torah schools. With the possible exception of Galatians 4:19, τεκνία occurs only in the Johannine literature in the New Testament, once in John (13:33) and seven times in I John (2:1, 12, 28; 3:7, 18; 4:4; 5:21). The author of I John was apparently drawn to the term by the importance of its context in John (the new commandment) and its use in the Old Testament, and therefore used it repeatedly in his letter to the Johannine community.

Aune, David Edward. *The Cultic Setting of Realized Eschatology in Early Christianity*. Supplements to Novum Testamentum, Vol. XXVIII. Leiden: E. J. Brill, 1972.

Baumbach, Günther. "Gemeinde und Welt im Johannes-Evangelium." *Kairos*, XIV (1972), 121-36.

Becker, Jürgen. *Das Heil Gottes: Heils und Sündenbegriffe in den Qumrantexten und im Neuen Testament*. Studien zur Umwelt des Neuen Testaments, Bd. III. Göttingen: Vandenhoeck & Ruprecht, 1964.

Betz, Otto. *Offenbarung und Schriftforschung in der Qumransekte*. Wissenschaftliche Untersuchungen zum Neuen Testament, VI. Tübingen: J. C. B. Mohr, 1960.

_____. *Der Paraklet: Fürsprecher im häretischen Spätjudentum, im Johannes-Evangelium und in neu gefundenen gnostischen Schriften*. Arbeiten zur Geschichte des Spätjudentums und Urchristentums, II. Leiden: E. J. Brill, 1963.

Bickerman, Elias. "La chaine de la tradition pharisienne." *Revue biblique*, LIX (1952), 44-54.

Borgen, Peder. *Bread from Heaven: An Exegetical Study of the Concept of Manna in the Gospel of John and the Writings of Philo*. Supplements to Novum Testamentum, Vol. X. Leiden: E. J. Brill, 1965.

Bousset, W[ilhelm]. *Jüdisch-Christlicher Schulbetrieb in Alexandria und Rom: Literarische Untersuchungen zu Philo und Clemens von Alexandria, Justin und Irenäus*. Forschungen zur Religion und Literatur des Alten und Neuen Testaments, n.F., Heft VI. Göttingen: Vandenhoeck & Ruprecht, 1915.

Boyancé, Pierre. *Le Culte des muses chez les philosophes Grecs: Études d'histoire et de psychologie religieuses*. Bibliothèque des Écoles françaises d'Athènes et de Rome, Fasc. CXLI. Paris: E. de Boccard, 1937.

Brown, Raymond E. *The Gospel According to John*. The Anchor Bible, Vols. XXIX and XXIXa. Garden City, N.Y.: Doubleday & Company, Inc., 1966-70.

_____. "The Paraclete in the Fourth Gospel." *New Testament Studies*, XIII (1966-67), 113-32.

Bultmann, Rudolf. *The Gospel of John: A Commentary*. Translated by G. R. Beasley-Murray, R. W. N. Hoare, and J. K. Riches. Philadelphia: The Westminster Press, 1971.

_____. *The Johannine Epistles*. Translated by R. Philip O'Hara with Lane C. McGaughy and Robert W. Funk. Edited by Robert W. Funk. Hermeneia. Philadelphia: Fortress Press, 1973.

304

Burkert, Walter. *Weisheit und Wissenschaft: Studien zu Pythagoras, Philolaos und Platon*. Erlanger Beiträge zur Sprach- und Kunstwissenschaft, Bd. X. Nürnberg: Verlag Hans Carl, 1962.

Carrington, Philip. *The Primitive Christian Catechism: A Study in the Epistles*. Cambridge: At the University Press, 1940.

Charlesworth, James H., ed. *John and Qumran*. London: Geoffrey Chapman, 1972.

_____, and Culpepper, R. A. "The Odes of Solomon and the Gospel of John." *Catholic Biblical Quarterly*, XXXV (1973), 298-322.

Clarke, M. L. *Higher Education in the Ancient World*. Albuquerque: University of New Mexico Press, 1971.

Conzelmann, Hans. "Was von Anfang war." *Neutestamentliche Studien für Rudolf Bultmann zu seinem siebzigsten Geburtstag am 20. August 1954*. Edited by Walther Eltester. Beihefte zur Zeitschrift für die neutestamentliche Wissenschaft, XXI. Berlin: Alfred Töpelmann, 1954.

Crönert, Wilhelm. "Die Epikureer in Syrien." *Jahreshefte des Österreichischen archäologischen Institutes in Wien*, X (1907), 145-52.

Cross, Frank Moore, Jr. *The Ancient Library of Qumran and Modern Biblical Studies: The Haskell Lectures 1956-1957*. Rev. ed. Garden City, N.Y.: Doubleday & Company, 1961.

Culpepper, R. Alan. "Education." *International Standard Bible Encyclopedia*. Rev. ed. Grand Rapids, Mich.: Wm. B. Eerdmans, [Forthcoming].

Daube, David. "Rabbinic Methods of Interpretation and Hellenistic Rhetoric." *Hebrew Union College Annual*, XXII (1949), 239-64.

Davies, W. D. *The Gospel and the Land: Early Christianity and Jewish Territorial Doctrine*. Berkeley: University of California Press, 1974.

_____. *Paul and Rabbinic Judaism: Some Rabbinic Elements in Pauline Theology*. 3rd ed. London: S. P. C. K. Press, 1970.

_____. *The Setting of the Sermon on the Mount*. Cambridge: University Press, 1966.

Delorme, Jean. *Gymnasion: Étude sur les monuments consacrés à l'éducation en Grèce (des origines à l'empire romain)*. Bibliothèque des écoles françaises d'Athenes et de Rome, Fasc. CXCVI. Paris: Éditions E. de Boccard, 1960.

DeWitt, Norman Wentworth. *Epicurus and His Philosophy*. Minneapolis: University of Minnesota Press, 1954.

_____. "Organization and Procedure in Epicurean Groups." *Classical Philology*, XXXI (1936), 205-11.

Dodd, C. H. "The First Epistle of John and the Fourth Gospel." *Bulletin of the John Rylands Library*, XXI (1937), 129-56.

_____. "Jesus as Teacher and Prophet." *Mysterium Christi: Christological Studies by British and German Theologians.* Edited by G. K. A. Bell and D. Adolf Deissmann. London: Longmans, Green and Co., 1930.

_____. "The Primitive Catechism and the Sayings of Jesus." *New Testament Essays: Studies in Memory of Thomas Walter Manson.* Edited by A. J. B. Higgins. Manchester: University Press, 1959.

Dombrowski, Bruno W. "HYḤD in 1QS and *to koinon*: An Instance of Early Greek and Jewish Synthesis." *Harvard Theological Review*, LIX (1966), 293-307.

Düring, Ingemar. *Aristotle in the Ancient Biographical Tradition.* Göteborgs Universitets Årsskrift, Vol. LXIII, 2. Göteborg: Elanders Boktryckeri Aktiebolag, 1957.

Fascher, Erich. "Jesus der Lehrer: Ein Beitrag zur Frage nach dem 'Quellort der Kirchenidee.'" *Theologische Literaturzeitung*, LXXIX (1954), 325-42.

Fischel, Henry A. *Rabbinic Literature and Greco-Roman Philosophy: A Study of Epicurea and Rhetorica in Early Midrashic Writings.* Studia Post-Biblica, 21. Leiden: E. J. Brill, 1973.

Forkman, Göran. *The Limits of the Religious Community: Expulsion from the Religious Community within the Qumran Sect, within Rabbinic Judaism, and within Primitive Christianity.* Coniectanea Biblica, New Testament Series 5. Translated by Pearl Sjölander. Lund: C. W. K. Gleerup, 1972.

Freed, Edwin D. *Old Testament Quotations in the Gospel of John.* Supplements to Novum Testamentum, Vol. XI. Leiden: E. J. Brill, 1965.

Fritz, K[urt] von. "Mathematiker und Akusmatiker bei den alten Pythagoreern." *Sitzungsberichte der Bayerischen Akademie der Wissenschaften: philosophisch-historische Klasse*, Jahrgang (1960), Heft XI.

_____. *Pythagorean Politics in Southern Italy: An Analysis of the Sources.* New York: Columbia University Press, 1940.

Früchtel, Ursula. *Die kosmologischen Vorstellungen bei Philo von Alexandrien: Ein Beitrag zur Geschichte der Genesisexegese.* Arbeiten zur Literatur und Geschichte des hellenistischen Judentums, II. Leiden: E. J. Brill, 1968.

Furnish, Victor Paul. *The Love Command in the New Testament.* Nashville: Abingdon Press, 1972.

_____. *Theology and Ethics in Paul.* Nashville: Abingdon Press, 1968.

Gaiser, Konrad. *Platons ungeschriebene Lehre: Studien zur systematischen und geschichtlichen Begründung der Wissenschaften in der Platonischen Schule.* Stuttgart: Ernst Klett Verlag, 1963.

306

Georgi, Dieter. "The Records of Jesus in the Light of Ancient Accounts of Revered Men." *Society of Biblical Literature: 1972 Proceedings*. Vol. II. Edited by Lane C. McGaughy. N.p.: The Society of Biblical Literature, 1972.

Gerhardsson, Birger. *Memory and Manuscript: Oral Tradition and Written Transmission in Rabbinic Judaism and Early Christianity*. Translated by Eric J. Sharpe. Acta Seminarii Neotestamentici Upsaliensis, XXII. Uppsala and Lund: C. W. K. Gleerup, 1961.

_____. *Tradition and Transmission in Early Christianity*. Translated by Eric J. Sharpe. Coniectanea Neotestamentica, XX. Lund: C. W. K. Gleerup, 1964.

Goldin, Judah. "A Philosophical Session in a Tannaite Academy." *Traditio*, XXI (1965), 1-21.

Goodenough, Erwin R. *By Light, Light: The Mystic Gospel of Hellenistic Judaism*. New Haven: Yale University Press, 1935.

_____. "Wolfson's Philo." *Journal of Biblical Literature*, LXVII (1948), 87-109.

Guthrie, W. K. C. *History of Greek Philosophy*. 3 vols. Cambridge: University Press, 1962.

Haacker, Klaus. *Die Stiftung des Heils: Untersuchungen zur Struktur der johanneischen Theologie*. Arbeiten zur Theologie, 1. Reihe, Heft, LXVII. Stuttgart: Calwer Verlag, 1972.

Hadas, Moses. "Gadarenes in Pagan Literature." *The Classical Weekly*, XXV (1931), 25-30.

_____. *Hellenistic Culture: Fusion and Diffusion*. New York: Columbia University Press, 1959.

Hammond, N. G. L., and Scullard, H. H., eds. *The Oxford Classical Dictionary*. 2nd ed. Oxford: Clarendon Press, 1970.

Harnack, Adolf [von]. "Das 'Wir' in den Johanneischen Schriften." *Sitzungsberichte der Preussischen Akademie der Wissenschaften*, XVII (1923), 96-113.

Hengel, Martin. *Judentum und Hellenismus: Studien zu ihrer Begegnung unter besonderer Berücksichtigung Palästinas bis zur Mitte des 2. Jh. v. Chr.* Wissenschaftliche Untersuchungen zum Neuen Testament, X. 2 Aufl. Tübingen: J. C. B. Mohr, 1973.

_____. *Nachfolge und Charisma: Eine exegetisch-religionsgeschichtliche Studie zu Mt 8,21f. und Jesus Ruf in die Nachfolge*. Beiheft zur Zeitschrift für die neutestamentliche Wissenschaft und die Kunde der älteren Kirche, Beiheft XXXIV. Berlin: Verlag Alfred Töpelmann, 1968.

Hijmans, Benjamin Lodewijk, Jr. ʼΑΣΚΗΣΙΣ: *Notes on Epictetus' Educational System*. Assen: Van Gorcum & Comp. N.V., [1959].

Houlden, J. L. *A Commentary on the Johannine Epistles.* Harper's New Testament Commentaries. New York: Harper & Row, 1973.

Iwry, Samuel. "Was there a Migration to Damascus? The Problem of שבי ישראל." *Eretz-Israel,* IX [W. F. Albright Volume, edited by A. Malamat] (1969), 80-88.

Jaeger, Werner. *Paideia: The Ideals of Greek Culture.* Translated by Gilbert Highet. 3 vols. New York: Oxford University Press, 1939-44.

Jeremias, Gert. *Der Lehrer der Gerechtigkeit.* Studien zur Umwelt des Neuen Testaments, Bd. II. Göttingen: Vandenhoeck & Ruprecht, 1963.

Johnston, George. *The Spirit-Paraclete in the Gospel of John.* Society for New Testament Studies Monograph Series, XII. Cambridge: At the University Press, 1970.

Jones, Peter Rhea. "A Structural Analysis of I John." *Review and Expositor,* LXVII (1970), 433-44.

Käsemann, Ernst. *Exegetische Versuche und Besinnungen.* 2 vols. Göttingen: Vandenhoeck & Ruprecht, 1960.

_____. *The Testament of Jesus: A Study of the Gospel of John in the Light of Chapter 17.* Translated by Gerhard Krodel. Philadelphia: Fortress Press, 1968.

Kirk, G. S., and Raven, J. E. *The Presocratic Philosophers: A Critical History with a Selection of Texts.* Cambridge: University Press, 1963.

Klein, Franz-Norbert. *Die Lichtterminologie bei Philon von Alexandrien und in den hermetischen Schriften: Untersuchungen zur Struktur der religiösen Sprache der hellenistischen Mystik.* Leiden: E. J. Brill, 1962.

Klein, Günter. "'Das Wahre Licht scheint schon': Beobachtungen zur Zeit- und Geschichtserfahrung einer urchristlichen Schule." *Zeitschrift für Theologie und Kirche,* LXVIII (1971), 261-326.

Klinzing, Georg. *Die Umdeutung des Kultus in der Qumrangemeinde und im Neuen Testament.* Studien zur Umwelt des Neuen Testaments, Bd. VII. Göttingen: Vandenhoeck & Ruprecht, 1971.

Kragerud, Alv. *Der Lieblingsjünger im Johannesevangelium.* Oslo: Osloer Universitätsverlag, 1959.

Kuhn, Heinz-Wolfgang. *Enderwartung und gegenwärtiges Heil: Untersuchungen zu den Gemeindeliedern von Qumran.* Studien zur Umwelt des Neuen Testaments, Bd. IV. Göttingen: Vandenhoeck & Ruprecht, 1966.

Lauterbach, Jacob Z. *Rabbinic Essays.* Cincinnati: Hebrew Union College Press, 1951.

Leroy, Herbert. *Rätsel und Missverständnis: Ein Beitrag zur Formgeschichte des Johannesevangelium.* Bonner biblische Beiträge, XXX. Bonn: P. Hanstein, 1968.

Lesky, Albin. *A History of Greek Literature*. Translated by James Willis and Cornelis de Heer. New York: Thomas Y. Crowell Company, 1966.

Lorenzen, Thorwald. *Der Lieblingsjünger im Johannesevangelium: Eine redaktionsgeschichtliche Studie*. Stuttgarter Bibel-studien, LV. Stuttgart: Verlag Katholisches Bibelwerk GmbH, 1971.

Lynch, John Patrick. *Aristotle's School: A Study of a Greek Educational Institution*. Berkeley: University of Cali-fornia Press, 1972.

Marrou, H[enri] I[rénée]. *A History of Education in Antiquity*. Translated by George Lamb. New York: Sheed and Ward, Inc., 1956.

Martyn, J. Louis. *History and Theology in the Fourth Gospel*. New York: Harper & Row, Publishers, 1968.

_____. "Source Criticism and *Religionsgeschichte* in the Fourth Gospel." *Jesus and Man's Hope*. Vol. I. Pittsburgh: Pittsburgh Theological Seminary, 1970.

Meeks, Wayne A. "The Man from Heaven in Johannine Sectarianism." *Journal of Biblical Literature*, XCI (1972), 44-72.

_____. *The Prophet-King: Moses Traditions and the Johannine Christology*. Supplements to Novum Testamentum, Vol. XIV. Leiden: E. J. Brill, 1967.

Milik, J. T. *Ten Years of Discovery in the Wilderness of Judaea*. Translated by J. Strugnell. Studies in Biblical Theology, No. 26. London: SCM Press, Ltd., 1959.

Morrison, J. S. "Pythagoras of Samos." *Classical Quarterly*, N.S. VI (1956), 135-56.

Muirhead, Ian A. *Education in the New Testament*. Monographs in Christian Education, No. II. New York: Association Press, 1965.

Murphy-O'Connor, Jerome. "The Essenes and Their History." *Revue biblique*, LXXXI (1974), 215-45.

Mussner, Franz. "Die johanneischen Parakletsprüche und die apostolische Tradition." *Biblische Zeitschrift*, N.F. V (1961), 56-70.

Nauck, Wolfgang. *Die Tradition und Charakter des ersten Johannesbriefes: Zugleich ein Beitrag zur Taufe im Urchristentum und in der alten Kirche*. Wissenschaftliche Untersuchungen zum Neuen Testament, III. Tübingen: Verlag J. C. B. Mohr, 1957.

Neusner, Jacob. *From Politics to Piety: The Emergence of Pharisaic Judaism*. Englewood Cliffs, N.J.: Prentice-Hall, Inc., 1973.

_____. *The Rabbinic Traditions about the Pharisees Before 70*. 3 Parts. Leiden: E. J. Brill, 1971.

Osten-Sacken, Peter von der. *Gott und Belial: Traditionsge-schichtliche Untersuchungen zum Dualismus in den Texten aus Qumran.* Studien zur Umwelt des Neuen Testaments, Bd. VI. Göttingen: Vandenhoeck & Ruprecht, 1969.

Philip, J[ames] A. "The Biographical Tradition--Pythagoras." *Transactions of the American Philological Association*, XC (1959), 185-94.

_____. *Pythagoras and Early Pythagoreanism.* Phoenix Supplementary Volume VII. Toronto: University of Toronto Press, 1966.

Platthy, Jenö. *Sources on the Earliest Greek Libraries: With the Testimonia.* Amsterdam: Adolf M. Hakkert, 1968.

Riesenfeld, Harald. *The Gospel Tradition.* Philadelphia: Fortress Press, 1970.

Robinson, James M., and Koester, Helmut. *Trajectories through Early Christianity.* Philadelphia: Fortress Press, 1971.

Roloff, Jürgen. "Der johanneische 'Lieblingsjünger' und der Lehrer der Gerechtigkeit." *New Testament Studies*, XV (1968), 129-51.

Sasse, Hermann. "Der Paraklet im Johannesevangelium." *Zeitschrift für die neutestamentliche Wissenschaft*, XXIV (1925), 260-77.

Satake, Akira. *Die Gemeindeordnung in der Johannesapokalypse.* Wissenschaftliche Monographien zum Alten und Neuen Testament, XXI. Neukirchen-Vluyn: Neukirchener Verlag, 1966.

Schnackenburg, Rudolf. "On the Origin of the Fourth Gospel." *Jesus and Man's Hope.* Vol. I. Pittsburgh: Pittsburgh Theological Seminary, 1970.

Schweizer, E[duard]. "The Concept of the Church in the Gospel and Epistles of St. John." *New Testament Essays: Studies in Memory of Thomas Walter Manson.* Edited by A. J. B. Higgins. Manchester: University Press, 1959.

Seeberg, Alfred. *Der Katechismus der Urchristenheit.* Theo-logische Bücherei, Bd. XXVI. Munich: Chr. Kaiser Verlag, 1966 [originally published in 1903].

Smith, Dwight Moody, Jr. *The Composition and Order of the Fourth Gospel: Bultmann's Literary Theory.* Yale Publications in Religion, X. New Haven: Yale University Press, 1965.

_____. "The Use of the Old Testament in the New." *The Use of the Old Testament in the New and Other Essays: Studies in Honor of William Franklin Stinespring.* Edited by James M. Efird. Durham, N.C.: Duke University Press, 1972.

Smith, Morton. "A Comparison of Early Christian and Early Rabbinic Tradition." *Journal of Biblical Literature*, LXXXII (1963), 169-76.

Smith, Morton. "Palestinian Judaism in the First Century."
    Israel: Its Role in Civilization. Edited by Moshe Davis.
    New York: Harper & Brothers, 1956.

Stegemann, Hartmut. *Die Entstehung der Qumrangemeinde*. Bonn:
    Rheinische Friedrich-Wilhelms-Universität, 1971.

Stendahl, Krister. *The School of St. Matthew and Its Use of the
    Old Testament*. 2nd ed. Philadelphia: Fortress Press, 1968.

Thesleff, Holger. *An Introduction to the Pythagorean Writings
    of the Hellenistic Period*. Acta Academiae Aboensis,
    Humaniora, XXIV, 3. Åbo: Åbo Akademi, 1961.

_____, ed. *The Pythagorean Texts of the Hellenistic Period*.
    Acta Academiae Aboensis, Humaniora, Vol. XXX, 1. Åbo:
    Akademi, 1965.

Tiede, David Lenz. *The Charismatic Figure as Miracle Worker*.
    SBL Dissertation Series, No. 1. N.p.: Society of Biblical
    Literature, 1972.

Unnik, Willem Cornelius van. "First Century A.D. Literary
    Culture and Early Christian Literature." *Nederlands
    Theologisch Tijdschrift*, XXV (1971), 28-43.

Vaux, R. de. *Archaeology and the Dead Sea Scrolls*. London:
    Oxford University Press, 1973.

Vermès, G[éza]. "The Qumran Interpretation of Scripture in Its
    Historical Setting." *The Annual of Leeds University
    Oriental Society*, VI (1966-68), 85-97.

Williamson, Ronald. *Philo and the Epistle to the Hebrews*.
    Arbeiten zur Literatur und Geschichte des hellenistischen
    Judentums, IV. Leiden: E. J. Brill, 1970.

Wilson, Bryan R., ed. *Patterns of Sectarianism: Organisation
    and Ideology in Social and Religious Movements*. London:
    Heinemann, 1967.

Wolfson, Harry A. *Philo: Foundations of Religious Philosophy
    in Judaism, Christianity, and Islam*. 2 vols. Cambridge,
    Mass.: Harvard University Press, 1947.

Wycherley, R. E. "The Garden of Epicurus." *The Phoenix*, XIII
    (1959), 73-77.

_____. "The Painted Stoa." *The Phoenix*, VII (1953), 20-35.

_____. "Peripatos: The Athenian Philosophical Scene."
    Greece and Rome, VIII (1961), 152-63; IX (1962), 2-21.

Young, Franklin W. "A Study of the Relation of Isaiah to the
    Fourth Gospel." *Zeitschrift für die neutestamentliche
    Wissenschaft*, XLVI (1955), 215-33.